Indexed in

EGLI 1992

Indexed in

Indexed in

Idiom

D0849457

The Family in Italy
from Antiquity to the Present

EDITED BY DAVID I. KERTZER
AND RICHARD P. SALLER

THE FAMILY
IN ITALY

from Antiquity to the Present

YALE UNIVERSITY PRESS

NEW HAVEN AND LONDON

Designed by Nancy Ovedovitz and set in Fournier type by The Composing Room of Michigan, Inc. Printed in the United States of America by Edwards Brothers, Inc., Ann Arbor, Michigan.

Library of Congress Cataloging-in-Publication Data

The Family in Italy from antiquity to the present / edited by David
I. Kertzer and Richard P. Saller
p.   cm.
Papers from a conference, "The Historical Roots of the Western Family: The Evolution of Family Relations in Italy," which was held in Bellagio.
Includes bibliographical references and index.
ISBN 0-300-05037-2
1. Family—Italy—History—Congresses.   I. Kertzer, David I.,
1948– .   II. Saller, Richard P.
HQ629.F36   1991
306.85′0945—dc20   91-12478
CIP

The paper in this book meets the guidelines for permanence and durability of the Committee on Production Guidelines for Book Longevity of the Council on Library Resources.

10   9   8   7   6   5   4   3   2   1

CONTENTS

ACKNOWLEDGMENTS

During the four years in which the conference "The Historical Roots of the Western Family: The Evolution of Family Relations in Italy" and the resulting volume were planned and came to fruition, many offered support and advice. The Wenner-Gren Foundation for Anthropological Research provided the initial commitment of funds and encouragement to pursue the project. The Rockefeller Foundation made available its villa in Bellagio as the location for the conference; the gracious hospitality of the staff there made it easy to concentrate on intellectual discussion and also to enjoy the splendid setting. The National Endowment for the Humanities, an independent federal agency, granted the additional financial support needed to make the conference possible. To all three we are grateful.

In addition to the authors whose names appear on the following pages, Samuel Cohn, John Davis, Jack Goody, Diane Owen Hughes, and Richard Smith participated in the conference. The chapters, and especially the introduction, benefited from their perceptive contributions to the discussion. The skill and patience of our translator, Lydia Cochrane, deserve special thanks. We would also like to express our thanks to Ellen Graham, whose encouragement and sage counsel at Yale University Press have been so valuable, and to Cynthia Ayres, whose editing of the manuscript text in several different languages was a tour de force. And to the Yale University Press readers we are indebted for valuable suggestions and corrections.

CONTRIBUTORS

MARZIO BARBAGLI, professor of sociology at the University of Bologna, has written widely on Italian education, family, politics, and social mobility. His books include *Educating for Unemployment: Politics, Labor Markets and the School System, Italy, 1859–1973* and *Sotto lo stesso tetto: Mutamenti della famiglia in Italia dal XV al XX secolo.*

JANE FAIR BESTOR has carried out anthropological fieldwork in Iran. She is writing a doctoral dissertation at the University of Chicago on the kinship structure and marital strategies of a Renaissance Italian princely house, the Dieste of Ferrara.

CAROLINE B. BRETTELL, an anthropologist on the faculty of Southern Methodist University, is the author of several books, including *Men Who Migrate, Women Who Wait: Population and History in a Portuguese Parish* and *We Have Already Cried Many Tears: The Stories of Three Portuguese Migrant Women.*

EVA CANTARELLA, professor of Roman law at the University of Milan, is the author of *Pandora's Daughters: The Role and Status of Women in Greek and Roman Antiquity* and *Secondo Natura: la bisessualità nel mondo antico.*

DAVID COHEN, professor of rhetoric at the University of California, Berkeley, is the author of *The Athenian Law of Theft* and *Law, Sexuality, and Society: The Enforcement of Morals at Classical Athens.*

MIREILLE CORBIER is directeur de recherche at the Centre National de la Recherche Scientifique in Paris. She was trained in epigraphy and is the author of *L'aerarium Saturni et l'aerarium militare: Administration et prosopographie sénatoriale* and *Indulgentia Principis.* She has written extensively on family, public finances, literacy, and food in the Roman Empire.

WILLIAM A. DOUGLASS is coordinator of the Basque Studies Program at the University of Nevada, Reno. His books include *Emigration in a South Italian Town: An Anthropological History* and (with Jon Bilbao) *Amerikanuak: Basques in the New World.*

ANTHONY H. GALT, professor of social change and development and anthropology at the University of Wisconsin—Green Bay, has conducted ethnographic and historical research in both Sicily and the southern Italian mainland. He is the author of *Far from the Bell Towers: Settlement and Society in an Apulian Town.*

PETER GARNSEY, reader in ancient history at the University of Cambridge and fellow of Jesus College, works primarily on ancient and comparative social and economic history. His recent books include *The Roman Empire: Economy, Society and Culture* (with Richard Saller) and *Famine and Food Supply in the Graeco-Roman World.*

DAVID I. KERTZER, William R. Kenan, Jr., Professor of Anthropology at Bowdoin College, has conducted both ethnographic and historical research in Italy on politics, religion, and family life, and has done theoretical work on age stratification and on ritual and politics. His most recent books include *Ritual, Politics, and Power* and (with Dennis Hogan) *Family, Political Economy, and Demographic Change: The Transformation of Life in Casalecchio, Italy, 1861–1921.*

JULIUS KIRSHNER is professor of history at the University of Chicago and editor of the *Journal of Modern History.* Among his previous publications is *Pursuing Honor While Avoiding Sin: The "Monte delle Doti" of Florence* (1978). He is currently working on a study of matrimony and patrimony in Renaissance Florence.

CHRISTIANE KLAPISCH-ZUBER teaches at the Ecole des Hautes Etudes en Sciences Sociales, Paris. She has published extensively on the social history of medieval Italy and the history of population and family. Her books include *Tuscans and Their Families* (with David Herlihy) and *Women, Family, and Ritual in Renaissance Florence.*

RICHARD P. SALLER, professor of history and classics at the University of Chicago, is the author of *Personal Patronage under the Early Empire* and coauthor (with Peter Garnsey) of *The Roman Empire: Economy, Society and Culture.*

BRENT SHAW is professor of history at the University of Lethbridge (Alberta) and the author of numerous articles on Roman social and economic history, including family history.

MICHAEL SHEEHAN, C.S.B., is a senior fellow of the Pontifical Institute of Mediaeval Studies and professor at the Centre for Medieval Studies of the University of Toronto. He is the author of *The Will in Medieval England* and the editor of *Aging and the Aged in Medieval Europe.*

LUIGI TITTARELLI is associate professor of demography at the University of Perugia. He has written extensively on demographic processes, households, and infant abandonment in the eighteenth and nineteenth centuries.

SUSAN TREGGIARI is professor of classics at Stanford University. Her books include *Roman Freedmen during the Late Republic* and *Roman Marriage: Iusti coniuges from the Time of Cicero to the Time of Ulpian.*

SYLVIA JUNKO YANAGISAKO, associate professor of anthropology at Stanford University, is the author of *Transforming the Past: Kinship and Tradition among Japanese Americans* and coeditor (with Jane Collier) of *Gender and Kinship: Essays toward a Unified Analysis.*

The Family in Italy
from Antiquity to the Present

Chapter 1

RICHARD P. SALLER AND
DAVID I. KERTZER

Historical and Anthropological Perspectives on Italian Family Life

This volume presents a joint effort by historians and anthropologists to advance the study of European family life. Italy was chosen as the focus for several reasons. As the center of an ancient empire and then of Western Christendom, Rome and Italy have influenced the rest of Europe. The roots of Western family life are not to be discovered in Italy alone, yet it has rightly been the focus of debate and is the place to begin. Italy also offers the advantage of being the only place in western Europe for which adequate evidence exists to document family life both before and after the establishment of Christianity, through the Middle Ages, and into the modern era. In addition, features of modern Italian family organization have been at the forefront of discussion concerning the possible existence of a distinctive Mediterranean family system contrasting with those of northwestern and central Europe. As one of the few areas in Europe where both historians and anthropologists with historical interests have investigated family formations of the past, Italy holds great potential for collaboration between the disciplines.

The conference from which this volume originated was organized in the hope that participants would construct a developmental account of family life in Italy over two millennia. Thus it was intentionally situated between the two broad categories of influential works in family history—the collections of historical studies of family practices in diverse times and places (such as Laslett and Wall 1972; Goody, Thirsk, and Thompson 1976; Wall, Robin, and Laslett

We wish to thank all of the conference participants, whose discussion served as a basis for this introduction. In particular, we are grateful to John Davis for providing us with the notes to his conference summation, to Caroline Brettell for her helpful comments, and to Jane Fair Bestor, whose valuable suggestions for rewriting nearly warrant her inclusion as a coauthor.

1983; Netting, Wilk, and Arnould 1984) and the broad developmental syntheses of European family life over the centuries (notably Ariès 1962 and
Shorter 1975, and more recently Goody 1983, Herlihy 1985, and Boswell
1988). Each category presents its own strengths and weaknesses. The broad
syntheses allow readers to see major changes over the long historical sweep,
giving attention to large issues, such as the impact of Christianity and the
reintroduction of Roman law. But these works have been subjected to criticism
by specialists unconvinced by the analyses of their own periods. The collections have brought together specialist studies to compare family life in different
societies. The scattered nature of the contributions, however, precludes a developmental account; the comparisons lead instead to typologies as a means of
generalization.

The aim in bringing together Italian specialists on the ancient, medieval, and
modern periods was to combine the strengths of both kinds of family studies, to
achieve historical depth and avoid geographical disparateness. This volume
meets these goals to some extent. Eva Cantarella's chapter is an illustration of
how to write a developmental account of one important issue in family law—
homicides committed for the sake of honor in cases of adultery. Other chapters,
although less ambitious in chronological scope, allow the reader to identify
continuities and changes over time Although the chapters do not add up to a
systematic developmental history of the family in Italy, they point to a picture
of diversity of family values and practices within and between Italian communities that amounts to a fundamental critique of both developmental accounts
and typological analyses. The diversity has important consequences for the
historian: it may make *the* history of *the* Italian family impossible to write, but it
also may lead to a more complex and sophisticated, and ultimately a more
satisfying, understanding of family life. Many of the chapters stress that families in the past did not have a single kinship system or heirship system or set of
familial values imposed on them; rather, in managing family life they drew on a
surprisingly wide cultural repertoire from the past. Some of the changes and
continuities in those cultural repertoires can be followed more clearly than
others.

METHODS AND APPROACHES

Comparison plays a prominent role in this volume, reflecting a variety of
goals. Comparisons across time have, of course, long been a staple of historical
research, part of the standard attempts to describe continuities and change.
Thus inheritance laws of eighteenth-century Italy may be compared with those
of the Napoleonic period and these, in turn, compared with those of the newly
unified state to plot the course of change. This sort of comparison is common

enough in these pages, but less orthodox comparisons are also in view. Using different historical periods and different societies as a kind of data base, they shed light on the peculiarities of historically specific family arrangements and suggest why such family systems have the characteristics they do. More abstractedly, such comparison—which treats historical cases together with and in the same way as ethnographic comparison—promises to advance our general understanding of social processes, the ways societies work and how they change.

The value of this collection for cross-historical comparison lies in its historical depth, which allows testing of hypotheses concerning historical continuities and change. It has been suggested, for example, that the cultural complex centering on the concept of family honor, often described for medieval and modern Italy, derived from Islamic influence. But David Cohen's work (1991 and in this volume) demonstrates the existence of familiar Mediterranean notions of honor not only in classical Rome but also much earlier in classical Greece. Eva Cantarella traces legal attitudes toward and practices concerning the murder of adulterers from Roman times up to the twentieth century, showing some striking lines of continuity as well as change (see below).

Whereas medieval and modern historians look back in time to determine what has changed and what remains of past forms, the classical studies in this volume look at studies of later periods to provide new perspectives on their work. Richard Saller, for example, is stimulated by Reinhard Sieder and Michael Mitterauer's (1983) study of eighteenth-century Austrian peasant families to question the relation of actual inheritance practice in Roman times to the formal laws and norms governing inheritance. In Austria only a minority of successions conformed to the preferred paradigm, and the reasons—partly demographic—are applicable to the Roman case as well.

Finally, comparison puts European family history in perspective by bringing to light provocative similarities between European and non-European societies. It also puts the historical changes and cross-societal European differences in clearer perspective through contrast with the vast range of possibilities that comparison with non-European societies permits. As Jack Goody observed from an Africanist's point of view, the big differences our contributors have discerned in family organization between different parts of Italy and between Italy and other European societies are but minor variations on a theme. One area might have had nuclear families and another stem families, yet they all practiced monogamy.[1]

1. See Goody 1990 for his account of the similarities of the Eurasian family systems.

The historiography of European family life can be seen as structured by a series of typologies, reflecting theories of the key elements that defined family systems in the past. Frédéric Le Play's (1871) distinction between stem families, identified with the peasant past, and nuclear families has exercised a tremendous influence over the past century. Studies of European families have offered revisions of these types and revisions of the revisions. Peter Laslett and the Cambridge Group for the History of Population and Social Structure initiated an avalanche of historical household studies from the early 1970s with a new household typology and with a repudiation of Le Play's equation of the peasant past with complex family household organization (Laslett and Wall 1972; Wall, Robin, and Laslett 1983).

It is in the context of these influential typologies and of British historical demography that some of the exceptional interest in the nature of family organization in the Italian past, and in its evolution, must be understood. The early efforts of the Cambridge Group to characterize the history of the family in Europe relied heavily on fourteenth- and fifteenth-century Tuscan data to identify a type of family different from that found in northwestern Europe. This model Tuscan family, derived from the work of David Herlihy and Christiane Klapisch-Zuber (1978), was marked by two features: a low female age at marriage and a high incidence of multiple-family households. Debates followed about both the antiquity and the longevity of this family system. Do we see here evidence of a different family system in Mediterranean Europe, in contrast to an ancient nuclear-family system in northwestern Europe? If so, how, why, and when did family organization in the different parts of Europe diverge? And what can be said about the multiple-family system's subsequent history? How did it change and why?

These last questions lead to a consideration of the advantages and disadvantages of typological approaches in family history. The advantage of an approach such as that used by the Cambridge Group is clear: it facilitates comparison across societies and spurs research. Moreover, anomalies raise provocative questions, generating new directions for research. But the limits to typological approaches of this sort are also significant. First, entire geographical areas are characterized as types: the stress is on differences between large regions. Yet the following chapters reveal major local variations that make it difficult to identify a single type that could reasonably be characterized as "the Italian family" at any given time. In addition to differences between Italian communities, separate social groups living in the same communities were characterized by quite different family systems—for example, the large multiple-family household system of the sharecroppers coexisted with the smaller, usually nuclear families of their agricultural wage-laborer neighbors in nineteenth-century central Italy (Kertzer 1984).

Second, household typologies presume a strong functionalist model in which certain traits are tightly linked to other traits. This presumption is hard to justify in light of the chapters in this volume. In particular, Marzio Barbagli demonstrates that although both Sardinia and most of mainland southern Italy had nuclear-family household systems in the modern era, women's age at marriage was typically high in Sardinia and frequently low on the mainland. In Tuscany, although the multiple-family system described by Herlihy and Klapisch-Zuber was characterized by a low female marital age, by the eighteenth century the same area had a high female marriage age. Instead of emphasizing types, then, it may be more profitable to consider how particular characteristics arise and change—an approach that may challenge some of the most basic guiding concepts in family history, such as inheritance and dowry. Caroline Brettell's broad survey of Mediterranean practices of property transmission demonstrates the complex social realities that such simplifying labels as "partible inheritance" may cover. And Julius Kirshner, asserting that "dowries customarily accompanied brides into marriage in late medieval Italy," explores changes in the law regulating the transmission of non-dotal property to Florentine wives to show that affirmation of a dotal system does not provide an adequate understanding of women and property.

A central concern of historians and anthropologists alike is the relation between ideology and practice, between social norms and behavior. From the anthropologist's perspective, a primary virtue of the ethnographic approach is that it permits the researcher to distinguish statements of norms and ideals from people's behavior, in a way not possible using survey-based methods. Historians and others using historical materials, however, often confront daunting obstacles in understanding this relation. The historian's sources, especially for the distant past, generally offer statements of ideals and norms rather than data on people's actual behavior. The historian's task becomes even more problematic with the realization that the opposition between ideals and behavior is overly simplistic, since practice contributes to the creation of ideals and norms.

The classical chapters illustrate these problems. Although Peter Garnsey explores the various definitions of parental concern in past cultures through the ancient medical literature on infant nutrition, no systematic information is available to enable us to judge how the advice literature affected or reflected practice. Similarly, Saller reviews the development of testamentary law but cannot say how frequently particular legal instruments were used. Whereas

Mireille Corbier argues that Roman marriage and adoption can be interpreted within an ideological context valuing political alliance, Susan Treggiari shows both that Roman ideals were more complex and that the scattered examples of marriage arrangements do not follow the ideals and laws in a straightforward manner. Eva Cantarella's and David Cohen's chapters consider the relation between the ideal of honor and the practice of adultery from antiquity to the present. Much of the evidence, particularly for the Roman world, consists of laws and speeches invented as rhetorical exercises. What do the laws and mock orations reveal either of people's actual attitudes or of their behavior? Does the banning of revenge murder for crimes of honor indicate a change in popular attitudes toward the appropriateness of such retribution? Or does the legalization of revenge killing necessarily imply that such retribution had become more common? Cantarella points to subtle distinctions among ideal, norm, and practice. The medieval Church preached against homicide *honoris causa* and Italian laws of the sixteenth and seventeenth centuries tried to appropriate the punishment of adulterers as the state's domain, but popular social norms discouraged cuckolds from availing themselves of the law for fear of being ridiculed; the actual frequency of such homicides is beyond our knowledge for this period and most others.

Brent Shaw's chapter perhaps presents the most challenging instance of the relation between ideals and practice. He deploys a huge but unsystematic data base—the thousands of funerary inscriptions giving age at death—to trace changes in Roman ideology regarding age and gender from the pagan to the Christian periods and from the city to the countryside. His conclusions address some of the most fundamental questions in family history, and yet doubt is likely to persist because of the difficulty of inferring ideals from funerary commemorations, especially when those are expressed in brief and stylized forms. What the valuation of the deceased on a stone reveals about family relationships among the living is not necessarily obvious.

Historians of later periods face the same problem. Both Michael Sheehan and Julius Kirshner acknowledge that they cannot accurately judge the impact on behavior of the doctrinal and legal changes they trace. As more data become available for more recent periods, some resolution to the problem is possible: the strength of William Douglass's careful and detailed analysis is to show that the ideal of the multigenerational household had greater impact in eighteenth-century Agnone than a superficial survey of households might suggest.

Finally, some of the chapters move beyond the question of the correspondence between ideal and behavior to examine how ideals were manipulated in practice. Cohen recognizes that in Roman society the "ideology of male honor and female chastity . . . existed in a dynamic tension with other patterns of values, beliefs, and practices." Perhaps the most illuminating discussion in this regard comes from Christiane Klapisch-Zuber, who demonstrates the coexistence of the two different systems of kinship from Roman and canon law in late medieval Florence, the exploitation of which allowed citizens to meet individual goals.

In historians' recent embrace of anthropology, one of the principal attractions has been the anthropological emphasis on the study of symbols. The work of Clifford Geertz has become a familiar touchstone for many social historians (Kertzer 1987), but has had less impact on European family history. This book suggests that further attention to symbols and symbolic systems is an important complement to both social organizational and jural approaches to the history of the family.

Jane Fair Bestor's chapter illustrates how the study of symbolic thought regarding family bonds can enrich our understanding. She investigates the complex nexus of theories of procreation, symbols of kinship, and conceptions of familial relations as affected by Christian cosmology through the Middle Ages. Symbolic thought about procreation influenced not only the perception of paternal and maternal bonds, with the father-child link commonly given priority because semen was regarded as the force giving form to new life, but also religious beliefs about God the Father and political attitudes toward the *patria,* or fatherland. Yet Bestor warns against a facile assumption of transference of symbolic relations from one domain to another, because such thought was neither uniform across the culture nor wholly consistent.

If such central symbols of kinship and family life as blood, semen, seed, and milk are widespread and almost commonplace, they will have to be interpreted with delicacy and sophistication, since they interacted with thought in other domains in subtle and sometimes contradictory ways.

Family history has become more nuanced in recent years through a recognition of the effect of the life course on familial relationships and roles. It is not enough to ask what the position of women was in the families of the past, as if a teenage bride and an aging widow had the same relationship with other members of the family. Treggiari discusses the consequences of age most explicitly in connection with Roman marriage arrangements. An evaluation of the influence exercised by the bride-to-be on the choice of a spouse must take into account the "incalculable difference" made by the age of the bride; whereas a twelve-year-old girl might have no voice in the decision about her first marriage, later in life, as a widow or divorcée without a living father, she was able to make an independent choice of a husband.

Douglass offers a refinement of the joint-household system from the perspective of life course. He argues that, where demographically possible, fathers lived with adult married sons in Agnone. This joint household, however, characterized only the interval between the marriage of the sons and the death of the parents. Douglass contrasts this temporary joint household, specific to a particular stage of the life course, with the more enduring joint households in the *mezzadria* regions farther north in Italy.

Brettell's analysis of the devolution of property within the family also emphasizes matters related to life course: patrimonies were distributed among the next generation in a stem-family pattern, not to conform with a stem-family paradigm, but "because parents want at least one child to remain at home, work on the farm, and assist them as they get older." If the age and condition of the older generation affected the inheritance arrangements, so too did the age and condition of the beneficiary. Saller's chapter explores the uses made of the broad flexibility that Roman law gave testators in the transmission of their property. Given the large proportion of child heirs, it was important that testators be able to make different arrangements depending on the age and competency of the heir. Furthermore, the Roman law of trust was developed to permit testators to cope with the uncertainties of the life course in an era of high mortality. Roman parents were aware that an infant heir might not live long enough to manage its inheritance, and they regularly made alternative arrangements accordingly. Where possible, then, historical accounts of family life should incorporate not only a life-course perspective but also the historical actors' perceptions of the life course.

THE SOCIAL AND CULTURAL CONTEXT OF FAMILY LIFE

A history of family life should incorporate not simply a description of its features but also an understanding of how families interacted with the wider environment. Only by examining the larger social and cultural context can we make sense of the course of changes in European family life during the past millennia. Family historians over the past two decades have paid greatest attention to the economic and demographic forces that have shaped family practices. Recently interest has increased in two institutional and ideological forces, the church and the state, and in ideologies structuring beliefs about gender roles.

ECONOMIC AND DEMOGRAPHIC FORCES

Family historians commonly portray families as the principal adaptive mechanism people have to cope with a political and economic system. Where family units are also productive units, the requirements of production affect family form and family relationships. Where individuals, and not families, are the productive units, families serve to pool income and to meet such economic needs as housing, food, and child rearing. Given this relation, changes in the economic system may stimulate changes in the family system, and people occupying different positions in the economy may exhibit different patterns of family organization.

Close study of Italian family history reveals possible connections between the organization of economic activities and family practices. Just as the development of sharecropping in some areas led to the proliferation of multiple-family households, due to the landowner's interest in maximizing the number of family workers on the land, the growth of the agricultural wage-laborer population in the eighteenth and nineteenth centuries led to an expanding population of people living in smaller, less complex family units (Kertzer 1984). In this volume Barbagli argues that the more prominent family role played by Sardinian women compared with Sicilian women may be partially attributable to the pastoral nature of the Sardinian economy; men were frequently away from the home village for long stretches of time, leaving the women in control. Anthony Galt's study of Locorotondo relates changing economic behavior to a major transformation in the devolution of family property: the Locorotondesi began to provide houses for sons, rather than daughters, as the intensive labor of fathers and sons together became necessary to develop new agricultural lands.

The impact of demographic forces on family life over millennia encompasses both dramatic and subtle processes. Devastating plagues like the Black Death of the late medieval period had a major impact on families, both directly through the loss of family members and the fragmentation of families, and indirectly through economic effects, notably the sudden availability of large areas of farmland and a great demand for labor. The interaction between family practices and other demographic forces may be less striking but more significant in the long run. For instance, the Roman cultural pattern of late age at marriage for men, combined with high mortality, had a profound bearing on the configuration of authority in the Roman household: the law may have given fathers striking power over their children for as long as they lived, but death took most fathers away before their children reached adulthood (Saller 1987 and in this volume).

Whereas demographic forces affected the way in which cultural norms and values were translated into behavior, the cultural context must be taken into account in understanding demographic forces. To take an obvious contrast, E. A. Wrigley and Roger Schofield in their magisterial study of early modern Britain (1981) argued for a connection between the length of life-cycle service and economic prosperity: in times of economic difficulty the period of service tended to increase, thus raising age at marriage and reducing the reproduction rate. The logic of their argument presumes a set of cultural values inapplicable to southern Italy, where values of honor and shame, with their stress on female chastity, put a quite different, negative complexion on life-cycle service.[2]

Historians need to be sensitive not only to the implications of general demographic rates, but also the vagaries of mortality and the sexes of children in individual families. Normative statements favoring sons in transmission of the patrimony must be evaluated in a context in which a substantial minority of families (perhaps 20 percent) in ancient Rome and medieval Tuscany had only female heirs. Using mid-nineteenth-century Perugian evidence, Luigi Tittarelli examines the effect of household size and sex balance in particular households on the timing of sharecropper children's marriages. He finds that where adult household members were plentiful in this patrilocal society, daughters' marriages were encouraged but sons' marriages were discouraged.

THE IMPACT OF THE CHURCH

The Church has been brought to the center of attention by recent histories of European family life, although its influence remains surprisingly neglected in studies of the modern period. Jack Goody (1983) and David Herlihy (1985), for example, both portray the Church as decisively shaping the European family, albeit in entirely different ways. Goody suggests that the Church's extension of the incest prohibition was responsible for a major change from endogamy to the exogamy characteristic of medieval and modern Europe, as the Church disrupted traditional lines of patrimonial transmission and enriched itself. Herlihy, on the contrary, claims that the Church not only did not disrupt traditional family practices, but was responsible for the uniformity of families across the social hierarchy. Neither of these theses is easy to sustain in view of the evidence from pre-Christian Rome. Proving that the Church had a decisive impact on preexisting marriage patterns is difficult, since endogamy, although legally permitted, was not normal in either a prescriptive or a behavioral sense before the fourth century (Shaw and Saller 1984; Treggiari this volume; compare Corbier this volume). As for moral uniformity, Herlihy exaggerates the change brought by the Church by misrepresenting the Roman situation: before the establishment of Christianity most Romans lived in simple families, based on monogamous marriages and reciprocal bonds of duty between father, mother, and children. Even slaves, who had no legal capacity to marry, formed

2. We summarize here part of the argument of Richard Smith's conference paper, "Child and Young Adult Female Labor in the Household: Patterns in Late Medieval Northern and Southern Europe."

de facto marriages and were regarded as bound to their children by obligations of *pietas* (piety).[3]

The extent and nature of the Church's influence on family life remain far from clear. Official pronouncements regulating elements of family life can be traced, but it cannot be assumed that these were put into practice by the people. That the Church did not always have its way is demonstrated by studies documenting the persistence of endogamous marriages in various isolated communities of Italy (see Merzario 1981). Where new Church policies and values coincide with changing family practices, what was cause and what effect are not always obvious. Shaw's study shows that under Christian influence Roman imperial funerary commemorations were increasingly devoted to young children, but in this regard Christianity was following a previously established pattern, in which urban children were more likely to receive a funerary monument than their counterparts in the countryside. The theological premises leading to the creation of a celibate clergy, discussed by Michael Sheehan, did have a discernible impact on family life in Italy. In sixteenth-century Perugia, for instance, eighteen hundred of the three thousand members of religious orders were women, and according to Tittarelli, a quarter to a third of these were from elite families. Here and elsewhere, to send a daughter or a son to join the Church was a strategy commonly employed by elite families to keep their patrimonies and lifestyles intact.

The influence of the Church on marriage practices in Italy ought to interest historians of modern times as much as those who study the more remote past. Provocative questions await systematic scholarly attention. Those who minimize the influence of the Church in contemporary Italian family life may cite Italy's fertility rate, one of the lowest in the world, in spite of the Church's unceasing opposition to birth control. Yet compared with its northern European neighbors, Italy today has little nonmarital cohabitation and, though divorce is now legal, a low divorce rate. And the most widely read magazine in Italy is *Famiglia Cristiana,* a paean to the traditional family values of the Church. In short, scholars who recognize the Church's prominent role in the long-term evolution of family organization and family values in the ancient and medieval world would be rash to ignore the role of the Church in shaping contemporary attitudes.

3. Herlihy's claim (1985, 3) that the father was excluded from his *familia* is directly contradicted by the very legal text he cites (*Dig.* 50.16.195f.).

STATE INTERVENTION IN FAMILY LIFE

Long ago Henry S. Maine (1861) represented the history of European society as the history of the growth of civil power at the expense of that of family units. In this volume the issue of attempts by the state or other suprafamilial political entities to wrest control from family groups recurs regularly throughout the centuries. Augustus's law against adultery of 18 B.C. presents two common threads of the story: the state's desire to monopolize means of violence at the expense of family autonomy, and increasing state intervention in the private sphere.

Cohen and Cantarella both take the *lex Julia de adulteriis* as a starting point for their studies. Both show that this law, usually interpreted as a law against adultery, in fact served to limit violent retribution against adulterers. Whereas the adulteress's husband and father formerly had been permitted to punish the offenders on their own, from 18 B.C. only the father could take punishment into his own hands, and only in limited circumstances. In place of private retribution Augustus substituted public trial and state-administered punishment. The struggle between the state and families over control of violence has continued into more recent periods, as is evident in Klapisch-Zuber's chapter. Like Augustus, fourteenth-century Florentine officials sought to widen state control over the retaliatory violence exercised by kin groups. The historical juxtaposition of Augustan Rome and late medieval Florence highlights the weakness of any view (sometimes implicitly assumed, though not explicitly stated) suggesting a unilinear progression in the growth of state power at the expense of the family. Cantarella's chapter traces the widening and contracting latitude in retaliatory actions allowed to families over two millennia, as the state was sometimes more and other times less tolerant of "crimes of honor."

In considering the second, broader theme of state intervention into family life, Cohen stresses the lex Julia de adulteriis as a turning point in state appropriation of a new regulatory sphere, the family. The law was just one aspect of Augustus's larger program of social engineering, which included privileges and penalties to encourage childbearing. Later emperors issued more legislation governing family life and restricting fathers' discretion within their own households. When this trend was later combined with Christian doctrine concerning sexuality and marriage, the result was a long and powerful tradition of regulation in a sphere that formerly had been largely left to families.

Roman emperors were gradually drawn by their interest in family welfare into enforcing previously unwritten obligations, such as the maintenance of young children by parents and the maintenance of elderly parents by their children. By the modern period, welfare provisions of the state come to the fore of scholarly attention, from studies on the impact of child labor laws to the regulation of infant abandonment. As the rich materials on the imperial *alimenta* in Roman Italy and public welfare entities in Renaissance Florence show, however, we should not think of state welfare provisions for families as a modern innovation, replacing family and church-administered organizations that served the same purposes in the past. The long-term history of secular political control of family welfare provisions has yet to be written.

GENDER AND FAMILY

Recent studies of gender have suggested vital new directions for family history. Male authority and the commonality of male and female outlooks are no longer assumed. Scholarly interest is now focused on the different ways in which social life is structured by gender differences and on the different ways in which gender divisions are conceptualized and symbolized. These matters permeate the following chapters. Three general issues deserve a brief preview: the history of patriarchy; the nature of parent-child relations; and the symbolism and behavior related to concepts of family honor and female purity.

The assumption of patriarchy underlies much earlier work on family history: male authority over the household was largely assumed, and the family was seen as a unitary group seeking common goals. Insofar as intrafamily conflict was examined, it tended to be conflict between father and sons and among the sons, especially over matters of inheritance. Women were presumed to have been both legally and socially subservient to men. Nothing reveals the assumption better than the way the term *household head* was used: in European societies complete families could have only a male as head; moreover, in dealings between the family and other units—whether state, church, or other families—only men could ordinarily speak on behalf of the family, only men could commit the whole family to any obligation or course of action. As the chapters in this book make clear, however, the character of family relations has been far more complex than simple patriarchy. Two basic questions recur: what is the history of the formal norms and laws regulating male authority over females? and what has been the actual balance of power between males and females in families?

The emergence of gender parity is too easily assumed to be a recent phenomenon. The following chapters show that women's legal rights with respect to family and property have not moved in a single direction over the past two thousand years, but have gone through periods of development and decline. By the classical Roman period women were generally free of the legal authority of a husband and had property rights comparable to men's. In spite of the later influence of Roman law, this remarkable legal independence did not endure. As

Kirshner demonstrates, in late medieval Florence women's control over their own non-dotal goods was gradually whittled away by statutes in favor of their husbands.

How did these changing laws affect relationships between male and female family members? Anthropologists such as Susan Rogers (1975) have pointed to the need to look beyond the formal rules and norms to discover the nature of gender stratification systems in European peasant societies. This is also true for ancient Rome. Legal and literary evidence indicates that not all Roman wives took full advantage of the independent property rights allowed by law. On the other side, by comparing legal and literary evidence Treggiari demonstrates that the *paterfamilias* did not always utilize to greatest effect his legal right of final approval of his children's marriages; in reality, the women of the family were heavily involved in the matchmaking.

Here arises the more general issue of what it meant to be household head. The head could be conceived in different ways: as an owner, a trustee, a head of a board of governors, or in some circumstances no more than a figurehead. The distinction was discussed in antiquity by Roman jurists, who claimed that whereas classical law concentrated strong rights of ownership of family property in the paterfamilias alone, the ancient rules of succession treated the father's *sui heredes* (his heirs, usually his children) as virtual coproprietors (*Dig.* 28.2.11). This bit of antiquarianism from the jurist Paulus is dubious as history, but illustrates a continuing awareness of varying conceptions of headship.

Another central issue, the gender division of extradomestic labor and women's influence in the sphere of family decision making, is not as easily documented as property rights, because it was not a matter of law. Brettell refers to northwestern Portugal, where women's positions were enhanced through their relation to land, both as cultivators and as owners. Although Italian women's ownership rights have received attention, the extent to which Italian women's direct contribution to the extradomestic family economy gave them a more powerful position in their families remains to be systematically studied.

Life-course perspectives offer new insights into the old questions of patriarchy, since they expose the inadequacy of thinking in unitary terms of male versus female power. For example, the same patrilocal system that made the young married woman a relatively powerless dependent in the household could grant considerable influence to the older woman, who as mother-in-law acquired a growing corps of younger adult female dependents. In such a situation familial conflict might well be between females. A family decision made by a young husband overruling his wife, for example, should not necessarily be interpreted simply as evidence of patriarchy, or male control, since the decision might have been initiated by his mother. This situation in turn points to a more general pattern in the female life course: a woman who gives birth tends to acquire a new and higher status for herself, and as her children age, she may acquire greater power through them. This pattern obtained in ancient Rome (Dixon 1988) and was later explicated by such writers as the medieval theologian Jacobus de Varagine (Bestor this volume).

An awareness of gender affects consideration of all family relationships, including those between parents and children. Indeed, there should be some hesitation about framing the issue in gender-free terminology. The history of parent-child relations is, more precisely, the history of four potentially very different relationships: mother-son; mother-daughter; father-son; and father-daughter.

This history has often been written in terms of an evolution from parental indifference toward infants in the past to contemporary concern for children. First popularized by Philippe Ariès (1962) and further developed by Lloyd DeMause (1974) and Edward Shorter (1975), this argument holds that "in traditional society, mothers viewed the development and happiness of infants younger than two with indifference," a state that Shorter (1975, 168–170) saw as prevailing among the popular classes from ancient times into the early nineteenth century. One of the bases for this indifference is said to have been the high levels of infant mortality: parents could not afford to make a large emotional or economic investment in a newborn, whose chances of death before a first birthday were one in three or four.

The hypothesis of parental indifference is flawed in fundamental ways: it makes no gender distinctions; and, more broadly, its premise of a unilinear progression is impossible to sustain in the face of the evidence. The debate over indifference often focuses on infant abandonment. Exposure of newborns was commonplace in ancient Rome, with females almost certainly at greater risk than males. But Garnsey rejects the idea that exposure constitutes proof of parental indifference, suggesting that "stern realism" would be a more appropriate description of parental attitudes toward infants. His examination of the medical advice literature reveals a concern among parents for the welfare of their infants, even if we today would regard some of the advice as fatally misguided. To the advice literature could be added other direct expressions of Roman parents' sentimental attachment to infants. The unilinear story is also belied in other ways. The ancient Romans were aware that exposure was acceptable in some ancient cultures, but that for the Egyptians and the Jews in particular it was not. The effect of later Christian teaching against exposure is not easy to interpret; while discouraging exposure, it did not preclude abandonment of newborns on the steps of foundling homes, which often led to death. From the beginning of the foundling homes in the fifteenth century, Italy witnessed upsurges in infant abandonment from time to time; as many as one of every three newborns were abandoned in such cities as Florence and Milan in the mid-nineteenth century. This is part of a wider pattern found elsewhere in eighteenth- and nineteenth-century Europe (Boswell 1988). Rather than arguing that the upsurges are evidence for a decline in parental concern, we would do better to admit, as Garnsey suggests, that parental concern and indifference are variable cultural constructs for which there is no single index.

The mass abandonment of infants in the modern era contradicts one of the most familiar popular images of Italian family life, namely, the fierce devotion of the mother toward her children, and the corollary asymmetry between the mother's relationship with her children and that of the father. Bestor analyzes de Varagine's thirteenth-century explanation of the perceived asymmetry in terms of procreation and socialization of offspring. Sylvia Junko Yanagisako's chapter expresses a common understanding of modern Italian family life, in which the mother serves as emotional center of the family and is preoccupied with both the family's welfare and its unity. The perception of asymmetry in parent-child relations has not always prevailed on the Italian peninsula. In classical Rome, the mother's position in the family was ambiguous; if she was married in the usual way (*sine manu,* that is, without moving into the power of her husband), she did not legally become a member of the familia of her husband and children (Dixon 1988). Although for practical purposes Roman mothers certainly were members of their husbands' and children's households, several characteristics of family life among propertied Romans—relatively frequent divorce, wet nursing, and child care by slaves—may have distanced some mothers from their children.

The Roman mother's relationship with her children was also influenced by her having, like the father, independent powers of testation, with the result that her children looked to her to secure their future prosperity and social standing. This points to the broader matter of the effect of economic roles and organization on family relations. The chapters in this volume point to fundamental distinctions of gender and class and to wide variation by period and locale. Saller's chapter traces basic changes in inheritance practices in the Roman period alone, from a strongly agnatic system giving women little freedom of testation in early Rome (fifth century B.C.) to the classical system (from the second century B.C.), which recognized a wider circle of cognates as heirs and gave women a surprising freedom of testation. Unfortunately, the Roman sources are not adequate to allow the historian to document related developments in the affective relationships between parents and children from the fifth to the second century. De Varagine assumed in the late thirteenth century that patrimonial succession tied sons more closely to fathers than to mothers (Bestor this volume), but the historian should beware of making facile assumptions about the connection between emotional bonding and economic ties.

If the Roman legal evidence provides a better indication of the flexibility in the transmission of property between generations than of the actual patterns of devolution, by later periods varied patterns of inheritance can be documented up and down Italy. Where patrilocality prevailed, the transmission of property through sons was in harmony with the desire to preserve the family estate intact, whereas property given to daughters was thought to be lost from the family of origin. These attitudes may have had a symbolic as well as a material dimension, women being associated with nondurables in medieval times and men with the durable goods of production (the house, the estate, even the tomb). In Yanagisako's study of family firms of Como she finds this distinction again in the contemporary period, with the connection between a reluctance to have daughters enter the firms and the notion that married women are under the control of their husbands.

The cultural complex of honor and shame has been the focus of anthropological research in Mediterranean Europe for as long as anthropologists have worked in the region. Indeed, in a recent review essay Stanley Brandes (1987, 122) characterized honor and shame as "the bread and butter of Mediterranean studies." A summary or critique of the large anthropological literature is beyond the scope of this introduction,[4] which focuses on the larger questions of historical evolution confronted in the following chapters.

Anthropologists have occasionally considered how and why (but not where) the honor complex originated in southern Europe, but their discussions have been largely speculative, based on theoretical considerations rather than historical data.[5] The concept of family honor is itself complex, incorporating such facets as sex, status, and domination, which have received varying emphases in different times and places. Whatever the variation, a striking conclusion from the following chapters is the resilience of the value placed on honor in Italy throughout the centuries, especially the notion that a family's honor is tied to the virginity and sexual fidelity of its daughters and wives. Cohen presents the evidence from ancient Rome for three central elements of this sexual ideology: the emphasis on female chastity, its importance for men's honor, and the community's ambivalence toward unbridled male sexuality. Cohen concludes by pointing out how the sense of honor later came to be linked to

4. Readers interested in pursuing this subject might begin with Gilmore 1987, Blok 1981, and Herzfeld 1984.

5. Notable is the stimulating work of Jane Schneider (1971) and that of Jane and Peter Schneider (1976). They weave together political, economic, social organizational, and cultural factors in a sophisticated account of the honor complex, focusing on Sicily.

broader Christian ideas of sin. Thus in medieval times sexual crimes were interpreted not only as threats to family honor but also as violations of the honor of God (Ruggiero 1985). Cantarella's chapter traces the shifting legal protection granted to those who, in response to a slight to their family honor, murdered adulterous offenders—a thread running through the legal tradition from Augustus until 1981, when special consideration for murder honoris causa was eliminated from the Italian code.

Cohen's three elements produced a long-enduring double standard for the genders, with family honor threatened principally by the illicit sexual behavior of its women, not its men. The Augustan law defined the crime of adultery in terms of the status of the woman—that is, on the basis of the honor of her family. Cantarella shows how the apparent trend in nineteenth-century law codes toward a single standard for the two genders is deceptive. Sanctions were developed for unfaithful husbands, but they were different from those for unfaithful wives; the extenuating circumstance of honoris causa was extended to murders by mothers and sisters, but only murders of female family members, not males. The justification was that the illicit sexual behavior of another woman in the family cast doubt on their own reputations. The legal innovations are suggestive, but much work remains to be done to understand the historical development of male and female attitudes toward these highly gender-biased honor codes.

Within this long tradition, nonlegal evidence of changing attitudes can be found. Latin has no word for *cuckold,* a term that in Italian (*cornuto*) later acquired such resonance as a term of derision. Moreover, in Roman times a wife who engaged in extramarital sexual relations in some instances rendered her husband not so much a victim as an accessory, on the grounds that the husband must have been a pimp rather than a dupe. Whereas late medieval literature portrays the cuckold as a laughably impotent figure, in Roman literature he is represented more as a debased character willing to sacrifice his and his wife's moral standing for the sake of gain.

A final consideration in a historical account of the honor complex is regional diversity. Here much firmer evidence exists for the recent period than for the ancient and medieval worlds. Southern Italy has traditionally been associated more with strong notions of family honor than has the north—a pattern manifested in different ways. By the time of unification, crimes of honor were much more common in the south than in the north. Furthermore, demographic historians have shown that a woman who had an illegitimate child in southern Italy was generally excluded from future marriage and went on to have a succession of illegitimate births; in the north, by contrast, a woman with an illegitimate child thereafter often married and gave birth to a series of legitimate children. When the north-south differences in the honor complex arose, and under what influences, remain important questions for the history of family life in Italy (see Schneider 1971 for one analysis).

Gender ideologies, the impact of church and state, property transmission, the timing of marriage in the life course—these are but a few of the topics related to family life considered in the following chapters. The reader, we hope, will find the richness of method and approach stimulating. And if the collection does not satisfy the desire for a comprehensive narrative, we trust that the points of comparison and contrast between the chapters will provoke questions and further research into how and why patterns of family life in Italy changed.

Part One

ANTIQUITY

RICHARD P. SALLER

Introduction to Part One

The Roman family occupies an important place in Western social and political thought as a paradigm of authoritative, orderly social relations. Leading social and political theorists have used their perceptions of the Roman family as bases for schemes of social development or decline. In the sixteenth century Jean Bodin in his *République* praised the unlimited power of the Roman father as the foundation of social order and claimed it as justification for the absolute sovereignty of kings; he believed that Roman history showed how the decline of that power inexorably led to a decline in social order. In the nineteenth century Sir Henry Maine drew extensively on his knowledge of the early Roman family and state to explain the evolution "from Status to Contract." More recently, as the earliest historical society of western Europe, Rome has served as the starting point for histories of the family in Europe (Goody 1983; Herlihy 1985). To assess the impact of Christianity, an understanding of pre-Christian family life is essential.

The characteristics traditionally associated with the Roman family and kinship system stress males. The kinship system implied by the earliest laws was agnatic—that is, for inheritance and other purposes kinship was traced through males; the kinship line came to an end with females. The family is envisaged as highly patriarchal: the *paterfamilias* (the oldest living male ascendant in the family) was endowed with *patria potestas*, legal power that encompassed the power of life and death over his children and his sons' children, and a monopoly of ownership of property within the family. Potestas over sons ended with the death of the father (there was no age of majority); daughters upon marriage moved from the potestas of their fathers to the authority, or *manus*, of their husbands (or husbands' fathers, if still alive). When the paterfamilias died, his wife, sons, and any unmarried daughters became legally independent, or sui juris, and each of the sons became a paterfamilias in his own right. From these legal principles some historians have imagined the Roman family as an authoritarian unit of three or more generations under the rule of the paterfamilias.

The patriarchal image was derived from Roman law handed down from the early republican period of the fifth century B.C. Because the earliest contemporary historical sources were written much later, in the second century B.C., it is impossible for the historian today to know how well the early legal rules corresponded to the social practices of the fifth century. The Romans of the later classical period looked back with nostalgia to the early republic as a time of stable families under strong paternal authority, uncorrupted by the vices of their own day. Classical Romans like Cicero recognized the quite different realities of family life in their own time of the first century B.C. The paterfamilias continued to have potestas over his children, but adolescent sons were sometimes not easy to control. Fathers had the right to approve or veto sons' and daughters' marriages, but as Susan Treggiari shows, fathers did not always play the dominant part in matchmaking. Most wives did not marry into the manus of their husbands, but remained in the power of their fathers. When their fathers died, they became independent of male authority and had the right to own property and to dispose it as they wished. Among the elite, divorce was easy and common and wives could take the initiative by delivering notice to their husbands of their intent to dissolve the marriage. The first emperor Augustus insisted on witnesses to divorce as a precondition for identifying adultery, a preoccupation of Augustus and other propertied men, which is discussed by David Cohen and by Eva Cantarella.

Contemporary evidence for the second century B.C. indicates that the strictly agnatic principles of early law were giving way to bilateral kinship reckoning. Recognition of cognates as well as agnates in inheritance was facilitated by the discretion allowed to testators to choose their heirs through written wills, which I show were employed in a myriad of ways to supersede the residual rules of succession. With a written will a Roman could manipulate the kinship network imposed by the accidents of birth. Mireille Corbier demonstrates that Roman law and mores allowed far more flexibility in constructing kinship than did later European societies. A Roman could break the agnatic link with a son by emancipation or create one through adoption; he could replace (or add) one set of affines with another by divorce and remarriage. The narrower incest prohibitions of Roman law permitted wider choice of spouses than later canon law did. Nevertheless, as Plutarch noted, even before the establishment of Christianity Roman marriage tended to be more exogamous than in the eastern Mediterranean.

Roman social historians continue to debate the extent and causes of changes in family life throughout the imperial age. Some detect an increasing value attached to marriage and children, which they attribute to Christianity. Brent Shaw's study of patterns of funerary inscriptions may appear to support this view, but he argues that the trend was part of a complex of social developments of which Christianity was only one aspect. In this respect, Shaw is one of a group of historians looking beyond Christianity to find the roots of the change in the pre-Christian empire. Other historians are skeptical about claims of change in the valuation of children or of the conjugal couple. Peter Garnsey in his chapter on infant nutrition recommends examining changing cultural expressions of attachment rather than attempting to measure the attachment or indifference to children. The debate is not likely to be decisively resolved, but the standards of argument and evidence are rising, and recent, closer analyses of the ancient evidence make the earlier grand theses of social evolution untenable. Future research is likely to follow the lines suggested by Shaw's chapter in seeking to discover and explain regional variations within Rome's vast empire.

Chapter 2

RICHARD P. SALLER

Roman Heirship Strategies in Principle and in Practice

Throughout antiquity the great majority of men spent their lives working the land, and land was the predominant form of wealth and the preferred investment. The transmission of that wealth from one generation to the next was the primary determinant of a Roman's position in a society in which high rank was not automatically inherited but rested on possession of property. Social status more broadly defined was even more closely tied to wealth, encompassing sections of the population that fell outside the hierarchy of rank. Insofar as rank and status were de facto inherited, the reason lay in the transmission of property within the family—a matter that preoccupied Romans.

Propertied Roman families faced a problem general to traditional agrarian societies with a limited supply of land: how to plan the coordination of their productive and reproductive functions? That is, how were Roman families to produce enough children to continue the family line in the face of high mortality, and at the same time avoid too many children, with the consequent fragmentation of the patrimony and decline in social status? On the basis of work by Jack Goody, Keith Hopkins, and others, this problem could offer at least a partial insight into the notable failure of the Roman senatorial aristocracy to reproduce itself. Senatorial families disappeared and were replaced by new families at an astonishing rate of up to 75 percent per generation, because to avoid dividing their estates too many ways in a thoroughly partible inheritance system (sons and daughters receiving full shares), they had quite small families. Given ancient mortality rates, the family bearing only two or three

In addition to the conference participants, Suzanne Dixon, David Johnston, and Christoph Paulus deserve special thanks for offering their comments and especially their legal expertise.

children was likely to avoid the risk of division, but also unlikely to produce a surviving male heir (Hopkins 1983, chaps. 2–3).

There is surely something to this logic, and Roman authors give the impression that aristocrats typically kept their families small, even if limitation had to rely on such distasteful practices as infant exposure. Yet the law and the demographic parameters make the matter far more complicated. This chapter suggests some of the complexities of the family life course that affected transmission of patrimonies and considers how Roman law was developed to meet those complexities, in part by bringing to the surface assumptions about the relation between law and practice often left submerged.

SOURCES

The Roman historian studying transmission of property between generations has a peculiar set of sources to work from: an assessment of all that follows must be colored by an awareness of the limitations of the sources. No archives of testamentary documents have survived from the western empire. Some wills on papyrus have been found in Egypt, but it is hard to know how representative of the empire as a whole the Egyptian papyri are. From the west, fragments of testaments have been preserved in inscriptions, but nearly all concern testators' instructions regarding funeral arrangements. An exception is the famous but fragmentary "will of Dasumius," which was wrongly attributed to Dasumius and erroneously restored by Theodor Mommsen (Champlin 1986).

The historian is left with juristic sources, which have much to say about inheritance, and the scattered comments of literary figures. The juristic materials fall into several categories. First and best known perhaps are the textbooks, the *Institutes* of Gaius (mid-second century after Christ) and of Justinian (nearly four centuries later). The *Institutes* offer a textbook set of rules, and as such they encourage too simple a view of inheritance. A better source is the *Digest,* a compilation of excerpts from the treatises of the classical jurists, especially of the late second and early third centuries. The excerpts go well beyond the textbook rules, giving opinions about cases real and imagined. Sometimes the real cases can be distinguished by the specificity of names and circumstances, but more often the distinction between real and imagined cannot clearly be made—a problem for the historian interested in typical testamentary practice rather than in the jurists' clever powers of deduction. The historian can take some comfort in the comment of Celsus that "the law ought to be related to those things which happen often and easily rather than those which occur very rarely" (*Dig.* 1.3.5). But of course the jurists are at best interested in common occurrences among the propertied classes. What proportion of the population that encompassed, we cannot know. David Daube's assertion that nine-tenths of the population were more or less propertyless seems extreme, and many of the cases in the *Digest* and the few extant documents concern modest sums rather than senatorial fortunes (Crook 1973, 39). One other caution about the *Digest:* the procedure of excerpting means that the passages are out of context. How far the Justinianic compilers distorted their excerpts or interpolated new phrases into them to suit their own Byzantine interests is a subject of debate among Romanists. Finally, imperial rulings are preserved in the codes of Theodosius and Justinian of the fifth and sixth centuries, respectively. From them it is possible to identify significant legal developments in the later empire that might have been retrojected into the classical materials.

Fortunately, we are not entirely dependent on legal sources. Roman literature, especially the letters of Cicero, Pliny, and Fronto, contains numerous references to and the occasional extended discussion of inheritance cases of the day. These authors were from, and wrote for, the narrow circles of the imperial elite, and yet after allowing for their special point of view we must draw on them to compare law and practice. It must be conceded, however, that there is not enough literary discussion to make systematic comparison possible. Therefore, since the sources for the Roman Empire are so heavily juristic—not archival documents or court records—it is critical to reach some preliminary theoretical understanding of the relation between the jurists' rules and principles, and social practice.

LAW AND SOCIAL PRACTICE

As one who is neither a lawyer nor a philosopher, I cannot offer anything original on the subject of law and social practice, but I should like to draw attention to some of the views of those who have written about Roman law and society. In *The Concept of Law,* H. L. A. Hart critiques John Austin's analysis of law in terms of "elements of commands and habits" (Hart 1961, 18). Since commands and habits seem to underlie much of the layperson's (and social historian's) concept of law, Hart's argument deserves our attention.

Law is often conceived as a system of restraints on behavior, which some philosophers have tried to reduce to a set of coercive orders (Hart 1961, 27–42). This notion seems to inform the repeated comments of Jane Gardner in *Women in Roman Law and Society* to the effect that law "is about what people may or may not do, not what they actually do" (Gardner 1986, 3). In other words, law is a body of rules that people may or may not obey. As will be seen, this concept covers parts of the Roman law of inheritance, but not most of it.

If law embodies a society's habits, then Roman law can be interpreted as a guide to Roman mores. Arnaldo Momigliano advocated this view twenty-five years ago when he congratulated a gathering of Roman lawyers and historians on overcoming the disciplinary boundaries separating them. It was only fitting, since "a large part of what is called the sociology of the ancient world is in fact custom or law, seen in a synchronic rather than a diachronic arrangement" (Momigliano 1966, 242). This assertion cannot be accepted at such a high level of generality, since it is possible to find in the evidence for Roman succession numerous instances of disparities between law and practice, or even between legal prescriptions and social norms.

In the face of such disparities, the notion of law as habits can be saved by seeing law as gradually responding to prevailing attitudes and practice: the law "therefore gives a general guide to social standards" (Dixon 1988, 41). The disparities occur in the lag time (sometimes measured in centuries) before the law is changed to conform to new mores. This approach is attractive, because in numerous areas of Roman law general legal rules were anticipated by individual behavior and social values. The legal instruments and rules regarding inheritance can be seen as evolving over the centuries of the empire in this way. But, again, this is only part of the story: some laws were issued in attempts to turn the tide of mores viewed as deleterious by the emperors.

Moreover, the most notable feature of the Roman law of succession is that it did not prescribe or allow just one pattern of behavior, but presented an array of instruments and rules that permitted testators to pursue an almost infinite variety of goals. For this reason, David Daube, Mireille Corbier, and others have interpreted Roman testamentary law as a liberator that freed Romans to disperse their estates outside the family if they wished. Alan Macfarlane emphasized this freedom in his sweeping attempt to account for the differences in demographic patterns and household organization between northern and southern Europe in the early modern period. Written Roman law in the southern regions permitted household heads to leave all their land to a single child, and that possibility "seems connected to the pattern of extended households" (Macfarlane 1980, 10). But any strong claim for legal determinism—it is not clear whether Macfarlane is advancing a causal argument—would be unwarranted. As Corbier has rightly stressed (1985, 520), the testamentary freedom enjoyed by classical Romans was considerably restrained by social pressures and goals. Roman law in itself cannot explain a particular pattern of devolution of property.

A skeptic might even argue against Macfarlane that in the face of social pressures and custom the law had so little impact on the way people behaved that it is irrelevant to the social historian. The legal historian H. F. Jolowicz expressed just this view on wills and guardianship in Greek-speaking Egypt: the Greeks were perfectly happy to accept fluid informality and ignore legal forms. But in his view the correspondence between law and behavior in the Roman world was much closer, because "the Romans, being lawyers, could not rest satisfied with such a position" (Jolowicz 1947, 88). An assertion based on such a stereotype may not seem convincing today, but extreme skepticism seems unwarranted in the case of the Romans. Of course, some areas of the western empire and some strata of the population were unaffected by Roman law. There were also spheres of daily life where formal powers in law, such as the father's right to execute his child, had little bearing on behavior (Saller 1986). Then as now, however, there were certain crises or transitions in life in which law and legal documents were expected to come into play—the most important being the transmission of one's property after death. Propertied Romans clearly did believe that wills and other documents would determine or at least influence outcomes during these transitions—hence their creativity in developing legal instruments to guide their property into the desired hands after their death.

Rather than viewing the law of succession as restraining, or liberating, or reflecting mores (it did all of these things, too), this chapter emphasizes the instrumental nature of the law. Hart noted that "such laws do not impose duties or obligations. Instead, they provide individuals with faculties for realizing their wishes, by conferring certain legal powers upon them to create, by certain specified procedures and subject to certain conditions, structures of rights and duties within the coercive framework of the law" (Hart 1961, 27). The reference to realizing wishes may sound similar to Corbier's version of testamentary law as potential freedom from social norms, but there is more to it. The *Digest* illustrates the ingenious use of legal instruments not only in pursuit of freedom from social norms but also in strategies to cope with various contingencies on the way to meeting social norms. The ways in which Romans did—and did not—manipulate their flexible legal instruments have much to tell about their principal concerns and aims in the transmission of patrimonies from one generation to the next.

TESTAMENTARY LAW AND PRACTICE

By the classical period the Roman law of succession consisted of several layers of rules from different periods, organized on different principles and reflecting different conceptions of kinship (Crook 1967, chap. 4; Thomas 1976, pt. 6).

It is reasonably assumed that the oldest stratum is reflected in the law of intestacy found in the Twelve Tables (451–450 B.C.). If a Roman *paterfamilias* died without a valid will, the order of succession was (2) *sui heredes,* or "his own heirs" (those who became independent of paternal authority on his death, usually his children and possibly grandchildren by sons, but also a wife married *cum manu*); (2) *proximus agnatus,* or "closest agnate" (nearest relative linked by males, most commonly brothers, sisters, or paternal uncles); and (3) *gentiles,* or clansmen of the same name (names being transmitted from fathers to children) (Watson 1975, chap. 5). This system was based on agnatic ties, giving no recognition to kinship links through women.

The Twelve Tables allowed for the possibility of a written will by a testator who wished to supersede the rules of intestacy. How common the written will was in the fifth century B.C. is impossible to know, but several centuries later propertied Romans expected to write wills and intestacy was avoided. Nevertheless, the intestate rules giving first claim to all sui heredes continued to reflect certain elements of Roman mores and expectations at a general level. All sons and daughters were thought to deserve a substantial share of their father's estate, even if not the equal shares that came to those whose fathers died intestate. That underlying sentiment can be found in the apologetic clauses included in some wills: for instance, the father who asked his daughter "not to be angry because I shall have left a more substantial inheritance to your brother, who, as you know, will be sustaining great burdens and will be discharging the legacies which I have made above" (*Dig.* 31.34.6). The need for explicit comment on a lesser share for a daughter, whether in a real will or the jurist's imagination, suggests that a larger share for sons or eldest sons was not taken for granted (as also in *Dig.* 32.27.1).

Even if most propertied Romans left wills to distribute their estates unevenly, the rules of intestacy did not become an irrelevant archaism. Wills had to be written in fixed formulas and could easily fail on technicalities, leaving the deceased intestate. It seems unlikely, therefore, that the Romans would have tolerated a system of intestacy widely at variance with their broad standards for equitable division of patrimonies. Furthermore, from the end of the republic close relatives were able to bring a *querela inofficiosi testamenti* ("complaint of an unduteous will") against a will that flouted standards of equity and responsibility without good cause. If a testator did not name all children in his will or explicitly disinherit them for bad behavior, sons or daughters could bring a complaint partially to break the will so that the rules of intestacy would come into operation. The testator could preempt the complaint by leaving to sui heredes at least a quarter of what would have been due to them on intestacy. The rules were far more complex than just stated (for example, sons had to be disinherited by name, but daughters could be disinherited in a general clause), but the point is that the querela can be understood only against the background of a belief in the continuing legitimacy of the rules of intestacy. These rules were rooted in a conviction that a Roman father was morally obliged to include all his children in the settlement of his property (Renier 1942). Here the law is a reflection of mores and a restraint. The invention of the remedy is also evidence of deviance from the mores. According to Ulpian, "it must be known that complaints of undutiful wills are frequent: to all parents as well as children it is permitted to dispute an undutiful will" (*Dig.* 5.2.1).

After sui heredes, the proximus agnatus stood next in line to inherit, followed by gentiles. The property interests of agnates were further recognized in the early law of *tutela,* or guardianship. Both women and minors no longer in paternal power came under the guardianship of the nearest agnate, unless otherwise arranged, on the principle that the *tutor* should be the one who stood to inherit the property from those who by definition could not have sui heredes. At a general level, emphasis on agnatic relationships in property transmission and guardianship corresponded with Roman elite thinking about dignity and honor, which were transmitted through the *familia* marked by the nomen (Saller 1984). Although sui heredes remained at the center of moral and legal ideas about succession, by the end of the republican era in the mid-first century B.C. both the rules of succession and conceptions of family honor had broadened beyond agnatic kin.

THE PRAETORIAN EDICT, COGNATES, AND THE DOMUS

Contemporary sources for Roman social history in the second century B.C. indicate that kinship reckoning and property transmission were not strictly along agnatic lines. The written will was being used by women as well as men to leave estates to other kin. A close reading of the second-century historian Polybius led Suzanne Dixon to conclude that in his day "it was usual for women of the propertied classes to make wills. The general expectation that a mother should regard her children as her proper beneficiaries is likewise established, whatever her legal relation to them by the rules of *agnatio*" (Dixon 1985b, 170). The importance of women in the transmission of patrimonies became such a concern that in 169 B.C. the lex Voconia was passed to bar women from being named as heirs to estates of the top property class (100,000 sesterces or more). They could still take legacies, but not in an amount greater than the principal heir received. The lex Voconia represents law as restraint, but as it turned out, one that was ineffective because it ran counter to the strong feeling that fathers ought to provide for their children, daughters as well as sons. The Romans soon displayed their creativity in adapting legal instruments to circumvent the law—as Dixon has neatly put it, "breaking the law to do the right thing" (Dixon 1985c).

The real direction of change was marked not by the Voconian law, but by the praetor's edict. The praetor was the annual senior Roman magistrate who interpreted and developed the law by issuing an edict outlining how he intended to interpret the law. During the late republic praetors were denying unjust claims based on the letter of the *jus civile* in favor of equitable settlements. In the middle or late first century B.C. the contemporary sense of equity in succession led praetors to include in the edict a new title, "Unde cognati" (Watson 1971, 181). As a result, cognates were formally recognized in the residual rules of succession. The new order was children, *legitimi* (closest agnate as recognized in earlier law), followed by *cognati,* husband and wife. Among close kinship ties agnatic links were still given preference, but the recognition of kinship bonds to and through mothers, as well as that of husband and wife, must have eliminated gentiles from succession in most cases.

The legal change was part of a broader trend toward taking account of non-agnatic kin in considerations of honor and posterity. Whereas Cicero in the mid-first century B.C. repeatedly referred to familia and nomen as markers of honor, 150 years later Pliny focused on the respectability of the *domus* (house), which in addition to agnates encompassed cognates who did not share the same nomen. Posterity, which seems to have had agnatic connotations in the republic, came specifically to include descendants through daughters in the early empire (Saller 1984, 348). The jurist Callistratus expressed Roman notions of posterity: "we conceive and produce sons and daughters so that from the continuing stock of both we may leave a memory of ourselves for all time" (*Dig.* 50.16.220.3). The Roman law of succession evolved in response to social mores regarding rights of cognates, but the change was very slow. The closeness of the mother-child bond received full recognition in the *jus civile* only in two laws, the Senatus consulta Tertullianum and Orfitianum of the second century after Christ—three centuries after the literary evidence shows mothers passing on estates to their children through written wills and two centuries after the praetorian edict gave a claim to cognates, including mothers and their children (Crook 1986; Dixon 1988, 54–60).

WILLS, TRUSTS, AND STRATEGIES

Written legal instruments, already available under the Twelve Tables of 451/450 B.C., were developed to a high degree of sophistication and flexibility over the next millennium. The law of testaments combined "freedom and formality." As David Johnston (1988, 3) has recently described, "civil law provided that formal requirements must be met. No will was valid if it was not duly made and witnessed, if it did not begin with the institution of an heir in prescribed form; no legacy was valid if it did not follow the institution and itself satisfy the time-honored wordings." As long as the formalities were met, the written testament in principle allowed the testator nearly unlimited freedom, until the development of the querela inofficiosi testamenti at the end of the republic; even then, testators could dispose of three-quarters of their estates as they pleased. If social pressures and family strategies added extralegal constraints, Romans were still notable for their dispersion of wealth beyond the family (Corbier 1985).

In spite of the freedom allowed in testamentary law, the formal requirements apparently chafed. Throughout the centuries of the imperial era jurists developed a different legal instrument, the *fideicommissum,* or trust. The fideicommissum was available by the Ciceronian age as an extralegal means of circumventing the Voconian law. If propertied fathers were barred from naming a woman as heir, they could institute a male third party as heir and instruct the heir by a fideicommissum to hand on the estate to the woman (often a daughter) as a gift. Initially the instructions had no legal standing, and the testator could rely only on the heir's *fides,* or faith. A famous ethical discussion from Cicero (*De finibus* 2.55, 58) points to the weakness of the republican trust. Publius Sextilius Rufus instituted Quintus Fadius Gallus as heir with the agreement, it was believed, that he hand over the estate to Rufus's daughter, who was ineligible to be named heir under the Voconian law. Gallus disavowed the agreement and claimed responsibility to uphold the laws, including the Voconian. Cicero and other contemporaries saw this as self-interested hyperlegalism, but the daughter had nothing beyond Gallus's good faith to stand on. A generation later Augustus saw such behavior as a flagrant breach of morality and instructed the magistrates to enforce fideicommissa. Trusts could take the form of either attachments to formal testamenta or informal documents to stand in place of testamenta. Over the centuries of the imperial era the latter sort of fideicommissum developed as a legal instrument, subverting the older testamentary system. Eventually, in the Justinian period the alternative forms of succession were brought together in a single form resembling the fideicommissum more than the testament (Johnston 1988).

If the fideicommissum was initially used to transmit property to those who had no capacity to receive in civil law, its attractions went much further. It was a legal instrument in which form was unimportant: whereas a flawed testament would fail and give way to intestacy, the trust had the advantage of respecting the intent of the testator as long as that could be discerned. This feature was valued, as is evident from the opening of a will quoted as an example by the second-century jurist Scaevola: " 'I, Lucius Titius, have written this, my will with no legal adviser, following the reason of my own mind rather than excessive and wretched pedantry; and if I should happen to have done anything without due legality or skill, the intention of a sane man ought to be held valid at law' " (*Dig.* 31.88.17, in Johnston 1988, 139). As a will, this document was invalid, but because of the opening it was construed by the jurist as a trust and respected. The advantage of putting intent above form was patent (the corresponding disadvantageous potential for ambiguity was easily overlooked by nonlawyers). Consequently, after Vespasian and Hadrian closed the loopholes so that those incapable of taking under civil law also became incapable of taking under trusts, the popularity of trusts continued to grow. Precisely because the fideicommissa embodied intent without the structure of formalities and were developed in the early imperial period, it is especially interesting to examine how they were manipulated in the pursuit of certain ends; because they were so flexible, to ask how they were not used is also meaningful.

GOALS AND STRATEGIES

Discussions of Roman heirship strategies may have been too heavily influenced in the English-speaking world, consciously or unconsciously, by knowledge of the early modern period. For example, trusts bring to mind the English development of perpetual entail, a legal instrument designed to keep the family estate intact as it passed on to a son in each succeeding generation. Practical problems often interfered (Bonfield 1979), of course, but the long-term goal was clear: the ideal was the indefinite transmission of the patrimony through the hands of eldest sons. Such grand strategies for posterity or lineage can too easily distract attention from the more immediate difficulties faced by testators.

The magnitude of the short-term obstacles to ideal inheritance patterns is suggested in a provocative study of Austrian farmers by Reinhard Sieder and Michael Mitterauer. Their examination of the evidence for areas in which primogeniture was the paradigmatic form of succession revealed that only about one-third of the successions conformed to the paradigm. In ultimogeniture areas characterized by smaller holdings, the rate of conformity was much lower, under one-tenth. Various events in the course of family life could derail the patrimony from the preferred line of transmission. Some fathers had no sons. Another common cause of deviation was the remarriage of the widow and the addition of a stepfather, introducing a new family into the circle of prospective heirs (Sieder and Mitterauer 1983, 312).

The Austrian and Roman cases are not precisely comparable, and of course quantitative generalizations are beyond the Roman historian's grasp. But the

Austrian evidence suggests that looking for material related to short-term problems of succession would be worthwhile. A survey of the *Digest* does indeed show that many of the stock clauses in Roman wills and trusts were intended to deal with the problems Sieder and Mitterauer discovered in Austria. Several features of Roman family life, demography, and law made the transmission of property to the next generation less than straightforward; some, like high mortality, would be found in most premodern societies, whereas others were more culturally specific.

First, the typical age structure of the Roman family raised problems. A broad survey of the relationships between commemorator and deceased preserved on Roman tombstones has revealed in Italy and the provinces of the Romanized west a typical Mediterranean pattern of late male and early female marriage (Shaw 1987a; Saller 1987). There is a noticeable shift from commemoration by parents to commemoration by spouses for men in their late twenties and early thirties and for women in their late teens and early twenties. The best explanation for the shift is that these were the typical ages at marriage. Among the senatorial elite the typical ages were probably about five years younger for both men and women. For all statuses attested in the inscriptions, there was a common Mediterranean age gap between men and women of seven to ten years. This information, together with a reasonable guess at life expectancy at birth ($e_0 = 25$ using the Coale-Demeny table for Level 3 West), enabled us to generate a model population of families with the aid of the Cambridge Group's computer simulation.[1] An analysis of the model population offers a rough idea of the numbers and types of living kin for a Roman of a given age. Some of the resulting numbers are sensitive to certain arbitrary parameters that were fed into the program, but the proportion of living fathers depends heavily on ages at marriage, for which we have ancient evidence (see table 2.1).

This table clearly has implications for the limits of paternal power (Saller 1986, 1987). Although *patria potestas* lasted for the lifetime of the father, it was less oppressive than often thought because most adult Romans did not have a living father. In light of Sieder and Mitterauer's study, it also has powerful implications for patterns of succession. At the death of their fathers, nearly half

---

1. Besides the mortality rates from Coale and Demeny (1983), first marriage was assigned in the simulation so that 67 percent of women were married by age twenty-two and 67 percent of men by age thirty-two. In the absence of ancient evidence, levels of fertility were assumed to be the same as those used by the Cambridge Group for the History of Population and Social Structure for eighteenth-century England, giving a mean age at maternity of twenty-seven. The simulation has been criticized (see Smith 1989 on the criticism of Ruggles 1987). If Ruggles's criticisms were valid, the demographic features of the Roman family stressed in this chapter would be exaggerated rather than diminished.

TABLE 2.1

Percentage of Romans at a Given Age
with a Living Father

Senatorial Order		Ordinary Romans	
Age	Percentage	Age	Percentage
5	85	5	84
10	69	10	68
15	55	15	54
20	43	20	41
25	32	25	30
30	20	30	19
35	12	35	12
40	6	40	6

of Roman children were legally *impuberes*—that is, under the age of puberty, defined as twelve for girls and fourteen for boys. An additional quarter were between puberty and twenty-five years old, the age at which Romans were judged fully responsible to manage their own property. Only a minority of Romans inherited as full adults; consequently, guardianship of children must have been a far more important social issue than commonly realized.

The complexity of the situation was increased by the odd contradiction within the Roman family: the wife's independence from her husband's authority and her full property rights, juxtaposed with the children's lifetime submission to paternal authority and their consequent inability to own property as long as their father was alive (barring emancipation). This meant that the mother could very well be a financial force in the family in her own right. It also meant that although children were thought to deserve shares of their mother's financial resources upon her death, if she predeceased her husband, her children would not normally have the capacity to inherit in their own name.

The intricacies of succession were further complicated by remarriage. Although remarriage was hardly unique to Roman society, it surely was a bigger factor in classical Rome than in later Christian societies because of the ease of divorce. Roman historians disagree about the frequency of divorce, but the case made by Michel Humbert (1972) that it was common among the elite seems convincing (the arguments of Raepsaet-Charlier (1981–1982) to the contrary are flawed in my judgment). Yet it must be conceded that no good evidence exists for the vast majority of the population, and ordinary Romans may have had less incentive to divorce and remarry (Kajanto 1969, whose evidence cannot prove his conclusion). Nevertheless, divorce at all levels was probably more common than in later periods, when the Church exercised considerable influence to maintain marriages. Furthermore, the attitude toward remarriage changed under the influence of Christianity. Although classical attitudes were ambivalent, to increase the rate of childbearing Augustan marriage legislation penalized men and women who did not remarry following divorce or the death of a spouse. General considerations, then, suggest that the breakup and the reconstitution of families were more common in the classical period than later. As in other societies, the new relatives acquired through remarriage were perceived as threats to normal succession. According to Jolowicz, the threat of the stepmother has been overstated, and as a stereotype, the evil *noverca* certainly was subject to exaggeration. The figures of Sieder and Mitterauer, however, give a sober indication of the disruptive potential of stepparents and siblings.

Roman law attempted to meet the dangers inherent in remarriage through the institution of *tutela* of impuberes, or guardianship. Tutela was regarded as a "masculine duty" from which mothers were traditionally barred (*Dig.* 26.1.16.18). It was conventional for fathers to name their most trusted friends ("amicissimos et fidelissimos") in their wills as tutors for their underage children and to reward them with a legacy for their troubles (*Dig.* 27.1.36 pr.). If no tutor was named in the will, the nearest agnate as *tutor legitimus* was the next choice. If neither type of tutor was available, the magistrate was responsible for appointing a tutor and exacting security for the return of the estate from him. The state saw itself as having an interest in protecting the *pupillus,* or underage heir (*Dig.* 26.6.2.2). But a tutor was no guarantee against threats to the child heir's estate, since tutors themselves had a reputation for embezzling. For the honest man, tutela was regarded in classical times as an onerous burden in the interests of the child. The tutor stood to make personal financial sacrifices in the service (see, for example, *Dig.* 34.3.10.8), and if convicted of dishonest management upon final accounting, he suffered *infamia,* or disgrace. In view of the pervasive need for tutors and the problems raised by their guardianship, it is not surprising that the title "De administratione et periculo tutorum" (26.7) is one of the longest in the *Digest,* or that a body of law about legal excuses evolved.

If the extensiveness of tutela created certain problems, its limits created others. Tutela came to an end when the pupillus reached the legal age of puberty, after which the heirs no longer needed the approval of a tutor to enact valid transactions. Propertied youths under the age of twenty-five received some protection in law. Through *restitutio in integrum,* if a youth was taken advantage of in a transaction, the court could order that it be nullified and affairs restored to what they had been. The institution of *cura* developed throughout the imperial era: in the early empire the *curator* gave nonbinding advice on financial management; in the early postclassical era the curator's approval became a requirement for a valid transaction. One can imagine that in the early empire a testator might well have been concerned at the prospect of his youthful heirs having wide discretion over the patrimony as early as age twelve. The testator could, however, employ legal instruments to alter the residual rules concerning age.

Finally, as the law of succession grew more complex and allowed more kin to make claims, the possibilities of a Roman's estate passing in some unforeseen direction also increased. Consider the case described by Modestinus (*Dig.* 49.14.9): a man named his sister heir to three-quarters of his estate and his wife and father-in-law to the remaining shares; his will was voided by a posthumous son; consequently, the entire inheritance devolved upon the son, who died shortly thereafter, and then on his mother. Given ancient mortality rates, the case of the posthumous child, and more specifically one who lived just long enough to disrupt the testator's plans, was not as rare as might be thought (perhaps one in fifty, or enough to worry a Roman in such an important matter). In another example (*Dig.* 28.16.47), "a man, who had a son and a daughter who were both *impubes,* having instituted the son as his heir, disinherited the daughter and substituted the daughter to the son if he died before reaching puberty; but he substituted to the daughter, if she had died before she married, his wife and his sister. Since the daughter died first while *impubes* and then her brother while *impubes,* I ask whether the inheritance belongs to the wife and the sister." Here the testator's wish that his estate go to his wife and sister in the event of the deaths of his children before adulthood seems clear enough, but because he failed to anticipate all the permutations of order of death, his wish was frustrated.

One of the reasons for such unforeseen diversion of the patrimony lay in the rather strict biological view the jurists took of kinship. It is commonly said now that the Roman newborn became part of the family through the ritual act of the father raising up (*tollere*) the infant to signify acceptance (expressed, for example, by Veyne 1987, 9), rather than through the biological event of birth. From the legal point of view this is patently false, as is evident in an example given by Scaevola. "A man had repudiated his wife when pregnant and taken another; the first wife gave birth and exposed the son; someone else rescued him, and he was brought up and always called by his father's name; during his father's lifetime neither father nor mother knew that he was alive; on the father's death, his will was read in which he neither disinherited his son nor instituted him as heir; the son was acknowledged by his mother and paternal grandmother, and took possession of the father's inheritance as the legitimate heir succeeding on intestacy" (*Dig.* 40.4.29). Here, then, is another illustration of why testators might be concerned about an unexpected outcome of dogged application of intricate rules.

In sum, before a Roman could start realistically thinking about his or her future generations of posterity, there were many demographic, legal, and social contingencies to face in guiding his or her property into the hands of his or her living kin. Testators might find themselves in several basic situations. Presumably the simplest would be that of the testator who had lived a long life and produced children who had grown into responsible adults with children of their own. The direction in which the estate would descend could be comfortably predicted. Even if one or another of the children was favored in a written will, the division of the property among the primary heirs in case of failure of the will might not seem too unfortunate. Property owners sometimes anticipated death by dividing the estate in advance and then confirming the arrangement in the will (*Dig.* 10.2.20.3, 10.2.39.5, 14.3.19.2, 32.37.3, 41.10.4.1). The simulation model, however, shows that only a fraction of Roman testators were able to transmit their patrimonies in such a simple, direct fashion.

Testators who anticipated that they might die before their children reached adulthood had to make more difficult decisions about whom to trust and how to arrange the devolution of their property. It was probable that one parent would die before the children were adults, but not both. For a wife who had faith in her husband, the matter was fairly straightforward: she could bequeath the property to her children or to her husband. Either way, the husband would assume ownership of the property and pass it on to the children upon his death (that is, when they became independent and could own property themselves). If the wife wished to add legal force to that faith, she could charge her husband with a fideicommissum to restore the property to her children—a practice well attested in the *Digest* (31.77.7, 32.41.12 [a foster child], 35.2.95 pr., 36.1.17.11, 36.1.20 pr., 36.1.80.10, 36.3.7). There were variations on this practice: the husband might be allowed usufruct of the wife's property (*Dig.* 31.34.7), or he might be instructed to give the child an allowance (*Dig.* 33.1.25). Needless to say, not all fathers deserved such trust; some defrauded the fideicommissum established on behalf of their children (*Dig.* 36.1.52). During the late empire the *dominium* of the father over maternal property left for the children continued, but his discretion was drastically reduced to protect the children's interests (Dixon 1988, 58–60).

When the husband predeceased his trusted wife, the traditional prohibition on women fulfilling the duty of tutela required more legal gymnastics. A husband who had complete faith could disinherit his children and institute his wife as heir with a charge to restore the property to the children. Historians tend to think of disherison as a penalty for unfilial behavior (as it often was), but jurists were also aware that "many men disinherit their children not as a mark of disgrace nor to prejudice them, but so as to provide for their interests, as, for example, where they are *impuberes,* and they give them the inheritance by *fideicommissum*" (*Dig.* 28.2.18, Ulpian). The transmission of property in this way—from father to mother to children—appears repeatedly in the *Digest* (31.88.2, 35.1.77.3, 36.1.76.1, 36.1.80.14, 36.2.26.2, 37.77.12). The trust between spouses implicit in this arrangement was highly valued: "The Emperor Marcus [Aurelius] ruled in a rescript that the words in which a testator had provided 'that he did not doubt that his wife would deliver to the children whatever she had taken' [namely, from his estate] should be taken as a *fideicommissum.* This rescript is highly salutary to ensure that the honor of a well-conducted marriage, and confidence that children are held in common, does not deceive a husband who thought too highly of the mother" (*Dig.* 31.67.10).

Aside from a fideicommissum, the husband could give legal force to his faith by instituting his children as heirs but giving his wife *usufructus* and *usus* of the property together with the children. This strategy, in evidence from the late republic, was a convenient means of entrusting management of the inheritance to the mother and taking care of her needs, and at the same time protecting the children's ownership (see Cicero, *Pro Caecina* 11–12; compare *Dig.* 7.2.8; for later times, *Dig.* 33.2.37). Alternatively, the testator sometimes asked simply that his wife and child hold his property in common (*Dig.* 31.89.3, 36.1.80 pr.).

That the mother was often the natural choice as guardian because she had her children's interests most at heart is reflected in the attempts of husbands to leave management of their children's estates in their wives' hands even before they legally could serve as their children's tutor. Some husbands instructed the tutor to heed the wife's wishes, which occasionally put tutors in an awkward dilemma, caught between the will of their ward's mother and their own best judgment about the child's interests (*Dig.* 4.4.47 pr., 26.7.5.8, 38.17.2.23). In spite of the legal niceties, mothers were de facto supervising their children's property as early as the late republic (Cicero, *Verrines* 2.1.105f.; Seneca, *Consolation to Helvia* 14.3; see Dixon 1988, chap. 3). But the law was not irrelevant, and ignoring legal rules carried risks, as in a case of Scaevola's (*Dig.* 46.3.88; compare 3.5.30.6). There were other compromises to compensate for the mother's inability formally to act as tutor. Her husband's will might grant her the choice of residence for their children (not legally binding) or the choice of a husband for their daughter (*Dig.* 33.1.7, 23.2.62 pr.).

The threat to the mother's devotion posed by remarriage was not taken lightly. Augustan legislation intended to encourage marriage and childbearing made conditions prohibiting marriage or remarriage on bequests void. But it was acceptable to bequeath property to one's wife on condition that she not remarry as long as the children were impuberes (*Dig.* 35.1.62.2). Gradually the law came to accept mothers as tutors. Around A.D. 100 the jurist Neratius allowed that mothers could petition the emperor for special dispensation to act as tutor for their children. In the later empire this possibility was generalized, but only if the mother took an oath that she would not remarry—an oath that was more compatible with the new Christian attitude toward remarriage (Dixon 1988, 65). As in other matters of succession, what had been an individual arrangement through legal instruments in earlier periods became a legal rule under the Christian emperors.

Hostility and distrust between husband and wife increased the need for careful manipulation of legal instruments. The mother who anticipated predeceasing her children's father faced the problem that the children were likely to be in the potestas of the father, who would therefore acquire anything left to them. The law offered solutions to this obstacle. The mother could leave the property to the children on the condition that they be emancipated from the father's power (*Dig.* 5.3.58). The father could not be compelled to do so, but his refusal would cost his family the bequest (*Dig.* 30.114.8, 35.1.92). The father in such circumstances would naturally be eager to acquire the property (as in Pliny's account of Regulus and his son in *Ep.* 4.2); if he did meet the condition, the law tried to honor the mother's intention by preventing the father from retaking control of his child's affairs (*Dig.* 26.5.21.1). We hear of other relatives, especially grandmothers, who included the emancipation condition in their wills to ensure that their property reached the children for whom it was intended (*Dig.* 27.10.16.2, 28.7.18, 35.1.77 pr., 35.1.93). The emancipation condition was the extreme example of how the diffusion of property in Roman families could undermine the monopoly of potestas granted to the paterfamilias in law (Saller 1988). When late imperial law came to recognize and protect children's property while it was technically in the father's dominium, this and other legal devices may have become less necessary.

When the father predeceased his wife, the residual legal rules kept the children's property from the control of their mother. The father could name a tutor whom he trusted, perhaps a relative (such as the child's older brother, paternal uncle, or maternal grandfather) or a friend (*Dig.* 26.7.39.8, 31.70.2, 35.2.14.3, 22.3.26, 26.7.32.6, 27.3.9.1, 31.77.7, 9, 30). If the father neglected to name a tutor, his wife and freedmen were obliged to request one from the magistrate, and cognates, affines, and friends were allowed to bring such a request (*Dig.* 26.6.2). Because tutela was regarded as a burden, volunteers were not always forthcoming, but in a slave society a whole class of men was subject to compulsion. A freedman, who was in his ex-master's debt for the favor of manumission, was obligated to serve as tutor for his master's children (*Dig.* 37.14.19). What the freedman lacked in status he often made up for in experience as the master's agent or financial manager. A freedman who was not formally appointed tutor might be asked to stay on with the children in return for a legacy or annuity (*Dig.* 40.5.41.16; also 33.1.13, in which a grandmother entrusts management of an inheritance to a freedman on behalf of a grandson; 32.37.5 for an uncle).

Through tutela the state and the magistrates worked to protect the interests of countless underage heirs, but the normal rules of tutela were not satisfactory in some circumstances. In classical law the mother did not enjoy the same right as the father to name a tutor. The mother's choice might nevertheless be respected for the property she herself left (*Dig.* 26.2.4, 26.3.2 pr.). Alternatively, the mother could resort to a fideicommissum. Pollidius, for example, "was made heir by a woman relative and asked to restore to the woman's daughter at a certain age whatever he obtained from the estate. The mother explained in her will that she did this in order to entrust her daughter's affairs to relatives rather than to tutors. . . . The mother had chosen the remedy of fideicommissum to avoid the dangers of *tutela*" (*Dig.* 22.1.3.3, Papinian). As in this case, a woman's relatives were natural choices for such a trust (*Dig.* 36.3.18 pr.). Yet trust was a very personal matter that sometimes flew in the face of stereotypes; "a woman who had left two sons in the power of their father and married another man instituted her second husband her heir and asked him to restore her inheritance to her children or to the survivor of them after the death of their father." To everyone's surprise, the distrusted father emancipated the sons before his death; the emperor Marcus Aurelius ruled that the estate could then be restored in accord with the woman's implicit intention (*Dig.* 36.1.23 pr.). Though the law generally tended to protect children's property from stepparents, legal instruments were flexible enough to override many rules.

The law of tutela, as suggested above, established age limits that might be unsatisfactory to fathers, mothers, and other relatives. A testator who was nervous at the thought of a teenage son making decisions about his patrimony could use the fideicommissum to raise the age. A husband might leave his property to his wife to be restored to their son at age twenty-five, who perhaps would receive any profits in the meantime (*Dig.* 36.2.26.2). Sixteen or eighteen or twenty or the occasion of marriage might be deemed the appropriate times for restoration (*Dig.* 33.2.37, 34.3.28.8, 35.1.10 pr., 36.1.48, 36.1.76.1, 36.2.30). The fideicommissum could operate in the opposite way, instructing the child instituted heir to hand over the estate to another's management, as in Scaevola's example: "A man instituted as heirs his son to three-quarters and his wife to one-quarter and imposed on his son a fideicommissum that he should hand over his inheritance to his stepmother. Of her, however, he asked that she should take thought for the youthful weaknesses of his son and pay him ten aurei a month until he reached his twenty-fifth year, but when reached that age she should hand over to him half the inheritance" (*Dig.* 33.1.21.2). The manipulation of legal instruments to meet personal circumstances at odds with the usual stereotypes is again in evidence here.

Testators had to use their discretion and judgment in deciding at what age their ultimate heirs would be responsible; some decided that they could not predict or could not trust their normal heir at all. Fideicommissa offered solutions to such difficulties. A testator could leave property to a third party with instructions to restore it to the beneficiary when he or she began to demonstrate a sense of responsibility (*Dig.* 34.4.30 pr.). A woman who distrusted her sons but did not want to take the extreme action of disinheriting them instituted the sons as heirs and instructed them to surrender management of the estate to a third party until the property could be divided among the grandchildren when they reached age twenty-five (*Dig.* 36.1.80.1).

Added to the testator's concerns about whom to entrust with management of his or her estate was the unpredictability of high mortality. Parents writing wills had to expect that not all young children would reach adulthood and produce their own families; nor could it be taken for granted that a guardian would live to finish his term of duty. If matters were left to the residual rules of intestacy, the estate could move in unforeseen directions. Wills, therefore, commonly named a substitute to the main heir; if the heir died as a pupillus, the substitute would have a claim (Thomas 1976, 491–93). This sort of instrument was known as a pupillary will, and it became void when the pupillus reached puberty (*Dig.* 30.92.2ff.). The institution of an impubes son, with the testator's brother's sons named as substitutes, presumably was not uncommon (*Dig.* 34.9.16 pr.). A testator daunted by all the permutations created by the vagaries of mortality might place the estate in the hands of someone close, with general instructions to pass it on in accordance with good judgment to whatever descendants survived. Papinian offers an illustration (*Dig.* 36.1.59.2): "I request of you, my dearest wife, that when you die you restore my inheritance to my children or to one of them or to my grandchildren or to such of them as you wish or to my kinsmen, should you wish to choose any from among my whole kindred (*cognatio*).' "

I have outlined the legal rules and the possible uses of Roman legal instruments to emphasize the almost endless number of ways written wills and trusts were devised to cope with the structures of the legal system, the uncertainties of death, and the peculiar configuration of personal relationships enjoyed by each testator. In view of the extraordinary flexibility of the legal instruments to further the testator's specific wishes, it is highly significant that Roman trusts were not developed in the classical period to transmit family estates indefinitely down through the generations. The recent findings of David Johnston's study of Roman trusts (1988, 77–78) are worth quoting:

> For family settlements it is quite remarkable how little evidence of any kind there is in classical times. The jurists supply only five instances, of which the following is typical: "A testator instituted his brother heir and requested that his house should not be sold but that it should be left in the familia . . ." [*Dig.* 31.69.3]. This text, and another with almost identical wording, have modest ambitions. The dispositions they attest do not lay claim to controlling the fate of the property for many generations. Instead they are content to provide that the immediate beneficiary should not have free disposal but be required to leave the property to a member of the family. The same may be said for other texts with different wording. There is in fact only one text which aims for more: "I wish my house not to be sold by my heirs nor to be pledged by them but to remain intact with them and their sons and descendants for all time . . ." [*Dig.* 31.88.15]. The words are in Greek, which may be significant: if the writer was familiar with any legal system, it may well have been a system other than Roman.

The one exceptional case, it should be added, concerned a house rather than a patrimony.

Roman law did not permit settlements in perpetuity: the testator could direct his or her property only as far as one generation beyond those living. But the evidence does not suggest that Roman testators were interested in pushing the legal instruments to that limit. Plenty of examples attest to the desire of testators to guide their property past the hands of their immediate beneficiaries, but in most cases the concern was limited to how the property would be distributed among the living. Papinian provides an illustration: "A father appointed his sons as heirs and wrote as follows: 'I ask you, my daughter, that, having accepted from my inheritance as your portion a hundred aurei and my Tusculan lands, you restore to your mother your share of the inheritance'" (*Dig.* 31.77 pr.). Here, as in the great majority of such instances, the trust allowed the testator to express his wishes as to who among his immediate circle of kin and friends would benefit from his property in the event that his heir or legatee died. Curiously, when Romans did include clauses expressing an interest in the perpetuation of their nomen, the instructions to keep particular properties within the nomen usually concerned freedmen who bore their ex-master's name, rather than his direct descendants (Johnston 1988, 88–97). The interest in family settlements in perpetuity, as we understand them, began to appear only in the Byzantine period (Johnston 1988, 116).

The concept of heirship strategies brings to mind the preoccupations of later European nobilities intent on preserving a consolidated patrimony in the male line forever. Roman preoccupations were less grandiose. Though some Roman aristocrats were certainly interested in their own posterity, the manipulation of legal instruments was directed toward more immediate problems, which are too easily underestimated: the pupillus and the tutor ought to loom much larger in our social (and economic) histories of the Roman world.[2] That Romans' manipulation of trusts was focused on the relatively short term is one aspect of a more general paradox: the Romans had enormously flexible legal instruments and institutions to perpetuate their lines and names (most obviously, adoption), but they cannot have exploited them to the fullest. Otherwise, imperial aristocrats would have been far more successful in social reproduction.

This summary of succession has shown Roman law to have been partly an embodiment of social norms, partly a restraint to enforce those norms of family obligation, and partly a means to free oneself from those obligations. The law was also an instrument to deal with demographic, legal, and personal contingencies. The patterns of manipulation reveal some familiar family features, especially the confidence placed in mothers, whatever their incapacities in law. But other patterns are specifically related to characteristics of Roman society, for example, the extensive property rights of women and the role of freedmen.

How far did the establishment of Christianity alter the relevant characteristics? Much remained the same, and late imperial law can often be seen as the culmination of earlier tendencies—for instance, the laws protecting the children's interest in their maternal estate. But the new official attitude toward widowhood and remarriage did have consequences: the first Christian emperor abolished the long unpopular Augustan marriage law requiring remarriage; once the widowed mother was no longer under legal pressure to remarry, she could more easily be considered a satisfactory official guardian for her children.

One final general consideration. The richness and complexity of Roman law gave Romans the potential to reach highly diverse goals. This calls into question the argument that Roman law had a powerful impact on southern Europe

---

2. The conservative Roman attitude toward investment, with a preference for land, is well-known. That a considerable proportion of estates in the Roman world were under the management of tutors must have contributed to that conservatism, since they were obligated, at the risk of their own estates, to guarantee a safe return on the investment of their wards' fortunes, and the safest investment was land.

when it was reintroduced centuries after the fall of the western empire. Roman law could be used to validate any number of patterns of devolution of property (though the querela inofficiosi testamenti would not allow primogeniture in its narrowest sense). Roman legal instruments could have been employed to continue customary practices of partible inheritance, which the Romans themselves judged proper, at least at an abstract level. Roman law offered a highly diverse and flexible tool kit: the tool kit by itself does not explain very much; what needs to be explained is why later southern European societies decided to use the tools in the way they did.

Chapter 3

PETER GARNSEY

Child Rearing in Ancient Italy

The history of childhood in European history takes off in the early modern period, around the sixteenth century. Historians of classical antiquity and the Middle Ages have until recently shown little interest in the topic, largely because their preoccupations have traditionally been different.[1] Shortage of evidence is not an adequate reason or excuse for this neglect. The reconstruction of infant life in early modern Europe is admittedly also a hazardous business. Indeed, Peter Laslett opted to study household size and composition because of the lack of data on infancy. His forthright criticism includes both primary sources (such as personal diaries) and secondary sources (such as advice literature): "It is well known how intractable the analysis of any body of documents of this kind can be; so untidy is it, so variable, so contradictory in its dogmas and doctrines, so capricious in what it preserves and what it must leave out" (Laslett 1977, 66). Linda Pollock is perhaps more representative of early modern social historians in her willingness to work with the sources, while admitting their deficiencies: "We still know little about how parents actually reared their children" (Pollock 1983, 203, 212, 234).

For antiquity, scattered literary discussions and references, though different from the early modern diaries, serve a similarly limited purpose. Between the literary texts, and such diverse sources as papyri recording wet-nurse contracts in Egypt, stone epitaphs for dead infants, and skeletal remains, we do not lack

Among those who helped me improve this chapter, I have special reason to thank Keith Bradley, Robert Sallares, and Greg Woolf. Robert Hinde and Keith Wrightson provided invaluable bibliographical assistance.

1. In addition to the monographs by Néraudau (1984), Boswell (1988), and Wiedemann (1989), useful contributions on a smaller scale include Bradley 1980, 1986; Brind'Amour and Brind'Amour 1971, 1975; Dixon 1988, chap. 5; Golden 1988; Rousselle 1983, chap. 3; and Wiesehöfer 1988. I am grateful to Josef Wiesehöfer for sending me a prepublication copy of his article and for permission to cite it.

information (of variable quality and quantity, to be sure) on parent-child attitudes, birth rituals, the treatment of babies, feeding patterns, and the nutritional status of infants. Again, the secondary literature from antiquity includes works whose influence on adult behavior and attitudes toward children in later periods of European history has been profound: they range from Soranus's *Gynaecology* to the various treatises wherein Augustine expounds the doctrine of original sin.[2]

Antiquity has not been a closed book to social historians who are not by training ancient historians. One thinks on the one hand of the work of Michel Foucault on sexuality and, on the other, of histories of pediatrics, breast feeding, and wet nursing, which have serviceable opening chapters on antiquity (Foucault 1984; Still 1931; Abt and Garrison 1965; Fildes 1986, 1988). The judgments of ancient attitudes and practices that are found in such works, however, are often superficial and inappropriate. Philippe Ariès, the founder of modern childhood history, for example, writes: "This feeling of indifference towards a too fragile childhood is not really very far removed from the callousness of the Roman or Chinese societies which practised the exposure of new-born children. We can now understand the gulf which separates our concept of childhood from that which existed before the demographic revolution or its preceding stages. There is nothing about this callousness which should surprise us: it was only natural in the community conditions of the time" (Ariès 1962, 37).

The approach of Ariès and those influenced by him (Hunt 1972; DeMause 1974; Shorter 1975; Stone 1977) is colored by an assumed ancient (or medieval) "before," with which is juxtaposed a modern "after" and an early modern transition. Such schematization carries obvious dangers; it gives the impression, for example, that attitudes and behavior toward children in ancient and early modern societies were sharply contrasting. But the issues are similar: crucially, a high rate of infant mortality was a shared feature of all premodern societies, and it should not simply be assumed that classical, medieval, and early modern societies coped with this in different ways. As it is, the behaviours that are usually taken as barometers of parental attitudes, in particular, the abandonment of unwanted babies, wet nursing, and swaddling, occurred in all the societies in question (though not necessarily to the same degree or for the same reasons from one society to another or, within any individual society,

2. The influence of Christianity on attitudes toward childhood is too large a subject to be treated here. Continuities with and divergences from the Jewish and pagan traditions merit exploration. (Keith Thomas has some suggestive comments on baptism as a *rite de passage* [1971, 36].) The main theme is the comprehensive reorientation of attitudes about childhood that was achieved by the church fathers, in particular, Augustine (see Currie forthcoming).

from one social class to another).[3] Thus it is quite wrong to suppose that the abandonment of infants was practiced to a significant extent only in ancient communities, or in ancient pagan communities.[4]

In fact, the whole procedure of inferring attitudes from behavior is problematic. The sources pose a number of problems, of which the first and most obvious is that the behavior in question is often flimsily recorded and (in any case) cannot be quantified. We do not and cannot know how common the exposure of children was in Greco-Roman antiquity (Patterson 1985; Boswell 1988, 46–49), or what proportion of abandoned children survived. In addition, parental behavior must be placed in a cultural and socioeconomic context if it is to receive anything but a superficial interpretation. Advocates of the "indifference thesis" are vulnerable to the criticism that their analyses are one-dimensional. Nor are their critics themselves entirely immune, for example, in their response to Lawrence Stone's judgment of a culture that practiced wet nursing as bleak and non-caring (Stone 1977, 65). These critics maintain that personal diaries reveal a quite different society, in which the high mortality rate "led not to indifference but to a persistent anxiety for their children in the face of the hazards of illness and accident" (Wrightson 1982b, 109), a society in which "affection and deep concern" for children was conspicuous (Macfarlane 1986, 52; compare Pollock 1983, 58). The effectiveness of such responses depends on the size and representativeness of the sample, both in this case strictly limited. The part of Stone's argument that pertains to the miserable and brutal life of the poor, who swaddled, smothered, and abandoned their children, remains untouched.[5]

Likewise, one cannot achieve any major breakthrough by summoning up from antiquity touching epitaphs and stray anecdotes to show that sometimes dead babies were mourned and surviving infants valued (among the elite and

3. With regard to antiquity, I have in mind mainstream Graeco-Roman society. I am aware, for example, that exposure was not practiced by the Jews (cf. Tacitus, *Hist.* 5.5) or the Egyptians (Diod. 1.80.3; Strabo 17.2.5; Masciadri and Montevecchi 1982).

4. It might even be argued that the standard classification of abandonment as a form of infanticide (cf. Scrimshaw 1983) is inappropriate in the case of pagan antiquity, because values and institutions (e.g., slavery) ensured a significant degree of "circulation" of the abandoned, and therefore a reasonable survival rate. For abandonment in the (Christian) late Roman Empire, see Boswell 1988, 69–75, 138–179. Wrightson (1982a) suggests for the Christian Era, with special reference to the early modern period, that a Christian social morality, especially its condemnation of illegitimacy, increased the rate of abandonment. For Italy, from the late Middle Ages onward, see, e.g., Trexler 1973a, 1973b (Florence); Tittarelli 1987 (Perugia); and Hunecke 1989 (Milan). Daly and Wilson (1984) argue, in a comprehensive comparative survey, that two-thirds of the societies of the contemporary world are infanticidal.

5. The division of society into rich and poor with which Stone operates is, of course, an oversimplification.

the upwardly mobile). Such evidence can do little more than justify the assertion that "there was no general absence of tender feeling for children as special
beings" (Boswell 1988, 37). A more significant riposte to the indifference thesis
is to show, as Fildes does for the early modern period, that wet nurses did not
invariably neglect the infants in their care, and that wet nursing might have
been resorted to as a means of spacing children close together or of reducing
absence from full-time employment (Fildes 1988).

With respect to Greco-Roman antiquity as well, the recourse to a wet nurse,
and other aspects of the regimen imposed on infants, must be explained with
reference not just to parental emotions, but also to the socioeconomic circumstances of individual families and to cultural practices and social values. The
cultural context in particular tends to get short shrift in the history of childhood. In the matter of the abandonment of children, the *rites de passage* of birth
and (infant) death thus provide an essential part of the background against
which to assess the decisions of parents.[6]

To summarize, a better understanding of childhood in antiquity is of importance not only in itself, but also as a contribution to a better founded "history of
childhood"—better founded in the sense that it would not privilege the quest
for "conscious human emotions" at the expense of the analysis of the norms
and practices and the socio/economic conditions of the society in question.

NEONATES: THE DEAD AND THE UNWANTED

The newborn were survivors of that most dangerous operation, birth. Or
they were temporary survivors. Many neonates—most according to Aristotle—died in the first days: "Most are carried off before the seventh day, and that
is why they give the child its name then from the belief that it has now a better
chance of survival" (*Hist. An.* 588a5). On the basis of comparative evidence,
and assuming an average expectation of life at birth of twenty-five years, one
can calculate that in ancient Rome 28 percent of those born alive, or 280 out of

6. Rites de passage have been studied (see especially, for Rome, Brind'Amour and
Brind'Amour 1971, 1975), but as far as I know, they have not previously been brought centrally
into the debate about parental attitudes. But see Golden (1988, 156), referring to the role of
"customary and well-accepted child-rearing practices" and "more or less elaborate ritual practices and eschatological beliefs," which reduce anxiety and "help parents come to terms with
their grief." Wiesehöfer (1988, 23) comes close to my argument when he infers from the legal
texts and the underrepresentation of infants in funerary inscriptions "dass jene Kinder eben noch
nicht also vollwertige soziale Persönlichkeiten angesehen wurden und als Träger familiärer
Traditionen ausfielen" (that such children were not yet acknowledged to be full members of
society and were judged deficient as bearers of family traditions).

1,000 children, died in the course of the first year, and around 50 percent died
before the age of ten (compare Hopkins 1983, 225).

The concept of infant mortality rate as customarily used by demographers
refers to numbers of deaths in the first year of life proportionate to live births.
Some historians of childhood use the term rather more loosely to cover the first
five or six years of life (Pollock 1983, 25). This does not matter much, as long as
the five-year period is not treated as monochrome, as if parents can be assumed
to have responded to the death of an infant in the same way, whatever its age.
The reconstructions of Ariès and of his adherents envisage parental indifference and neglect persisting in a kind of steady state throughout the period of
infancy.

One would expect parents to be more deeply affected by the deaths of older
children than those of the very young. This is confirmed by the early modern
English and American diaries, at least for the diary-compiling classes (Pollock
1983, 141). The Roman evidence appears to be corroborative. But we need to
ask not just how individual parents reacted to the premature deaths of their
children (a question that brings us face to face with the exiguity and problematic nature of the evidence), but also what kind of behavior was normative
and culturally sanctioned.

Funerary monuments and epitaphs suggest in the first place that a lower
evaluation was placed on neonates and young infants than on older children
and adults. Of more than sixteen thousand tombstones from the city of Rome
and elsewhere in Italy that recorded ages at death, only 1.3 percent were those
of babies under twelve months. The proportion rises significantly for children
between the ages of one and four (expected: 21 percent of all deaths; observed
13 percent). That is to say, all children under five were underrepresented in
commemorations, but by far the most pronounced underrepresentation was
that of infants in the first year of life (Hopkins 1983, 225). Of course, a child
who did not receive commemoration in an epitaph was not necessarily denied a
formal burial. In some Roman North African samples, there is an interesting
discrepancy between tombstone commemorations and actual burials. At the
town of Sitifis, 39 percent of all burials ($N = 228$) were of children under one
($N = 88$), and 62 percent those of children under ten ($N = 141$) (compare
Saller and Shaw 1984, 130 n. 27).

Funerals of babies were simple and accomplished with dispatch (Néraudau
1984, 373–392). Plutarch, talking of his own Greek society, says that infants
who died young, presumably before the naming ceremony (see below), did not
receive the normal burial rites (*Mor.* 612). Sources for Rome suggest that the
dead were escorted at night with torches outside the city walls, to diminish their
terror (according to Seneca, *Hercules Furens* 849ff.) or to dispel pollution (Serv.

Ad. Aen. 11.143). Fear of pollution did not prevent parents in certain societies (for example, early Rome) from burying their babies in or under the house. This practice, and the custom of not cremating babies who had yet to cut teeth (Pliny, *Nat. Hist.* 7.72; cf. Juvenal 11.139–140), suggest that the very young were considered not yet to have made the transition from nature into the human community.

Displays of grief at an infant's funeral were considered inappropriate. It was enshrined in law that children under twelve months should not be mourned at all, whereas those between one and three years might receive some measure of mourning (*Frag. vat.* 321). The inference is not that babies were never mourned, or that parents were indifferent. Instead of parental indifference or worse (the scope for moralizing at the expense of past societies is endless), we might prefer to talk of stern realism in the face of high levels of fetal, perinatal, and infant mortality.

The rites de passage associated with birth should throw light on social attitudes, not merely those of individual parents. Another dimension is added to the argument if parents experiencing one of the great crises of human existence are seen as members of a wider community, carrying out ritual customs and practices imposed by tradition (compare van Gennep 1960, chap. 5).

A Roman child was named on the *dies lustricus,* on the eighth day after birth for girls and the ninth for boys, in what was at once a ceremony of purification (as its name indicates) and a ceremony of admission into the household (Paulus 107–108L; Macrobius, *Sat.* 1.16.36; Brind'Amour and Brind'Amour 1971, 1975). Until that day, the child was, as it were, in limbo, "more like a plant than an animal" (Plutarch, *Quaest. Rom.* 102.288C). During the ceremony the child was subject or subjected to a succession of "ritual dangers," corresponding to the physical peril it had faced in the first week of life. As has been seen, Aristotle made a straightforward connection between the postponement of the naming ceremony (held on the seventh day, in his account) and heavy neonate mortality.[7]

The birth rituals were designed, at different levels, to clear pollution from the newborn and its mother, protect them against the evil powers, assess the baby's capacity to survive, and test the willingness of its parents, particularly the father, to bring up the infant. The child (in its fetal as well as newborn state)

---

7. It cannot be assumed that rituals were invariably carried out as ordained by law or custom. See Scheper-Hughes 1985, 311, on the postponement of naming (and christening) at Alto do Cruzeiro; cf. Berry and Schofield 1971 on the variety of ages at baptism in early modern England, in spite of official regulations that countenanced a delay of up to seven days before c. 1650 and up to fourteen days thereafter.

was ringed around by a host of supporting deities, for which Varro, filtered through Augustine, is our main source. The Carmentes were the Fates, Postverta and Prorsa presided over regular and breech births, Diespater and Lucina had responsibilities for the birth, Vaticanus presided over the first cry, Opis placed the newborn on the ground, and Levana raised it again. Intercidona, Pilumnus, and Deversa were represented by three men who guarded the house of the newborn with ax, pestle, and broom. Inside, Cunina watched over the child's cradle, Rumina the feeding at the breast, and Potina and Educa the baby's drinking and eating, while Paventia protected it from terror (Augustine, *De civ. D.*4.11; compare 6.9). Augustine was eager to lay bare the farcical fragmentation of the pagan pantheon. But *we* can see a community engaged in a desperate battle against hostile powers to reproduce itself.

Seen in this light, birth was a time of acute danger and a source of pollution and disruption, met by a complex of rituals designed to define and limit both the dangers to child and mother and the anxieties of the family. Thus thinking in terms of parental indifference to, or distancing from, the newborn child becomes difficult, and judging the attitude and behavior of parents by our own values more obviously improper.

The problem of the unwanted child is also clarified if set against this background. *Infanticide,* which is often used as an umbrella term embracing exposure, abandonment, and actual killing of babies (inaccurately, according to Boswell 1988, 41–45), is a stumbling block for some who are otherwise unconvinced by the indifference thesis. Hopkins rejects the inference from the tombstones that Roman parents "passively tolerated, or pretended not to care about the death of babies and young children." But he goes on to admit that "infanticide" gives rise to "nagging doubts" (Hopkins 1983, 225).

The counterpart to the official recognition of the newborn child by its father, symbolized by his lifting the child from the ground (*tollere, suscipere*), was its rejection, which led to ritual exposure. This is clearly illustrated for the world of classical Athens by a playful passage in Plato's *Theaetetus.*[8] Socrates, acting as midwife to Theaetetus, who is laboring to give birth to a truth, asserts that the

---

8. Because of the need to focus on Italy I have made only limited use of the Greek evidence. This is an embarrassment, as there are interesting comparisons to be made (cf. Brind'Amour and Brind'Amour 1975). Moreover, the Greek and Roman worlds grew closer together under the political domination of Rome, and there were cultural consequences, for example, in the realm of medicine. What cultural classification should be assigned to the prescriptions of Soranus and Galen, both Greek doctors who practiced in Rome? A full study of Greek initiation rites for children should consider not only the Amphidromion, but also the Anthesteria and Apaturia festivals (see, e.g., Deubner 1959). In addition, the complex classificatory vocabulary applied to children from birth to the end of infancy has implications for conceptions of childhood. See Aristophanes of Byzantium frag. 1, ed. Nauck, p. 88. I owe this reference to Eva Cantarella.

product must be inspected and put to the test as if it were a newborn baby undergoing the *amphidromia* rite (compare Vernant 1983, 152–156; Parker 1983, 48–66; Hamilton 1984): "Well, we have at last managed to bring this forth, whatever it turns out to be; and now that it is born, we must in very truth perform the rite of running around with it in a circle—the circle of our argument—and see whether it may not turn out to be after all not worth rearing, but only a wind-egg, an impostor. But perhaps you think that any offspring of yours ought to be cared for and not put away? Or will you bear to see it examined and not get angry if it is taken away from you, though it is your first-born?" (Plato, *Theaetetus* 160c–161a).

The implication is that the physical condition of the baby and its prospects for survival and good health primarily determined whether it was "worth rearing." This is also the only motive offered, five centuries later, by Soranus, for not bringing up the child:

> Now the midwife, having received the newborn, should first put it upon the earth, having examined beforehand whether the infant is male or female, and should make an announcement by signs as is the custom of women. She should also consider whether it is worth rearing or not. And the infant which is suited by nature for rearing will be distinguished by the fact that its mother has spent the period of pregnancy in good health, for conditions which require medical care, especially those of the body, also harm the fetus and enfeeble the foundations of its life. Second, by the fact that it has been born at the due time, best at the end of nine months, and if it so happens, later: but also after only seven months. Furthermore by the fact that when put on the earth it immediately cries with proper vigor; for one that lives for some length of time without crying, or cries but weakly, is suspected of behaving so on account of some unfavorable condition. Also by the fact that it is perfect in all its parts. . . . And by conditions contrary to those mentioned, the infant not worth rearing is recognized. (Soranus, *Gyn.* 2.10)

Was this "merciless selection" (Etienne 1976, 131), stern realism, or something else? A physically imperfect child had little chance of surviving to adulthood, and the sooner it died, the more easily its loss could be borne—if, that is, we allow Roman parents some human emotions, as Plato apparently allowed their Greek counterparts.

Physically weak babies were born to and rejected by rich and poor alike. Only the poor systematically abandoned babies, because they could not feed them. Feeble by nature or doomed to malnourishment—these categories merged together. An anthropologist studying destitute women in a north Brazilian shantytown noted their habitual "equanimity and resignation" as they sent their superfluous babies into "circulation" through informal adoption or abandonment—or just let them fade away. But maternal passivity could give way to intense grief at the loss of a particular child in whom hopes had been invested. If there was neglect, it was "selective," and a product of grim necessity (Scheper-Hughes 1985).

To return to classical antiquity, for children who could not be supported from available resources, the rate of abandonment probably fluctuated seasonally (so that an autumn baby, conceived in the winter month of Gamelion, self-evidently a popular month for marriage in Athens, had a better chance of being reared than one born in the spring before the harvest). The prevailing economic climate (the size of harvests and the incidence of drought and shortage) was also a determining factor.

The fateful decision might be made on other grounds, for example, the illegitimacy of the child (who thus infringed political, religious, or moral rules). Among those with wealth and high status, the desire to keep property intact in a society where partible inheritance was practiced might also provide sufficient motive.[9] Finally, the sex of the child was sometimes of consequence.[10]

Only those suffering from physical weakness or deformity are likely to have met with direct infanticide more or less invariably. Other unwanted babies were often preserved (compare Powell 1988, 354–357; Boswell 1988, 129) or given some chance of survival. The important points are these: the rejection of a child normally occurred before he or she was (culturally) considered to have achieved the status of full humanity (compare Harris and Ross 1987, 7); and that rejection was integrated into a sequence of rituals designed to protect the newborn (and its mother) in its most vulnerable period. Far from holding them cheap, Romans placed a high value on their babies (compare Schama 1987, chap. 7).

THE SURVIVING INFANT: SWADDLING AND FEEDING

Indifference and neglect become even less appropriate descriptions of parental attitudes toward children once the newborn had survived the perinatal crisis and secured formal admission to the family. In the words of the Hippocratic Corpus: "Curriers stretch, rub, brush, wash; that is the treatment given to children" (Hipp. Corp., *On Regimen* 1.19). It was important that the child be beautiful, well proportioned, and healthy.[11]

9. The three reasons for infanticide outlined thus far are considered by Daly and Wilson (1984) in their full comparative survey to have been the most significant. For a critique of their methodology and assumptions, see Hinde 1987, 99–100.

10. For references to female infanticide in antiquity, see Eyben 1980–1981, 16–17; for general discussion, see Dickemann 1975.

11. The themes of this and the following sections are given preliminary treatment in Garnsey 1989.

Much of the attention given to the survivors was misguided and not conducive to their good health and future prospects. Greeks and Romans, including their leading scientists—Hippocrates, Aristotle, Soranus, and Galen, and the rest—were groping in a thick fog of ignorance, which incidentally did not lift until about a century ago. Soranus's *Gynaecology* was authoritative as late as the nineteenth century. One's reaction to such works is to wonder whether children were not safer in the hands of humble midwives than those of fashionable doctors. There is some overlap, however, between ancient and modern wisdom in the matter of the feeding and care of children.

The twisted wisdom of the medical profession began to have an impact on the newborn baby soon after birth—at least among those families who patronized such doctors. Soranus, it is true, disapproved both of dousing the baby in cold water (a custom among Germans, Scythians, and some Greeks) and of washing it with wine (pure or mixed with brine) or with "the urine of an innocent child." He favored cleansing the child with salt, possibly combined with honey, olive oil, or the juice of barley or fenugreek or mallow, and then bathing it twice in lukewarm water (Soranus, *Gyn.* 2.12–13). But the swaddling that immediately followed and continued for around three months was potentially dangerous, if coupled with confinement indoors and, as the child became more mobile and independent, an inadequate weaning diet. An off-the-cuff remark of Galen's about the habits of Roman women, that they "stay indoors, neither engaging in strenuous labour nor exposing themselves to direct sunlight" has implications for early infancy (Galen, *De venae sectione adversus erasistratum liber,* Kühn 164, translated in Brain 1986, 25).

The main disability to which such infants were liable was rickets. The etiology of rickets is complex. Genetic background, diet, and lack of exposure to sunlight are all possible factors. People have contracted rickets in a Mediterranean climate in modern times (Belton 1986; compare Lapatsanis, Deliyanni, and Doxiadis 1968; Doxiadis et al. 1976), as well as in antiquity.[12] Soranus, who quite obviously did not understand the condition, writes:

> When the infant attempts to sit and to stand, one should help it in its movements. For if it is eager to sit up too early and for too long a period, it usually becomes hunchbacked (the spine bending because the little body has as yet no strength). If, moreover, it is too prone to stand up and desirous of walking, the legs may become distorted in the region of the thighs.
>
> This is observed to happen particularly in Rome; as some people assume,

12. Grmek (1983, 118–120) finds rickets rare in antiquity before the Roman period brought the growth of huge cities and with it, pauperization and dietary change in an urban context. Cf. Garnsey (n.d.).

because cold waters flow beneath the city and the bodies are easily chilled all over; as others say, because of the frequent sexual intercourse the women have or because they have intercourse after getting drunk—but in truth it is because they do not make themselves fully acquainted with child rearing. For the women in this city do not have sufficient devotion to look after everything as the purely Greek women do. Now if nobody looks after the movements of the infant the limbs of the majority become distorted, as the whole weight of the body rests on the legs, while the ground is solid and hard, being paved in most cases with stone. And whenever the ground upon which the child walks is rigid, the imposed weight heavy, and that which carries it tender—then of necessity the limbs give in a little, since the bones have not yet become strong. (Soranus, *Gyn.* 2.43ff.)

After describing the techniques of swaddling and putting the baby to bed, Soranus turns to food:

Now, after putting the newborn to bed subsequent to the swaddling, one must let it rest and, in most cases, abstain from all food up to as long as two days. . . . After the interval one must give food to lick . . . , honey moderately boiled . . . , one must gently anoint the mouth of the newborn with the finger, and must then drop lukewarm hydromel into it. . . .

From the second day on after the treatment, one should feed with milk from somebody well able to serve as a wet nurse, as for twenty days the maternal milk is in most cases unwholesome, being thick, too caseous, and therefore hard to digest, raw, and not prepared to perfection. Furthermore, it is produced by bodies which are in a bad state, agitated and changed to the extent that we see the body altered after delivery when, from having suffered a great discharge of blood, it is dried up, toneless, discolored, and in the majority of cases feverish as well. For all these reasons, it is absurd to prescribe the maternal milk until the body enjoys stable health.

Therefore we ought to censure Damastes, who orders the mother to give the newborn the breast immediately, contending that it is to this end that nature too has provided for the production of milk beforehand so that the newborn may have food straightaway. And one must also blame those who follow his opinion in these things, like Apollonius called Biblas. . . . If, however, a woman well able to provide milk is not at hand, during the first three days one must use the honey alone, or mix goat's milk with it. Then one must supply the mother's milk, the first portion having been sucked out beforehand by some stripling (for it is heavy) or squeezed out gently with the hand, since the thick part is hard to suck out and also apt to clog up in newborn children on account of the softness of their gums. (*Gyn.* 2.17–18)

Distrust of colostrum has a long history in Europe and persists in present-day Third World societies (Jelliffe and Jelliffe 1978). Yet colostrum is about three times as rich in protein as mature human milk (Stini 1985, 203ff.) and has important protective functions in the first six weeks of life: its antibodies and proteins guard the newborn against infections, particularly in the gastrointestinal tract (Fildes 1986, 81, compare 199–204).

Aristotle assumed that the child would be given the breast from the first day and had nothing to say against colostrum (*Gen. An.* 776a). Evidently the medical profession in Soranus's day was divided on the subject, though Galen makes no comment. Like other medical controversies, this would have had limited impact outside an upper-class clientele. Ordinary people may have regarded colostrum as acceptable or rejected it as bad milk. There is no way of telling. What is clear is that the denial of colostrum would have significantly reduced the life chances of the children concerned.

MOTHER OR WET NURSE?

Nutritionists are agreed that maternal milk is the best food for the newborn baby; that in developing countries supplementary or substitute foods, whether traditional (and often of low nutrient content) or commercial, jeopardize the health of the infant; and that even in advanced societies the early introduction of supplementary foods increases the infant's vulnerability to infection and food allergy. The contemporary debate is over requirements and how best to test dietary adequacy. By recent WHO and FAO estimates, the average baby needs to take in 120 kilocalories of milk per kg of body weight in the first three months, falling to 110 kcals at six to eight months and 106 kcals at one year. Such levels of milk production, however, are beyond the capacity of average mothers, whether in advanced or poorer societies. Department of Health and Social Security figures are lower by more than 10 percent, but are still too high, judging from many contemporary societies, where babies apparently in reasonable health take in a "less than adequate" volume of milk. An alternative approach, which seeks to measure milk requirement with reference to growth patterns, confirms that official estimates are unrealistically high, especially for the three- to nine-month-period, sandwiched between periods of high growth velocity (Whitehead and Paul 1981, 1988; Whitehead, Paul, and Cole 1982, 1989; Paul et al. 1988). The discussion continues.

The medical writers of antiquity were agreed that mother's milk was best for babies, other things being equal. Galen writes: "They require a completely moist regime, since their constitution is more moist than that of other ages. . . . Thus nature herself planned for children and provided them with mother's milk as a moist sustenance. And mother's milk is equally best for all children, provided it be not by chance diseased, and not least for the child of the best constitution, whom we are now discussing, for it is likely that his mother's

whole body and her milk are free from disease. So that those children who are
nourished by their mother's milk enjoy the most appropriate and natural food"
(Galen, *Hyg.* 7.22).

For psychological as well as nutritional reasons, however, the milk of a
woman who had given birth two to three months previously was believed to be
of better quality than that of the more recently delivered mother. Soranus
makes this point with the aid of a quaint simile from gardening:

> But if circumstances allow a choice of women able to suckle, one must select
> the best, and not necessarily the mother, unless she also shows the attributes
> characteristic of the best nurses. To be sure, other things being equal, it is better to
> feed the child with maternal milk; for this is more suited to it, and the mothers
> become more sympathetic toward the offspring, and it is more natural to be fed
> from the mother after parturition just as before parturition. But if anything
> prevents it one must choose the best wet nurse, lest the mother grow prematurely
> old, having spent herself through daily suckling. For just as the earth is exhausted
> by producing crops after sowing and therefore becomes barren of more, the same
> happens with the woman who nurses the infant; she either grows prematurely old
> having fed one child, or the expenditure for the nourishment of the offspring
> necessarily makes her own body quite emaciated. Consequently, the mother will
> fare better with a view to her own recovery and to further childbearing if she is
> relieved of having her breasts distended too. For as vegetables are sown by
> gardeners into one soil to sprout and are transplanted into different soil for quick
> development, lest one soil suffer by both, in the same way the newborn, too, is apt
> to become more vigorous if borne by one woman but fed by another, in case the
> mother, by some affliction, is hindered from supplying the food. (Soranus, *Gyn.*
> 2.18)

The attention given to wet nursing by the medical writers, and the controversy it aroused among the educated classes, indicate that wet nursing was
common at least among the wealthy in Rome and in the empire at large (see
Gellius, *Noctes Atticae* 12.1; Tacitus, *Dial.* 2.39; Ps.-Plut. *De lib. educ.* 5). Moreover, the rich employed wet nurses (usually slaves or humble free women) not
only for their legitimate children, but also for infant slaves, including no doubt
some they had themselves fathered (for example, Bradley 1986, 211).

Why wet nurses? According to Lawrence Stone, many infant and child
deaths resulted from the indifference and neglect of their parents. In the case of
the rich, they "sent their children away to wetnurses for the first year, despite
the known negligence of nurses which resulted in a death rate double that of
maternally fed babies" (Stone 1977, 65). Doubtless some parents in all ages

have deserved Stone's strictures, or have fitted Bradley's more sensitive characterization: "It is within this area of class mentality that perhaps the best explanation for the prevalence of wetnursing is to be found, therefore, because the custom provided parents with a mechanism which operated against the over-investment of emotion in their children, or a cushion against the foreseeable loss of children and the accompanying emotional trauma. By driving a wedge between parent and child, wetnursing fulfilled for the parent a self-protective function, diminishing the degree and impact of injury in the event of loss in a society where such loss was commonly experienced" (Bradley 1986, 220).

Parental feelings were complex, and any generalization about motives is suspect. Behind Soranus's discussion lies the assumption that wet nursing was an efficient means of rearing children, and this no doubt influenced rich parents and slave owners alike. Other considerations varied from a mother's vanity to the desire for more children, or for more closely spaced children. It was appreciated in antiquity that lactation inhibited pregnancy (Aristotle, *Hist. An.* 587b; *Gen. An.* 777a). That nurturing the newborn imposed a heavy burden on the mother was also recognized.

Maternal death and incapacity would have increased the demand for wet nurses significantly in rich and poor households alike. Poor families, however, could hardly compete with the rich for wet nurses. If no nurse was available in the family, or among friends and neighbors, the poor would have had recourse to such grimmer remedies as early weaning (see below), abandonment, or sale.

Nor should we forget the displaced babies of the wet nurses themselves: Soranus (*Gyn.* 2.20) pronounced that women who had given birth two to three months previously made the best nurses. As Richard Trexler wrote regarding late medieval Florence, "Infants put out to nurse were given to mothers whose own infants had either died, been abandoned, or themselves been given to wetnurses. The lives of the innocents, like those of any child put to nurse, depended on the death or dislocation of cohorts" (Trexler 1973b, 260).

Only a minority of families had the luxury of choice whether to employ a wet nurse. Insofar as wet nursing was standard practice among the propertied classes and not among the poor, then the latter scored over the rich—for a baby who is fed by his or her own mother is endowed with greater resistance to disease. This advantage must be weighed against the possibility that many humble mothers were chronically malnourished and unable adequately to feed their babies, who were in any case likely to have been small at birth and fragile afterward. "Undernourished mothers have undersized babies and undersized babies have high mortality rates" (Stini 1985, 218).

WEANING

Modern nutritionists and health experts familiar with contemporary developing countries are very aware that infants being weaned (those who have survived the crises of pregnancy, birth, and the neonatal stage) are particularly vulnerable to disease. There are two periods of particular danger (Whitehead 1980; Whitehead and Paul 1981; Whitehead, Paul, and Cole 1982; Wharton 1986). The first, beginning around three months, coincides with the initial introduction of supplementary foods that are nutritionally suspect and unhygienically prepared and administered. The characteristic features of this critical period are increased morbidity and, in particular, the prevalence of "weanling diarrhea." This stage begins earlier for children prematurely weaned or fed artificially more or less from birth, and their chances of survival are much slimmer. The current wisdom is that supplementary foods are rarely needed and should not be introduced before the end of the third month. This can be accepted as a rule of thumb, even if vigorous debate continues about the length of time breast feeding can completely satisfy the infant's requirements, and whether indeed those requirements can be generalized, given differences in sex, size, pattern of baby activity, growth velocity, and metabolic needs. A complication is the capacity of infants (and indeed humans of all ages) to adapt to lower than "desirable" nutrient intakes.

The second period of high vulnerability to disease occurs when the supply of breast milk is lagging well behind need and the child is increasingly dependent on inadequate weaning foods. This period begins, typically, at about nine months, when there is a significant upturn in the velocity of growth, and may be prolonged for more than a year. It is often characterized by nutritional deficiency, a high susceptibility to infection, and malnutrition.

For information on weaning foods in classical antiquity, we turn to the prescriptive works of the medical writers. Soranus talks of "crumbs of bread softened with hydromel or milk, sweet wine, or honey wine," and later also of "soup made from spelt, a very moist porridge, and an egg that can be sippled" (*Gyn.* 2.46). Galen prescribes "first bread, and then vegetables and meat and other such things" (*Hyg.* 10.31). Ordinary people would have depended on cereal as the basic weaning food. The well-off family had a distinct advantage at the weaning stage because of its access to a wider range of foodstuffs, including some that were rich protein sources. But the phasing out of milk in favor of solid food would undermine the child's health if it happened too early. The ordinary family had the choice of transferring the infant to cheap solid food that was low in protein, or delaying the weaning process (always supposing that breast milk was still available).

In all this, the weaning timetable was of crucial importance. Galen prescribes milk alone until the baby has cut its first teeth (in about the seventh month), and thereafter a gradual introduction of solid food until the end of the second year (*Hyg.* 9.29, 10.31). Soranus's treatment is more detailed:

> Those women are too hasty who, after only forty days, try to give cereal food (as do those for the most part who find nursing a burden). Yet, on the other hand, it is also bad not to change to other food when the body has already become solid—not only because the body becomes moist and therefore delicate if fed on milk for too long a time, but also because in case of sickness the milk easily turns sour.
>
> For this reason, when the body has already become firm and ready to receive more solid food, which it will scarcely do successfully before the age of six months, it is proper to feed the child also with cereal food. . . .
>
> As soon as the infant takes cereal food readily, and when the growth of the teeth assures the division and trituration of more solid things (which in the majority of cases takes place around the third or fourth half-year), one must stealthily and gradually take it off the breast and wean it by adding constantly to the amount of other food but diminishing the quantity of milk. . . .
>
> One should not, however, pay attention to Mnesitheus and Aristanax, who maintain that one should wean a female six months later because it is weaker; for they do not realize that some female infants are both stronger and fleshier than many males. . . . (*Gyn.* 2.46–48)

In sum, Soranus knew of babies denied the breast in the second month, but like Galen, favored the introduction of solid food in the seventh month. He envisaged final weaning in the course of the second year; he disapproved of advice to delay the weaning of girls, presumably into the third year.

Both authorities, as already indicated, wrote for a social milieu in which the hiring of wet nurses was common. So did later medical writers (notably Aetius, Oribasius, Paulus of Aegina), who made similar recommendations (compare Fildes 1986). Wet-nursing contracts in Egypt ran from six months to three years, with two years the most typical (Bradley 1980). People who could afford wet nurses in principle could also provide a supporting diet of solid food of reasonable quality; the extent to which they did so cannot be determined. The risks involved in late weaning did not apply so much to this class as to those ordinary and poor families who could offer only a decreasing quantity of mother's milk and inadequate supplementary foods.

Early weaning, however, posed the greatest danger. In other pre-modern societies, and in the contemporary Third World, it is associated with poverty, working mothers, and urbanization. The combination of the mother's poor diet and her need or obligation to work in the fields or in the cities leads to reduced milk output, at a time when the child needs to build up and preserve passive immunity (Schofield 1979, 103). As a mid-sixteenth-century French doctor, Simon de Vallambert, wrote, "Long before the first teeth appear, even before the age of three months, the women of the countryside, and the poor women of the towns, give bouilli to their children, because if the latter took no other nourishment beside milk, they would not be able to go so long without sucking as they do, during the time when mothers are absent and held down by their work. . . . Because of their continual labour and poor life, these mothers do not have a lot of milk, so that they would not be capable of feeding the child if he did not take other nourishment in addition to milk from the breast" (cited in Fildes 1986, 247).

The emotional lives of families in past societies is a most elusive subject. Yet bold assertions are made about affective relationships within the Roman family to the effect that parents, in the face of high mortality at birth and early infancy, showed indifference to or distanced themselves from their infants, and displayed sheer cruelty and callousness toward those babies they did not want to bring up. Infants who survived the perinatal period were turned over to wet nurses even if the mother was both available and capable of feeding her own child. Why? Apparently to prevent mother-child bonding, preserve the figure, follow the fashion that high society dictated, or maximize the mother's child-bearing potential. The lack of systematic treatment of infant diseases in the medical sources is interpreted as betraying a casual attitude on the part of both doctors and parents to the suffering of children.

Parental indifference, neglect, and cruelty did exist, but not as general or distinctive features of Roman society. One can begin constructing an alternative theory by citing individual cases of anxious or grief-stricken parents (from literature and gravestones). In spite of the problematic nature of some of the sources, they suggest that in certain social circles some parents cared deeply about their children from birth. A more effective strategy would take cognizance of socioeconomic factors, including the poverty of the mass of the population and the lack of adequate methods of birth control, and yet would see infant-rearing practices as culturally defined and sanctioned. In the first days of life, the baby hovered in a kind of no man's land, the object of purifying, protective, and testing ritual. If it survived the ordeals imposed by nature and by man until the dies lustricus, the eighth or ninth day after birth, it was named and formally accepted by the father and other family representatives—always supposing the family had the will and the resources to prolong its existence. The three most prevalent reasons for rejection of a baby were its poor fitness potential, inadequate parental resources, and illegitimacy.

Rejection of one child did not necessarily carry adverse implications for the treatment of those admitted into the family and receiving the formal commitment of the parents to its care. From this time onward, the chief point of interest becomes how much the child-rearing methods of Roman parents undermined the health and survival prospects of their children. In the Roman world of the high empire, at least in the circles in which Soranus and company moved, babies were frequently denied colostrum, the hiring of a wet nurse was expected, swaddling was standard practice, weaning foods were nutritionally inadequate (though wealthier families may have provided more varied and nutritious fare), early weaning was common enough to be singled out for criticism, and late weaning recommended; other sources, especially papyri, suggest that late weaning was often practiced. Given the close connection between infant feeding practices and infant malnutrition, disease, and mortality—obvious to anyone familiar with contemporary developing countries—we may confidently hypothesize a high incidence of undernourishment and disease among the under-five population of Rome and the Roman world.

It is not my present purpose to test this particular hypothesis. That would require an analysis not only of the conventional medical literature, but also of paleopathological evidence, both cumulative deficiency disease in children (porotic hyperostosis and cribra orbitalia, bone damage traceable frequently to iron deficiency anaemia) and periodic stress at the fetal, neonatal, and older infant stages (as revealed in a dental condition known as enamel hypoplasia). For the present, I confine myself to the observation that the regimen prescribed for infants by fashionable doctors, and the unsatisfactory nutritional status achieved by many infants so treated, are to be accounted for with reference not to theories of affective relationships, but to the social norms and cultural practices of a prescientific society.

Chapter 4

BRENT SHAW

The Cultural Meaning of Death: Age and Gender in the Roman Family

Dis Manibus T. Flavi Romuli, vixit annis X, mens. VIIII,
dieb. XII fec. T. Flavius Primigenius et Flavia Romula
filio carissimo.

"I have before me a Latin funerary inscription, carved from a single block, made for a single purpose. Yet nothing could be more variegated than the evidences which there await the probing of the scholar's lancet" (Bloch 1953, 145).[1] The celebration of death in the Roman world by what has aptly been called the "epigraphical habit" produced the historical document of which Marc Bloch speaks. The inscribed tombstone is indeed one of the most characteristic and prolific artifacts of Latin civilization. It was an integral part of the behavior formed by a Latin culture that defined "being Roman" in the lands of western Europe and North Africa in the first six centuries of the Christian Era. The gravestone is surely the most numerous example in the entire corpus of public monuments inscribed with writing that have survived from the Roman world. The broader category of inscribed objects, of which tombstone epitaphs are only a part, also includes records of civic and military careers, texts of government decrees and edicts, religious texts, markers for lands and roads, and so on. These inscriptions have never actually been counted, but a reason-

I am grateful to those who offered their criticisms of this chapter, especially Peter Brown, William Douglass, Mark Golden, and Ian Morris.

1. The inscription in the epigraph is from the *Corpus Inscriptionum Latinarum* 6:18189: "To the infernal spirits of Titus Flavius Romulus, who lived 10 years, 9 months, 12 days, set up by Titus Flavius Primigenius and Flavia Romula to their beloved son."

able guess would place the total at about one-third of a million items. Inscribed tombstones constitute perhaps as much as three-quarters, or more, of all these inscriptions. In terms of sheer numbers, therefore, the funerary stones (which normally contained such basic information as the name, age at death, and relatives of the deceased) offer an unparalleled opportunity "to read" many social aspects of the Roman world in bulk (Saller and Shaw 1984, 124; Millar 1983, 80–81).

The tombstones were indeed set up "for a single purpose": to memorialize the dead. The preparation of a tombstone, however, was not the result of some natural behavior, an automatic response triggered by death. It was a cultural act—even more artificial than the relationships and sentiments it recorded. The cultural significance of the celebration of death, as pioneers like Philippe Ariès and Michel Vovelle have insisted, was as mutable and relative as any other aspect of human action (Ariès 1974, 1981; Vovelle 1974, 1982, 1983; for subsequent treatment by historians, see, for example, Gittings 1984 and McManners 1981). The death of an individual evoked an emotional response, sentiment that is reified in the tombstone. It should be made clear here that by *sentiment* is meant a rather neutral type of valuation of the person that might have structural origins, as well as purely emotive ones. I do not signify by it any specific type of changed emotion. So, for example, shifts in emphasis between husbands and wives in funerary dedications should not be taken to indicate that husbands loved wives more than husbands, or vice versa (Hopkins 1987, 115 n.5). What is signified is the valuation of the social persona of the deceased—the value of the place he or she had in the overall networks of power of the whole society in which the family had an integral function. The act of placing a tombstone, of having it inscribed, was integrally connected with the webs of duties and feelings concerning the dead and, by extension, a mirroring of their status while still among the living. The dead, even those within rather well defined social or economic groups, were decidedly not seen in a democratic or egalitarian way. Some were seen as worthier of public commemoration than their brothers and sisters. The core argument of this chapter is that it is precisely this social valuation that is recorded on the tombstones strewn across countless memorial landscapes of the Roman west.

First, however, a commonly accepted idea about the value of these tombstone data should be dispelled. Although this inquiry involved a massive counting operation (nearly fifty-five thousand such inscriptions were tabulated) the aggregate "statistics" on ages at death produced cannot be used (or rather abused) to produce dependable demographic profiles (for example, mortality rates) of Roman populations. The fundamental methodological problem was recognized long ago: the patterns of mortality and life expectancy produced by analyzing the "mortality figures" cumulated from the ages at death recorded on tombstones do not bear a consistent relationship to any known human population. As Keith Hopkins put it in his now-classic analysis of the problem: "There is no means at our disposal for correcting the distortions due to *the habits of commemoration.* The only conclusion possible is that, even on the assumption of a stationary population (which is a fragile assumption), ages at death derived from Roman tombstones cannot be used to estimate expectation of life at birth or at subsequent ages" (Hopkins 1966, 246 [my italics]; he reiterates, and strengthens, his arguments in Hopkins 1987). The reason the age-at-death figures recorded on tombstones are so skewed from one region and group to the next stems from the basic social context of their existence: the stones were set up, usually by close relatives and friends of the deceased, not for the purpose of maintaining a demographic record, but in order to mark the place of the body and the memory of the deceased. This particular valuation of persons in death was not constant across all regions and social groups of the western empire, nor through time. What the tombstones do tell us in a rather simple and direct manner, therefore, is precisely about those different social valuations—a story often obscured by the drive to produce mortality statistics for the Roman world (such being the main impetus behind the elaborate studies of Szilágyi 1961–1963, 1965–1967, and those of Frier 1982, 1983). To measure these different social valuations, I collated and tabulated tens of thousands of data from tombstones in the Roman world according to age sets (by decades, or deciles) and gender. These data were then analyzed for different social, regional, and ideological groups in Roman society. Finally, to assess possible temporal variations, where practicable the data from the earlier period of Roman imperial history (roughly from the beginning of the first century A.D. to the mid-third) were distinguished from those of the later empire (from the mid-third century A.D. to the end of the sixth).[2]

There are, it must be admitted, some not inconsiderable methodological problems involved in interpreting the data—problems of context. For example, tombstone inscriptions that contain the age at death of the deceased constitute only a portion of all funerary epitaphs, many of which merely provide the name and some other attributes of the deceased. Moreover, any given population might have tended to specify age at death more for boys than for girls, or fathers as opposed to mothers. If we are to use tombstones that contain ages at

---

2. The tables included in this chapter represent a relatively simple tabulation of some of the results of this larger analysis. The more complex charts, some sixty in number, which give the complete breakdown of emphasis for every decile between the ages of ten and one hundred, for males and females, were simply too lengthy to justify inclusion here. It is my intention to publish these results separately.

death as our only basis of analysis, we run the real danger of underestimating concern in death signaled in this way for certain groups. Sample tests, however, revealed a distinct tendency to include age at death for those groups in the population that were already "preferred"—for example, young boys as opposed to young girls (in the city of Rome). Although it is not possible artificially to correct this problem in the data, its cultural context seems reasonably clear: specifying age at death was a further public valuation indicating the greater social importance attributed to that person in death. Another problem of method is posed by high infant mortality levels that might skew our analysis. In the funerary epigraphy, the deaths of infants are rather uniformly absent from commemorations (table 4.1). In all cases they represent a very small proportion of all burials (and hardly a true indication of infant mortality levels). Infants clearly did not merit the effort required of formal recognition in burial. With these caveats in mind, we can proceed to analyze the large body of Roman tombstone data in order to highlight the differential valuation placed at death on different age groups and on males as opposed to females. What I am proposing here is less a generative model of family formation than a simple quantification of some of the publicly expressed valuation of a person that was produced and strengthened in the process of the formation of Roman families. The main questions that I shall ask are: (1) What regional, ethnic, and cultural variations are found in respect of these factors? (2) What variations exist among social groups (for example, slaves, soldiers, freedmen)? and (3) What changes happened over time, especially those evident from a comparison of pre-Christian and Christian periods and social groups?

But first, a few general observations on Roman families. The Roman Empire in the west at its putative height produced at least two characteristic family types. One certainly existed as an ideological ideal for the elite, and also informed some of its behavior. This was the extended agnatic lineage, with males linked in a long series of generational chains, hoarding power and property and passing them down to their male descendants. The ideal was fossilized in the corpus of the Roman law, which emphasized the existence of this sort of upper-class "property family" both in its concerns with the power of the paternal head of the family, and with the devolution of property through inheritance. The other sort of family is more difficult to sight, though it too can be seen in the developing body of laws throughout the second century A.D. and later, which systematically chipped away at the authority of the father, at principles of agnatic descent, and at the strict gentilicial devolution of property—all in favor of a much looser, cognatic, individualized unit centered principally on parents and children (Saller 1984; compare Saller and Shaw 1984). Philippe Moreau (1986, 187) has remarked on "the loss in importance, as

TABLE 4.1

Infant and Child Burials as a Percentage of All Commemorations

Region or Social Group	1-3 Centuries				3-6 Centuries					
	0-12 Months		1 Year		0-12 months		1 Year		T(-1)	T(+1)
	Male	Female	Male	Female	Male	Female	Male	Female		
Africa: Towns	0.2	0.1	0.4	0.2	0.4	0.2	0.6	0.4	0.8	1.5
Africa: Castellum Celtianum	0.0	0.0	0.0	0.0	0.0	0.0	0.0	0.0	0.0	0.0
Africa: Lambaesis	0.1	0.2	0.4	0.1	0.7	0.2	1.0	0.7	0.5	0.9
Spain	0.2	0.0	0.7	0.2	0.4	0.1	0.6	0.4	0.2	0.9
Gaul	0.5	0.2	0.7	0.2	0.3	0.0	3.0	3.0	0.6	2.6
Noricum/Raetia	0.5	0.0	0.4	0.3					0.5	0.4
Rome: City	0.9	0.5	2.4	1.4	1.0	0.7	2.1	1.5	1.5	3.8
Ostia	1.8	0.0	2.2	2.7	1.7	0.7	3.6	1.7	2.1	5.1
Northern Italy: Towns	0.4	0.5	1.7	0.7	0.7	0.4	1.4	1.5	1.0	2.7
Slaves: Rome	1.0	0.6	3.4	1.8					1.6	5.2

Category						
Slaves: Western empire	0.7		1.4	1.6	1.0	3.0
Freedmen: Rome	0.4	0.2	1.3	0.5	0.6	1.8
Freedmen: Western empire	0.4	0.3	1.1	0.9	0.7	1.7
Christians (ICUR 4)	1.7	1.9	3.9	2.1	3.7	6.0
Christians (ICUR 5)	2.0	1.8	3.2	2.9	3.8	6.1
Christians (ICUR 6)	2.5	2.5	2.2	0.9	5.1	3.2
Christians (ICUR 7)	1.6	2.4	2.0	2.8	4.0	4.7
Christians (ICUR 8)	0.2	0.9	3.0	2.8	1.1	5.8
Christians: Gaul, Belgica	4.9	0.7	3.5	3.5	5.6	6.9

1

Note: T(−1) = total percentage for infants under age one (1–12 months); T(+1) = total percentage for children at one year of age (13–24 months). Sources: Africa (towns), Szilágyi 1967, 25; Africa (Castellum Celtianum), Szilágyi 1965, 313–314; Africa (Lambaesis), Szilágyi 1965, 311–313; Gaul, Szilágyi 1961, 134–42; Noricum/Raetia, Szilágyi 1962, 317–21; Rome (city), Szilágyi 1963, 131–132; Ostia, Szilágyi 1963, 133–34; northern Italy (towns), Szilágyi 1962, 298–303; slaves (Rome), Szilágyi 1963, 149–50; slaves (western empire), Szilágyi 1962, 322–323; freedmen (Rome), Szilágyi 1963, 150–51; freedmen (western empire), Szilágyi 1962, 323–324; Christians (ICUR 4), Ferrua 1964; Christians (ICUR 5), Ferrua 1971; Christians (ICUR 6), Ferrua 1975; Christians (ICUR 7), Ferrua 1980; Christians (ICUR 8); Ferrua 1983; Christians (Gaul, Belgica I), Gauthier 1975.

primary groups of reference in the domain of kinship, of two formations which are mentioned most frequently when one is considering the phenomena of kinship in Roman society: the *gens,* a unilineal descent group, and the *familia,* a group whose main axis was the juridical authority of its male head. The diminution in importance of these earlier family types favoured the emergence of two other groups: the complex family, created by remarriage, and the cognate family or cognates, centered on one person, and including relatives in both the male and female lines, and other persons linked to them." As Moreau himself notes, the emergence of these new family types among the elites of Roman society also affected the consciousness of the social actors involved— as can be deduced from the modification of their sentiments toward the obligations and expectations invested in kinship relations.

If the complex family, created largely through the processes of death, divorce, and remarriage, became typical of the central and regional upper classes of the western empire (Bradley 1987a), then the small, or simple, family was almost certainly more typical of the mass of the urban-centered populations. The vast bulk of our literary texts, generated by the propertied upper classes of Roman society, however, tend to stress their ideals and some of their actual behavior, at the expense of what was actually happening in the society at large. The use of evidence more relevant to the vast majority of the population of the western empire seems to indicate, first, that in terms of basic obligations, and even basic living units, these families were what we would call a nuclear or elementary type—families where the primary bonds of obligation, of living, and of economic relations were centered on the parent-child unit. Marriages were not arranged or manipulated as they were for the upper classes, but were subject to different economic considerations. Though some girls married in their early teens, or before, most probably married in their late teens and early twenties. Males were marrying for the first time rather later, in their middle to late twenties (Saller and Shaw 1984; Saller 1987; Shaw 1987a). This outline of the basic structure of the Roman family is, however, rather skeletal. There are still unresolved questions about the sorts of values that were attached to this kind of family, and about the basic social and economic contexts in which it developed. It is precisely here that the evidence of inscriptions can help us map some of this lost history of values.

There are, of course, the mandatory caveats. Even valuation of the deceased was not an unfettered personal act, untrammeled by other social constraints. One can study the degree to which those who buried the dead tended, for example, to show preference in signaling the decease of males, as opposed to females. If one assumes that there were equal numbers of males and females in the commemorating population, and equal numbers of male and female dead, then the trends that emerge in terms of signaled memorials should be a relatively good guide to gender preference. But these criteria clearly do not hold in all cases. Soldiers, for example, tended to live in communities that, for the most part, consisted of males. It can come as little surprise, then, that of all social groups the military displayed extraordinary "male preference," specifically those between the ages of twenty and fifty, who were part of the armed forces of the state (see table 4.5). As we might expect, they also consistently placed the lowest social value on infants and children in death (no more than 3–4 percent of all dedications). Although these are genuine values, and ones that are accurately reflected in the epigraphical record, they were determined to a large degree by the simple absence of families. A second countercase is provided by the slaves who set up funerary monuments to themselves in the major urbanized administrative centers of the west. An elite type of slave, they were the closest Roman society came to having a managerial class. Because of their professional service functions, the internal composition of these servile service corps was predominantly male (Weaver 1972; Treggiari 1975; Bradley 1987b, 73–74), which is simply reflected in their funerary commemoration habits.

If we are to acquire a more reliable indication of the linkage between social values and family structure, we must turn to less artificially constructed populations. A detailed analysis of the tombstone dedicators has revealed one important fact: almost all were drawn from the narrow circle of the nuclear, or elementary, family. Among most urban civil populations in the western Roman Empire, 80% or more of all commemorators were the spouses, parents, children, or siblings of the deceased (Saller and Shaw 1984; compare Shaw 1984 for later imperial patterns). This analysis could be advanced by examining the emphases various regional and social groups placed, in funerary commemoration, on distinct age groups, especially on the most telltale elements of the population: the very young and the very old (see tables 4.2 and 4.4). Those who placed relatively great public value in death on children were all from larger urban centers or from Christian backgrounds (tables 4.1 and 4.2). A few Christian social groups were exceptions, but the groups that emphasized children less tended to be drawn from rural or frontier regions (for example, Dalmatia, Noricum, or Raetia), from the ranks of the Roman army, from certain types of servile groups, and finally, from specific geographical zones (notably Spain).

The major factor that seems to lie at the heart of this division is the traditional urban-rural dichotomy that was a principal characteristic of the economy and society of the Greco-Roman world. In some cases, the disparity was marked (the city of Salonae in Dalmatia, for example, compared with its surrounding rural region, 21.7:15.2 percent). The populations of the larger

TABLE 4.2

Percentage of Tombstone Epitaphs Dedicated to Children under Ten Years of Age by Region and Social Group

Region and Social Group		Region and Social Group	
Christians: Rome (*ICUR* 6)	40.8	Slaves: western empire	17.3
Christians: Spain	40.8	Christians: Rome (*ICUR* 4)	15.4
Christians: Rome (*ICUR* 7)	39.4	Dalmatia: general	15.2
Christians: Africa (Haïdra)	38.4	Military: Pannonia	13.3
Ostia: general	38.3	Africa: Altava	12.6
Christians: Rome (*ICUR* 5)	38.9	Africa: Theveste	11.6
Christians: Gaul (Viennensis)	36.8	Noricum/Raetia	11.1
Christians: Rome (*ICUR* 8)	36.7	Military: northern frontiers	10.7
Christians: Rome	33.8	Spain: urban centers	9.2
Slaves: Rome	32.3	Africa: Northern Proconsularis	8.7
Rome: general	29.5	Africa: Lambaesis	8.4
Northern Italy: urban centers	27.0	Africa: Cirtan Federation	7.8
Christians: Africa (Mactar)	25.2	Africa: small centers	7.7
Dalmatia: Salonae	21.7	Spain: general	7.1
Freedmen: Rome	21.4	Africa: Western Proconsularis	4.4
Christians: Carthage	21.2	Military: Rome (elite units)	4.0
Southern Italy: urban centers	20.1	Military: Lambaesis	3.2
Africa: Carthage	19.8	Africa: Cirta (rural)	1.6
Gaul	19.5	Africa: Castellum Celtianum	0.6
Slaves: Carthage	19.2		
Christians: Gaul (Belgica I)	19.1		

Note: *ICUR* = The cemeteries and catacombs covered by the specified volume of *Inscriptiones Christianae Urbis Romae* (Ferrua 1964–1983).
Sources: In addition to the sources for table 4.1, see also Christians (Spain), Vives 1969; Christians (Africa, Haïdra), Duval 1975; Christians (Gaul, Viennensis), Descombes 1985; Christians (Africa, Mactar), Prévot 1984; Dalmatia (Salonae), Szilágyi 1962, 303–304; Christians (Carthage), Ennabli 1975, 1982; southern Italy (urban centers), Szilágyi 1963, 134–141; Africa (Carthage), Szilágyi 1965, 315–316; slaves (Carthage), Szilágyi 1967, 25–29; Dalmatia (general), Szilágyi 1962, 304–305; military (Pannonia), Szilágyi 1962, 311–317; Africa (Altava), Marcillet-Jaubert 1968; Africa (Theveste), Szilágyi 1966, 238–239; military (northern frontiers), Szilágyi 1961, 128–134, 137–138, *Journal of Roman Studies* 44–59 (1954–1969), "Epigraphy," *Britannia* 1–16 (1970–1985); Spain (urban centers), Szilágyi 1963, 144–147; Africa (Northern Proconsularis), Szilágyi 1966, 235–236, 244–245, 252–253, 255–257, 260; Africa (Cirtan Federation), Szilágyi 1965, 309–311; Africa (small centers), Szilágyi 1967, 25; Africa (Western Proconsularis), Szilágyi 1965, 316–321, 250–251, 258–259; military (Rome, elite units), Szilágyi 1962, 325–326; military (Lambaesis), *Corpus Insriptionum Latinarum,* vol. 8, nos. 12590–13213, 24678–24876; Africa (Cirta, rural), Szilágyi 1965, 313–314, 1966, 236–237, 240–241, 243–246, 249–250;Africa (Castellum Celtianum), Szilágyi 1965, 313–314.

urban centers of northern Italy tended to emphasize children and infants more than did those of the cities of southern Italy (27.0:20.1 percent)—and both were outstripped by the city of Rome (29.5 percent). In some cases the impact of urbanism was not as great, for example in Spain, where urban-dwelling groups manifested only a marginally greater propensity to celebrate infant and child deaths (9.2:7.1 percent). Nevertheless, even in Spain the influence of an urban environment was discernible. Any attempt to measure this urban-rural difference immediately encounters a problem: certain social groups (the very poor) or regions (the countryside) are severely underrepresented—they simply did not produce epigraphical records for us to study and analyze. In fact, there is so little epigraphy from the Italian countryside or from its small towns that the sort of comparison I am attempting is almost unfeasible (Millar 1986). Nonetheless, urbanity is the factor that affected all social groups regardless of the relation of their own proper characteristics to family formation. Freedmen in the large urban center of Rome, for example, expressed this public valuation of children more than did the freedmen who were scattered in the smaller administrative centers elsewhere in the empire (21.4:13.7 percent). Slaves in Carthage, the great administrative capital of North Africa, emphasized their children in this manner more than slaves did in small urban centers of the African provinces (19.2:17.3 percent), whereas the slaves of the imperial metropolis of Rome revealed a greater public valuation by far than those at Carthage (32.3:19.2 percent). The same factor can also be observed with Christian populations (see below). Those in a remote and mountainous rural region of Gaul (northern Viennensis, abutting on the western Alps around Vienne and Grenoble) had markedly less tendency to celebrate children in death than did Christians in the more urbanized zones of Gaul, for example, those of Belgica Prima (19.2:36.8 percent). The urban factor was therefore pervasive and virtually uniform in its effects. The degree of the urban effect, however, was specific to a given cultural area or region—one type of effect was rather uniform within Spain, Gaul, or North Africa, but not across those broad regions and cultural groups.

As a distinct region of the empire, Italy reflects patterns of family development consistent with the western empire as a whole, only with greater intensity than those, for example, in North Africa. The city of Rome and its port city of Ostia, by far the single largest urban agglomeration in the empire, outdistanced all other centers and regions in Italy (and, a fortiori, the regions of the west outside Italy) in emphasizing the celebration of children in death. The rest of Italy commensurately outdistanced the other regions of the west as a whole. Nevertheless, the same disproportion between countryside and city holds for Italy itself. The emphasis placed on children among non-Christian populations in North African contexts ranged from less than 1 percent to about 20 percent (Castellum Celtianum to Carthage), with most town centers and groups crowding around the 10 percent range, or less. For Italy, however, the whole range is moved considerably upward, running from a low of approximately 20 percent to a high of about 40 percent for non-Christian populations, with most groups clustering around the 27 percent figure. Once again, though, small centers in the north and south ranked lowest, with the purely rural regions surrounding them falling lower yet, and the principal urban centers of the peninsula, like Ostia and Rome, at the very top. Even low-ranking social groups, like slaves and freedmen, if they happened to live in large urban centers, participated in the trend to emphasize the valuation of children. In that case, they were more likely to commemorate their young in burial than were the free populations of any given rural district.

To track the infant and child preference across time, it is perhaps easiest to begin with the Christian populations of the western empire by comparing them systematically with the pre-Christian populations in the same cultural or regional settings (table 4.3). Most Christian epigraphy dates from between the mid-fourth and the mid-fifth centuries A.D. An analysis of these inscriptions clearly shows two forces at work: the continued and manifest impact of urbanity and the influence of ideology. To return to table 4.2, we can see immediately that Christian groups are predominant. As a whole they placed a greater emphasis on children than earlier social groups from the same region did. Spanish populations may indeed have placed a relatively low public importance on children in death, but Christianity apparently made a considerable

TABLE 4.3

Percentage of Tombstone Epitaphs Dedicated to Children under
Ten Years of Age in the Earlier and Later Empire

Region	*1–3 Centuries* *(ca. A.D. 1–250)*	*3–6 Centuries* *(ca. A.D. 250–500)*
Rome	27.7	34.0
Northern Italy	19.5	21.1
Spain	6.9	7.7
Africa: Carthage	16.9	22.5
Africa: Cirta	5.5	11.4
Africa: small centers	6.9	8.4

Sources: See tables 4.1 and 4.2.

difference (40.8:7.1 percent), over and above the earlier effect of urbanism on these same populations (17.3:9.1 percent). The same observations apply to other populations where such a comparison was possible.

There seems little doubt that the urban environments of the western empire encouraged a different valuation of children. But we cannot achieve an appreciation of this simple fact by constantly harping on the underrepresentation of infants and children in burial commemorations (underrepresented, that is, when compared with probable death rates for infants for a typical Roman population). This underrepresentation is surely true for all commemorating populations in the empire. The significant difference that should be measured, surely, is the shift from communities that placed relatively little emphasis on children in death to those who made a substantial effort (out of their total effort in this regard) to commemorate them. In the traditional Latin culture of central Italy it seems that infant deaths were perceived quite differently from the deaths of adults, regardless of other factors. In formal legal terms, they were thought to deserve much less grief than older persons (*Frag.vat. 321 = FIRA* 2:536; compare Néraudau 1984, 373–392, 1987, 195–196). So, too, their deaths were conceived of as polluting and dangerous, given their innocence, and so were a matter for the interior of the household rather than a public ceremonial (Wiedemann 1989, 177–182). Infant burials were therefore internal and surreptitious, performed in secret in the dead of night. What literary evidence we have, however, does indicate a changed attitude that took more account of children in the core of Roman society (Néraudau 1984, pt. 2, 1987, 195–204). The one reason that has been consistently advanced for this shift is a form of compensation theory—as fathers in the high ruling elite of Roman society lost their autonomous political powers in the transition from republic to principate, they retreated inward to their families to find consolation in their children (Néraudau 1987, 206–207, hewing an old line of Paul Veyne's). But this supposed lack of political power touched so few that it does not qualify as a serious explanation for a phenomenon that, after all, affected most urban-centered populations of the western empire.

This emphasis on descendants within the family in death is even greater than the bare figures seem to indicate. In almost all the samples where the test was made, the celebration of the deaths of more elderly persons was overwhelmingly dominated by those whose deaths almost had to be marked: church officials and central or local state officials. The urbanized zone of south and central Gaul produced a reasonable emphasis on children, but was far outstripped by Christian populations from a more northerly and less urbanized zone of a later period (36.8:27.7 percent). Perhaps the most radical shift discernible in the whole of the western empire, however, was in North Africa.

There a very rural and traditional society valued the elderly and the fact of seniority at the expense of the young—consistently producing some of the lowest rates of commemoration of the young in the whole empire. In the small hamlet of Castellum Celtianum to the northwest of Cirta, in what is today east central Algeria, commemorations of children were virtually absent in contrast to those of the very elderly. Christian Mactar and Haïdra, two typical mid-range African towns of the period (located in what is today central Tunisia) greatly altered their valuations of children over those of the pre-Christian period (25.2–38.4:5–7 percent). Christianity seems to be the controlling factor in this shift in social valuation that pervaded the towns and countryside of the Latin west. The change was rather radical in North Africa, but it was also marked in every other case in the western empire, though to varying degrees.

The valuation given in the commemoration of the elderly, at the other end of the scale, is of course largely the converse of the patterns we have just observed (see table 4.4). To some degree, this must be related to the desire to give public recognition to elderly persons of power and prestige in the community. As Michel Vovelle noted in his study of American colonial tombstones, those set up in the earlier period of the seventeenth century were mainly to older males who held positions of high status and prestige in the society (Vovelle 1980, 537). The patterns in the Roman data, however, are more difficult to discern, in part because of the much smaller absolute numbers. But in general the factors involved in child emphasis seem to be inverted. In their emphasis on seniority, urban and Christian populations were toward the bottom end of the scale; non-Christian and rural populations tended more to the top. Rural African towns like Castellum Celtianum and Thagaste ranked very high in their recognition of the elderly, as did the rural regions of Spain. That the Christians of eastern Gaul (northern Gallia Viennensis) also placed so high seems to contradict the emphasis Christians usually gave to children and the young—but in this case the ranking only shows the degree to which the remote mountainous terrain and the frontier marginality of the region, even after tempering by Christian ideology and behavior, were resistant to this type of change. Traditional patterns of public respect for the elderly in commemoration apparently reinforced the material and ideological factors that were the opposite of those that led to emphasis on children. But the "choice" that these particular populations displayed in their emphasis on seniority was not fortuitous. The pattern is a social one that must surely be linked to the different forms of family organization that dominated in the countryside, especially of North Africa, where vertical lineages found in the deep countryside (in so-called tribal social groups) influenced the valuation of persons, emphasizing the great importance of senior ancestors at the expense of juniors, especially infants and children (Shaw 1984,

TABLE 4.4

Percentage of Tombstone Epitaphs Dedicated to Those in the 70th Decile (60–69) by Region and Social Group

Region and Social Group		Region and Social Group	
Christians: Gaul (Viennensis)	16.0	Freedmen: western empire	6.8
Africa: Castellum Celtianum	13.4	Africa: Carthage	6.7
Africa: Theveste	13.4	Slaves: Carthage	6.1
Africa: Cirta (rural)	12.4	Gaul	5.2
Africa: Western Proconsularis	11.2	Southern Italy: urban centers	5.1
Africa: small centers	10.9	Christians: Rome	4.1
Africa: Northern	10.8	Military: northern frontiers	3.9
Proconsularis		Northern Italy: urban centers	3.0
Africa: Altava	10.8	Freedmen: Rome	3.0
Military: Lambaesis	10.5	Christians: Rome (*ICUR* 5)	2.9
Africa: Cirtan Federation	10.4	Rome: general	2.8
Africa: Lambaesis	9.7	Christians: Rome (*ICUR* 4)	2.7
Christians: Carthage	9.1	Christians: Rome (*ICUR* 8)	2.6
Spain: urban centers	8.8	Slaves: western empire	2.6
Noricum/Raetia	8.8	Dalmatia: Salonae	2.6
Spain: general	8.7	Christians: Rome (*ICUR* 6)	2.5
Christians: Africa (Mactar)	8.2	Christians: Rome (*ICUR* 7)	2.2
Christians: Africa (Haïdra)	8.1	Military: Rome (elite units)	1.2
Christians: Spain	8.0	Ostia: general	0.9
Dalmatia: general	7.6	Slaves: Rome	0.3
Military: Pannonia	7.5		
Christians: Gaul (Belgica I)	6.9		

Note: *ICUR* = the cemeteries and catacombs covered by the specified volume of *Inscriptiones Christianae Urbis Romae* (Ferrua 1964–1983).
Sources: See tables 4.1 and 4.2.

480–481). Such a valuation was a direct reflection of the distribution of power in this region of the empire, both through kinship networks and through formal political institutions. It produced African peculiarities in which formal public power was attributed to groups of elders (*seniores*) both in pre-Christian communities and in the Christian church, in a way that was unparalleled elsewhere in the western empire (Shaw 1982).

This leads to some preliminary remarks on the valuation of children as part of the family and on intrafamilial relationships. First of all, such a valuation cannot be explained as stemming from some purely emotional context. The changed social context produces the changed emotional valuation. The picture produced by an analysis of this large batch of data is so consistent that no other conclusion seems reasonably possible. In his study of commemoration of death in colonial America, Vovelle noted that the average age of the deceased recorded on tombstones tended to fall over time, not because of an actual change in the age profile of the whole population, but because the elderly "without disappearing, are drowned in a flood of younger men who had acquired the right to be mourned" (Vovelle 1980, 537). The emphasis on children was merely the final step in this process. The greater valuation of children, and one must suspect, the relative devaluation of seniority, seems to be associated with the following general characteristics that cut across peculiar regional and social factors:

1. The greater the degree of urban development or urbanity in living habitat, the greater the degree of emphasis on the value of children, primarily from parents (with the rare involvement of grandparents, or others).

2. Cities of major rank in each regional context are a watershed of sorts. These populations reveal a sometimes astonishing break with the surrounding rural populations in their valuation of children.

3. As time advanced, and where such changes can be measured, between the first two and a half centuries after Christ and the mid-third to sixth century, the emphasis on these sorts of family ties strengthened perceptibly. This temporal strengthening, however, varied in degree relative to the degree of urban or rural background of the populations. Among rural social groups, the trend toward an increased emphasis on children was weak (though perceptible), whereas in the cities it was quite marked.

4. Christian groups valued their children over and above the level attributable to time and city living.

With these factors in mind, we may now turn to an analysis of our second dimension, that of gender preference (table 4.5). Here we can ask the same questions as above: Does an urban as opposed to a rural setting make any consistent difference in gender preference? Do distinct regions and social groups have their own peculiar characteristics? Does the advance of time change this preference in any discernible way? And, finally, can any special impact be attributed to the factor of Christian ideology? First, however, one methodological point must be made. In all the samples from various social groups and geographic contexts, those specific populations, as has been argued above, tended to place special value on certain sectors of the whole age range of their population. This may have altered over time, or those peculiar ranges may have been further strengthened. Age sets outside these ranges are therefore not our concern here, and for two reasons. Since the commemorating populations

TABLE 4.5
Male Preference in Specified Social Groups
(index: 1 = 0.1 percent)

Age	0–10	11–20	21–30	31–40	41–50	51–60	61–70	71–80	81–90
Slaves									
Rome	+92	+25	+33	+24	+18	−1	+2	−1	0
Carthage	+77	+55	+64	+26	+70	+9	+22	+19	+29
Western empire	+16	+16	+37	+7	+28	+5	+5	−1	+5
Freedmen									
Rome	−57	−24	−50	+5	+17	+15	+11	+11	+5
Western empire	+40	+7	−41	−9	+8	+3	+23	+20	+1
Military									
Rome (elite)	−2	+21	+222	+387	+164	+23	+12	+3	+12
Northern frontiers	+20	+32	+108	+183	+132	+61	+14	+11	+16
Pannonia	+20	+15	+41	+87	+70	+65	+37	+17	+11
Lambaesis	+22	+14	+86	+137	+164	+105	+83	+50	+39
Christians									
Rome	+10	−10	−1	−1	+6	+13	+9	+10	+1
Northern Italy	+48	−22	−55	+14	+117	+7	+7	+41	+7
Spain	+16	−16	−48	−21	+16	+90	+26	+64	+16
Gaul: Belgica	+118	−28	+21	+14	+42	+14	+28	0	—
Gaul: Viennensis	+53	+31	−54	+23	+31	+15	+44	+8	+23

(continued)

TABLE 4.5
(Continued)

Age	0–10	11–20	21–30	31–40	41–50	51–60	61–70	71–80	81–90
Africa: Carthage	+60	−31	+16	−46	−61	0	−61	0	+30
Africa: Mactar	−14	+23	+45	+46	+22	+7	+22	+15	+23
Africa: Haïdra	−12	+11	+70	+12	+47	+24	+12	0	+23
Urban									
Rome	+72	+11	+14	+34	+28	+14	+13	+8	+6
Ostia	+114	+32	−3	+8	+20	+2	−3	−4	+3
Northern Italy	+42	+26	+2	+24	+54	+40	+14	+18	+8
Spain	+28	+12	+10	+2	−12	−2	+28	+30	+12
Carthage	+41	0	+29	−11	+19	+13	+19	+20	+15
Cirta	+2	+27	+22	−8	+5	+19	+19	+20	+16
Rural/Provincial									
Spain	+6	0	+5	+14	+23	+8	+24	+23	+17
Gaul	+37	+34	+13	+10	+28	+9	+25	+20	+16
Noricum/Raetia	+9	+32	+28	−8	+5	+20	+24	+26	+4
Dalmatia	+31	−6	+37	+79	+47	+9	+9	+8	+10
Cirta (rural)	+1	+2	+2	−1	+10	+23	+28	+7	+17
Castellum Celtianum	+2	−5	+8	−10	+9	+34	+30	−3	+22

Note: The figures in this table represent a measure of the difference between the percentage of funerary dedications made to females as opposed to males in each age group. Positive figures are the degree of male preference; negative figures the degree of female preference. The figures for Christians (Rome) are cumulative totals derived from the volumes of *ICUR*.
Sources: see tables 4.1 and 4.2.

undervalued those other age sets, they are small in absolute numbers (and so not susceptible to great change). Their undervaluation in terms of numbers is also a direct reflection of the qualitative concern with the expression of public sentiment for them. In the analysis that follows we must therefore first specify for what age ranges a specific population was concerned to express its valuation, because those ranges will reveal whether there was also, so to speak, a change of heart with respect to gender preference. Modern historians have frequently noted that there were strong cultural reasons in the Roman world for those who were commemorating the dead to signal their preference for males: parents, for example, tended to prefer sons over daughters (Hopkins 1964–1965, 323–324 and fig. 2, 1966, 261–264). This was also true of the eastern Mediterranean, where it can be measured (Boyaval 1976, 223–224, 1977). It goes without saying that almost all social and regional groups of the period were strongly male dominant and male oriented. My pursuit of the problem is therefore a matter of emphasis: to what degree certain regions or social groups showed greater or lesser preference for males.

Let us begin with the imperial metropolis of Rome. As has been shown, the value emphasis in this city was on the younger deciles in the whole population (those under thirty). If we look at gender emphasis in this group we see that as time advances from our earlier period (first to mid-third century) to our later (mid-third to sixth century), the preference of males over females diminishes noticeably, indeed so much so that females in their teens and twenties shift from being decidedly not preferred (male emphasis factors of +25 and +22) to actually becoming the favored gender (male preference falling to −23 and −7 in those ranges). In his comparative study of colonial American tombstones, Vovelle noted much the same sort of trend. Women were scarce at first (4 percent in the seventeenth century), but gradually achieved greater recognition in death (28 percent by the nineteenth century): "a progression . . . expressing an evolution in practice which although far from arriving at equality between the sexes, does reflect a progressive reevaluation of the position of the woman as companion or loved one." Vovelle rightly warns that "the final inequality in death reflected the inequality of a patriarchal society still dominated by men" (Vovelle 1980, 535–536). In the Roman case, the impact of Christianity does not seem to have greatly exaggerated this trend. The average preference among Christians for males in each of the first three deciles was +11.9, −6.8, and −1.1, which although not as radical a shift in the direction of female preference as in the population as a whole, clearly followed and shared in the general movement in time. Measurable Christian populations for northern Italy are provided by the urban centers of Aquileia, Ravenna, and Mediolanum (Milan). We can sense the movement over time in emphasis on small children by comparing these Christian children with those of the general populations of urban centers in northern Italy in the first six centuries A.D. In these latter populations, the decile emphasis on age groups is located at the lower end of the scale (the first four decades). Here we witness a general movement over time similar to that of Rome (table 4.4). In every case the movement is away from strong male preference, either mitigating (in the deciles under ten and forty this movement is from $+70$ to $+28$, and from $+36$ to $+10$, respectively) or dramatically reversing that preference (in the decile under twenty, for example, male preference falls from $+41$ to -8, and in the decile under thirty from $+72$ to -3). Once again, the Christian sample from these major urban centers, though a small one, reveals some, though not all, of this same movement (table 4.4). The degree of male preference for those under ten, $+48$, falls midway between the early and late samples for northern Italian centers in general. For the critical teens and twenties, however, the male preference in these urban Christian communities falls to negative values of -22 and -55. Since the sample is rather small it is hardly a firm basis for sure deductions; the results, however, do seem in line with a trend toward greater equality between the sexes in terms of valuation at death. But the same samples also suggest that, with respect to gender preference, Christians were following trends already well established in the general urban population.

To ask the same question of provincial populations, we might consider those of Spain and North Africa. Spanish populations in general emphasized mainly the middle decades of the whole population: those in their twenties, thirties, and forties. In analyzing the preference for males or females in these age groups as we look at the general mix of commemorations spread over the first to sixth century, no clear shift emerges; if anything, male preference seems uniformly to be strengthened. But in this case Christians as a distinct group reveal a marked difference. In the critical middle decades there was a wholesale shift from male to female preference, with indexes of male preference falling to uniformly negative values of -16, -48, and -21, respectively. But the Spanish Christians were an exception—the dominant trend was a strengthening of male preference over time. For North Africa, we must distinguish between the larger urban centers, where age preference tended to be located in the early to middle decades of the whole population, and the rural populations, where the emphasis was on the middle to later decades. To begin with the urban centers, we might select two of the largest: Carthage and Cirta. The story in both is the same. When the degree of preference for males over females is compared for the earlier and the later periods of history, we find a marked strengthening in the preference for males. Even in the decile of the thirties, where in both cases females were initially preferred (perhaps a sign of the large ex-servile element in our epigraphic samples?), the preference falls off with the passage of time, that is, from female to male (from -15 to -6 in Carthage and from -13 to $+3$ in Cirta). The same is true, only with greater emphasis, among the rural populations, as we move from the earlier to the later period. Here the critical deciles are still the later ones, from the thirties and forties to the seventies. In every decile the preference for males over females either remains constant (for the seventies at $+27$) or increases, from a factor of three for the fifties ($+23$ to $+26$) to a factor of twenty for the sixties (from $+8$ to $+28$). Among these provincial populations, therefore, in the critical age sets that they emphasized, (with the exception of the Christians) time does not have the discernible mitigating impact that is perceptible in Rome and in Italy. Males remain on the whole the preferred sex, and this preference seems, oddly enough, to grow stronger through time. Why?

For both North Africa and Spain, the slight movement toward increased elementary family organization is much less pronounced than elsewhere in the west; the rural regions of both areas certainly seem to stand in marked contrast to the core urban centers of the empire. The more severe forms of family sentiment, and of gender relationships and age hierarchies, that we find in literary sources do not appear to be anomalous. The Roman family attested by our best literary source for North Africa, Saint Augustine, seems to have been characterized by peculiarly harsh paternal relationships that may be placed at one end of the extremes of family sentiment (Shaw 1987b). If this observation is matched with what can be documented, in rather colder fashion, from the tombstone evidence, we can see that the region of Numidian Africa from which Augustine came (western Proconsularis, centered on the towns of Thubursicu Numidarum, Madauros, and Thagaste) had one of the lowest valuations of children of any region even within North Africa (4.4 as opposed to 8.7 percent for northern Proconsularis; 7.8 percent on average and 11.4 percent for Augustine's time for the Cirtan Federation), and that it contrasted sharply with the urban metropolis of Carthage (19.8 percent on average, 22.5 percent for Augustine's time). Hence, at least for some regions and social groups, the effects of Christianity and development through time were not uniformly beneficial for females. The generalized boxing in of relationships within the elementary family may have encouraged a structurally greater emphasis on children, but at the same time may have served only to perpetuate the rather traditional place of girls and, even more so, of married women. This seems to have been equally true of the eastern Mediterranean at this time (Boyaval 1976, 223; the tombstones of the village Akhmim in Egypt, all of them set up by Christians except for one stele, display the greatest discrepancy between those for males and those for females of all his Egyptian samples). As has been pointed out in another context, the powerful structure of the patriarchal family itself may have been strong enough to determine the work position of women, as much as any forces impinging on the family from outside, even economic ones (Howell 1989).

One might also note that these profoundly rural regions were marked not just by strongly traditional sentiments and family forms, but also by traditional labor regimes. Paradoxically, where "modern" family structures and sentiments were most prevalent were at the heart of regions that had broken with that pattern, notably with respect to the critical role slave labor played in the process of their development. In this regard, the factors of Christianity, slavery, and urbanization seem to be strongly correlated. We must then wonder if the joint impact of these forces somehow modified traditional family patterns. Not one of them taken in isolation offers a whole explanation. Slavery could have been one of the important contributory factors—out of urban servitude flowed a new population, freedmen and their descendants, who had to constitute (or reconstitute) families de novo in an urban environment where their labor was organized along lines that would reinforce nuclearity (Patterson 1982, 5–9; for definitions of family in the context of a slave society, see Fox-Genovese 1988, 24, 37–99). It cannot be accidental that the large numbers of freedmen who contributed to the creation of these urban proletariats produced one of the finest examples of nuclear family sentiment from the Roman world. This evidence consists of the closest analogue we have from Roman society to the modern family snapshot. These pictures are part of the iconographic element of the tombstone alluded to at the beginning of this chapter. In the last century of the Roman Republic, from the fluid and dynamic relations that evolved in the community of upwardly mobile ex-slaves emerged a novel iconographic form: the tombstone that featured a relief sculpture composed of the portrait busts of the family whose members (or at least one of whom) were commemorated in the written text. It is particularly significant that urban freedmen should have been in the vanguard of the production of this novel type of popular art. That the family is intended is clear not only from the type of the portraiture itself, but also from the reliefs so obviously being modeled on the frontage of an actual house. The *domus aeterna* became a replica of the *domus temporalis* (Zanker 1975 is the critical study; compare Kleiner 1977, 1987a, 1987b).

The emphasis of the iconography on these otherworldly homes is entirely on the husband, wife, and children (Zanker 1975, 294ff.). In this respect, the iconography of these family-oriented stones, if we may call them that, contrasts sharply with that of the typical pictorial stones commemorating soldiers, many of whom did not have families (compare the funerary portraits typical of urban freedmen in Kleiner with those typical of soldiers: Anderson 1984; Franzoni

1987; Saller and Shaw 1984, 141–142). These were two reasons why freedmen should especially emphasize this type of family. One, already referred to above, is that they had little other choice; as former slaves they had no ascendant family tradition. Then again, they would have wished to stress the fact of family, as other symbolic parts of their tombstone iconography also suggest, because of its status value. By visually portraying their families they proclaimed their normality, their status as citizens, and their social position as free Romans (Zanker 1975; there was also a bare economic reason: children protected freedmen against the possible testamentary claims of their former masters). But it is interesting to see that, although by setting up these memorials freedmen did mimic the upper classes to a certain extent, the form they created was substantially one of their own making (for elements of imitation and originality, see Zanker 1975, 276–277, 280). "Marriage and family were understandably closely linked to the main social objectives of the freedmen. The simple social fact of a genuine marriage made their new status as citizens manifest. No wonder then that the relief sculptures on the tombstones particularly emphasize this point. Numerous reliefs show the married couple, alone or with children, and, occasionally, with other relatives and dependents in the form of a larger family group" (Zanker 1975, 285). Zanker's point is substantiated to a considerable degree by the preferences signaled in the funerary epigraphy—at Ostia, for example, where the corpus of funerary stones is dominated by freedpersons, the commemorations reflect both a great emphasis on children (38.3 percent of the total) and a preference for sons over daughters in that age group (24.8 percent to 13.4 percent). Indeed, the position of the son is especially prominent in these family pictures—a further demonstration of the important social function that these images of family had for persons who were attempting to emphasize publicly the fact of family (Shaw 1987a, 41; compare Zanker 1975, 289, 294–296).

To understand better why freedmen, who were thrust into the circumstances of family formation, should coalesce primarily into the elementary family, we must surely take into account a fundamental transformation in the Roman social world that has been greatly neglected (Finley 1980, 147–148). This was the creation of the large class of formally free urban plebes, who dominated the populations of the great urban centers of the later empire (for the changing labor regimes that matched this shift, see Hahn 1981). For the great urban populations, which included large numbers of freedmen and their descendants, the material circumstances of their family economy and of their work situation must have encouraged and reinforced the structure of the simple family (Brunt 1980; Kampen 1981; Treggiari 1982b). Most of the million or so inhabitants of the metropolis of Rome, for example, would have been constrained to earn their livelihood by the direct application of their own labor. It is surely no accident that the leading ideologues of the new Christian morality surrounding sexuality and marriage, men like the holy Hermas, the priest Hippolytus, and Pope Callistus, were drawn from this same urban slave and free population (Rousselle 1988, 101–105; Brown 1988, 59–72; on Callistus's social background, see Gülzow 1967). Significant numbers of this slave and free population were involved in nonlegal forms of marriage known as *contubernium* (army slang meaning "tenting up," equivalent to the modern slang "shacking up," and with much the same pejorative connotation) and concubinage (*concubinatus* [bedding down together], again with pejorative connotations). In the pre-Christian Roman world such relationships were regarded either as additions or as alternatives to a formally recognized marriage. Although urban slaves and freed persons engaged in these de facto marriages, they rejected a pejorative categorization of them. Instead, they hypostatized their own marital unions (that is, monogamous and permanent liaisons) as the only acceptable form of marriage. The sort of marriage relationship encouraged by their economic situation therefore took its place in the process of family formation (Treggiari 1981a; Rawson 1974; on the Christian reaction, see Rousselle 1988, chap. 6). The precise role of Christian ideology in this matrix is complex, obscure, and still open to question.

The previous caveat is in order because we all have an ingrained tendency to overestimate the impact of Christian belief and practice. One should not forget that this influence was itself strongly contextual. In its own most powerful milieu, that of the urban environment, Christianity did function as an ideology. But when isolated in the remote countryside, Christianity could become sublimated to the more dominant milieu of its background, and whatever effect it had might be marginal indeed, as seems to have been the case, for example, in northern Gallia Viennensis, the remote montane zone of eastern Gaul. Nevertheless, among some major urban populations with both the passage of time and the advent of Christian belief and behavior, the gap in preference between males and females celebrated in death narrowed, and the emphasis descended to the young, especially children. There is perhaps no better single symbol of this whole shift than a reused gravestone found at Carthage. On one side of the stone, the side used first, is the funerary inscription of a Roman soldier: *D.M.S. M[arco] Val[erio] Petrao, I Alae Gemellianae. Ex Provincia Tingitana. V[ixit] an[nis] XXX. H.S.E.* [To the Infernal Ghosts. (This stone is dedicated) to Marcus Valerius Petraus, from the First Gemellian Cavalry Wing. From the Province of (Mauretania) Tingitana. He lived 30 years. He lies here]. A memorial, obviously, to a male who died in middle age. On the opposite side of the stone, which was used again much later by Christians, is the following inscription: *Gloriosa vixit annu I fidelis in pace* [Gloriosa, who lived one year, faithful in the peace (of our Lord)]. A Christian, a girl, an infant. The shift is indicated not only on those three planes, but also in the workmanship of the two inscriptions. Whereas the soldier's memorial is recorded in the fine, polished lettering of a craftsman, the infant girl's inscription, like all the others found at the site, is in the simple, abbreviated, and crudely produced format of the urban proletariat, many of whose members were likewise memorialized at the Basilica of Mcidfa at Carthage (Ennabli 1982, no. 75 and photo, p. 89).

In reflecting on the nature of this massive shift in the public valuation of men, women, and children in Roman society in the west, we might conclude by returning to the text of the "typical" gravestone cited at the beginning of this chapter. We can now see that the sentiments it embodies are wholly atypical of the vast majority of the inhabitants of the western empire. Though often taken as an indication of normal sentiments, stones like these in fact represent the exceptional urban milieu of the great metropolis that was the heart of the empire. These primary bonds, vested in a form of nuclear family, are surely also tied to a type of individualism provoked by the economic and political forces that pervaded the typical Roman town and city in the west. It would be a mistake to categorize such novel sentiments as our sort of individualism, though the family life and structure that were part of Roman urban environments were integrally linked to the new values (Foucault 1986, 41–43, 78–80, on individualism). It is perhaps significant that Michel Vovelle was able to note much the same developmental pattern in his study of American tombstones of the colonial period: "Toward the middle of the eighteenth century, first the world of the patriarchs gave way to one which included the young adult men and began to make way for women. Then, around 1780, there appear children, increased numbers of young mothers and girls, and adolescent boys" (Vovelle 1980, 540). The nexus of social and economic forces impinging on the American family were different in kind and scope from those of the Roman Empire; but the pressures engendered by developing urban milieux by economic structures that emphasized the importance of the labor of the individual were similar. This peculiar nexus of forces brought to the fore ideals, and behaviors, that might properly be considered typical of a certain family structure that we in the West have come to accept as our own. I should emphasize here, however, that I am not arguing for a crude sort of evolutionary derivation of our small family from theirs—but merely for a convergence of similar types of economic forces producing similar results (Shaw 1984, 489–490). The lights did indeed finally fade on a Roman society in the west—one of our questions, however, should be where they faded last. The answer would seem to be that Roman-type behavior endured the longest in the urban centers of northern Italy and the lowlands of northwestern Europe along the communications corridor of the Rhine (Shaw 1984). When Michelet's "rebirth" began in this zone, it was marked precisely by a reemergence of typical urban life, and with it not wholly new forms of family relationships.

Chapter 5

SUSAN TREGGIARI

Ideals and Practicalities in Matchmaking in Ancient Rome

In pagan Roman society, at least among the members of the propertied classes, it was expected that all girls would marry—and be married for most of their childbearing years. If necessary, they would marry several times. A concurrent belief held by both moralists and statesmen with an eye on citizen manpower was that men were reluctant to marry. They might postpone unduly the performance of their duty to father legitimate children, or they might not wish to marry at all. But as far as we can tell, lifelong bachelors were in fact a rarity among the upper classes. The Augustan marriage laws laid down ages at which both men and women were to be married and parents. We do not know for certain the ages between which the unmarried were penalized, but we know the ages prescribed for parenthood; between twenty and fifty for women and between twenty-five and sixty for men. This suggests that society expected upper-class women to marry in their late teens and men in their early twenties and that entering a new marriage after fifty and sixty, respectively, was abnormal. Lower down in society, circumstances prevented some people from forming valid marriages. For two centuries soldiers had no capacity to marry, and their epitaphs show that a sizable proportion failed to form families even after their retirement (Saller and Shaw 1984). It has been suggested that poverty deterred the laboring classes in the city from marriage (Brunt 1971, 136–140). Slaves lacked the legal capacity, but they often formed unions that became valid Roman marriages if both partners were freed and became Roman citizens. Most of the empire's population until the early third century A.D. were noncitizens, who married according to their own laws but could not contract Roman marriages.

This chapter concerns Roman citizens, starting about 90 B.C., the period of the enfranchisement of the remaining noncitizens south of the Po, and ending in the early third century A.D., when the whole population of the empire received citizenship; the state and society subsequently (though not consequently) broke down in anarchy, and our sources almost dry up. Within this period, the social stratification of Italy was distinctly marked. Members of the Senate in Rome formed an aristocracy of service and held the highest status. But membership of the Senate was not hereditary. Some families recurred, some in every generation; others produced only one attested senator (Hopkins 1983, 31–200). Senators were distinguished from the next order, that of the *equites,* by their constitutional functions. But socially the two groups were closely linked: father and son (until the early empire, when three generations of males from a senator counted as senatorial), or two brothers or husband and wife might come from different orders. In turn, the equestrian order overlapped with the lesser aristocracies of Italian towns. Men moved up and down between these groups in wealth and function; women moved up and down by marriage; wealth moved between generations and individuals, often through women. The literary and juristic sources compel us to focus our attention on these groups. Epigraphy provides data on lower social groups, but allows us only to see who married whom, which does not permit us to do more than infer why a choice was made (Weaver 1972; Treggiari 1981b). In discussing the material on the upper classes, I focus on the conventional criteria that society acknowledged and on the more complex and detailed consideration that took place in practice. We must first admit that the authors available are doubly restricted: by being male (with the exception of the poetess Sulpicia) and by the genres in which they wrote. Adaptations of Greek New Comedy, love poetry, epic, lyric, satire, forensic and political speeches, formal history, and works on rhetoric and philosophy do not render the type of information that an early modern historian can glean from family papers and personal memoirs, not to mention the quantifiable data and interviews available to the sociologist. Biographies are more informative, at least on outsiders' and posterity's perceptions of motivation. Our best sources are the large collection of Cicero's letters (mostly written for the named correspondent alone) and Pliny's letters (unfortunately, composed with an eye to revision and publication). The jurists are practically silent on choice of marriage partner. We must also take account—as we would for a later period—of reticences, for instance, matters that the writer thought improper to mention to a particular reader, and of the omission of those that were taken for granted. (For a fuller discussion, I refer the reader to Treggiari 1991, 83–160.)

IDEOLOGY

Philosophers discussed whether the philosopher should marry (and the schools differed on the answer), and rhetoricians taught boys to debate whether a particular man should marry (Quint. 3.5.8). Many upper-class young men were confronted with such questions in the schoolroom. They might also have come across the moralist's question, Should one always obey his father? Philosophers were divided. Some said one should always obey; others that obedience was not required; still others that the duty to obey depended on the nature of the order. Among acts that were morally indifferent and that the son should normally perform at his father's request was taking a wife. But if ordered to marry a wife who was publicly dishonored, of loose life, or likely to be prosecuted on a criminal charge, the son might refuse (Gell. 2.7).

The question was not posed in this way for Roman daughters. But Ulpian (late second to early third century A.D.), in discussing the consents necessary for a valid engagement, gives a clue that their moral position was seen as parallel to that of sons. For a valid betrothal, the man and woman who were to marry had to consent, and their fathers also, if they had paternal power. If a daughter was in her father's power, *filiafamilias,* her consent to an engagement to which her father consented might be assumed, unless she explicitly expressed dissent (*Dig.* 23.1.12 pr.). We should note that the obverse of this applied: if the woman made the engagement, her father's consent was assumed unless he explicitly denied it (*Dig.* 23.1.7.1). Ulpian gives it apparently as his personal opinion that for a daughter in power to be allowed to reject an engagement proposed by her father would be improper, unless the man was unworthy because of his moral character, low social status, or disgraceful occupation (*Dig.* 23.1.12.1). This seems precisely parallel to what Gellius says.

LEGAL PROTAGONISTS

The sweeping legal powers of a *paterfamilias* are striking to modern scholars, as they were to Gaius when he wrote his elementary textbook on private law in the second century A.D. A man and a woman had the right to marry in Roman law, *conubium,* if they were of age, not within the prohibited degree of relationship, and either Roman citizens or the equivalent (that is, the man was a citizen and the woman belonged to a state that had reciprocal rights of intermarriage with Rome) and neither was otherwise debarred by statute, imperial ruling, and so on. Any children born to them and acknowledged by the father would then be "right children," *justi filii,* to their father. They would be Roman citizens like him, and his heirs if he died intestate. They would also come under his paternal power, *patria potestas,* at birth. This meant that he had the power of life and death over them. This was rarely exercised, however, and usually with social safeguards, such as consultation with a family council. It was of more relevance in ordinary life that any property *filiifamilias* acquired legally belonged to their father, that they inherited automatically if he died without making a will, that their legal personality was part of his, and that the act of one could imply the consent of the other. Now it should be noted that the restrictions on the son or daughter went along with privileges. It should also be noted that, although the law involving filiifamilias remained of great interest to lawyers throughout the classical period, particularly in relation to sons and daughters engaged in business, there are relatively few allusions to it in literary sources, and we do not find fathers invoking their rights in order to control recalcitrant children. (It is significant that Roman boys practiced rhetorical exercises that involved a non-Roman form of disowning sons, *abdicatio,* not the real Roman practice of *emancipatio;* but compare Quint. 7.4.11.). There is nothing to show that Marcus or Quintus Cicero thought of reminding their disobliging sons of the powers they no doubt held over them. Affection is the usual theme; duty appears more rarely than it would in the harangues of an eighteenth-century father; patria potestas is notable for its absence. It was also possible for a child to be freed from power: this may have begun as a mode of disinheritance and a mark of disgrace, but it continued as a convenience and often as a privilege. More important, as has been conclusively shown, a high proportion of filiifamilias had lost their fathers to death before they themselves reached adulthood (Saller 1987). When freed, by whatever means, a son became the head of his own household, paterfamilias (even if he was a baby). A daughter became independent (sui juris). In the period from Cicero to Ulpian, we must be conscious that if a paterfamilias were alive, his consent would be legally required for the marriage of a child in his power. But we need not assume that the father, by virtue of patria potestas, played the dominant role in the choice of partner.

Our evidence, however, coming from men rather than women and from fathers rather than sons, emphasizes the role of the father, particularly the father of a young woman, in making a match. Fathers were said to betroth their daughters (for example, Tacitus, *Agr.* 9; Suetonius, *Aug.* 63.2). Cicero reports to Atticus in 67 "we have engaged Tullia to C. Piso Frugi, son of Lucius" (*Att.* 1.3.3). Tullia was then about nine, and we would not expect her to have taken a leading role in the choice of a husband.

Legally, engagements did not matter much, since they were unenforceable and damages could not be sought for breach of promise. Socially, it was allowable to repudiate a fiancé(e), though not to make a habit of it. The sources most frequently attest engagements as broken for reasons of political advantage (to cement a new alliance) or dynastic planning (in the Julio-Claudian family). But such motives might be masked by decent protestations that new evidence had come to light about the noncitizen status or moral unsuitability of the destined husband or wife (Seneca, *Ben.* 4.35.1; Tacitus, *Ann.* 12.3f., 8). For this chapter, evidence was sought from accounts of the making of both engagements and marriages, since each represented choice of a marriage partner (*conjunx*).

The consents required to make a marriage were the same as those for an engagement: each conjunx had to consent to the marriage as did the paterfamilias of either or both of them: "A valid marriage is impossible unless all consent, that is those who are united and those in whose power they are" (*Dig.* 23.2.2; Treggiari 1982a). Lawyers down to Justinian (sixth century) consistently stated that the consent of the paterfamilias was needed. This was particularly natural when the marriage was that of a son in power, for his children would be in the power of the grandfather and would have a strong claim on his estate. It would be unfair for the son to bring in heirs without the father's consent. Similarly, if the daughter not only married but passed under her husband's control, *manus,* which was analogous to paternal power, then she automatically left her father's power and all her property and future acquisitions went to her husband: her father's agreement to this arrangement was logically necessary. If, however, the daughter did not enter manus, she remained in her previous condition, as *filiafamilias.* Although her children belonged to her husband's family and had no legal claims on her father, he retained control over her and her property. A tension was set up between her legal and economic relationship with her father and a socio-moral and economic relationship with her husband. Moreover, the father could subsequently will a divorce.

No ratification of marriage by any outside party was needed and no particular form marked the giving of consent. The presence of the bride was required, but that of the husband could be dispensed with and a letter or messenger could express his consent. The patresfamilias were not required to attend: written consent or an oral message was certainly sufficient. It is probable that tacit consent also sufficed. When Cicero's daughter Tullia (probably filiafamilias [Dixon 1984, 90]) married for the third time, her father was in the Near East and had probably not even yet heard of the engagement. He had given Tullia and her mother, Terentia, permission to make the final decision, but far from approving the specific candidate, had just written to back another man. "There was in all cases a presumption of consent, even an irrebuttable presumption, where a parent acquainted with the facts did not take the opportunity to protest; for it is difficult to draw any substantial distinction between a positive consent which may be tacit and an absence of opposition which must be accompanied by knowledge" (Corbett 1930, 60). Sometimes fathers of daughters authorized the bridegroom in advance; sometimes they implied consent by handing over or promising dowry. How the father of a son demonstrated his consent in real life is not directly attested, though in comedy fathers sometimes ask for the hand of a woman for their sons by an archaic formula (Plautus, *Trinummus* 499ff.). Probably the father's consent was usually expressed orally to the son or implied by his acceptance of the dowry. But it may also have been tacit (compare the words of the praetor's edict [Watson 1967, 41]). Subsequent paternal acquiescence to a marriage often seems to have been sufficient, even if the father was unaware of its inception. On the other hand, the legal theory was that no one, whether a son or daughter in power or not, could be forced into marriage (*Dig.* 23.2.21; *Code of Justinian* 5.4.12, 14). But if a son was pressured by his father into marrying a wife whom he would not have married had he exercised his own free will, the marriage was still valid; it was argued that the son had chosen not to disobey (*Dig.* 23.1.22).

SELECTORS AND SELECTION PROCEDURES

Apart from the paterfamilias (father or paternal grandfather), no other family member had to give legal consent. An independent woman did not need the consent of her legal guardians for marriage (though she would for entry into manus or transfer of dowry [Gardner 1986, 18]). A man of full age, if independent, was completely free. Nor was application to a public authority involved. So in legal theory, a person of either sex above the age of puberty (twelve for a girl, fourteen or sexual maturity for a boy) could enter into marriage of his or her own volition as long as he or she was not under paternal power.

Blood relations had moral authority, however, and the approval of both parents was desirable. It was a pity that when the forty-year-old Brutus made his second marriage to his cousin his mother, Servilia, disapproved (Cicero, *Att.* 13.22.4). Rhetoricians might argue for young people's acquiescence in a parent's choice (Seneca, *Controv.* 2.3.2). But equally they could say that young men and women should have liberty in marrying and might, if necessary, disobey a father (*Minor Declamations* 257.5).

Conversely, it was proper for a father, even a paterfamilias, to consult friends, kinsmen, and especially his wife before taking action in so important a matter as the arrangement of the marriage of a son or daughter (Cicero, *De Or.* 3.133; Livy 38.57.6–8; Pliny, *Ep.* 1.14). There were social checks on his legal and moral authority, because legal requirements and moral imperatives were not the only considerations. Affection could increase the degree of freedom allowed to a child. Cicero certainly did not intend to force his own choice on his adored daughter. Even in the most manipulative families, we must allow for this element. Caesar was noted for his fondness for his only child, who seems to have married unusually late. (She was born c. 83 and married in April of 59 B.C.)

The age of the prospective husband or wife made an incalculable difference. This was related to his or her position in the family group. We have just seen the weight given, by authority and affection, to the opinion of the long-widowed mother of a mature man. Servilia's views were taken into account, but not obeyed. A young girl at first marriage with surviving parents was at one extreme. At the other end of the continuum was the divorcée or widow (*vidua*), without parents. When a wellborn and virtuous lady, long single and once a mother (her child or children had presumably died), decided to marry the old, sick, and disreputable Domitius Tullus, in spite of her own advanced years, she was severely criticized (Pliny, *Ep.* 8.18.7–10). But certainly no one was entitled to stop her, any more than sons or kin could stop the widowed Pudentilla marrying the young Apuleius (Apuleius, *Apol.*). Young men at first marriage had more freedom than women. Caesar at sixteen discarded the financée who had probably been found for him by his late father and made the politically risky choice of the daughter of Cinna, apparently on his own initiative (Suetonius, *Caes.* 1). Young men with fathers alive or dominant uncles or mothers could be subject to more pressure. Older and established men had the widest choice (including the privilege of choosing young women who had not been married before) and were least likely to need to attend to the views of relations.

Practical considerations also influenced search and choices in many ways. What contacts and ways of finding out information did the candidate for marriage or his or her relatives and friends have? What could the candidate offer and realistically hope to find in a conjunx? Our best-attested instance of a search illustrates some angles. I refer to the arrangement of Tullia's third marriage, in 51/50 B.C. (Treggiari 1984). This example illustrates the importance that a father attached to doing his duty by his daughter, his willingness to mobilize all his resources of friendship with a variety of men and women, and the ways in which his choice was modified by practicalities (his own absence, the shortage of suitable men who were available) and the competing plans of the woman herself and her mother. It is naturally a one-sided view. We would wish to have a sheaf of letters from Cicero's wife, Terentia, to her friends or kin, or tape recordings of their conversations. Tullia herself had circulated in society since at least about 60 B.C. and must have had a circle of women friends, male acquaintances, connections of her first husband, and perhaps of her divorced second husband, on whom she could call for advice and suggestions. Probably she had already met Dolabella, whose previous wife, if she was called Fabia (Quint. 6.3.73), must have been related to Terentia's stepfather (Asconius

91C). All this gives us some idea of how a search would be conducted by and on behalf of a daughter.

When a man sought a bride, particularly a virgin, his female relatives were best placed to advise him. Although ancient custom allowed children of both sexes to be present at dinner parties, they were usually segregated from adults, and adult men probably had little occasion to meet young girls, except the daughters of intimate friends. But mothers of sons, visiting other women, were well placed to review nubile daughters. A mother would also receive cautious advances from mothers of daughters and other interested matrons (*Minor Declamations* 306.27–28, 360.1).

Although young girls were not encouraged to be forward, they were brought up to accept marriage as their career and they must have had an interest in the choice of husband. A father might concede that in selecting a son-in-law he was concerned with grandchildren, but for his daughter the choice affected the whole of her life (Fronto, *Ep. ad Amicos* 2.2 [Loeb ed., 1:292]). "A man who gives his daughter in marriage to a man who uses insulting language and has often been repudiated (by fianceées or wives) will have done a bad job in looking after his daughter's interests" (Seneca, *Ben.* 4.27.5). Girls may have been allowed social contact with potential husbands under responsible chaperonage and their thoughts were perhaps turned in a suitable direction, so that they gave some encouragement to eligible men. Aunts, married elder sisters, and matrons who were friends of the family could help a virtuous adolescent to be noticed by other women and recommended to suitable *partis* or to appear where she might attract suitors. Boys and girls met at dinners and on religious occasions, and girls had elder brothers who would know most of their contemporaries in the city upper class from school, the army, or the lower offices. Pomponia cannot have been unusual in marrying the brother of a school friend of her elder brother's (although her marriage to Quintus Cicero may have been her second marriage [Nepos, *Att.* 5.3]).

The greater freedom allowed to matrons, divorced women, and widows meant that they could take some initiative in finding new husbands. A few examples are described by our sources, neutrally or for censure. Sulla (a new widower) was deliberately picked up at the Games by the patrician Valeria, who was wellborn, good looking, and recently divorced. After informing himself about her family and her past, he embarked (with her full cooperation) on a passionate flirtation and speedy marriage (Plutarch, *Sull.* 35.3–5). Livia Ocellina wooed Galba, and Agrippina the Younger pursued his son (who already had a wife [Suetonius, *Galba* 3.3, 5.1]). The second instance was shocking, but Cicero was not scandalized when a divorced woman was said to be proposing marriage to the precocious younger Q. Cicero. The elder Quintus merely checked up on her reputation and family, as usual (*Att.* 15.29.2, 16.2.5; see further Treggiari 1985).

CONVENTIONAL CRITERIA

In formulating their choice, the makers of a match could rely on categories established centuries before by moralists reacting to what they took to be the common views of society. We can distinguish between an idealistic and an alleged worldly list of qualities to be sought in a marriage partner. These differ little from those approved by the corresponding groups in later ages, except that in the fourth or seventeenth century A.D. shared religious beliefs achieved a prominence not seen in classical Rome.

In the late fourth or early third century B.C., the Aristotelian Theophrastus in a lost work on marriage asked whether a wise man would marry: "When he had laid down the conditions, if she were beautiful, of good character, with honorable parents, and if he himself were rich and healthy, then sometimes the wise man would enter on marriage, he at once adds the rider: 'but these things rarely all come together in a marriage' " (Jerome, *Adv. Iovinian.* 1.47 = 313C). The question became a commonplace and the criteria standard. Attacking conventional behavior in the first century A.D., the Stoic Musonius Rufus says,

> Therefore those who contemplate marriage ought to have regard neither for family, whether either one be of high-born parents, nor for wealth, whether on either side there be great possessions, nor for physical traits, whether one or the other have beauty. For neither wealth nor beauty nor high birth is effective in promoting partnership of interest or sympathy, nor again are they significant for producing children. But as for the body it is enough for marriage that it be healthy, of normal appearance and capable of hard work, such as would be less exposed to the snares of tempters, better adapted to perform physical labour and not wanting in strength to beget or to bear children (Lutz 1947:13B)

He then insists that there should be virtue on both sides. Isidore of Seville in the seventh century similarly lists four criteria for assessing possible husbands (manliness, family, looks, speech), and three for wives (birth, good character, beauty) (*PL* 83.812; compare *Etymologiae* 9.7.28).

The philosophers' lists fit well enough with the categories in which writers usually think. Dido is attracted by Aeneas's *virtus* (manliness, courage, prowess), birth, face, and words (Vergil, *Aeneid* 4.3–5). The full list for a man might include birth and background (home town and connections), wealth, morals, and affection for the bride (Ovid, *Her.* 20.221–228). Pliny, responding to Junius Mauricus, who asked him to help find a husband for his niece, recommends

Minicius Acilianus. He describes in turn his origin, relatives, character, and looks. Pliny adds coyly that Acilianus's father is rich, important for the sake of the future children (*Ep.* 1.14).

For a woman, a complete list would include looks, charm, wealth, birth, fertility, and chastity. "But who would really want to marry such a paragon?" says Juvenal (6.161–183). Statius pictures a bride who not only is highly educated and compatible in character with her bridegroom, but also meets all other qualifications: "figure, candor, charm, financial standing, blood, position, looks" (*Silv.* 2.7.81–86).

But the conventional list was so general that it served only as a guide to the categories that had to be considered. Not only would a man's scores in the four conventional areas have to be taken into account, but also subtler points (not only the general prestige of his family but also the effectiveness of his living kin). And this was only a beginning. One then had to calculate whether the woman and her family had enough to offer him in exchange. It might be seen as a coup for the inferior to win someone better qualified, but such a match might disgrace the superior. Moralists disapproved of unequal matches for various reasons. The domineering rich wife became a stock character in Latin literature. Relative worth might appear different to the two interested groups or individuals (Treggiari 1984, 422ff.).

Disparity of birth between a husband and wife was to be avoided by all classes. To marry someone less wellborn than oneself was discreditable and might be held against the children (Tacitus, *Ann.* 15.59.8; Horace, *Sat.* 1.6.36). Patrician descent through the male line retained its theoretical superiority, but plebeian nobility (descent from a holder of high office) and maintained distinction were also important. By the late Republic, the maternal lineage was almost as important as the paternal. Brutus's propaganda exploited the heroic deeds of his maternal ancestor Ahala as well as the first Brutus (Cicero, *Att.* 13.40.1; compare Vergil, *Aeneid* 11.340–341). The tendency to count distinction in the female line can only have been heightened by the circumstance that in the formative period of the Principate the claims of the emperors depended so much on their ancestresses: Augustus's on his link to Caesar through his grandmother, Tiberius's link to his stepfather and eventually adoptive father, Augustus, through his mother, Gaius's descent from Augustus's daughter Julia, and so on.

We sometimes hear of fathers choosing to override the claims of rank. So Augustus, when looking for a third husband for Julia, considered equites (Tacitus, *Ann.* 4.39.5; Suetonius, *Aug.* 63.2). Earlier, the future Augustus's friend M. Agrippa, a parvenu but a man whose influence would have allowed him to pick and choose (says his biographer) among the bluest blood in Rome, deliberately chose the daughter of the eques Atticus. No doubt Atticus's wealth as well as his connections recommended him (Nepos, *Att.* 12.1–2).

Romans also valued riches particularly in a wife, for they would allow her to give a generous dowry. An injection of cash was valuable to a young man seeking a political career. Cicero twice in 44 hinted that it would be to his and Quintus's advantage for their sons to marry since they would no longer need to pay the young men an allowance (Cicero, *Att.* 15.29.2, 16.1.5). The gynecologist Soranus observed that men investigated carefully the financial position of a potential bride, although a woman's capacity to be a mother was more important (1.34). Moralists loved the theme of avarice. Seneca in his treatise on marriage related an improving remark that he probably attributed to Porcia, daughter of Cato. "When she was asked why she did not marry again after losing her husband, she replied that she could not find a husband who wanted her more than her property. In this remark she elegantly showed that wealth is chosen above virtue [*pudicitia*] in a wife, and that many marry wives with their fingers not their eyes" (Jerome, *Adv. Iovinian.* 312C). Although moralists attacked the motive, it was recognized by ordinary people as natural and not discreditable. Allegedly, when Cicero was criticized by his ex-wife Terentia for having married Publilia out of passion, his secretary Tiro defended him by saying that he had married for money (Plutarch, *Cic.* 41.3–4). The Romans could see wealth as compensation for relatively undistinguished birth or lack of other attractions (Suetonius, *Galba* 3.3; Plautus, *Mostell.* 281; Apuleius, *Apol.* 92; *Dig.* 32.41.7). Lack of dowry made a woman hard to establish and usually meant that she would have to marry down, unless her poverty were offset by beauty or high birth (Seneca, *Controv.* 7.6.18; Plautus, *Aul.* 191). On the other side, the bridegroom's wealth had to be adequate to maintain the woman in the style to which she was accustomed and to secure the interests of children (Cicero, *Att.* 13.22.4).

Good looks in a woman as a qualification frequently figured on moralists' lists of what men desired, with the rider that they should prefer such solid qualities as health and strength (Musonius 13B). In real life other men were criticized for being attracted by beauty and charm (Cicero, *Sest.* 110; Plutarch, *Cic.* 41.3; Tacitus, *Ann.* 5.1.3, 12.3.1), but the motive was considered normal in oneself (Cicero, *Att.* 12.1). Good looks in a man were also relevant. A girl's health and potential fertility were to be estimated as well (Soranus, *Gyn.* 1.9.34, trans. Temkin, p. 32). A previously married woman could sometimes point to a childbearing record (Lucan 2.330–333; Tacitus, *Ann.* 1.41.3, 12.2.3, 12.6.1–2, 14.1.2).

The moralists identified good character as the prime qualification for marriage. This had long been a commonplace of literature as well as philosophy.

Because forecasting the character of a relatively sheltered girl was difficult, the emphasis was on the moral character of her parents. This applied, as we see in Pliny's letter of recommendation, to young men as well. Because the moral character of parents indicated the kind of upbringing a son or daughter had received, such an emphasis was not unreasonable. The mother's chastity, in particular, was no doubt expected to be passed on to a daughter (a belief proved spectacularly wrong in the imperial family).

Less is said about the sexual morality of young men. Instead, their intellectual abilities, eloquence, and career prospects received attention. This reflects the usual division between the spheres of men and women. Ideally, the wife led a sober and retired life governing her household and bringing up children. Her major virtue was pudicitia, chastity and love for her husband, which enabled her to make him happy and guarantee him legitimate children who resembled him. The husband was expected to shine in the wider world. For the Roman upper class, this meant a life of public service, which made courage, self-discipline, intelligence, and oratorical skills important.

CONSIDERATIONS OF CLASS, CONNECTIONS, AND RELATIONSHIPS

So far, I have concentrated on criteria openly acknowledged by our sources. Another area of concern is occasionally illustrated by remarks in the sources and can be deduced from attested marriages. Attention has been focused recently on endogamy (Thomas 1980; Goody 1983; Shaw and Saller 1984). The upper classes (consistent with their acknowledged interest in high birth) seem to have married within their own fairly extensive group (Dixon 1985a). As far as our evidence shows, members of senatorial families rarely married below the equestrian class. But social mobility was sufficient to allow a steady influx of new blood. It must be remembered that a son of a local decurion or of a freedman might become an eques and then marry a *senatoria*. Augustus was worried enough about the social mobility of individuals (rather than mobility over generations) to pass a law discouraging the sons, daughters, and grandchildren by sons of members of the Senate from marrying ex-slaves. Clearly, that a rich and successful freedman might marry a lady of equestrian family was not wildly improbable.

There was also intermarriage within particular sections of the upper classes (Cicero, *Att.* 6.1.10; Pliny, *Ep.* 1.14; compare Wiseman 1971, 60–61; Syme 1958, 2:601–606). Special ties of political interest were sometimes sought through a particular marriage. Renunciation of enmities was occasionally ratified by a marriage (for example, Livy 38.57). Convenient though such a dramatic gesture might be, it is doubtful that two men would have committed themselves to the long-term effects (transfer of a daughter and of dowry and the possibility of children) unless the marriage was also advantageous from other points of view. Similarly, marriage sometimes cemented an alliance with short-term political action in view. The most famous instance is the marriage arranged between Pompey and Caesar's daughter Julia. Caesar himself married Calpurnia and successfully backed her father L. Calpurnius Piso for the consulship of the following year. (This is the order of events given by Plutarch.) Cato attacked these marriages as a prostitution of politics: it was intolerable that leadership should be pandered and that men should bring each other into governorships, commands, and power by means of women (Plutarch, *Caes.* 14.5; Appian, *Bella Civilia* 2.14). The marital network here reinforced political connections. Repeated intermarriages between certain families have tended to make scholars search for lasting political alliances. But in the restricted circles of the top senatorial families repeated intermarriage was likely to occur anyway, and personal and economic motives probably played a part (see Brunt 1988, 453).

Lastly, there was marriage between close relatives, whether blood relations or relations by marriage, for which there were two possible economic motives. One was to keep the money in the family and the other was to ensure that a poor woman was not left unmarried or forced into a misalliance. The first type may be represented by the marriages between cousins that are attested in certain families in the late republic. The second type is exemplified by the cousin marriages of Appius Claudius's sisters. One was taken off her brother's hands (he said) by Lucullus, her mother's second cousin, with no dowry at all (Varro, *Rust.* 3.16.2). Another married a first cousin, Q. Metellus Celer (cf. Livy 42.34.3f.).

Family sentiment also played a part. For the dynastically minded aristocrats of the late republic or early principate, endogamy had other advantages. Augustus organized multiple and permutated endogamy, aiming at the perpetuation of his line through his only daughter and the maximum concentration of Julian blood in possible successors. Claudius eventually married his brother's daughter because he could not risk her taking her genes outside the family. She carried the line of Augustus and Julia (which he himself did not) and of the popular Germanicus. The disadvantage of marriage with close kin was that it reduced the options for broadening a power base or fortune (Plutarch, *Quaest. Rom.* 108; Augustine, *De civ. D.* 15.16).

During the pagan period, marriage with first cousins was practiced, but not habitually preferred (Shaw and Saller 1984). Marriages between the children of two brothers were relatively uncommon, but not criticized. Otherwise, Livy would not attribute such a match to Ligustinus (Livy 42.34.3f.), and Cicero would condemn Antony's marriage to Antonia. Marriages between the children of two sisters or of a brother and a sister, that is, marriages across agnatic boundaries, are hard to trace, but may have been commoner. In a peasant society, if two brothers inherited property from their paterfamilias and wanted to keep it together or reunite it (for one generation) after their own deaths and if they had only one child each, but of opposite sex, then the simple solution of matching the cousins presented itself. The grandfather's estate was kept together; no dowry went out of the immediate family, but no new dowry came in. The father of the only daughter saw himself succeeded in due course by grandsons of the same *nomen*. If the brothers each had a son, the expedient of marrying one to his female cousin immediately became less attractive. By the second century B.C., although ancestral property might be kept in the family as long as possible, the main family house and land could easily be passed on as a unit to one member, perhaps the eldest son, as happened in Cicero's family, and the younger compensated with other property. The specific economic motive for marriage of *fratres patrueles,* avoiding fragmentation of land, no longer applied. Diversification of holdings, complicated testamentary dispositions, and dotal contracts offered more flexibility. Perpetuation of the name may have continued to be a motive. On the other hand, if two brothers were both intent on maximizing their *affinitates* for the sake of political careers, it made good sense for them to deploy their children to make new connections.

The marriage of a brother's daughter and a sister's son could also be useful if the brother had no son. Augustus had recourse to this expedient. But where the brother had a son of his own, the main feature of such a marriage was to double the bond between two patrilineal families. The same was true of marriages between a brother's son and a sister's daughter, which also restored the woman to her mother's natal family. Better still, a marriage between children of two sisters created a marriage tie between two patrilineal families previously linked only by the blood tie of the sisters. But by this period it is important not to concentrate attention on the male line. Affection between sisters, married into different families, probably resulted in close contact between their children. Since matchmaking was a pursuit of a network of matrons at least as much as it was that of thoughtful patresfamilias, cousin marriage sometimes resulted. We can call the motive family affection.

MOTIVES OF AFFECTION

In marriage within the family group, the original affection of young people who knew each other well gave a practical basis for a new relationship (Apuleius, *Met.* 4.26). A shared childhood was one of the few justifications for the beginning and growth of affection. Prior affection was, however, a familiar enough motive for Augustus to take it into account. In his speech on the Papio-Poppaean law (A.D. 9) Dio makes him say, "I allowed men outside the Senate to marry freedwomen, so that if anyone was inclined to such a marriage by love or familiarity he might do it lawfully" (56.7.2). Augustus's concession seems to have been only a restatement of what was previously allowed: his innovation was to deny such marriages to *senatorii*. Dio is right in remarking that the law made room for emotional motivation in making a marriage. A remarkable instance of this is furnished by the new laws on manumission. The general rule was that owners under the age of twenty could not free slaves and that slaves under thirty could not be freed, unless a special case was made. Among reasons recognized as valid was a young man's wish to marry his slave woman (Gaius, *Inst.* 1.18f.). Lawmakers thought that allowing men to follow their own feelings would encourage them to marry.

Falling in love at sight is what young men in comedy do (without always intending marriage): it remained more acceptable for men than for women (for example, see Statius, *Silv.* 1.2). Love, more specifically, physical passion and the focusing of intense feeling on one individual with the expectation that she will respond with an exclusive affection, was the raison d'être of the extramarital affairs idealized by the elegiac poets. Some of the virtues demanded of mistresses (fidelity, commitment to a long-term exclusive relationship) were clearly patterned on the virtues expected in a wife. By the Augustan period, the romantic themes developed by the poets in portraying extramarital affairs in their turn influenced the literary portrayal of the ideal relationship between husband and wife. This can be seen clearly, for instance, in the language used by Ovid and Pliny when they were separated from their wives.

It is difficult to prove that a growth in individualism and an increased tendency to seek for personal happiness in private life had led to heightened expectations of emotional rewards in marriage around the time of Cicero. That is, such a trend cannot be quantified or precisely dated. But in the middle of the first century B.C., for which our sources are much richer than earlier, we have vivid portrayals, sometimes idealized (Lucretius 3.894–899), sometimes as realistic as we can expect (Cicero, *Att.* 1.18.1), of the joys of life in the close family circle of husband, wife, and children. When there is friction between husband and wife, the whole household is upset (Cicero, *Att.* 5.1.3–4). After harmony was lost between Cicero and Terentia, instead of continuing to avoid each other (which would have been comparatively simple, given the number of houses they owned), they considered divorce and remarriage (probably for both of them) the best solution.

Three elements come together. First, the idealization of marriage as a mutual support, involving fidelity, self-sacrifice, mutual respect, public displays of closeness, and trust. Second, perhaps increased expectations of personal happiness, both in career satisfaction (Hopkins 1983, 79–94) and in private life. Third, a romanticism spreading from the literary portrayal and the actuality of erotic relationships with social equals, high-class demimondaines, and social inferiors.

If this reconstruction is accepted, then such views of the ideal nature of marriage itself must have had some impact on the selection of a husband or wife. In societies where first marriages are usually arranged by parents or other kin and where the couple are very young (and perhaps do not meet until the wedding), it is hoped that proper sentiments will develop after the marriage begins. Traditional Hindu society is an obvious example. Rome is not. In society at large most girls probably married in their late teens (Shaw 1987a). They could legally marry at twelve (some married before that), and women of the imperial family and senatorial order sometimes married around the age of menarche (thirteen to fifteen). At this level, the girl's thinking probably was done for her, but that does not mean that parents failed to consider the potential affective relationship between her and the suitor. Moreover, the man was normally fully adult. In the late republic a young eques generally married in his late twenties; from the Augustan period on, a man who intended a senatorial career married at about twenty-two or twenty-three. The average age at marriage in society as a whole was the late twenties (Saller 1987a). Such evidence as we have suggests that most young men chose for themselves (with some consultation with parents) and that they took their reaction to the bride into account (but compare Seneca, *Controv.* 2.3.2, for the scenario of the young man who marries his father's choice and finds his wife satisfactory). At a woman's second marriage, she, like the divorcée who made a set at young Q. Cicero, would consult her own wishes. We find the Greek Plutarch emphasizing the importance of a good start to the sexual relationship on the wedding night for the development of an emotional attachment (*Mor.* 756E). Such a view would probably have seemed reasonable to his Roman readers. Certainly some rapid divorces of the late republic and early empire could tentatively be ascribed to the realization that the chemistry was wrong and the personal relationship had not developed satisfactorily: we might put Cicero's brief marriage to the young Publilia in such a group. But older couples had the opportunity to know before marriage whether sexual attraction existed between them (Statius, *Silv.* 1.2). There is some evidence for courtship practices (kisses and amorous conversation) even for the arranged marriage of a virgin bride (Ovid, *Am.* 2.1.5; Ovid, *Her.* 21.197f.; Augustine, *PL* 83.811; Ambrose, *PL* 15.1854).

Unlike people in early modern English society, the Romans did not (as far as we know) explicitly say that at least liking was necessary before a woman should accept a proposal. But they did allow her to reject an engagement (on the pretext of moral inadequacy), and Cicero's words about Tullia, "I'm afraid my daughter could not be brought to consent to him," suggest that personal liking or dislike had great weight. We might as well be listening to a father receiving a proposal from a suitor in a nineteenth-century novel.

Conversely, the writings attributed to Rome's one female erotic poet, which circulated in her high aristocratic circle, would have shocked the Victorians. Sulpicia, daughter of two patricians, the younger Servius Sulpicius Rufus and a Valeria, ranked as high as any woman outside Augustus's family in the 20s B.C. She moved in the circle of poets her uncle had collected; like them, she was educated and sophisticated and wrote charming and passionate elegies ([Tibullus] 3.13–18). She appears to be as yet unmarried; she is surrounded by friends, particularly her uncle (3.14.5), who worry that she will marry beneath her (3.16.5f.); she is not allowed to do what she wants (3.14.8); the man she is in love with (who is concealed under the Greek name Cerinthus) may prefer some common whore to her, "Servius' daughter Sulpicia" (3.16.3f.), and she has to be careful to preserve her reputation (3.13.2); but she is passionately in love (3.18.6). She exults in the consummation of her passion and asserts the appropriateness of the match. What does her reputation matter? "It delights me to have sinned, I am sick of wearing a calm face to deceive rumor: let it be said that I have been a worthy woman with a worthy man" (3.13.9f.). I suggest that these are the preliminaries to an eligible marriage. What is striking is how a marriage for which the groundwork may well have been laid by Messalla, Valeria, and numerous well-meaning elders is presented by a protagonist in the guise of a romantic affair. The subject is the private preliminaries to marriage. Compare the kisses once concealed and the subject of rumor that became licit when Stella and Violentilla married (Statius, *Silv.* 1.2.30). In her verses, Sulpicia explores the same themes of romance and eroticism as do her male contemporaries, always leaving us in doubt about what is real and what imagined. But unlike the men, she can play with the tension between her claim to freedom and the anxious concern of her family, between the danger of making a silly mistake (3.16.2) and passion, between reputation and love. It could be argued that all this is the fantasy of an extramarital affair, a fling with a man ineligible for matrimony, the obverse of the liaisons of Horace with various insubstantial hetaerae. But it makes better sense as an assertion of the claim of a highborn woman to experience love before marriage with a future husband (see Lowe 1988). Given that Sulpicia is unique, proof is impossible, but one thinks of the independent conduct of an earlier generation of aristocrats, such as Valeria

Polla or Servilia, and of the elegant part-fantasies produced by poets of the Augustan and other ages on the occasion of weddings (for example, Horace, *Odes* 4.1).

Choice may always in practice be relatively restricted, but it was not restricted in the Roman upper classes in quite the way that the schemata of the moralists would lead us to expect. The Romans did not select *conjuges* simply by reference to objective criteria: individual choice and the opportunities and limitations imposed by circumstances were the most important factors. Nor do modern divisions of history into periods apply. The constitutional and political nature of Rome and its empire went through a profound change in the transition from republic to principate. Autocracy may also have helped set literature on a new track. The emperor attempted social engineering. The Julian and Papio-Poppaean laws on the intermarriage of the orders led to a drop in the usual marriage age for senators, put pressure on people to marry, and encouraged intervention of third parties and the state in family matters. The Julian law on adultery and fornication attempted to control sexual practices. People may thereafter have married earlier and more often, and been discreet in courtship. But there was no fundamental division between the ideals and the practice of selection of husbands and wives among the aristocracy between the time of Cicero and the time of Ulpian.

Chapter 6

DAVID COHEN

The Augustan Law on Adultery: The Social and Cultural Context

In A.D. 19, during the reign of Tiberius, a Roman woman of praetorian rank, Vistilia, wife of Titidius Labeo, was convicted of adultery. The accusation itself represents nothing novel, for the prosecution for adultery of women of exalted social status was far from unknown during this epoch. What makes Vistilia noteworthy, however, is that she had inscribed herself on the aedile's list of public prostitutes. The immediate reasons for this action are transparent: the *lex Julia de adulteriis coercendis,* promulgated by Augustus in 18 B.C. (the same year as his sweeping reform of family law in the *lex Julia de maritandis ordinibus*), specifically excluded professional prostitutes, actresses, and women who worked in public houses from its scope. Vistilia, then, had attempted to remove her private life from the regulation of the law by exploiting a loophole in the statute. Although Vistilia's ploy did not protect her from prosecution and conviction, her case was either representative or notorious enough that a senatus consultum closed the loophole by ruling that no woman whose father, grandfather, or husband had been a Roman knight could prostitute herself (Tacitus, *Ann.* 2.84).[1]

What is one to make of this case of a Roman matron from the elite inscribing herself as a common prostitute so as to carry on her adulterous liaisons in peace? We will never know whether a desire to protest an unpopular law or simple depravity motivated Vistilia in particular, but Suetonius's description of

I should like to thank Richard Saller for his many helpful comments and criticisms during the revision of this chapter.

1. This may be the senatus consultum referred to by Papinian at *Dig.* 48.5.11.2, whose language ("evitandae poenae adulterii gratia") is close to that of Suetonius's description of Vistilia's case ("ad evitandas legum poenas").

the case suggests that at some point circumvention of the law in this manner became flagrant and rendered legislative action necessary (*Tiberius* 35.1ff.). Indeed, Tacitus indicates that the failure of traditional sanctions created the loophole in the first place. In former times, he comments, the shame of inscription on this list would have been punishment enough. Although Vistilia's case has rich implications for certain legal historical topologies (Daube 1978), I would like to explore instead its place within the Roman legal and social context, and the relation of this, in turn, to the broader problem of how ancient legal systems regulated the social problems arising out of such illicit sexual behavior as adultery. More specifically, the following analysis addresses two main questions:

First, are we to apprehend Vistilia's behavior as yet another example of the corruption of traditional Roman mores? In particular, does such behavior testify to the weakening, or absence, of norms associated with the values of honor and shame, which regulate female sexuality?

Second, under what theoretical rubric can the Augustan legislation on adultery best be comprehended? Ought one to view Roman legislation on adultery as an attempt to enforce morality for its own sake, that is, as an articulation of categories of moral transgression that the state will not tolerate? Or does Augustus's legislation represent a massive attempt at social engineering, an expansion of state power over sexuality and the family for the sake of power and knowledge itself, analogous, say, to the developments sketched by Michel Foucault in volume 1 of *The History of Sexuality* and in *Discipline and Punish,* and by Jacques Donzelot in *The Policing of Families?*

THE LEGAL CONTEXT

The Augustan legislation on adultery stands in stark relief to the treatment of marital sexuality in the preceding legal period. Most Roman law scholars from Theodor Mommsen and Hans Bennecke to David Daube and Dieter Nörr hold that prior to the lex Julia de adulteriis Roman legislation was largely unconcerned with adultery. That is, apart from censorial or other public action in exceptional cases, the law refrained from interfering with the right of the family to deal with adultery and its consequences. Augustus's lex Julia de adulteriis changed all of this in ways nothing less than revolutionary. In a subsequent chapter Eva Cantarella discusses these changes in detail, so here it suffices to indicate that the law established a permanent court to punish a broad range of extramarital sexual activities. For most women, the law prohibited all extramarital sexual relations, but slaves, prostitutes, and practitioners of certain base professions remained outside its scope. Men could suffer the penalties for adultery or *stuprum* if they engaged in intercourse with married women or unmarried women who did not fall into these low-status classes. The law also introduced important innovations for the treatment of adulterers and adulteresses taken in the act. Again, Cantarella takes up this question in detail, but it is important to note that a cuckolded husband could under no circumstances kill his wife, though he might kill her partner if that man were of sufficiently low status. Further, the adulteress's father could put both her and the adulterer to death only if they were taken in the very act of intercourse in his house or the husband's house.

The dramatic and far-reaching provisions of this legislation, only briefly sketched here, contrast sharply with the behavior of Roman matrons who registered themselves as prostitutes to escape its provisions. Is one to imagine a morally degenerate society resisting imperial attempts to reinject moral standards that have become utterly alien to it? Such an interpretation fits well with literary topoi about the degeneracy of the age: "Ubi nunc lex Julia? Dormis?" (Juvenal 2.37). Before accepting such conventional interpretations, however, one ought to reconsider the social norms informing sexual practices and their relation to the Augustan legislation. Though our evidence for both attitudes and conduct is woefully inadequate, certain patterns may tentatively be suggested.

HONOR AND SHAME

Richard Saller (1991) has demonstrated the importance of conceptions of personal honor and shame for understanding Roman attitudes toward authority, corporal punishment, and bodily integrity. In many other respects as well, Roman conceptions of the proper spheres for competitive male activity correspond to general Mediterranean patterns concerning the determinants of social status and the sexual division of space, labor, and power. This is not the place to elaborate Roman conceptualizations of public and private space, the social, economic, and political roles of men and women within these spheres, and so on. Rather, I should like to focus on one particular question within this general context: Can one usefully apprehend the constellation of Roman sexual and social norms, values, and beliefs involving illicit sexuality through a conceptual scheme derived from comparative Mediterranean studies of honor and shame? More specifically, can such a scheme illuminate the social context of the Augustan legislation on adultery? I began this chapter with the case of Vistilia because, like other such exempla of sexual laxity, it suggests that, whatever the relevance of honor and shame for early republican Rome, the society of the early empire oriented itself according to other values. The argument that follows suggests that however striking such cases may be, they can mislead the historian into taking the part for the whole.

To begin with, the case of Vistilia, if accurately reported, recounts the actual conduct of a particular Roman woman. Anthropologists at least since Bronislaw Malinowski have recognized that many societies manifest sharp divergences between the ideological representation of sex and gender and actual social practices. Malinowski (1929, 496–572) found in his investigation of Trobriand sexuality that although Trobrianders represent their society as abhorring incest, particularly brother-sister incest, as an unthinkable sexual abomination this does not mean that, Trobriander claims to the contrary, such cases never occur. What is more significant, such occurrences do not invalidate the norm, nor do they imply that Trobriand informants all lied about their culture. Rather, in the realm of sex and gender the norms of practice and the norms of ideology typically operate in a state of conflict, ambiguity, and tension. Their dynamic interplay forms the social context that individuals manipulate, interpret, avoid, and occasionally defy, according to their particular purposes. In turn, whichever strategy individuals choose to pursue in relation to this normative context, by orienting their conduct accordingly they contribute to the reproduction of the social system.[2] In short, examples of moral degeneracy do not tell the whole story. One must view them instead within the larger context of practice, purpose, and ideology of which they are a part.

As a heuristic device, three principles can be distinguished that frame the sexual ideology associated with honor and shame in many traditional Mediterranean societies.[3] First, a strong emphasis on female sexual purity, in particular, the virginity of girls as a prerequisite for an honorable marriage, and the exclusive possession by the husband of his wife's sexual and reproductive potential. Second, the community judges a man's honor to a significant degree according to the sexual purity of the women to whom he is related. Failure either to protect that purity or to avenge its violation is generally regarded as a humiliating failure of masculinity. Because of its capacity to bring ruin to a man

2. Readers will recognize a theoretical orientation toward the work of Pierre Bourdieu on social practice and that of Anthony Giddens on practical consciousness and agency. See Bourdieu 1977, 1–90, and Giddens 1986, chap. 1.

3. I should emphasize that the articulation of three principles is intended only to have explanatory force. One could just as well describe a single complex of associated values and beliefs. Further, I do not claim that this complex characterizes every Mediterranean society, or even every traditional Mediterranean society without exception. We are dealing here with a model, but a model that finds broad empirical support in studies of individual Mediterranean communities. For the most recent formulation of the issues, see Gilmore 1987.

and his house, women's sexuality is seen as a dangerous force that men must guard and restrict. Third, although active and dominant male sexuality is positively valued, there is some ambivalence about its unbridled exercise. The adulterer is a man who robs other men of their honor by seducing their wives, and though he enhances his masculinity by doing so, the socially disruptive force that adultery represents leads, particularly in certain contexts, to a negative valuation of men who destroy the homes of others.

FEMALE CHASTITY

The norms associated with honor and shame placed a high premium on the virginity of brides. Informants in traditional Mediterranean societies typically explain the early marriage of girls as a way of preventing "accidents" that might ruin a woman's chances of finding a husband (Maher 1974, 150; Sanders 1962, 158). Institutionalized in the vestal virgins, virginity also occupied an important place in the sexual imagination of Roman society. As this is well known, a few examples suffice to make the point. The rhetorical exercises embodied in the Elder Seneca's *Controversiae* (1.2.5, 1.2.8, 9.1.1, 9.1.4–6) reflect the belief not only that brides should be virgins, but also that those who lose their virginity through rape are nonetheless tainted and cannot (in theory) marry. Thus a girl who has been raped may be expected to attempt suicide (*Controv.* 3.5). To preserve their sexual purity, Plutarch explains, Roman girls are married very young (*Lyc.* and *Num.* 4; *Mor.* 138E).

As in traditional Mediterranean communities, chastity was also expected of married women (Giovannini 1986). In fact, claims Cicero (*Scaur.* 8), a wife should die rather than sacrifice her chastity. Women, of course, are seen as often falling short of these expectations: Seneca (*Consol. Helv.* 16.3), like other moralists, considers female unchastity as the greatest evil of his time.[4] Similarly, Juvenal (*Sat.* 6) speaks of the positive value of chastity and relates how wives constantly abuse it. Wives, he says, must be confined indoors to be kept pure.[5]

Mediterranean societies oriented toward the ideology of honor and shame characteristically judge female chastity according to a politics of reputation, whereby assumptions about a woman's private sexual conduct rest on inferences from her public behavior (Cohen 1991, chap. 4). Thus a girl who

---

4. Seneca argues that for a woman true chastity is an inner disposition. Thus a woman who is chaste because she fears the law or her husband is rightly numbered among the wrongdoers (*Ben.* 4.14.1).

5. Whether *Satire* 6 is the work of a misogynist or a parody of misogyny is irrelevant for my purposes, since in either case it reflects aspects of societal valuations.

lingers at the fountain, or takes too long returning from the stream or fields, is assumed to have had an illicit liaison (Du Boulay 1974, 112). In this way, the politics of reputation, from the standpoint of the subject, is largely one of managing appearances, based on one's knowledge of the conventional ways of drawing inferences from certain types of conduct. Further, women should avoid being the subject of gossip, since gossip will always find ways of interpreting innocent behavior in a bad light (Maraspini 1968, 180; Freeman 1970, 140). As Thucydides (2.46) has Pericles say, the best thing for a woman is not to be talked about at all, whether for good or bad. Roman sources in turn amply testify to the operation of similar patterns of normative expectations.

The ideological significance of chastity in Roman consciousness is manifest in the patterns of crucial events in their invented early history. According to Livy, the kings were turned out because of the violation of the matron Lucretia. Likewise, the decemvirs suffered the same fate on account of the rape of Virginia. That major historical upheavals were portrayed as arising from violations of chastity testifies to its centrality in the scheme of values.[6] Rhetoricians played upon the same normative expectations in their training. As one of the *Controversiae* (1.2.10) puts it, no woman is chaste enough if an inquiry has to be held concerning her. In another (2.7.2), a woman is accused of adultery by her husband solely on the grounds that another man left her money in his will. The *Controversiae* are, of course, rhetorical exercises involving highly contrived situations. Nonetheless, they aim at persuasion by invoking commonly held values, so though the events they depict may be spurious, they provide valuable evidence of attitudes and ideal norms. Other sources confirm this valuation of chastity. According to the law of *injuria*, for a man merely to follow a woman in the street called her chastity into question and thus gave rise to an action. As Ulpian (*Dig.* 47.10.15.22) comments, "assiduous proximity virtually reveals something disreputable." Similarly, Suetonius claims that Caesar divorced his wife upon mere rumor of adultery, because she should have been entirely free of suspicion (1.64). Cicero (*Cael.* 15.35) likewise attests the politics of reputation based on inferences about a woman's unobserved sexual behavior: the fact of close association with a man, he argues, raises a presumption of illicit sexuality that must then be disproved. Finally, Quintilian (4.2.69) says that behavior from which an inference of adultery may be drawn includes such circumstances as a woman celebrating or bathing with men, or even having close friendships with them.

Seneca (*Ben.* 9.5) also infers character and conduct from appearance when he describes a married woman who wears revealing clothes as having aban-

---

6. I am indebted to Richard Saller on this point.

doned modesty (*pudor*). Such women, he concludes, must be adulteresses. He also recounts what the politics of reputation require of a woman who wants to preserve old-fashioned female modesty: she must avoid being seen in public at all or serving as a subject for gossip. The best reputation for a woman, he claims in an argument reminiscent of Pericles, is not to have one (*Consol. Helv.* 19.6). Seneca was well aware, of course, of the discrepancy between the ideology of honor and shame and the way in which some Roman women lived. He recounts with contempt how a man is counted as a boor (*rusticus*) by other women if he refuses to let his wife appear in public in a sedan chair, open to the view of everyone (*Ben.* 1.9.4). The importance of such contradictions and conflicts in values cannot be overemphasized. Social norms and practices, as Bourdieu (1977, 1–90) has shown, do not constitute a logically coherent abstract system. We are doomed to misapprehend the patterned chaos of social life by imposing on it a uniformity that is not its own.

The assumptions underlying such judgments about a woman's sexual purity become explicit in one of the *Controversiae* (2.7.9), which echoes widespread Mediterranean sexual topoi. Woman's nature, the argument goes, is such that her best defense is never to have caused gossip and to be *believed* to be chaste. Accordingly, for women the one glory is *pudicitia* and to be seen to be chaste. Thus, the text continues, a woman who wants to avoid suspicion of adultery and to deter seducers, whose mere presence would arouse such suspicions, should go out dressed up only enough to avoid appearing unkempt. Her companions should be old, and she should go about with her eyes on the ground. If confronted with overattentive greetings, she should blush and appear confused, for such behavior is the guardian of her honor (*integritas*). This account of female chastity eloquently reflects the ideological stereotypes that dominate the Mediterranean imagination. The girls of Lebanon, Greece, and Andalusia must exercise similar care in regard to the greetings of men on the street (though the nuances may vary), and a woman who looks a man straight in the eye, or does not blush in the presence of a male stranger, is generally considered to be loose.

MALE HONOR AND FEMALE SEXUALITY

The ideology of honor and shame constrains women to avoid contacts with men that would damage their reputation. Failure to do so reflects on the males of their family: most immediately, on their husband, father, and sons, more remotely on their entire lineage. A substantial body of evidence indicates that this linkage of female sexuality and male honor informed Roman social practices as well. To begin with, the law of injuria, in the words of Ulpian, provided that "Every *injuria* is either inflicted upon the person, or involves one's honor or one's disgrace. It relates to the person when someone is struck, to one's honor when a matron's companion is led astray, and to one's disgrace when chastity is attacked" (*Dig.* 47.10.1.2). The husband or father of a daughter or wife so insulted is equally the object of the injuria and has an action in his own right against the wrongdoer.

As Cicero explains, a virtuous woman derives honor from her illustrious male relatives, but she also gives honor back to them through her reputation (*Rosc. Am.* 50.147). An adulteress, however, not only dishonors her husband, who has allowed her to be seduced by failing to guard her chastity, but also calls into question the paternity of her sons (*Controv.* 9.1.14, 1.4.12, 7.5.13–15). Such themes abound in Roman rhetorical exercises: in the case mentioned above, where a wife is accused of adultery because a man leaves her money in his will (*Controv.* 2.7.2), her husband's honor requires that he suspect adultery in spite of the lack of any other evidence of impropriety. Indeed, the mere approach of an adulterer to a married woman involves an insult (injuria) to the woman, to the integrity of her husband's house, and to her husband himself (2.7.5). The similar treatment of sexual approaches to women as injuria to their husbands or fathers in *Dig.* 47.10.15.15ff. testifies to the way the law utilized the same normative categories. Similarly, Cicero (*Scaur.* Fr. 2.6) refers to the disgrace of not protecting one's wife from other men. Indeed, Tacitus (*Ann.* 4.2ff.) tells us that when Sejanus set out to humiliate Drusus (who had slapped him), he could think of no better way than seducing Livilla, his wife. Tacitus further notes that by this adultery she degraded not only herself, but also her ancestors and her descendants.

This complex of values and beliefs, which links female chastity to the family as a whole, and particularly to its male inhabitants, finds particularly clear expression in another of the *Controversiae* (3.5): the man whose daughter is raped must salve his wounds, rebuild his household (*familia*), lament the despoiling of his house, console his daughter for her ravished virginity, and prevent her from taking her life. In this ideological context belong the principles of the law of injuria, whereby sexual insults or behavior that calls into question a woman's chastity is actionable by the males principally related to her. One finds the same argument in Cicero's *Pro Caelio* (13.32; compare 18.42). It is shameful, he argues, to attack a woman's reputation falsely. Attacking a woman, and the men connected to her, by questioning her sexual reputation brings disgrace on the males of the family. Thus, he concludes, virtuous women bring glory on a house, whereas adulteresses dishonor the men of the family. This belief finds what is perhaps its most extreme expression in the Roman instantiation of a classic Mediterranean pattern—judging the sexual purity of the wife by whether the children look like their father (Horace, *Odes* 5.21–24; Macrobius, *Sat.* 2.5; Juvenal 6.598–601; compare Brandes 1975, 228).

When men fail to preserve the chastity of their women, revenge provides the only means of erasing the stain. Of course, the ideology of revenge may vary widely from actual practice. In many Mediterranean societies informants assert that adultery or seduction inevitably results in the death of the daughter or wife and her lover. Frequently, however, such claims bear little resemblance to reality. In Rome, the lex Julia provided that under certain circumstances the father or husband could take direct revenge. That such instances sometimes occurred appears from passages in the *Digest,* which report that clemency was often granted to husbands who exceeded these statutory limits. In any event, at the level of ideology, violations of one's women requires revenge—this is a constant theme in the Elder Seneca's *Controversiae,* whether for adultery (1.4) or rape (1.5.1, 7.8.10, 9.1.1, 9.1.4–6). As one of the arguments (1.5.1) expresses this sentiment for a case of rape, "Revenge, fathers! Revenge, brothers! Revenge, husbands!" At the level of practice, however, there may have been considerable variation from such ideal norms. It is striking that the Augustan legislation tried to *force* husbands to take legal action, and Greek sources testify that some men preferred "to hide their shame in silence" (Aeschines 1.107).[7]

As in other Mediterranean societies, these same classes of male relations bear the primary responsibility for the protection of women's chastity (Pitt-Rivers 1977, 23; Campbell 1964, 271–278; Jamous 1981, 66; Brandes 1975, 227, 234–236). If they fail to wreak vengeance, in theory their honor suffers, though in practice, as Bourdieu has shown, norms can be manipulated to demonstrate that a particular case does not merit such a response. Another *Controversiae* (1.4f.) emphasizes the humiliation of a crippled husband unable to kill adulterers, who deride him. The standard also applies to brothers. In the *Pro Sestio,* Cicero shows how one can attack a man's reputation through his sister's illicit sexuality, and particularly through his knowledge of the transgression and his failure to act on it.[8] In another oration, he attacks a man's character by alleging that he tolerated his wife's lover, demonstrating that he was unfit for military leadership. Indeed, Cicero employs the same tactic again, attacking Verres for employing as a general a man who would tolerate such humiliation. He drives the point home by repeating again and again that Cleomenes was an *aemulus* for his own wife.[9]

The lex Julia nicely captures this contradiction in the restrictions it applies to

---

7. Similarly, Seneca argues that Augustus should not have made the debauchery of his daughter known. Seneca's words reveal the implicit complex of values: "In doing so, Augustus divulged that which he ought to have punished and equally to have kept secret. . . . Later he regretted that he had not veiled with silence matters which are disgraceful to relate" (*Ben.* 4.32.2).

8. Cf. the special role assigned to brothers in *Cod. Theod.* 9.7.2.

9. *Verr.* 2.5.41.107, 5.42.110, 5.47.124, 5.50.133. For a description of similar patterns of adultery, revenge, and cuckoldry in a later period of Italian history, see Ruggiero 1985.

men who may be overzealous in shedding blood to protect their honor, and in the threat of a charge of pandering against men who do not take action against their wives. That this legislation did not entirely succeed in limiting husbands' revenge appears not only from the homicide cases against husbands reported in the *Digest,* but also from literary sources that emphasize the dangers of adultery. Juvenal (*Satire* 10. 162–178), for example, expatiates on the dangers of adultery, dangers represented by the vengeance of the husband in the form of death, torture, and humiliation that go beyond the penalties that the law allows (compare *Dig.* 48.5.24.3). Valerius Maximus (6.1.3) also recounts the infliction of degrading and unmanning punishments when husbands take revenge: whipping, castration, sexual abuse, and so on. Clearly, in spite of the prevalence of topoi about moral degeneracy, such accounts rest on the premise that some husbands, at least, were not so depraved that they ignored their wives' adultery. For some men, the concepts of honor and shame still provided a normative orientation. Indeed, one ought to understand the lex Julia's limitation of the vengeance of the husband in this light. As Ulpian explains, the law limits the right of the husband to kill his wife and the adulterer, because a husband is naturally heated and impetuous (*mariti calor et impetus*) in such matters. A father, however, will take counsel for the good of his children before acting. Again, this only makes sense in a moral world where the natural impulse of the husband is to avenge adultery with blood—the world of honor and shame.

What all this means from the male point of view is that, as Cicero (*Cael.* 1.1) puts it, the desires of women must be restrained. If they are not, according to Cicero, the sexual misconduct of, for example, a mother brings dishonor to the whole family: it disgraces herself, the family, the lineage, and her son's name (*Clu.* 16. 188). According to the Mediterranean pattern, not only do women possess the power to wreak this havoc, but their nature constantly prompts them to do so. Juvenal's sixth satire, in a manner reminiscent of Aristophanes' catalogs of wives' deceits in *Ecclesiazusae, Thesmophoriazusai,* and *Lysistrata,* details at great length the way in which wives deceive and humiliate their husbands at every turn.[10] Mothers, he claims (231ff.), teach their daughters to delight in deceiving and despoiling their husbands, initiating these young women in the arts of adultery. The advice to husbands, as in so many other ancient and modern Mediterranean societies, is to keep their wives indoors if they want to keep them pure. "I hear the advice of my old friends: 'Bar the door and confine/restrain your wife.' But who will guard the guardians? The wife arranges accordingly and begins with them. High or low their passions are all the same. She who wears out the black cobblestones with her bare feet is no better than she who rides upon the necks of tall Syrians" (346–351).

10. See, e.g., 6off., 114ff., 232ff., 268ff., 306ff., 346ff.

Such passages accord well with the typical belief of Mediterranean men that their wives are prone to deceive them "forty times a day" (Campbell 1964, 278). As Stanley Brandes (1975, 228) reports, most Andalusian men maintain that their wives are either unfaithful or contemplating infidelity. Every man sees himself as a potential cuckold. One might modify this claim slightly to say that men talk in public as if they believed that their wives were unfaithful. The point is that such public discourse about the rampant and treacherous sexuality of women strongly resembles the male accounts of female infidelity at Rome or Athens. If one takes either Juvenal's tale of horrors or the anxieties of Andalusian husbands at face value, one would have to conclude that adultery was a nearly universal phenomenon.[11] The problem is that such accounts are cultural interpretations of ideology and not the objective reporting of social facts. Male ideology constrains men to view their wives in this way because of the enormous fear of the power of female sexuality to ruin them, and because of the difficulties of control, since male honor also requires that men spend their time out of the house, in the company of other men.[12] Juvenal's argument that chastity is a value that women constantly violate as they deceive their husbands at every opportunity should, like the catalogs of adulteries in the *Thesmophoriazusai*, be viewed in this context.

This interpretation finds support in two other stereotypical elements of the portrayal of the dangers of female sexuality. First, Juvenal, like other sources, expounds on the sexual insatiability of women.[13] The view of women as possessing an unquenchable sensuality constitutes an element of the complex of beliefs and values associated with honor and shame from Morocco, Algeria, and Turkey, to Greece, Italy, and Andalusia.[14] Not only does this sensuality fuel male anxieties about cuckoldry, but it has a darker side as well. Thus Juvenal recounts numerous stories of women who poison their husbands or other relations for depraved purposes. "Why tell of love potions and incantations, of poisons brewed and administered to a stepson, or of grosser crimes to which women are driven by the imperious power of sex? Their sins of lust are the least of their sins" (133–135; compare 610–661).

This murderous side of women's sexuality appears across the Mediterranean. Brandes recounts the widespread Andalusian male fear "that their wives

11. See Juvenal's inquiry whether a single Roman woman is worthy of her vows of chastity (6.60). Note Seneca's claim that adultery is the most common basis for the formation of marital unions (*Ben.* 1.9.4).

12. Note that the husband in Juvenal 346ff. does not even consider the possibility that he would guard his wife.

13. E.g., 114ff., 315ff., 364–374; and cf. Martial 6.67, who tells of a woman who surrounds herself with eunuchs because she wants sex and not babies.

14. Mernissi 1975, 4, 10, 16; Fallers and Fallers 1976, 258–259.

crave to destroy them" and drive their men to early deaths—either through
incessant sexual demands or poison—so that they may pursue their sexual
satisfaction unrestrained and enjoy their husbands' property (1980, 103ff., 224–
226; compare Du Boulay 1974, 123). The anxieties are mutual and self-
perpetuating, as John Campbell (1964, 276) demonstrates in relating how
Sarakatsani maidens vow to hide a knife and castrate their husbands on the
wedding night rather than submit. The cases in the early imperial period where
adultery, poisoning, marital and political treachery, and treason all come together can, like Juvenal and much of Suetonius, be read as a kind of ideological
narrative of male anxieties and fantasies about dangerous, insatiable women,
Roman equivalents of the Greek tales of Clytemnestra, the Danaides, or
Medea. Whether the accusations are accurate in particular cases is irrelevant for
an appreciation of their ideological content.

This brief discussion has made clear that Roman sources evidence a characteristic connection between male honor and female sexuality. These sources
also reveal how this connection depends on certain male conceptualizations of
women's sexual nature, conceptualizations widely shared by other traditional
Mediterranean societies. A final passage provides eloquent testimony to the
way in which the various elements of this complex of beliefs, values, and
practices interrelate. Tacitus (*Ann.* 3.33ff.) recounts a debate concerning
whether wives should accompany their husbands on service abroad. The first
speaker argues that women should remain at home. Women, he claims, must be
kept under control and away from politics. Otherwise, their deceitful, schem-
ing, and ferocious natures will cause great harm, for they will intrigue, insinu-
ate themselves into political affairs, dominate men, and bring ultimate ruin. The
second speaker proposes that women should be brought along but, significantly, shares the same underlying ideological premises as the other speaker:
women are indeed prone to cause trouble, but it is the duty of the husband to
control his wife. If she misbehaves, it is his fault. Further, if the husband is
away, the weaker sex will be vulnerable to their own drives and to masculine
desires. Men, he concludes implicitly, must control and guard their wives'
sexuality to prevent moral ruin. This linkage of male honor and the maintenance of the social order to a view of dangerous female sexuality that must be
regulated by men and confined to the private sphere places Roman society
squarely within the Mediterranean context of honor and shame defined above.

THE AMBIGUOUS STATUS OF THE ADULTERER

Roman society, like most other Mediterranean cultures, placed considerable
emphasis on public affirmations of masculine honor. Passivity and sub-
missiveness, whether sexual or social, undermine the dominant, active masculine principle upon which honor rests. Accordingly, as in classical Athens,

accusations of sexual passivity furnished a common means of attacking one's opponent's reputation.[15] It would seem to follow that one clear way of asserting one's masculinity would be to take the women of other men. In fact, this seems to be the case in both the ancient and the modern Mediterranean, which helps to explain why in both Athens and Rome some cuckolded husbands apparently sexually abused adulterers taken in the act. Yet though Don Juan, in the traditional understanding, enhances his honor by robbing other men of theirs, he is not a positively valued figure (Pitt-Rivers 1977, 23). Adultery may establish one's masculinity, but it also destroys families, encourages revenge and feud, and hence threatens the stability of the social order. Thus in many Mediterranean communities, though men may boast of their conquests in private to their closest friends, in public they do not express overt approval of it as a general practice.

One finds some evidence of this ambivalence at Rome. Cicero, for example, deprecates opponents by references to their sexual misconduct, like rape and stuprum, which reflect on a man's integritas and pudor (*Planc.* 12.29; compare Seneca, *Ben.* 7.2.21). The accusation he levels against Verres is typical: whereas in his youth he submitted to other men, as an adult he engaged in adultery and stuprum, ravishing the pudor and pudicitia of others (*Verr.* 2.5.13.34).[16] Seneca addresses the issue specifically when he argues that a man is wrong to require chastity of his wife while he himself is corrupting the wives of other men (*Ep.* 94.26; compare 95.57). Yet in so arguing he recognizes that many do not think this way, for example, men who desire the wives of others but suffer no one to look at their own wives (*De Ira* 2.28.7). In the same passage Seneca also refers to the competitive motivation that leads some men to adultery, when he comments that some men delight in adultery precisely because of the difficulty that it involves. These passages may explain why some men ran the considerable risks that adultery entailed, though the affective attachments which it could produce were surely a major factor. The fashionableness of adultery provided further impetus. Thus Seneca describes adultery as de rigeur among the elite: the man who grudges his wife the pleasure of appearing scantily clad in public is boorish (rusticus); if he refrains from adultery himself, or from giving money to his married paramour, he is viewed by other women as base and addicted to low pleasures and maidservants (*Ben.* 1.9.4).

Adultery, then, like other forms of illicit sexuality, could in some contexts be

15. See, e.g., Cicero, *Cael.* 3.6–8, where he argues that only those who keep their youth *integra atque inviolata* will become men of good reputation, and cf. *Sest.* 8.18, 17.39, 54.116. Suetonius (1.49) claims that Caesar's intimacy with King Nicomedes damaged his reputation for pudicitia and led to his being called Nicomedes' queen.

16. Cicero also recounts how a crowd gathered outside Verres's mansion, shouting out the names of the women he had debauched (*Verr.* 2.5.3.94).

considered conduct damaging to a man's reputation. Yet in other contexts neither these social norms nor the legal penalties of the lex Julia de adulteriis appear to have carried much weight with some Romans. Similarly, adulteresses may have, in theory, dishonored their families, but some women of elite status, like Vistilia, appear not to have given the matter much thought. Moreover, whereas some husbands aimed to lay murderous hands on any men they found with their wives, others appear to have ignored, or even profited from, their wives' adultery. What, if anything, can one conclude from these contradictions? Are they merely a sign of the moral confusion and degeneracy of the times?[17]

Three related factors help to account for these ambiguities and contradictions. First, as emphasized above, such conflicts are not exceptions requiring special explanation, but rather reflections of the nature of social life. Only by focusing exclusively on ethical or cultural ideals are scholars able to identify a coherent system of values. But as Bourdieu and others have convincingly shown, such objective moral systems have little to do with the actual societies that they purportedly regulate. Instead of attempting to explain away such conflicts by claiming that one group of sources is truly representative, whereas others are somehow aberrant, the historian should emphasize such cultural tensions. Roman society in this period was certainly not unique in manifesting them, for just these ambivalences and anxieties about male and female sexuality characterize other traditional Mediterranean communities. There was no single Roman attitude toward adultery, sexuality, or women, nor even a uniform attitude among the Roman elite toward these matters. Our sources reflect the complexity and richness of conceptualizations of sexuality and gender among individuals, and even within the same individual in different contexts.

Second, part of the ambiguity arises from the difference between ideal norms and the norms of social practice. Again, the historian risks reductionism by attempting to dismiss social practice as mere deviance from societal norms. The norms of practice together with cultural ideals and values constitute a dynamic system by which individuals orient their behavior and develop strategies for the manipulation of the normative expectations of their communities.

Finally, comparative evidence strongly suggests the unrepresentativeness of social elites. In many Mediterranean societies (as elsewhere), elites tend to be the most punctilious in matters of honor, but at the same time far less concerned than other social groups with community judgments and strictures on sexual freedom. This does not imply that they act outside the system of

---

17. Seneca claims that Romans no longer feel shame for adultery because it is so common. Pudicitia, he claims, is just regarded as proof of ugliness (*Ben.* 3.16.3). Cicero (*Cael.* 12.29) states that the vices and immorality of the age are a standard topos to be used against opponents.

honor and shame. On the contrary, they are among its most ardent supporters, for it buttresses their own social supremacy. This two-sidedness has typified most European aristocracies, and it surely plays an important role in the conflict one finds in Roman sources between evidence suggesting that traditional values were still intact and other testimonia indicating moral degeneracy. That an individual like Augustus preached the sanctity of the marital bond in public and may have violated it in private is not mere hypocrisy, but rather a characteristic feature of such culture complexes.

In short, our sources permit precious few (if any) generalizations about illicit sexuality in Roman society as a whole. Further, generalizations about the moral situation of the Roman elite should take into account the special nature of aristocratic values and practices. The evidence briefly reviewed above does not, in the end, support the view that the Roman aristocracy had abandoned traditional values and drifted into moral degeneracy. In fact, the values associated with honor and shame appear to have exercised considerable influence in evaluations of sexual conduct. This ideology of male honor and female chastity, however, existed in a dynamic tension with other patterns of values, beliefs, and practices. Neither Vistilia, nor the images of chaste and blushing matrons, by themselves tell the whole story.

THE FAMILY, SOCIAL POLICY, AND THE LEX JULIA DE ADULTERIIS

Scholars have advanced many interpretations concerning the legislative purpose behind the lex Julia. Jane Gardner (1986, 128) and Aline Rousselle (1988, 85–87) view it as intended "to preserve the chastity of women in marriage." Pal Csillag (1976, 54) holds that Augustus was responding to the utter disintegration of the Roman family and sexual morals. Thus, he concludes, the statute was designed by Augustus to be a powerful weapon against the corruption of the age. Nörr (1977) emphasizes instead the legislation's regulatory nature under the rubric of state planning. Such a view, in my opinion, best clarifies some of the puzzling features of this legislation. If the primary purpose of the law was to strike fear into the hearts of prospective adulterers, why did it sharply limit the greatest dangers that they could incur?

The literary sources discussed above portray the severest threat as residing not in legal penalties, but rather in the death or savage maltreatment that might result if an adulterer was taken in the act. The lex Julia, however, confined the father's right to a narrow set of unlikely circumstances and, in most instances, completely prohibited the husband's revenge (see Cantarella's chapter in this volume for a detailed discussion of the restrictions). Rather than enhancing the legal threat to adulterers, the lex Julia de adulteriis actually severely restricted it. Indeed, this restriction operated at the expense of the family, and it was surely this aspect that led Mommsen to call the legislation "eine der eingrei-fendsten und dauerndsten strafrechtlichen Neuschöpfungen welche die Geschichte kennt [one of the most intrusive and long-lasting creations in criminal law in all history]" (1955, 691).

This intervention into what formerly had been a largely autonomous famil-ial sphere may have aimed at restricting adultery, but not the way, for example, biblical legislation does. The biblical codes (Leviticus 20:10, Deuteronomy 22:22) also punish adultery by taking it out of the hands of the family, but they do so by superimposing a new, theologically determined sexual morality on the family-oriented values of honor and shame. The Deuteronomic and Levitical legislation punishes adultery with death not because of its contribution to social decay, but because it is an abomination, a sin, a transgression against God's commandment. Thus throughout the Old Testament prophets employ adultery as a metaphor for idolatry: Israel is the harlot or adulterous wife who turns away from God and goes whoring among the nations.[18] The Augustan legislation, however, addresses social concerns. Adultery is symptomatic of, and contributes to, the degeneracy of an elite who are perceived as failing adequately to reproduce themselves as a social group. The punishment of adultery thus falls under the category of social policy, not sin and trans-gression.

This difference is significant, for it represents an important moment in the Western legal and political tradition. In spite of sumptuary legislation and the like, in both classical Athens and republican Rome the family was perceived as a social unit enjoying a significant degree of legal autonomy. In this regard, the lex Julia's restriction of the power of the family tribunal and the right of vengeance, its provisions for mandatory divorce and prosecution, its encour-agement of informers, and so on, together with the Augustan marital legisla-tion, represent a massive and deliberate appropriation by the state of a new regulatory sphere: marriage, divorce, and sexuality. Mommsen was right to see this as a radical intervention, and as Nörr has pointed out, Augustus's contem-poraries also viewed it that way. To use a Foucaultian vocabulary, the family, and the marital, reproductive, and sexual relations that it embodies, became the object of legal categorizations, official discourses, and political strategies of normalization, an axis of power and knowledge in the development of a new form of government. In this view, the lex Julia concerns far more than ensuring

18. See, e.g., Ezekiel 23:1–4, 36–49. I quote in part: "For they have committed adultery, and blood is in their hands, and with their idols have they committed adultery."

the chastity of Roman women, far more than checking the moral corruption of the age. The appropriation of the family, sexuality, and reproduction for the purposes of state policy was not entirely successful, but it established a principle that, when adopted by a Christianized empire, would have far-reaching consequences.

Though beyond the scope of this paper, a few concluding remarks on the fate of the Augustan legislation on adultery may be appropriate. Like all such attempts, of course, the Augustan legislation necessarily failed to eradicate the conduct that it prohibited. Indeed, over the next centuries there was a growing trend toward severer penalties.[19] This movement perhaps culminated in the provision of Constantius and Constans in 339, which not only called for severe enforcement of the laws against adultery, but also decreed that adulterers be punished "as though they were manifest parricides," by being sown up in a leather sack and drowned.

The specific language of the provision is significant, for it refers to adulterers as the "sacrilegious violators of marriage." This statement appears to herald the shift in emphasis that Christianity brought to the prosecution of adultery. Constantine, of course, had already restricted to the immediate family the right to prosecute adultery, thereby reversing one of the major innovations of the lex Julia de adulteriis. It is noteworthy, however, that in doing so he placed the primary responsibility on the husband, whom he calls "the avenger of the marriage bed" (*Cod. Theod.* 9.7.2), a phrase taken up in the subsequent official discourse of adultery (*Const. Sirm.* 8; *N. Maj.* 9.1). In justifying ever severer punishments in the name of a sacred marital chastity, Roman legislation incorporated the notion of adultery as sin and transgression that informed the Old and New Testament traditions.[20] In this light, a provision enacted in 388 ordaining that a Jew who married a Christian woman be punished as an adulterer is surely significant (*Cod. Theod.* 9.7.5). This development reached its logical conclusion in legislation of Justinian, according to which a married woman convicted of adultery was to be confined in a convent for life. Because of the sanctity of marriage, however, if after two years her husband chose to remarry her, he could do so. Otherwise she remained immured.

In the end, then, the adulterer becomes less an offender who damages the social order by impeding the management of populations, and more a sacrilegious, heinous offender who destroys the chastity of the marriage bed and all

19. See, e.g., *Cod. Just.* 2.4.18 and 9.9.9 for the death penalty, and cf. *Const. Sirm.* 8, *N. Maj.* 9.1, and *Cod. Theod.* 11.36.4. for further evidence of the push toward severity.

20. The concern for the preservation of marriage is also evident from Constantine's no longer requiring the husband to divorce his wife when the accusation of adultery is based only on suspicion.

that it represents. He is now like the Jew who pollutes the Christian union of man and woman. With the revival of Roman law in later periods, these two layers of Roman strategies against adultery and sexual immorality provided a powerful heritage for those who would use the powers of church and state to create a legal and institutional framework that, in the name of seeking out sin, recognized no area of private conduct, discourse, or thought as beyond its reach. In the institutions of the penitential and the canon law, which regulated the entirety of sexual, reproductive, and marital life, the legal revolution of the Augustan legislation reached fruition in ways that its author had perhaps never imagined.

Chapter 7

MIREILLE CORBIER

Constructing Kinship in Rome:
Marriage and Divorce,
Filiation and Adoption

Dante interpreted the story of Marcia, who was given by Cato, her husband, to his friend Hortensius but returned to Cato when she was widowed, in terms of the return of the soul to God.[1] This poetic allegory invites us to take another look at the famous episode. Plutarch tells us that Hortensius, "desiring to be more than a mere associate and companion of Cato, and in some way or other to bring his whole family and line into community of kinship with him," asked Cato for his daughter Porcia (who was married to Bibulus) "as noble soil for the production of children." He promised that "if Bibulus were wholly devoted to his wife . . . he would give her back after she had borne him a child, and he would thus be more closely connected both with Bibulus himself and with Cato by a community of children" (trans. Perrin, Loeb Classical Library). When Cato refused to comply, Hortensius asked for his wife, Marcia, and obtained her. Widowed by Hortensius, Marcia returned to Cato, who took her back in what was, according to Lucan, a chaste union (Plutarch, *Cat. Min.* 25; Lucan, *Phars.* 2.326–391). Plutarch's rhetorical tone aside, this love story was based on situations that could actually occur in Roman society. As Claude Lévi-Strauss suggested (1983a, 1983b), the "view from afar" is appropriate for an appreciation of a society with its own logical system.

It is only too tempting for the historian to interpret the evolution of the family from the Roman era to medieval and modern days as a continuity—the historical roots of the Western family—a continuity that was, at most, affected

---

1. Dante, *Convivio* 4.28.13–19; *The Divine Comedy, Purgatorio* 1.4.78–84. See Goar 1987, 104–107.

by transformations on the sentimental level (in love or friendship) or the institutional level. The church, and later the state, regulated kinship and registered marriages, births, and deaths. In reality, there was a profound rupture between classical Rome and later ages. Unlike their European successors, on whom the church imposed strict rules of filiation and alliance, Romans enjoyed a large degree of liberty to create their kinship groups and also, through the use of testaments, to choose their heirs. They needed no dispensations from an external authority. Indeed, few rules were imposed: although the Roman state controlled statutes and regulated mores, the power of decision of the *paterfamilias* in the domains of family formation and development (marriage and the legitimization of children) remained central.

In comparison with later canonical prohibitions and familial customs, there was no "impossible marriage" (with a spouse of appropriate status). The range of prohibitions connected with kinship was extremely limited in Rome in the period examined here, the last two centuries of the republic and the first three centuries of the empire. Furthermore, access to marriage was not reserved to a limited number of siblings, as it was later in many noble, patrician, or peasant families of Europe. In Rome, celibacy was a personal choice, permitted to men only, and unfavorably regarded by the state authorities (who, under the empire, attempted to dissuade the elites from celibacy by limiting the successional rights of unmarried persons and treating similarly widows and widowers who did not remarry). All male siblings had an equal right to head a family, and all female siblings were married.

Remarriage was not "impossible" either. The Romans were monogamous, but successively. Marriage was not indissoluble, and remarriage was the normal future course for widows, widowers, and divorced persons alike—for divorce was written into the law. The cards were not dealt out once only: both men and women could play another hand. The Roman family had one more means of replenishing its ranks or constructing a kinship group other than marriage and remarriage—adoption, which the church nearly eliminated in western Europe for close to fifteen hundred years.

THE LIMITS OF INFORMATION

We must first emphasize the limitations of our evidence and of the results we can obtain from it. The Romans had a wide vocabulary in these matters and depicted the family and kinship from various points of view. Our descriptions of their social practices depend on juridical and literary evidence and on epigraphic documentation. These sources are in no way neutral and in each instance refer to particular facts, whose representativeness is uncertain. Both types of source lead us to study mainly the social elites.

REPRESENTATIONS OF THE FAMILY AND OF KINSHIP

The *familia* had two juridical definitions (Ulpian, *Dig.* 50.16.195.2, 4). A strict definition limited the family to the pyramidal group of men and women placed under the authority of the paterfamilias (or would have been so placed if he had not died). From the very beginning the term *familia* included goods and slaves, since its first meaning, derived from *famel,* "slave," was patrimonial. The broader definition equated the familia with a branch of the patrilineal lineage (the gens) and even with the gens itself by reference to one common ancestor. In all cases, the familia was defined agnatically. But the group of kin (Fox 1967, 148) was in fact bilateral and included all the *cognati* (only half of whom were *agnati*). Bilateral kinship was recognized as such by the law of succession up to the sixth Roman degree (second cousins) and even to the seventh degree (second cousins once removed) in the case of the children of cousins. A special status was accorded to relations by marriage (the *adfines*).

Domus is the most adequate term to indicate the unit of residence—the household—including the wife, who within free marriage (the form most common at the time) was not a member of the familia. The term, widely used during the empire, according to context could render the three senses of the physical house, the household, and the (noble) house. The same familia could thus include more than one domus, and in fact Plutarch, writing in the imperial age, speaks of coresidence among married sons or brothers as an old-fashioned custom (Plutarch, *Aem.* 5.6–10, *Crass.* 1.1–2).

Literary writers play on the various registers of agnate and cognate relations, juridical and domestic, through the polysemy of the terms *familia* and *domus* (Saller 1984). The agnati hardly enter their vocabulary, even though they were well aware of these major players in the drama of successional rights. Cognati appear more frequently, and blood ties, maternal and paternal, are strongly portrayed. But authors prefer terms that suggest proximity (*propinqui, proximi*), affection (*mei*), or accruing obligations (*necessarii*), and they are apt to divide intimates into groups designated by the nature of the bond in order to include forms of proximity other than kinship, notably friendship or even geographical proximity. Usage of the tripartite formula *propinqui, adfines, amici* is thus common.

JURIDICAL SOURCES AND SOCIAL PRACTICES

By and large, the Roman jurists show an interest in marriage, legitimate descent (natural or adoptive), and the kinship relations deriving from them because of their outcomes: *patria potestas,* the dowry, rights of succession, the exercise of guardianship, and so forth. This leads them to study situations that would deprive the union of its character as a *justum matrimonium,* and hence of its effects. They do not present their definitions and their expositions as a reflection of the Roman system of alliance and kinship. In an attempt to be exhaustive, they envision an entire range of theoretical possibilities that cannot always be related to concrete instances. The jurists also propose solutions to real *casus,* and their writings provide excellent evidence of social practices. The same concern for exhaustiveness, however, led the compilers to devote space to some cases that we cannot be sure corresponded to widespread patterns of behavior. How many granddaughters, for example, married their maternal uncle at their grandmother's urging? The children of one such incestuous union were legitimated by imperial rescript (Marcianus, *Dig.* 23.2.57a).

CAN FAMILY HISTORY BE CONSTRUCTED FROM EPITAPHS?

The historian of ancient Rome does not have parish records registering births, marriages, and deaths. Italy has passed on no registers of the census (a republican practice that continued to the Flavians) or birth declarations (introduced perhaps in the age of Augustus). Outside of Egypt, epitaphs and other inscriptions provide the only mass documentation on families, and it is highly selective. The study of such inscriptions poses a number of methodological problems that cannot be examined here. The first step is to read the epitaphs for what their authors wanted to say or to stress, which is usually the affective dimension. The next step is to attempt to make these texts tell us more by questioning what they fail to say and by seeking to develop them, as one does a mathematical formula. In this way, we can reconstitute possible genealogies and alliances on the basis of onomastics and the kinship relations that are given. The results are uneven, however.

Explicit mention. Some inscriptions reveal a double kinship link, like that in which a *gener* (son-in-law) honors his *patruus* (paternal uncle), showing probably a marriage between patrilateral parallel cousins. The same type of marriage is clearly indicated by the expression *uxor eadem soror patr(u)elis* (at the same time wife and patrilateral first cousin). The designation of one woman as *socrus et amita* by her niece and daughter-in-law of the same name indicates a marriage between cross-cousins. A man who presents his wife as *consobrina eademque uxor* has married his first cousin. When a woman is designated as *matertera* (maternal aunt) to her husband's brother's sons, it means—if the person dictating the dedication respected Roman kinship terminology—that she and her sister married brothers.[2]

---

2. *Corpus Inscriptionum Latinarum* (Berlin: W. de Gruyter) (hereafter cited as *CIL*), 6:17534 (in

Implicit. Kin can also be identified by onomastics. Sharing the same *gentilicium* is indicative of agnatic kin, both male and female, as with Cornelius and Cornelia. (Freedmen and freedwomen of the same owner also bore the same name, which can add to our difficulties when status is not identified.) Ramification of the gens is expressed by distinctive *cognomina* showing the branch (Cornelius Scipio) or subbranch (Cornelius Scipio Nasica). This traditional system, which was also adopted by new families in the imperial age, competed then with polyonymy showing the stratification of alliances. Nomenclature very soon made room for cognatic kinship, using the same terms to express alliance (on the maternal side) and adoption (on the side of the natural father). Not all the polyonymi of the second century A.D. were adoptees—that is, men who changed familia—but a number of them did incorporate the names of the relative or friend, whether male or female (though in classical Rome women could not adopt legally), who had designated them as heirs on this express condition (Syme 1982, 397–398). That friends could enter into the nomenclature reveals the high esteem in which they were held in Roman society.

Onomastics alone can suggest a marriage between close kin. It all depends on the social milieu. Statistically, a conjugal pair bearing the same name were likely the freed slaves of the same owner (or the owner and one of his freedwomen), but a similarity in gentilicium also could indicate a marriage between patrilateral cousins or at least between agnatic kin. The wife who bears as a cognomen her husband's *gentilicium could* (among other possibilities) be his patrilateral cross-cousin.[3] Finally, when a notable married a woman whose name (Antonia) was identical to that used for several generations by his family as a cognomen (Antoninus), we are tempted to see it as a reinforced alliance link even if we cannot specify the number of generations intervening between the original Antonii woman and the second, or the relationship between the two women.

Occasionally we can reconstitute a genealogy over several generations from nomenclature and the indications of kinship ties. An inscription at Allifae, in

---

Rome); *CIL* 6:8409 (for imperial slaves and freedmen); Giorges Fabre, Marc Mayer, and Isabel Rodà, *Inscriptions romaines de Catalogne,* 2 vols. (Paris: Publications du Centre Pierre, 1984–1985), 2:50 (in Aeso in Hispania Tarraconensis); Hermann Dessau, ed., *Inscriptiones Latinae Selectae,* 3 vols. in 5 (Berlin: Weidmann, 1892–1916) (hereafter *ILS*), in Historium [Vasto]); Stéphane Gsell and Hans-Georg Pflaum, *Inscriptions Latines de l'Algérie,* Tome II (Numidie cirtéenne), *Inscriptions de la Confédération Cirtéenne, de Cuicul et de la tribu des Suburbures,* vol. 1, *Rusicade et région de Rusicade, Cirta, Castellum Celtianum, Caldis, Castellum Tidditanorum* (Paris: Edouard Champion, 1957), 616 (in Cirta [Constantine]).

3. This is one possible explanation among others of the name of Lartidia Sex(ti) (filia) Cominia, wife of the senator T(itus) Cominius Proculus. Edmund Groag and Arthur Stein, *Prosopographia Imperii Romani saec. I, II, III* (Berlin: W. de Gruyter, 1933) (hereafter cited as *PIR²*), L 119 and C 1270.

Latium, gives the father, the two grandfathers, and one great-grandfather of a
clarissima (senatorial) girl named Acilia Gavinia Frestana. Prosopographers
now interpret this as indicating that her father, the senator Claudius Acilius
Cleoboles, married a matrilateral first cousin, perhaps identifiable as Acilia
Manliola, "clarissima lady," given in a twin inscription as the daughter of
M(anius) Acilius Faustinus (*ILS* 1134, 1133). The mother of Claudius Acilius
Cleoboles was indeed an Acilia Frestana, the sister of the same Acilius
Faustinus, whose gentilicium he bears instead of and in the place reserved for
the maternal name (Jacques 1986, 152, 173).

WHICH ROMAN FAMILY?

What could be more Roman than a casus examined in the *Digest?* Nevertheless, a judgment rendered by Marcus Aurelius and transmitted by the jurist
Scaevola concerns a *fideicommissum* left to her sons by the divorced wife of a
Roman senator originally from Sparta named Brasidas (*Dig.* 36.1.23 pr., Ulpian). Prosopographers have recently identified the protagonists of this family
story (Spawforth 1985). To be able to doublecheck epigraphic sources with
more informative juridical and literary sources is extremely rare.

Juridical texts stress stability. The model of the Roman family that they
describe, however, had been developed by gradually Romanized elites, whose
ancestors may have had other traditions: first by Italian families who became
Roman citizens, then by provincial families. The extension of citizenship to all
free men of the empire after 212 brought about the disappearance in Egypt of
marriage between brothers and sisters, which had been tolerated up to that
point, but thereafter was prohibited for Egyptians as well as for other Roman
citizens (Hopkins 1980; Lewis 1983, 43–44, 216). Although modern scholars
recognize the persistence of previous family structures at the provincial level—
for instance, the endogamic practices of the Lycians—they tend to see the
smaller Italian cities of the later republic and the early empire as miniature
Romes. The nature of our sources makes it difficult to isolate local familial
traditions. Still, the Etruscan custom of indicating the mother's name after the
father's had not yet disappeared, even in the age of Augustus, and it is one sign
of a different conception of the family.

The character of the documentation prevents us from reaching the mass of
the population, which, even in Italy, was never conceivably represented in
epitaphs. Epigraphy was used to extremely unequal degrees by the various
social groups. Consequently, the study of alliance and kinship remains limited
to the social elites—municipal, equestrian, and senatorial—and to the imperial
families, whose practices were the same as the other aristocratic families but
who had different aims and are the best known.

THE FREEDOM OF THE GAME: JURIDICAL PROCEDURES

Before we attempt to define what actually took place in society, we can start with the model provided by known procedures.

MARRIAGE

For Cicero and Augustine (who took his inspiration from Cicero), the family was the foundation of the state and of all human society, and marriage was the "seedbed of a city"—*seminarium civitatis* (Cicero, *De officiis* 1.54; Augustine, *De civ. D.* 15.16).

Legal marriage. "To take a wife in order to have children" was one of the definitions of legal marriage in Rome. Producing offspring benefiting from the status of *sui*—who would be first in line in inheritance from the father in case of intestate succession—distinguished marriage from all other forms of sexual relations, whether occasional or, like concubinage, associated with cohabitation. Hadrian's adopted son is reported to have answered his wife, when she complained of his extramarital affairs, with an ungallant "wife is a title of dignity, not of pleasure" (*Hist. Aug., Aelius* 5.11). Marriage, which was founded on the will of both spouses, remained a private act, as confirmed by the ritual question posed by the censor: "in your soul and conscience, have you a wife?" (Gellius, *Noctes Atticae* 4.20.3). Roman marriage was perceived as a lasting association, "a partnership for life" (Modestinus, *Dig.* 23.2.1), which was close to the definition of friendship, "a partnership for everything" (Seneca, *Ep.* 48). Unlike Christian marriage, however, in which initial consent united the couple for the rest of their lives, Roman marriage was founded on the continuing will of the spouses (and of their fathers).

Free marriage. The married couples holding hands in sign of conjugal understanding depicted on certain funeral monuments owned nothing in common. In the framework of free marriage, a practice that became frequent in the late republican period, the wife did not join the familia of her husband but remained in her father's familia. These spouses could not practice community property even had they wanted to, since gifts were forbidden between living spouses. By testament, however, they could name one another as their heirs or legatees. They also transmitted their estates to their children separately.

Kinship hindrances to marriage. In Christian Europe, to marry was, in principle, to leave one's real or spiritual kinship group. The monogamous and indissoluble marriage advocated by the Church was also exogamous. In western Europe, peasantry and aristocracy alike stubbornly resisted a model whose prohibitions they sought to turn aside through a system of dispensations. In Rome, the term *adfinis* designated both the kinsman by alliance and the proprietor of adjoining land, which without necessarily implying blood kinship, at least indicates geographical and social proximity. In the context of the ancient Mediterranean world, the Roman model of marriage that Plutarch presents (see Corbier 1987, 1273–1274) and that avoids the union of close kin stands in contrast to an oriental model. Classical Athens admitted marriage with one's niece (still attested in the imperial age) and even with an agnatic half-sister; in Ptolemaic and Roman Egypt the custom of marriage (for non-Romans) with one's sister, "born of the same father and same mother," developed; Lycians tended to marry their female cousins and their nieces. After comparing the strict exogamic constraints imposed by the Church in the west, however, Jack Goody (1983) came to consider the Roman model as endogamic.

The period of Roman history under consideration here is, in any event, the one in which matrimonial restrictions based on kinship were the least strict. Until the year A.D. 49, the closest permissible female blood relative was the first cousin (the fourth degree in Roman reckoning). From that year (when a senatorial decree legalized it to justify the union of Claudius and Agrippina) until 342 (when Constantius II abrogated this dispensation), it was legal to marry one's brother's daughter (the third degree in Roman reckoning). Marrying a direct ascendant or descendant was never permitted, nor was marrying a sister or a half-sister, agnatic or uterine, an aunt, paternal or maternal, or a niece or a great-niece on the sister's side. At the turn of the first century the four affines in direct line were prohibited as well (ascending, the ex-mother-in-law and ex-stepmother; descending, the ex-daughter-in-law and ex-stepdaughter), but not collateral affines (Moreau 1983, 118). Thus a man could marry his brother's ex-wife or his ex-wife's sister, or even the daughter born of another marriage of his stepfather or his stepmother, even if she had been brought up with him as his sister. This period was sandwiched between two others of more sweeping prohibitions, however. Until the third century B.C., it appears (Bettini 1988b) that no cousin could be one's bride: the *sobrina* (female second cousin; sixth degree in Roman reckoning) no more than the *consobrina* (first cousin; fourth degree in Roman reckoning). Although marriage with a first cousin was explicitly authorized in classical Rome (when the jurists recognized the right of a grandfather, acting on his own initiative, to unite a grandson and granddaughter under his potestas and born of different fathers), imperial legislation (in the west at least) began to question that right in the late fourth century. Sixth-century councils extended the prohibition to second cousins (Roda 1979; Goody 1983, 56).

Divorce and remarriage. Consensual marriage was the foundation of the principle that the conjugal bond could be dissolved. In reality, however, divorce and remarriage were made possible by the unique status of the wife and of her wealth, which, under free marriage, were not integrated into the family and the patrimony of the husband. The juridical texts, in fact, based recognition of the wife's right to the return of her dowry in the event of dissolution of the union (by death or divorce) on her need to remarry. The law even forbade any dotal agreement by which the spouses promised not to divorce. Marriage could be broken at will by either partner, acting *sui juris* or through his or her pater-familias if still under paternal power.

Filiation. The famous formula *is est pater quem nuptiae demonstrant* ("he is the father whom marriage designates") must be understood in the specific context of Roman paternity. The legitimacy of the child ensued from the just marriage of the parents—that is, from a marriage in conformity with law. But this necessary condition was not by itself sufficient: the Roman father still had the right to refuse a child borne by his spouse. Exposing the infant, however, was not considered abandonment: the father by doing so did not lose his rights over the child if a third party reared him (Boswell 1988, 63–65). The posthumous child posed a special problem for Roman society (Thomas 1986): since the father's rights could not be delegated, no one (neither the mother nor another relative) could deny the child the right to be brought up. The father himself was free, however, to renounce exercise of patria potestas and exclude a natural or adoptive child from his familia by emancipation, and he could transfer his rights to another by giving a son for adoption.

Adoption. The law made a distinction between *adoptio,* strictly speaking, which was the transfer of an individual *in potestate* from one paternal control to another by the will of the natural father, and *adrogatio,* by which a person sui juris placed himself under the potestas of another person of his own free will. Both procedures required ratification by public officials. Testamentary adoption, on the other hand, which is well attested in literature, was a private practice that permitted transfer of both a name and an estate. The practice does not figure in Roman juridical works; whether or not it was a true adoption and established a descent line between the adoptee and adopter is the subject of controversy among scholars today. Those who merely sought to do a kindness to a child could turn to a purely affective quasi-adoption (Nielsen 1987) of a young foster child (*alumnus*) born to a slave woman or a freedwoman of the household or taken in from outside.

The licit and the honestum. With divorce, remarriage, adoption, and strict control of filiation, the Romans seem to have enjoyed a broad range of choices in the game of alliance and kinship. Juridical procedures were not the only rules of that game, however. The value judgments occasionally expressed by Roman authors of the time suggest, to the contrary, that rules of social acceptance provided a counterweight to a theoretical liberty. Social practice stressed conformity to morality: *quid honestum sit* ("what is honorable"), as the jurist Modestinus wrote (*Dig.* 23.2.42).

ALLIANCE AND KINSHIP PRACTICES

Adfines. Even before procreation, marriage created kin called in Latin adfines. New ties were forged. Cicero justifies his remarriage precisely because he feels the need of new *necessitudines* (*Fam.* 4.13.4). Tacitus, a senator without ancestors, saw a large kinship group as a sign of belonging to an ancient family (*Ann.* 15.48.2). In Roman society rank depended on relations by blood and by alliance and on the patronage and support of friends (electoral influence, judicial solidarity, financial aid, and so forth), and wealth was acquired largely through inheritance (from kin, friends, and predeceased spouses). Matrimonial behavior thus was necessarily influenced not only by precise political aims but also by prospective inheritance and dowries and by the desire to consolidate or extend kinship and affinity networks. In Rome as elsewhere, a man married (or married his son to) the sister, the daughter, or the niece of a relative or a friend, or to the contrary, of an enemy with whom he wanted to make peace. The marriage of a *privigna,* a stepdaughter, brought the advantage of alliance for her father-in-law. There were no "bastards" to be provided for in this society, however. One unusual case seems to our eyes downright exotic. If Plutarch can be taken at his word, Hortensius took one occasion to theorize that sharing a wife could generate an alliance between three men—her father, her ex-husband, and her new husband—implicitly supporting the thesis of marriage as a "seedbed of a city." The idea that having children by the same woman creates a bond between two men also appears in Asconius, the commentator of Cicero, who implies that uterine kinship between offspring created a solidarity, if not a tie of alliance, between the two fathers (Asconius, p. 19 Clark). We have to accept on faith that the idea reflects genuine sentiment.

Remarriage. When we know more about a member of the elite than his or her epitaph tells us, we often know that he or she had several wives or husbands, often two or three, in Larinum as in Rome. Oppianicus (the "notable" presented in the *Pro Cluentio*) with his six wives and Vistilia with her six husbands hold the documentable records for the period, but we also find mothers honored in their epitaphs by children of two marriages (Moreau 1983; Bradley 1987a). That divorce and widowhood made remarriage possible for women as well as for men increased the chances of multiplying family ties of all varieties during a lifetime. Even when other pretexts were offered, the divorces known to us were often concluded with a view to remarriage, and the abandoned spouse often remarried as well. Men did not hesitate to marry a woman pregnant by another man (who retained control of the child). Unilateral divorce could be a dangerous game to play, however: one risked seeing the former *adfinitas* turn into *inimicitia*. Thus many a husband who wanted to leave his wife took pains to accuse her of adultery. On occasion, the repudiation of a wife also occurred after her father's death, as in the case of Pompey and Antistia. When Mark Antony repudiated his wife Antonia, however, he did not offend just a father-in-law, but his paternal uncle.[4] The divorce of Mark Antony thus offers a perfect illustration of a theme mentioned in Plutarch: the risk of failing to respect kinship obligations to which marriage with close kin could lead (Corbier 1987, 1273).

Alliance customs. In senatorial circles, the motivations behind matrimonial alliances changed with the transformation of the regime. Republican careers, punctuated by elections, required true political alliances; this explains why Cato disdained purely expedient matrimonial alliance, which seemed to him a kind of bribery (Plutarch, *Cat. Min.* 30, *Pomp.* 44.2–3). Marriage did not always shape politics in Rome, but marriages were often used for leverage—which is not to say that unions based on more personal aims were unknown. Under the empire, the mediation of the powerful was needed to settle the least controversy (MacMullen 1988, 60–84), and advancement and social promotion depended on a network of patronage and friendships that gave access to the favor of the great and, at the summit, of the ruler (Saller 1982). Inversely, when disgrace struck, the network of adfines and *familiares* that an individual had constructed might be systematically destroyed with him.

Representations of alliance. Alliance was represented both horizontally and vertically, as can be seen in funerals and on tombs. The noble families of the republic made much of their lineage. They cultivated their genealogical memory with stemmata painted in their atria and *imagines* bearing likenesses of their ancestors, which were carefully stored away to be brought out for funerals, when they were carried at the head of the funeral procession (Bettini 1988a, 176–193). Prestigious kinship relations acquired by the entry of women into the family (by marriage) and eventually of men (by adoption) were remembered as well.[5] At a great funeral procession in A.D. 22 for Junia, "Cato's niece, [half]-sister of Brutus, wife of Cassius," the images of twenty senatorial families were carried, showing the enormous kinship capital the family had accumulated (Tacitus, *Ann.* 3.76.1). Even families who were less prestigious but impor-

4. Cicero (*Phil.* 2.99) reproaches him precisely for having left *filiam eius, sororem tuam* (omitting the unnecessary specification *patruelem,* which would clearly designate this sister as a cousin).

5. If the Manlii took part in the *pompa* of Junia, it was, according to Koestermann (1963, 567), because of an adoption going back to the mid-second century B.C., known to Cicero, *Fin.* 1.24.

tant on the local level displayed reconstructed kinships (these went back only three or four generations, however). On the sarcophagus of P(ublius) Libuscidius Victorinus, "maternal uncle of Cl(audius) Fortunatus, maternal great-uncle of D(ecimus) Satrienus Cl(audius) Satrenianus, Roman knight," found at Canosa in Apulia and dated from the late third century A.D., the avuncular relation replaces genealogy: here it passes through men who are collaterals on the female side rather than agnatic ascendants (Chelotti et al. 1985, 84–86 n. 50). The double genealogy on the sarcophagus of the senator P(ublius) Paquius Scaeva and his wife Flavia (who lie side by side for all eternity on a double tomb), found and preserved at Vasto, is something of a rebus.[6] Given the placement of the epitaph on the internal walls of the sarcophagus, the two inscriptions, which were doubtless read and discussed by the couple during their lifetimes, then by their family and friends on the occasion of their funerals, were not destined for other readers, a rare fate for a funerary inscription. Scaeva and Flavia dictated rigorously symmetrical epitaphs. First they present themselves as first cousins; then they stress a pair of common great-grandparents rather than grandparents. Undoubtedly, they were cross-cousins: Scaeva's mother was already a Flavia. Each of them, speaking of him- or herself, enumerates three couples of parents, grandparents, and great-grandparents; each one, speaking of the other, recalls only the male ascendants, designating them by their cognomen alone as if they constituted an agnatic lineage. But their common great-grandfather cannot have been both a Paquius and a Flavius, and may not have been either, for in at least one lineage and perhaps in both there is one man (or several men) who is an ascendant by the female line. To date, the three family trees proposed (Torelli 1973, 350–351) provide several possible solutions to this puzzle, among which I do not propose to choose here. Scaeva and Flavia used symmetrical constructions, symmetrical lapidary formulas, and a play on homonyms (out of six couples, the names Flavia, Sinnia, and Consus each appear twice) to construct a handsome text, as if they wanted to keep the fragments of the family tree that united them and the various paths of their kinship before their eyes.

Certain members of the municipal elite sometimes used a second gentilicium that functioned as a unique cognomen; at other times they bore a

---

6. *CIL* 9:2845–2846 = 5244 = *ILS* 915 (at Historium [Vasto]): "P(ublius) Paquius, Scaeuae et Flauiae filius, Consi et Didiae nepos, Barbi et Dirutiae pronepos, Scaeua . . . [*cursus* here], consobrinus idemque uir Flauiae Consi filiae, Scapulae neptis, Barbi proneptis, simul cum ea conditus.

Flauia, Consi et Sinniae filia, Scapulae et Sinniae neptis, Barbi et Dirutiae proneptis, consobrina eademque uxor P(ublii) Paquii Scaeuae, filii Scaeuae, Consi nepotis, Barbi pronepotis, simul cum eo condita."

cognomen ending in -*anus* formed on the gentilicium, in order to credit a vertical alliance with a family that we know belonged to the same social milieu. The municipal registry of Canusium for the year 223 offers several examples of both formulas. Similarly, Minicius Acilianus, a young man from Brixia (Brescia) supported by Pliny, was the son of one Minicius and the nephew of someone named Acilius. Pliny is sensitive to the basic structure of the husband, the wife, and the wife's brother (defined by Claude Lévi-Strauss [1973] as "the atom of kinship"), to which he himself owed his fortune and his social promotion, since his maternal uncle had adopted him. Elsewhere Pliny suggests another promising structure (common in Roman society) that relied on the accumulated patrimonies, coupled with adoption or not, of a widowed mother and her second husband (Pliny, *Ep.* 1.14, 2.9, 2.13). The correspondence of Pliny, the first senator in his family, presents a quantity of friends (peers, superiors, and inferiors), a few colleagues, not many kin, and among the latter more kin by alliance than blood relatives, notably the noble and wealthy Pompeia Celerina, the mother of his late wife, with whom he kept up his former ties of adfinitas.

From alliance to lasting affinity. How indeed was it possible to assure the stability of the networks that were built up so carefully? The practice of early engagement provided the benefits of alliance before it was necessary to give anything (Treggiari 1984; Dixon 1985a). Without creating a strict obligation to marry, the Roman *sponsalia* established a tie between the two families, and the future son-in-law and father-in-law could already be called *gener* and *socer*. The union might never take place: for example, one of the engaged couple might die, one of the fathers might die, or the fathers might change their minds. Death and divorce also broke the chain of contracted matrimonial alliances. For the Roman jurist, the affinity tie was ruptured when the link was broken. But people avoided losing a prestigious alliance, which indicates that alliance was sought for itself. Men also attempted to establish ties through a divorced spouse. These are instances of merely individual behavior, however. How could one capitalize on alliances on the family level? In the first century B.C., when an Aemilius Lepidus gave his son in adoption to a Scipio, or when another Aemilius Lepidus (grandson of the first one), who had intentionally been named Paullus, married a Cornelia, they were recalling and repeating practices of exchange by marriage and adoption (stemma, p. 144) of the most prestigious branches (which had become extinct) of their two gentes: the Aemilii Paulli and the elder branch of the Cornelii Scipiones (the branch of the two "Africans") (Syme 1986). Not many families could maintain ties of affinity over two centuries in this manner.

Choosing a partner. As in many societies, in Rome the open marriage strategy and the closed one were not mutually exclusive.[7] They were often practiced simultaneously by a given family head in aid of his various children (also his children-in-law and even his nephews and nieces) and successively during his lifetime by an individual acting on his own volition or carrying out his father's desires. A family might also make use of various types of alliance, one after the other, at different stages of its rise to prominence. Individuals and family groups were thus familiar with the double game of close and distant marriage.[8] By marrying one of his daughters to a Scipio Nasica, her second cousin, did Scipio Africanus inaugurate the tradition of intermarriage between the various branches of the Cornelii that prosopographers have noted (Münzer 1920, 101–103)? By giving his other daughter in marriage to a Sempronius, he diversified his alliances. In the following generation, however, the union of his grand-daughter Sempronia with his nephew (by alliance) and grandson (by adoption), Scipio Aemilianus, played the role of a direct deferred exchange between Cornelii and Sempronii and ended a marriage cycle between Aemilii and Sempronii (stemma, p. 144).

Close marriage has inspired debate recently, and in my opinion, Brent Shaw and Richard Saller's approach (1984) in their criticism of Jack Goody's thesis (1983) is marred by not taking prosopography sufficiently into account (Corbier 1988, 196–197). In Roman society two forms of close marriage existed concurrently with distant marriage: marriage with consanguine kin and marriage into the kinship group by affinity.

The closest relative with whom custom authorized marriage during the two last centuries of the republic and in the early empire seems to have been the first cousin. Thus the timely decree of the senate in A.D. 49 authorizing the union of a niece and her paternal uncle did not lead Romans to adopt a form of marital relationship they considered incestuous. In any event, the perfectly legal but infrequent marriage of patrilateral parallel cousins had nothing in common with the preferential marriage known as arabian. The aim of isogamy, one of the characteristics of the latter type of union, does not seem to have interested the Roman elites. Some could use hypergamy as a means of social promotion and others hypogamy to garner a patrimony. Unions of patrilateral cousins can be found, however, in all strata of society above the middle level (as in the marriage of the centurion Spurius Ligustinus in the second century B.C. [Livy

---

7. "Exogamy enables them to diversify alliances and to gain certain advantages . . . while endogamy consolidates and perpetuates previously acquired advantages"; Lévi-Strauss 1983a, 135; 1983b, 1222 (trans. Neugroschel and Hoss).

8. I intend to develop these notions in a book in progress on alliance and kinship practices in Rome.

42.34] or the Roman epitaph dedicated by a gener to his patruus mentioned above) up to the senatorial aristocracy (as with the first marriage of Mark Antony) and the Julio-Claudian family (Drusus II and Livilla, Nero and Julia). This type of marriage in familia did not involve exchange strategies: though it facilitated the conservation of family patrimony, it did not enhance it. One could also marry a matrilateral parallel cousin or a cross-cousin, or even a cousin within the fifth degree (a first cousin once removed, the daughter of a consobrinus or consobrina) or sixth degree (a second cousin, or sobrina). All these combinations appear in the Julio-Claudian family.[9]

Marriages between cousins are difficult to spot using simple onomastic criteria: one consobrina out of four and one sobrina out of eight—female patrilateral cousins—bear the same name as *ego*. Only prosopographical studies that aim at reconstituting a family in its entirety (as far as the sources permit) can show clearly the matrimonial practices that have only recently interested historians of Rome.[10] (An excellent example of such a reconstitution is MacMullen 1988, fig. 15 following p. 76.) The genealogical trees that have been published, which concentrate on agnatic lineages, do not always list known daughters and their husbands, let alone their descendants, who supposedly appear on the stemmata of other familiae.[11] Thus a Servilia, wife of an Aemilius Lepidus, was her first cousin, as their mothers were sisters (the Juniae, the half-sisters of Brutus) (Hallett 1984, table 4).

Another form of marriage between close relatives—affines this time—was practiced among municipal families (like at Larinum) as well as in senatorial and imperial families: a married couple (or the surviving member of the couple) might decide to unite their children from previous marriages. It was even

9. See my study in "The House of the Caesars," in *Epouser au plus proche,* edited by P. Bonte (Paris: Editions de l'EHESS), in press.

10. Thomas 1981; Corbier 1982, 1988; Moreau 1983; Bresson 1986. Alain Bresson, Philippe Moreau, and I have works in progress on this topic.

11. Thus the stemma of the Calpurnii (*PIR²* C) omits the marriage of Calpurnia, the daughter of L(ucius) Calpurnius Piso, consul in 57, to L(ucius) Calpurnius Piso Galerianus (the son, natural or adoptive, of the Piso who conspired under Nero). Galerianus is presented by Tacitus (*Hist.* 4.49.4), however, as the "first cousin and son-in-law" of Calpurnia's father—a cousinship of uncertain degree, but one that invites us to eliminate the Calpurnii Pisones from the family trees used by Shaw and Saller (1984, 435) to demonstrate the absence of marriages "between cousins related within a legally recognized degree." The same might be said of the Aemilii Lepidi, of the Acilii Glabriones (mentioned above), and of the Annii Veri and the Aurelii (both of whom show the marriage between famous first cousins, Marcus Aurelius, an Annius adopted by an Aurelius, and Faustina). As for Shaw and Saller's last example, the Arrii Antonini, it may suggest a tradition of intermarriage between two families of Cirta, the Arrii and the Antonii, which quite possibly might have resulted on occasion in unions between close kin.

possible to draw up contracts for such future marriages. A couple might also
marry the son or the daughter of one spouse to the sister or the brother of the
other. Marriage was not the only means of creating kinship, however.

REMODELING THE FAMILY

Romans were not limited either to real ties founded in consanguinity and
affinity or to the order of the generations instituted by nature. Adoption allowed them a multitude of moves among which the most obvious one—giving
oneself a descendant—was the simplest. The freedom granted to the paterfamilias to remodel his agnatic descendants fascinated Roman jurists.

Adoption. In Rome, where men adopted other men (and rarely women),
adoption seems usually to have been aimed at transmitting a name, an inheritance, or a succession (quantities that anthropologists invite us to distinguish
carefully). Adoption, however, should not be perceived only in terms of the
continuity of the familia, including that of the familial cult, and the advantages
offered to the adoptee, who gained access to a patrimony and, eventually, a
rank that he otherwise could not have obtained. It was also a means by which
the paterfamilias could control a man, his wealth, and his descendants. In the
Julio-Claudian family several adoptions should be seen in this light.

Whom to adopt? One adopted non-kin, of course. But the most typical case
was the adoption of close relatives chosen either from among consanguines
(paternal or maternal) or affines (Corbier 1991). Maternal grandfathers and
uncles (or great-uncles) seem to have had a particular propensity for adoption.
Husbands often adopted a boy their wives brought from a former marriage.
Paternal grandfathers and uncles also adopted. Difficult to ascertain by
onomastics in that case, since the adoptee kept the same gentilicium, the
practice is attested by both juridical and literary texts. Augustus made an
agnate (his grandson) of a close affine, Germanicus (his wife's grandson), who
was also a more distant cognate (Augustus's sister's great-grandson) when he
obliged his own adoptive son, Tiberius, to adopt him.

Adoptees and their kinship group. The adoptee could appropriate the ancestors
of both lineages, the natural and the adoptive. He might find himself with
sisters on both sides who were forbidden as spouses, but who brought as many
potential brothers-in-law. Even then, an adoptive sister remained a possible
spouse if her father emancipated her or transferred her to another gens. This
meant that a pater could envision the marriage of his blood daughter and his
adoptive son. The adoptee rarely had an agnatic brother, as adoption usually
occurred in the absence of male offspring (Germanicus and Nero did, however).
The adoptee could nonetheless maintain close ties with his natural family:
Scipio Aemilianus is always presented as exemplary in this respect.

Marriage and adoption: complementary strategies. By combining the effects of adoption and marriage, Augustus, who had only a daughter, gave himself offspring of his blood who bore his name. Better still, his descendants also descended from his wife, Livia, with whom he had no children.[12] No head of family, prince or peasant, of the medieval or the modern age could have dreamed of creating a similar construction, for it was indeed a deliberate construction, carried out after mature reflection and in view of the transmission of power.

The concentration of family ties. When adoption of close kin was combined with close marriage (between either consanguines and affines), the result was to multiply an individual's potential interactions with kin (by blood, adoption, and alliance). It was precisely the accumulation of kinship ties closing the family in within itself (of which the Julio-Claudian family was the most complete model) that Augustine criticized at length in the *City of God* (15.16; see Corbier 1987, 1274). He states, among other things, that "the aim was that one man should not combine many relationships in his one self, but that those connections should be separated and spread among individuals, and that in this way they should help to bind social life more effectively by involving in their plurality a plurality of persons" (trans. Bettenson, Penguin 1972, 623). This reconfirms the importance that Augustine, faithful in this to Roman tradition, accorded to the enlargement of kinship.

Propinqui, adfines, amici. Romans were fond of recalling that a relative by alliance was first a relative by blood. They were also fond of using marriage to assemble their various offspring by previous marriages or adoptions, and they soon found ingenious ways to capitalize, on the simple level of nomenclature, on their entire kinship group—maternal kin and paternal kin by nature alike. But one could not capitalize on alliances forever: the old ones wanted renewal, and new ones were needed, for newcomers had their place in this game.

Roman society invented and developed multiple ties, which created reciprocal obligations. The ties recognized as the strongest seem to have been kinship and friendship (*amici cognatique, propinqui atque amici*). From friendship to alliance, and inversely, from alliance to friendship, was but a step. Anyone who wanted to become Cato's friend (Pompey), or reinforce his friendship with him (Hortensius), or prove his loyalty to Cato's memory (Brutus) apparently could find no better way to do so than to marry Cato (through a niece, his wife, or his daughter).[13] Such anecdotes remind us that the Romans paid continual

---

12. See Corbier, "House of the Caesars."
13. This recalls the famous declaration of the duc de Saint-Simon to the duc de Beauvilliers,

and careful attention to the creation of kinship ties. They did so partly with the aid of women through matrimonial alliance, which offered the possibility of replaying the game, thanks to remarriage (either when destiny intervened, with widowhood, or when the marriage was deliberately terminated, with divorce), and partly directly by giving themselves sons and heirs through adoption. By altering genealogical positions, they could also remodel their kinship group: they could give grandchildren the status of sons, transform collaterals into descendants, and so forth. By weaving a blood tie between non-kin, they created *consanguinitas* from the agnatic relationship. They could also construct their familia in direct line of descent with kin through women, born in other families. For someone who had no son of his own, this was perhaps the ideal formula. All of these were freedoms that the Church took away from their descendants in Europe and that modern states have not reinstated.

Translated by Lydia G. Cochrane

Alliance and Adoption: The Cornelii and the Aemilii Paulli
in the Third and Second Centuries B.C.

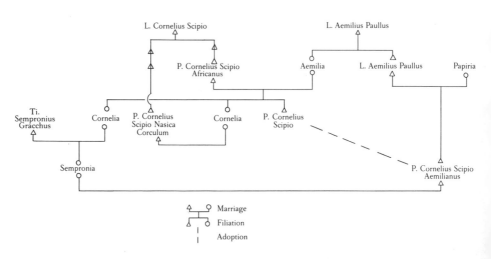

---

the hand of whose daughter he had come to request in marriage: "Fortune was not the attraction for me, nor even his daughter, whom I had never seen; it was rather himself and Mme de Beauvilliers whom I loved and wished to marry" (1953–1958; trans. Norton 1967, 1:160).

THE MEDIEVAL FULCRUM

JULIUS KIRSHNER

Introduction to Part Two

Caveat viator. Regional and linguistic diversity, a myriad of local customs, and a superabundance of manuscripts and archival documents produced from the thirteenth century on, the bulk of which remains to be critically edited, make generalizations about medieval Italian families hazardous. Establishing the genealogy of even a single family, let alone its history, can be a daunting task when, as commonly happened, a member of the family was known by several names, the spelling of names was inconsistent, and the same names were shared by contemporary and succeeding members of a family or by persons who were not related—all can readily lead the neophyte researcher to commit serious errors. These problems are compounded when we deal with families without surnames or with only toponymic surnames—namely, the overwhelming majority of families, typically located on the lower rungs of society. Moreover, when scribes drafted documents they often omitted the relationship, by blood or law, between seller and buyer, lender and borrower, guarantor and principal debtor, testator and beneficiary, and so on. A contract of sale cited as evidence for an economic market composed of autonomous agents acting voluntarily may turn out to be evidence for an intrafamily property readjustment required by law; a legacy to an ecclesiastic cited as an exemplary expression of religiosity may in fact be a gift to a relative.

The five chapters in this section affirm that a critical understanding of supralocal values and standards of conduct emanating from Christian doctrines and Roman and canon law is necessary for a nuanced analysis of local practice. These standards defined the purpose of the family, prescribed the rituals and procedures for the formation of new families, marked out the roles of their members, and provided the mechanisms both for the transfer of persons, symbolic capital, and property between different families and for the devolution of patrimonial fortunes. Jane Fair Bestor reviews the legacy of ideas from the classical world about man's and woman's roles in procreation and analyzes how these ideas were selected, elaborated, and related to wider thinking about kinship by medieval Christians. Michael Sheehan describes the militant campaign waged by the Church in the early Middle Ages to regulate sexual behavior and to establish virginity and chastity as preeminent virtues. The model Christian marriage was monogamous and indissoluble; it existed primarily for procreation and the rearing of offspring, and secondarily for the avoidance of fornication through the legitimate satisfaction of sexual desire. In addition, divorce, contraception, abortion, homosexual relations, and heterosexual sex for pleasure—acts that violated the reproductionist view of human sexuality— were classified as illicit and duly condemned and suppressed. Notwithstanding such medieval secular works as Boccaccio's *Decameron,* which furnish pleasurable and subversive depictions of a society in thrall to fornication and adultery, and a spate of recent monographs on the sexual exploits and imagination of medieval Italians (for example, Watson 1979; Lemay 1981; Ruggiero 1985; Rocke 1987), the persistence and operability of sexual regulations from the Middle Ages until quite recently is remarkable testimony of the enduring authority of the Roman Catholic Church and the willingness of secular courts to prosecute sexual offenses to staunch public scandal. Largely owing to the massive political action of thousands of women and the support of left-wing political parties, which overcame opposition from the Church, civil divorce and abortion were finally legalized in Italy in the 1970s.

Advocating a single standard of sexual behavior, medieval churchmen denounced an adulterous husband as vigorously as they did an adulterous wife and looked askance at a husband who married the woman whom he had bedded after the death of his first wife. The available evidence, admittedly sparse, suggests that secular courts were intent on punishing husbands found guilty of adultery. Just as an adulterous wife forfeited her dotal rights, an adulterous husband lost control over his wife's dowry and other goods. Yet thanks to the juridical principles, first formulated in Augustus's law on adultery of 18 B.C., the double standard reared its ugly head: the husband and father of an adulterous woman were authorized to kill (*jus occidendi*) her and her paramour with impunity, because they had dishonored both the father's and the husband's family. Eva Cantarella provides an insightful discussion of Augustus's law and the juristic interpretations it occasioned from the Middle Ages until 1981, when Italian legislators, after almost two thousand years, eliminated the jus occidendi from Italy's penal code. Although medieval Italian and Renaissance writers idealized adultery as an essential ingredient of love and portrayed women as essentially inconstant and sexually voracious creatures easily led into illicit liaisons, it is difficult to confirm whether adultery was as widespread as many historians believe. It is equally difficult to determine to what extent the comparative rarity of litigation involving adultery in the Middle Ages, as noted by legal historians, was due to the moral imperative that dishonored husbands from the upper reaches of society should not seek relief from a judge but should take matters into their own hands; to the fear of wives to commit adultery in face of the terrible consequences; or to the notorious unreliability of statistics culled from medieval judicial sources.

Florence in the late Middle Ages is the scene for Christiane Klapisch-Zuber's chapter on kinship and my own on marital property. Klapisch-Zuber shows how the communal government of Florence exploited Roman and canon law as a weapon to restore public order by breaking up lineage-based solidarity groups held responsible for the violent tenor of civic life. My chapter illustrates how the manipulation of Roman legal principles increased a Florentine husband's control over his wife's property. These legal innovations had lasting effects on Florence's political and social life. The refiguration of kinship groups allowed nascent public power to mature, helping set the stage for the Renaissance territorial state. Meanwhile, the men of the ruling class were legally fully entitled to use their wives' assets to maintain and enhance their families' status. Although neither chapter claims that the legal innovations in Florence, and their alleged causes, implications, and consequences, were entirely representative of what transpired in other communes of northern Italy, both do suggest that the Florentine case exemplifies general trends and can serve as a reference point for future comparative research.

Chapter 8

JANE FAIR BESTOR

Ideas about Procreation and Their Influence on Ancient and Medieval Views of Kinship

The subject of procreation greatly interested medieval writers, who discussed it in works on medicine, philosophy, theology, politics, and family life. Dante gives an account of procreation in *Purgatorio* 25 to explain the relation of the soul to the body and its faculties. In the *Defensor Pacis,* Marsilius of Padua compares the action of the human mind in forming the state to the processes of animal reproduction as described by Aristotle and Galen (1980, 63). Donald Weinstein notes that "the image of Florence as a woman in childbirth" was deeply rooted in myths about the city (1968, 16). From Dante to Leonardo Bruni, accounts of the origin of Florence reveal a structure of beliefs about procreation and filiation that dates back to classical antiquity.

Historians have examined medieval medical, philosophical, and religious ideas about procreation (for example, Hewson 1975; Lemay 1981; Needham 1959; Thomasset 1981) and their influence on such areas as the construction of gender roles (Bullough 1973; Maclean 1980) and the symbolism of devotional traditions (see especially Bynum 1982). A subject that remains to be considered is the role of theories of procreation in shaping attitudes toward familial relationships. This issue has been obscured by the concept of filiation, which historians have borrowed from Jack Goody's influential formulation of the

This chapter is dedicated to Nancy Helmbold, whose enthusiasm for classical studies has greatly enriched my studies. I thank Steven Epstein for encouraging my research on Jacobus de Varagine and Carol Delaney for several spirited discussions that helped me to clarify the issues in this chapter. I would also like to thank Cristelle L. Baskins, Lorraine Daston, John O'Malley, and the members of the conference for their helpful comments.

distinction between descent and filiation, or kinship (see Goody 1983, 222–225; Dixon 1985a, 354; Chojnacki 1985, 241–242; Herlihy 1985, 83). Filiation "denotes the relationship created by the fact of being the legitimate child of one's parents. . . . As a relationship in the internal domestic domain it denotes the specific moral and affective ties and cleavages between successive generations . . . that arise from the facts of begetting, bearing, and above all, exercising responsibility in rearing a child" (Fortes 1959, 206). Meyer Fortes's influential definition grounds kinship in biology. But anthropologists increasingly stress that the so-called facts of begetting and bearing are culturally constituted, and that the relationships established by these symbolically interpreted processes are "essentially connected," although not identical, to the domain of socially recognized kinship roles (Barnes 1964, 298).

The gendered character of Western theories of procreation raises the issue of what each parent supplies to the formation and growth of the child and the cultural meaning of their respective contributions (Weiner 1976, 17). Carol Delaney notes that the terms *paternity* and *maternity* are not semantic equivalents and states that in the West, "traditionally, even the physiological contribution to the child was coded differently for men and women, and therefore their connexion to the child was imagined as different. Maternity has meant giving nurture and giving birth. Paternity has meant begetting. Paternity has meant the primary, essential and creative role" (Delaney 1986, 495). But although this construction of procreative roles was very influential, it did not exhaust ways of thinking about parental contributions to the makeup of the child. Several theories of procreation coexisted in antiquity and were transmitted to Europe in the Middle Ages. They differed on two key issues implicated in ideas about parent-child relations: the contribution of each parent to the child and the transmission of inherited characteristics. This diversity of views concerning procreation does not allow scholars to assume that medieval family and kinship institutions reflected a single, consistently held view of parental roles in procreation.

In this chapter I briefly review several ancient theories of procreation and argue that Roman kinship symbols and rituals were congruent with cosmological speculation that attributed a generative role in procreation to the father and a nutritive role to the mother. I then show that early encyclopedias transmitted two competing models of procreative roles from antiquity. In discussions of heredity, medieval writers often ascribed a formative role in conception to the mother as well as to the father. But they usually defined parental roles in terms of a theory of procreation that emphasized the formative role of the father. I demonstrate that theologians and philosophers such as Thomas Aquinas and Jacobus de Varagine made this theory of procreation central to their account of the structure of emotional bonds within the family. Finally, I suggest that this theory also played a role in constructions of civic identity in medieval Italy.

THE CLASSICAL HERITAGE

Medieval Christian beliefs about procreation drew heavily on the legacy of ancient Greek and Roman authors, who frequently theorized about reproduction in their speculations concerning the nature of the cosmos. A striking feature of this legacy was the disagreement over the female contribution to conception. Greek and Roman theorists were convinced that the seed of the father contained a generative principle, but they were much less certain whether the mother also played a formative role (see Censorinus, *De die natali* 5).

Aristotle's views were widely influential both in antiquity and during the Muslim and Christian Middle Ages. Aristotle assumed that there can be only one active principle of creation—"there must be that which generates, and that out of which it generates"—and he assigned the active role in generation to the father (*Gen. An.* 1.729a). The male contributes seed, which provides the form or principle of movement that constitutes and sets the parts of the fetus, whereas the female supplies menstrual blood, which provides the undifferentiated matter of body.

Aristotle associated this asymmetrical view of procreative roles with a theory of bodily humors that ascribed the superior qualities of heat and dryness to the male and those of cold and moisture to the female. Although semen and menstrual blood are both residues of the blood that nourishes the body, the semen is concocted to a high degree by the natural heat of the male, whereas the menstrual blood remains less refined due to the naturally cold female constitution (*Gen. An.* 1.728a). Unless the semen is too weak to effect the formative action according to type, its movements gain mastery over the menstrual blood, thereby actualizing the attributes of the father or of the paternal ancestors. Otherwise its movements turn into their opposite and the fetus becomes a female, if the determination of sex is at issue, or inherits other attributes of the mother or of a more distant female ancestor (*Gen. An.* 4.767a–768b).

In contrast to Aristotle, the later Greek physician Galen believed that females as well as males contribute a seed in conception. To explain the transmission of inherited characteristics he relied on the principle of predominance, according to which the seed of higher quality with regard to a particular trait prevails in determining that trait (Blayney 1986, 234–236). But like Aristotle,

Galen also assumed that the maternal seed was colder and hence weaker and less perfect than that of the male. Accordingly, he described its main role as providing the male seed with nourishment in the initial stages of growth (Blayney 1986, 234), a view that conflicts with his account of the transmission of inherited characteristics.

Democritus and his follower Epicurus gave more scope to the female contribution in conception. Democritus thought that both male and female seeds were composed of small atoms derived from every part of the body; thus "each seed contained within it a complete set of those parts necessary for the development of the child" (Blayney 1986, 232). Through Epicurus, Democritus's theory of pangenesis influenced the Roman poet Lucretius (Blayney 1986, 231), who acknowledged his debt to Greek thinkers in the *De rerum natura* (*Rer. nat.* 1.136–139). This work in turn appears to have influenced the medieval encyclopedist Isidore of Seville. Lucretius (c.99–c.54 B.C.) states that a child always is created from the union of a paternal and a maternal seed. It resembles that parent, irrespective of sex, from whom it inherits more substance (*Rer. nat.* 4.1209–1217, 1227–1233). This substance may also transmit the traits of paternal or maternal ancestors (*Rer. nat.* 4.1227–1233).

Lucretius also uses the metaphor of love sowing the womanly fields to describe intercourse (*Rer. nat.* 4.1107). In its emphasis on the male as the active agent and the source of seed in procreation, this agricultural image recalls the views of Lucretius's older contemporary Varro (116–27 B.C.). To explain a Roman wedding rite involving the use of fire and water, Varro states that fire and water are the conditions of procreation. He associates Sky with heat, life, and semen, and Earth with coldness and female moisture (*L. L.* 5.55–59). Like Aristotle, he posits the male as the generative, life-giving principle and the female as the source of the material of the embryo. According to Augustine, Varro also defines the male as that which produces seed and the female as that which receives and nourishes it (*De civ. D.* 7.23). Varro posits these actions of giving and receiving as a more basic opposition between acting and suffering, to which he assigns cosmic dimensions: "he [Varro] says that the heaven is that which does, and the earth that which suffers, and therefore attributes the masculine principle to the one, and the feminine to the other" (*De civ. D.* 7.28).

In the *City of God,* Augustine lists the many gods thought by the Romans to participate in the conception and birth of the fetus (*De civ. D.* 7.3). They include Liber and Libera, or Ceres, the two gods responsible for "liberating" the male and female respectively by the emission of their seed. But Augustine indicates that although both sexes were commonly thought to contribute seed in procreation, Liber had conceptual and ritual primacy (*De civ. D.* 7.16, 21).

Varro's assumptions concerning procreative roles are congruent with the

Roman ritual of the *lectus genialis*. Paulus defines the lectus genialis as the bed "which is prepared during the nuptials in honor of the Genius, from whom it derives its name" (Festus 1975,70). Arnobius mentions the custom that "when you marry, you make little beds with a toga and you invoke the Genius of your husbands" (*Adv. Gent.* 2.67). According to Servius, the beds are "properly geniales that are prepared for young married people; they are so called from the bringing to the world of children, *a generandis liberis*" (Servius, *Aen.* 6.603, quoted in Dumézil 1970, 1:359). The texts by Paulus and Arnobius appear to be based on authentic rites honoring the Genius (Dumézil 1970, 1:359).

The interpretation of the Genius is relevant to understanding Roman views of procreation. Classical scholars once believed that in archaic times it signified the male procreative power, but Georges Dumézil rejects this theory. Instead he interprets the Genius as the "deified personality of the individual" (1970, 1:360), that is, of the male, since "the idea of a feminine Genius is strange" (1970, 1:44). Dumézil asserts that "it is not from the sexual point of view but from that of the *gens* that we are to understand the consecration of the nuptial bed to the Genius of the actual representative of the series" (1970, 1:360). But this argument presupposes that the male is the "agent of propagation" (1970,1:360), a belief that Dumézil assumes to be inscribed in nature.

To support his interpretation of the Genius, Dumézil cites Censorinus's description of it as a kind of individual tutelary deity (*De die natali* 3.1). But Censorinus also observes that the Genius, "whether because it sees that we are generated, whether because it is born with us, whether because it takes care of us once we are engendered and defends us, is called Genius from 'to be generated'" (*De die natali* 3.1). The common equation between blood and semen (see below), between the substance that sustains life and that which generates new life, suggests that the rite was aimed at ensuring that the plenitude of life in the husband, personified in his Genius, would be sufficiently great to engender offspring, especially offspring endowed with the same paternal *virtus*. It would have been a relatively easy step from the view of Genius as the personification of individual life force to that of Genius as the actual agent of procreation (Festus 1975, 70). By the Augustan era, Genius as the male power of procreation was paired complementarily with Juno in the form of Lucina, protectress of women in pregnancy and childbirth (Dumézil 1970, 1:293–294).

Gens and *familia* were closely linked concepts among the Romans. Richard Saller notes that in Roman literature the familia was construed more or less inclusively, sometimes taken as equivalent to gens and at other times more narrowly (Saller 1984,341; see also Isidore of Seville, *Diff. verb.* 1, *PL* 83, col. 38). Ulpian gives as one definition of the familia "those persons who proceed from the blood of the same ultimate ancestor (as we say the Familia Julia) as though from the fount of a certain memory. A woman is the beginning and end of her familia" (*Dig.* 50.16.195.1–4, quoted in Saller 1984, 338). The exclusion of the descendants of women from the familia indicates that the term in this sense signified not a bilateral descending kindred but an agnatic group. Literary usage was consistent with this definition (Saller 1984, 341). How are we to interpret this emphasis on blood transmitted from the apical ancestor as the primary symbol of agnatic unity?

Isidore of Seville (A.D. c.560–636) provides a clue to the privileged association of agnates with blood. In an exhaustive discussion of agnates and cognates taken primarily from Roman legal sources, he defines the term *consanguine,* or close agnate,[1] as follows: "consanguines are called thus because they were generated from one blood, that is, from the single seed of the father. For the semen of the man is a froth of blood like water poured onto rocks, which makes a pure foam, or like red wine, which stirred in a chalice, yields a white foam" (*Etym.* 9.6.4; see Gregorius Magnus in *Ezech.* 2,8 for a similar description of the paternal seed as a froth of blood, quoted in Reydellet 1984, 202 n. 326). The maximally concocted blood of which the semen is composed is the life-engendering and identity-transmitting substance par excellence.

Cicero's definition of *pietas* as "that which warns us to keep our obligations to our country or our parents or to others connected to us by blood" (*De Inv.* 2.22.66) confirms other classical sources that suggest that blood was central to the rhetoric of kinship in ancient Rome and symbolized the bonds to both paternal and maternal kin. The term *propinquus,* standing for closeness by blood, was commonly used in reference to both sets of kin. The spatial image of ego at the center of a kinship cluster structured by the proximity of blood ties thus coexisted with a linear model, that enshrined in the gens and familia, of agnatic bonds stretching back in time to a founding ancestor and forward in perpetuity. But blood was especially associated with the transmission of identity through males. This polysemicity was linked to a theory of procreation that ascribed asymmetrical meanings to paternity and maternity. The association of males with heat and accordingly with more highly concocted seed grounded a view of semen as the active, life-giving principle in conception.

ISIDORE OF SEVILLE AND THE
MEDIEVAL ENCYCLOPEDIC TRADITION

In the Middle Ages, encyclopedias popularized learned theories of procreation and concepts of family. This tradition is notable for its emphasis on

---

1. According to the Roman jurist Gaius, whose definition in the *Institutiones* 3.10 was probably the basis for Isidore's remark, "brothers born from the same father are agnates to each other and are also called consanguines, even if they did not have the same mother" (Zulueta 1946, pt. 1, 155). But Ulpian makes consanguines a distinct category between heirs and close agnates (Zulueta 1953, pt. 2, 123).

reproduction in the definition of parental roles. Particularly influential was Isidore of Seville's *Etymologiae l* (written circa 622–633), which remained a basic work of reference throughout western Europe from the seventh century to the Renaissance (Leyser 1970, 130; Sarton 1927, 1:471). Isidore assumes a perfect fit between words and the things they represent, and in book 9 he presents an exhaustive treatment of kinship relations primarily from an etymological perspective. His major sources were the *Digest,* in particular the *Institutes* of Gaius, and the works of Roman historians and grammarians, especially Servius (see Reydellet 1984, 1–29). In keeping with the importance Isidore attached to Roman civilization as a model of political and social organization for successor states, he depicts the family as "the Roman gens, presented as an ideal and universal type" (Reydellet 1984, 11).

Isidore posits an integral connection between gens signifying a people or nation and gens as kinship group (or extended familia). The first is an extension of the other produced through successive acts of generation: "The gens is a multitude arising from one source or separated from another nation according to its own gathering, as the people of Greece, of Asia. . . . The gens is called thus on account of the generation of families [the familia] that is, from to be procreated (*a gignendo*), just as nation (*natio*) comes from to be born (*a nascendo*)" (*Etym.* 9.2.1). In book 9 Isidore describes the familial structure productive of this social dispersion and explicates the principles of procreation that generate both family and nation. The source of the gens and familia is the father (*pater*), "he from whom arises the beginning of the family (*genus*); and thus he is called the *paterfamilias.* He is also called father because *patratione* having been completed, he procreates a child. For *patratio* is the consummation of the sexual act. . . . That which fertilizes (*crementum*) is the seed of the male, whence the bodies of animals and men are conceived."[2] But "*mater* is said because from her something may be made. For the mother is, as it were, matter, because the cause is the father" (*Etym.* 9.5.3).

In the *De differentiis verborum,* Isidore follows classical Roman usage in defining *genitor* as "a word of nature or of origin, for *pater* is a name of dignity and honor" (*Diff. verb.* 1, *PL* 83, col. 38). In book 9 of the *Etymologiae,* his association of *pater* with the reproductive function is consistent with earlier patristic usage, which grouped all agents of creation under this term. This usage and Isidore's elevation of the gens in the sense of nation to a primordial social unit

---

2. The verb *patrare* first meant "to act like a father" and then signified "bring to completion" and "achieve one's wishes" (and satirically, "to reach orgasm") (Hallett 1984, 27–28). In the Middle Ages, it sometimes signified "to procreate" (see Du Cange 1938, 213). The existence of a complex of words in Latin deriving from *pater* reveals the Romans' high valuation of fatherhood (Hallett 1984, 27).

are also consistent with the Vulgate translation of the Book of Genesis, in which the terms *pater, semen,* and *gens* are closely linked (see Reydellet 1984, 16–17, on Isidore's innovative use of the term *gens*). Abraham is appointed to be the father (pater) of many peoples (gentium) through the dissemination of his seed (seminis), also a metonym for his descendants.

Isidore's account in book 9 of parental roles may have been influenced by the strong bias toward the father in Roman law (Reydellet 1984, 188 n. 298), but it also accords with his plan of human social organization based on the biblical tradition and classical literary sources. In book 11 of the *Etymologiae,* which deals with man as a physical being, Isidore conceptualizes the pro-creative role of each parent differently (see also Reydellet 1984, 188). Recalling Lucretius in the *De rerum natura,* Isidore writes, "People say that children are born similar to their fathers if the paternal seed is stronger, and likewise to the mother if the maternal seed is stronger . . . those who resemble both are conceived from a mix of maternal and paternal seed equally. . . . From the paternal seed girls are born and from the maternal seed boys, because every offspring consists of a double seed, of which the greater part when it prevails determines the similarity of sex" (*Etym.* 11.1.145–146).

Isidore's definitions of parental roles in book 9 were frequently repeated in later works. They are found verbatim along with his conflicting explanation of heredity in another influential work, the *De universo libri XXII,* completed around 844 by the Carolingian educator Hrabanus Maurus (*PL* 111, col. 174 on heredity, cols. 185–186 on parental roles). The definitions of kinship roles, including pater and mater, are found in the *Lexicon* (c. 1050) of the eleventh-century grammarian Papias, who probably hailed from Pavia (Papias 1496). This work was composed for the instruction of youths in the liberal arts and was widely diffused in Italy and Germany through the Renaissance.

Later encyclopedists continued to rely on Isidore while incorporating new developments in medicine and philosophy. Isidore's influence appears, for example, in the English Franciscan Bartholomaeus Anglicus's encyclopedic work *De proprietatibus rerum,* written in the 1240s and translated into Middle English by John of Trevisa at the end of the fourteenth century. But Bar-tholomaeus's discussion of parental roles has been thoroughly Aristotelianized. Citing Aristotle, he writes that due to the male attributes of heat and dryness and the female attributes of coldness and wetness, "in the male [are] the virtues formal and of shaping and working, and in the female material, suffering, and passive" (Seymour 1975, 306). Consistent with these assumptions, the father is "head and well of begetting and engendering." He procreates children like himself in nature and shape, especially if the virtue of his seed exceeds that of the mother (Seymour 1975, 309). In contrast, the mother is called by the Latin term *mater* because she feeds the child with menstrual blood in her womb and later breast feeds the child with milk made from her blood (Seymour 1975, 302–303).

Like Isidore, Bartholomaeus explains the hereditary transmission of attributes from the perspective of the child differently from parental roles in procreation. The child is made of seminal matter that comes from all parts of the mother and father, although the mother's blood is cold and that of the father hot. If the virtue in the father's seed has mastery, then the child resembles the father; likewise with respect to the mother. But if the virtue is equally strong in both, then the child resembles both parents (Seymour 1975, 299).

In book 8 of his *Speculum doctrinale,* which concerns social organization and is modeled partly on book 9 of Isidore's *Etymologiae,* the Dominican scholar Vincent of Beauvais (c. 1190–1264) repeats Isidore's definitions of kinship terms almost verbatim. In this work, and especially in the *Speculum naturale,* Vincent also discusses theories of human procreation, excerpting the major authorities from Aristotle and Galen to Avicenna and William of Conches. He favors the view of Hippocrates and Galen that women contribute a seed in conception. But he asserts that the female seed is so little concocted in comparison to that of the male that philosophers assimilated it to the menstrual blood. He relies heavily on the authority of Ibn Sina (980–1037), who reconciled Galen's ascription of an active role to the female seed, however auxiliary, with Aristotle's belief in a single generating agent, the male. Vincent cites the *Canon* for the view that "there are two principles of generation of the human body: one, the sperm of the man, which holds the place of the maker; the other the sperm of the woman and the menstrual blood which hold the place of the matter" (*Sp. doc.* 14.27).

To sum up this brief survey, early encyclopedias indicate that in the Middle Ages a view of parental roles was widely disseminated in which the father was equated with the cause, or form, and the mother with the matter of the fetus. Isidore's perspective is consistent with that of Aristotle and his medieval followers, for whom every existing subject or substance is constituted by the union of form and matter. Form is the part of substance that endows matter, which exists only potentially, with actuality and hence individuality (see Bobik 1965, 49–80). Thus the informing agent plays a causal and generative role, and form constitutes the greater or superior part of substance, although matter is also an integral component. According to the Aristotelian Giles of Rome (c. 1243–1316), "because a carnal son has matter from his mother and form from his father, he is said to have his whole substance from his mother and father," but "because form is more in substance than matter, a son has more substance from his father than from his mother" (*De humani corporis formatione,* 25).

In this schema, which can be traced right through the Renaissance, the fathers are "the masters who have to fabricate the human image" (Alberti 1946, 172). But the encyclopedic tradition also shows that explanations of the hereditary makeup of children often took a more dynamic view of the mother's role in conception and ascribed an active role to her in the transmission of attributes. Philosophical, theological, and medical theories of procreation did not always coincide. Like their counterparts in antiquity, the majority of medical doctors in the Middle Ages adopted some version of the two-seed theory of conception, although they typically tried to reconcile their position with that ascribing a generative role solely to the father by assigning only a facilitating role to the female seed in conception. Moreover, preachers who invoked the stereotypic meanings of paternity and maternity derived from Aristotelian assumptions also described children as generated from the seed of both parents and therefore as proceeding from several lines of descent (for example, de Varagine's second sermon for the first Saturday of Lent in *Sermones Quadragesimales,* 1497, cc7 verso).

A profound inconsistency appears to have characterized medieval European views of procreation, an inconsistency that was sustained by the different contextual applications of each viewpoint. But the dominant framework for thinking about procreation among theologians and philosophers was the theory associated with Aristotle that ascribed creative agency to only one source, the male (Bullough 1973, 490; Thomasset 1981, 12). This theory was consistent with Christian cosmology, which transmitted pagan as well as biblical constructs of paternity and maternity to medieval Europe. Christianity uses procreative symbolism to define key relationships, both divine and human. Not only is Christ figured as the Son of God, "begotten not made" in the formula adopted by the Council of Nicaea, but also the themes of generation and filiation are repeated at a lower level in the spiritual hierarchy, that between the apostles and Christ's people (Grant 1969, 281). In the New Testament, Paul represents himself as a father procreating offspring by preaching the gospel (1 Corinthians 4:15). He also compares himself to a mother, who experiences the pains of giving birth until Christ is formed in his followers (Galatians 3:19) and who nourishes them with milk (1 Corinthians 3:1–2). Also in the New Testament, the word of God is symbolically equated with the creative seed (Luke 8:11).

Allegorical treatments of procreation that emphasize the creative nature of paternity and the nurturing role of mothers form a pervasive theme in medieval theological treatises, sermons, and devotional works (for a rich example, see Hrabanus Maurus, *De universo,* book 6). These works constituted a powerful force in shaping the attitudes concerning procreation not only of churchmen, but also of the laity to whom they ministered. The birth of Christ was used as a model for describing the births of kings and high ecclesiastical figures (see, for example, Lewis 1981, 67, on the birth of Philip Augustus (1165); Leyser 1968, 27, on Willigis, archbishop of Mainz from 975 to 1011). The Carolingian theologian Hincmar of Rheims (c. 805–882) describes the Catholic Church symbolically as a woman who receives and preaches the "leavening," or doctrine, of the Trinity and who thereby "ferments," or gives birth to the world (*Explanatio in ferculum Salomonis, PL* 125, col. 819). Bread making and cheese making as symbols of procreation occur in both secular and theological works and illustrate the commonality of lay and ecclesiastical perspectives. Although beginning in the twelfth century spiritual traditions celebrated the maternal contributions of flesh and milk to the infant and the very old association of women with nurturing and affection, they did not redefine maternal attributes but used them to expand the qualities associated with fatherhood (see Bynum 1982, 122).[3]

SYMBOLS OF KINSHIP IN MEDIEVAL ITALY

Medieval Italian kinship symbolism correlates with Giles of Rome's view that children are generated from the substance of both parents, but that of their father more than of their mother. As in Roman antiquity, blood held special significance as a symbol of kinship through males. In common Lombard usage, for example, the term *domus* referred to all those descended from the same blood (*Vocabularius iuris utriusque,* s.v. "domus"),[4] which in this context signified first and foremost all the descendants through males of a common ancestor, including not just agnates in the Roman sense but also bastards. But consonant with the maternal contribution of substance and the importance of the bilateral kindred, or *parentela,* in many aspects of life (see, for example, Herlihy 1985; Chojnacki 1985; Klapisch-Zuber this volume), blood symbolized kin relatedness on both sides. It was associated with the transmission of moral as well as physical attributes. Medieval Italians sometimes conceptualized the fellow feeling instilled by shared blood as a physical-moral force in almost a magical way: "our blood cannot help but feel the passion of its related blood, whether secret

---

3. This symbolism eventually had political as well as religious applications. The anthem "My heart is Inditing," used in the coronations of James II and George II of England and their consorts, incorporated Isaiah 49:23, rendered in the King James Version as "Kings shall be thy nursing fathers and queens thy nursing mothers."

4. This work was a handbook for students of law written around 1452. It is attributed to one Jodocus and was probably of German origin. I am grateful to Charles Donahue for this information.

or manifest" (Bernardi 1895, 2:150, quoted in Tamassia 1910, 118). Although theologians cited the opinion of doctors that "sperm is the most pure blood" to explain the etymology of the term *consanguinity* (Antoninus, *S.T.* 3.1.14 [1487 ed.]; see Thomasset 1981, 8), in the Middle Ages consanguinity signified the bond of those descended from the same trunk, whether through males or females. The term *consanguine* itself, relatively uncommon in classical Rome, became almost a synonym for *cousin* during the Middle Ages (Epstein 1984, 118).

Blood was also believed to be the source of milk, the greatest symbol of maternal nurture. Like blood, milk was also thought to transmit a mother's physical and moral characteristics to her infants (see, for example, Alberti 1946, 50). But milk was not a symbol of enduring kinship bonds, nor, in contrast to Islamic beliefs based on the same assumptions about blood, did the sharing of milk in itself create a kinship tie.[5]

THE ROLE OF PROCREATION IN THEOLOGICAL WRITINGS ABOUT THE FAMILY

In the thirteenth century, the rediscovery of Aristotle's scientific works introduced a new naturalistic tone into theological works and sermons (see Smalley 1952, 308–323). As part of this development, Christian philosophers and theologians began to introduce Aristotle's theory of procreation into their writings about affective bonds and moral obligations within the family. Albertus Magnus (c. 1200–1280) illustrates this trend in his commentary on the *Nicomachean Ethics*. There he discourses on the properties of male semen as described by Aristotle to explain the nature of love between father and child. Albertus's student Thomas Aquinas (1224/1225–1274) integrated Aristotle's theory of procreation, as well as his remarks on familial love in the *Nicomachean Ethics,* into a long theological tradition of reflection on charity.

In his *Commentary on the Sentences of Peter Lombard* (1254–1256) and again in the *Summa theologiae* (1265/1266–1273), Aquinas gives an account of the forms of natural love in relation to the dictates of charity. Aquinas assumes that the order of love in nature is well-ordered like that of charity, because both are works of divine wisdom (*S.T.* 2a2ae.26.6). Charity requires that we prefer that which represents the greater good and more closely resembles God. But the

5. Muslims consider a marriage between the offspring of a wet nurse and the children she nurses to be incestuous. In Iranian Baluchistan, where I carried out fieldwork in 1976, the relationship between children put out to nurse and their "milk mother" typically remains close throughout their lifetimes.

intensity of love is determined by the nature of the lover, and by nature "a man loves those closest to him and wills them good more intensely than those who are better and for whom he wills a greater good" (*S.T.* 2a2ae.26.7). If we compare the friendship of consanguines, which is based on natural origin, with other types of friendship, "the bond of natural origin is something prior and more fixed, because it has to do with the very substance of a human being, while others come after it and can be undone. Consequently the friendship of blood-relatives is more stable, though others can be stronger in respect of what is proper to each of them." Because the friendship of kin is more rooted in nature and prevails in those matters relating to nature, we are more obliged to provide kin with the necessities of life (*S.T.* 2a2ae.26.8).

The different parts of substance that parents supply to their children in procreation play an important role in Aquinas's discussion of love within the family. In the *Commentary on the Sentences,* Aquinas states that mothers love their children more than fathers do for three reasons. First, mothers labor more in the generation of their children, in which they give more of themselves. Second, they are more certain that their children are theirs than fathers. Third, unlike fathers they constantly keep their children with them and feed them, thereby adding social friendship to natural friendship. But this is also because mothers invest more of themselves in their children than fathers do. Since mothers love their children more, it seems that children should reciprocate. But according to Aquinas, more of the substance of the child comes from the father than from the mother, because the father gives the form and the mother gives the matter. Therefore a man naturally loves his father and the kin on his father's side more than his mother and her kin (*Sent.* 3.29.7).

Aquinas thus assumes that familial love is rooted in natural substance transmitted in procreation from parents to offspring. This love is innate, its innate character at best enhanced through social interaction. It is also asymmetrical. The disproportion between the maternal contribution to conception and the substance of the child is explained by the Aristotelian view of semen, which acquires its virtue from the soul of the father but alienates only a tiny portion of paternal substance, whereas the mother alienates considerable substance to her offspring in procreation.

The view of paternal and maternal roles expressed here indicates an underlying tension concerning the paternal role in procreation. Doctors and philosophers were certain about the nature of the male contribution and hotly debated the role of the female. Yet determination of paternal identity in any given case rested on presumption, thereby creating an element of uncertainty in the emotional relationship between father and child. Lack of certainty about the biological father led jurists to declare that the father is he whom marriage designates (*Vocab. iuris utriusque,* s.v. "pater").

In the *Summa theologiae,* Aquinas adheres strictly to Aristotle's position in the *Nicomachean Ethics* and does not cite the mother's role in procreation as a reason for loving her child more than the father does. But procreative roles remain the basis for Aquinas's argument that a man ought to love his father more than his mother in charity. Although both parents are principles of our natural origin, the father is a more excellent principle than the mother, because he is an active principle, whereas she is a passive and material one. Specifically, the power of the father's seed gives form to the matter of the body provided by the mother and prepares the matter for receiving a rational soul (*S.T.* 2a2ae.26.10).

Aquinas's views in the *Commentary* on the nature of a mother's love are cited in later treatises, such as the *Summa theologica* (c. 1454) of the Dominican Antoninus, prior of San Marco and from 1446 to 1459 archbishop of Florence (*S.T.* 1.6.2[1487 ed.]). But similar ideas were also incorporated into more popular rhetorical forms. For example, they occur in three sermons and in the Latin *Chronicle of Genoa from its Origins to 1297* by Aquinas's fellow Dominican Jacobus de Varagine (c. 1228/1229–1298), the archbishop of Genoa. De Varagine served from 1267 to 1277 and again from 1281 to 1286 as prior of the Dominican province of Lombardy. In this capacity he traveled extensively throughout northern Italy and Europe to attend general chapters of the order (see Monleone 1941, vol. 1, for details of his life). He is therefore likely to have been in touch with the major currents of scholastic thinking of his day. Although de Varagine was best known as the author of the *Legenda Aurea,* his sermons were also popular and were reprinted down to the end of the seventeenth century, not only in Italy but also in France and Germany.

De Varagine's sermons relating procreative roles to familial bonds seek to explain specific events of Scripture according to the natural principles of human affection. The sermons are all based on New Testament passages dealing with mothers who have lost sons, but much of their content applies to children of both sexes. De Varagine probably followed common practice and preached in the vernacular, only later writing his sermons in Latin for devout readers or as models for other preachers.

The third sermon on the slaughter of the innocents from the *Sermons on Saints* contains the sketchiest and probably the earliest formulation of de Varagine's views on paternity and maternity. De Varagine explains why the mothers, symbolized by Rachel, and not the fathers, symbolized by Jacob, were induced to cry over the death of their sons, a reference to Matthew 2:18. He argues that "a mother loves her child more and therefore mourns more when she loses it" and gives three reasons. First, "a mother gives more of her substance to her child than the father, and is seen therefore to have a greater part" (1497, Diii verso). Second, a mother labors more for her child than the father, and "that for which we labor more we love more." Third, a mother is more certain that a child is hers than the father, who loves his child less "as a doubtful thing" (1497, Diii). De Varagine's arguments are strikingly similar to those of Aquinas in his *Commentary on the Sentences* (*Sent.* 3.29.7). The similarity suggests that de Varagine was influenced by this work, whereas he probably did not know the *Summa,* which was roughly contemporaneous with the composition of the *Sermons on Saints* (see Monleone 1941, 1:113, on the dating of this collection).

De Varagine's use of the term *substance* in this context seems to belie his commonality with Aquinas and ultimate reliance on Aristotle, whether he knew Aristotle directly or through an intermediary. But a close reading of de Varagine's works shows that he uses *substance* interchangeably with *matter* (*materia*), which was one of the ordinary nonphilosophical senses of the term (see, for example, his description of the Virgin as "true and complete mother" in the second sermon for the first and second Saturdays of Lent). His view of maternity was orthodox: in a Lenten sermon he describes the Virgin as the true mother of Christ because she gave him the matter of her flesh, found a suitable place for him in her womb, and gave him appropriate nourishment, "for these three things make a true mother" (1497, ee verso).

In the third sermon for the sixteenth Sunday after Trinity (*Sermones de tempore*), based on the text "there was a widow" from Luke 7:25, de Varagine gives two additional reasons why a mother loves her child more than the father does. First, a woman naturally has more faults than a man because she is cold and humid, an argument developed in the first subtheme of the sermon. But these faults are removed when she bears children (no doubt especially sons), so that many women who were disliked by their husband are now loved on account of the children they procreate. Therefore, knowing that she is more loved by her husband and is relieved of her faults as a result of bearing children, a woman loves them more strongly (1497, p verso). Here de Varagine casts in doubt the possibility of realizing the medieval clerical ideal of mutual love between spouses and suggests that the relationship between husband and wife is mediated by the latter's procreative capacity. Second, de Varagine cites Augustine in the *De amicitia* and says that friendship grows from the habit of living together, speaking and conversing. Mothers live, talk, and converse with their children more than fathers; therefore, he implies, mothers have a stronger friendship with their children (1497, pii). This point introduces a more social view of the love between parents and children than hitherto evident in the sermons.

In spite of a mother's greater physical and emotional investment in her children, her lot is to be loved less, for de Varagine asserts that a child "naturally" loves his father more than his mother. He gives four reasons, considerably expanding Aquinas's treatment of this topic. First, "the father is the effective and formal principle in the carnal generation of his child." This statement, as well as an earlier allusion to "the philosopher" in regard to the mother's role in procreation, confirms de Varagine's reliance on the Aristotelian theory of procreation. Second, the son should inherit all the father's goods. Third, since the mother determines whether the status of the newborn is free or servile, the father is not associated with the transmission of liabilities, but only with the bestowal of such benefits as honors, offices, and dignities. In a legal marriage, the mother's status is irrelevant; the son of a servant girl and a king will have the royal dignity (1497, pii).

Finally, de Varagine considers the mother and father together in relation to their children. Both naturally love their offspring more than they are loved by them, and the reason is that parents give from their own nature to their children. Parents love their children as their own work, their own flesh, their own bodily members. The relations of giving and receiving substance have different emotional effects, a theme that is closely linked to medieval assumptions concerning the nature of love in marriage based on the story of Eve's formation from Adam. De Varagine draws on a natural image, that of sap welling up from the roots of a plant to its outer branches. The love of parents is just such a natural force, beyond their control, informing and suffusing their children as extensions of themselves. De Varagine also develops this theme in the *Chronicle of Genoa*. In apparent contrast to Aquinas, who attempts to legitimize the "natural" affections as part of God's creation, de Varagine follows Augustine in seeing the love between parents and children in itself as morally neutral because it is natural and therefore occurs without respect to the virtues and vices in children. It should therefore not be praised, but its absence should be detested (Monleone 1941, 2:204).

Among the theologians discussed here, beliefs about the transmission of shared substance from parents to children served to mark off the elementary reproductive group as a culturally defined "natural" unit. De Varagine's sermon for the Trinity season discussed above does not support Steven Epstein's claim that he viewed the tie between mother and child as "the foundation of life, overlooking any nuclear family or clan" (Epstein 1984, 68–69). De Varagine does, however, posit an asymmetry between the intimacy and warmth shared among children and their mother in the domestic context, and the establishment of social position in the world through resources transmitted by the father.

The popularity of this view is suggested by etymologies of the term *matrimony,* a topos in medieval discussions of marriage. Scholars derived *matrimony* from the mother because it enabled women to be mothers, conferring upon them the office of bearing and caring for children, in which they play a greater role than fathers (see Vincent of Beauvais, *Sp. nat.* 31,30; *Vocab. Iuris utriusque,* s.v. "matrimonium", Antonius de Bitonto 1495, sermon for the second Sunday after Epiphany). In contrast, they asserted that possession of the patrimony (*patrimonium*) was named after the father because the work of the husband is more necessary for its acquisition and management (Antonius de Bitonto 1495, sermon for the second Sunday after Epiphany).

PATERNITY AND MATERNITY IN CONSTRUCTIONS OF CIVIC IDENTITY

The concepts of paternity and maternity ordered thought and experience in a variety of medieval cultural domains. They played an important role in shaping ideologies of the family and occupied a central place in Christian cosmology and devotional traditions. Another area in which they figured was that of ideologies of the res publica. Legal and historical works represented the polity in familistic terms that often implicated assumptions about procreation. We have seen the medieval Christian groundwork for the natural basis of family and polity in the writings of Isidore of Seville. Isidore was undoubtedly inspired by the genealogical model of human society in Genesis, but he was also explicit about his debt to Roman sources. In defining the term *brother* (*frater*), Isidore notes that "they are brothers by cognation who are from one family (familia), that is, patria, which the Latins interpret in terms of paternity, since from a single root a great crowd of people is dispersed" (*Etym.* 9.6.9).

The urban myths of Florence reveal the close connection between ideas concerning the "natural" origin of the familia and that of the patria. Roman soldiers, imperial or republican, depending on the dominant political sentiment, plant their vivifying and form-endowing seed in Florence, personified as a woman and a mother. Through their seed they transmit the Roman virtues, the patriotism of Brutus, the chastity of Lucretia, to future generations of Florentines. Dante contrasts the "holy seed" of the Romans, that is, the descendants of Florence's Roman founders, to the lowborn and greedy men from Fiesole who have begotten pride and extravagance out of Florence, personified as a woman weeping over her sinful offspring (*Inferno* 16.73–75). Bruni traces the descent of the Florentines from Roman republican progenitors in order to endow them with an illustrious moral and political patrimony. Procreated at the height of the powers of their Roman ancestors, the Florentines inherited Roman nobility and virtues at their peak of excellence, a right to dominion over the territory they claimed, and an unquenchable thirst for the freedom granted by a republican constitution (Bruni 1978, 150). Discussion of the moral attributes and political values of the Florentines in such biological terms is a basic feature of medieval and Renaissance Florentine historiography (see Rubinstein 1942).

Beliefs about procreation strongly influenced the way medieval intellectuals conceptualized the character of familial bonds. Medieval Christian theologians appropriated and elaborated a view from antiquity of the father as sole generator, thereby encouraging an emphasis on the father as the chief agent in forming the identity of his offspring. This theory of procreation reinforced the father's superior authority in the family and provided cultural grounds for the ascendancy of the patrilineal principle among elites. But the assumption that the substance of the child was constituted from its mother as well as its father, and the transmission of a view of heredity that attributed an active role in generation to both parents, legitimized a situational stress on maternal kin ties in accordance with pragmatic interests, such as the acquisition of status, political support, and material resources. Finally, the definition of the family in terms of bonds of natural substance and the belief that the father played a formative role in procreation provided a model for medieval Italian polities. This model represented the socio-moral character of the polity as a biologically transmitted legacy from founding ancestors, who were frequently said to be Trojan or Roman warriors. It associated purity of descent, dependent on stable community boundaries, with social concord and the fulfillment of divinely sanctioned political goals that were legitimized by their exemplary origins. Thus the Florentines traced their virtues and political role in Italy back to Roman progenitors, of whom they were, according to a proclamation of the Signoria in 1424, "the sons, seed, blood and bone" (quoted in Rubinstein 1942, 225).

Chapter 9

MICHAEL SHEEHAN

Sexuality, Marriage, Celibacy, and the Family in Central and Northern Italy: Christian Legal and Moral Guides in the Early Middle Ages

In the opening paragraph of his description of monastic organization, the sixth-century author of the *Regula Magistri* chose the domestic household as the model for the two "divine households" of which he wrote: the local church and the monastery. His purpose was to provide a useful illustration of the hierarchical structure that he proposed to describe, yet the casual use of the comparison suggests a profound change that had occurred in sixth-century Italy.[1] He took for granted that two other structures that had appeared in the Roman world could be seen as parallels to and, to a certain extent, competitors with those households, which from the point of view of tradition and civil law were the motor and substance of society. The spread of the ideology that contributed to that change and its implementation in the Italy in which the Master lived are the objects of analysis in this chapter.

As the patristic period, the first era of theological reflection in the history of Christianity, drew to a close in the early fifth century, it was clear that Christian thinkers had arrived at a well-developed and somewhat original conception of mankind, its nature and its purpose. This conception was expressed with

---

1. Vogüé 1964–1965, 2:8. The perception of a development of this sort a century earlier is suggested by the collecting of the *Constitutiones sirmondianae* (Mommsen and Meyer 1905, 1:907–916) and the *Codex Theodosianus,* bk. 16.

different nuances in different parts of the Church, but in general terms it was consistent. One of the more important aspects of this ideology was the notion that both the human race and its individual members had histories.

That humankind had a history was clear from the Old Testament. The appearance of the human race was related to the creation of the rest of the world, but it involved a special exegetical problem having been described in two different ways. According to Genesis 1.26–29, the human race was created with an inherent gender distinction so that it could reproduce itself. The second account, Genesis 2.18–24, was more nuanced. It described the discovery of a need for adjustment within creation that became evident almost immediately. The first man needed a helpmate and companion, so a woman, a being similar to but distinct and somewhat different from him, was made from the first man himself. Furthermore, since the woman was both from and for the man there was to be both unity and hierarchy within their relationship. The first time that the couple was shown acting together, they made the tragic decision that produced an immense change. They became subject to a life of exhausting work and to death. In the sentence of the woman, the imperfection resulting from sin touched on both functions expressed in the accounts of her creation: because of her the human race would indeed increase and multiply, but at the cost of her suffering; she would bear the difficulties of her subjection to Adam because of her attraction to him (Gen. 3.16).

The very difference that attracted the couple to each other—the difference of which they learned when they became aware of shame—was disturbed, so that it was at once delightful and problematic. Furthermore, since it was the couple's difference, namely, their sexual powers, that allowed humanity to continue through time, the consequences of their original sin were seen to be passed on by that difference as well. Yet their prospect was not without hope, even in the Genesis account of the Fall. In time, the second or postlapsarian agenda was seen in a positive light, and the sad event that made it necessary came to be called a "happy sin." This was possible because of the arrival of a new Adam in the alternative agenda, Jesus Christ. He not only furnished the means whereby the evils consequent on the original sin could be removed, but he also provided an interpretation of the meaning of life and a teaching on human behavior that was to be implemented by all people. Some of this teaching touched the exercise of sexual powers.

First, Christ urged a self-discipline concerning sexual matters that reached even to one's innermost thoughts. Second, he suggested a way of life that did not involve the sexual bond, presented in such a way that it could be seen not only as honorable and desirable, but also as superior to the life of the married. Finally, although his instruction on matrimony was not developed, the implications of his teaching were to require an adjustment of major importance to marriage and, eventually, to the general organization of domestic life. As his doctrine was developed by his followers, marriage took on the sacred character of a mystery like the union of Christ and the Church. Marriage was seen as indissoluble and monogamous and, though these elements developed slowly, was presented as open to all men and women and to depend on the free choice of the spouses themselves. Christ made it clear that the claims of domestic life, though it forms the background to his conception of society, were secondary to the greater personal good of inheriting eternal life. He did not give an abstract analysis of the operative domestic group, but described it in simple terms: father and mother, wife and children, brothers and sisters, houses and lands (Matt. 19.29). He went on to note that the choice for eternal life would cause strife within the domestic unit (Matt. 10.34–36; Luke 2.51–53) and, in a rhetoric not our own, that the Christian might have to hate father and mother, wife and child, brother and sister to free himself to achieve his purpose. Furthermore, at that point in Mark's gospel where Christ chose the Apostles, he insisted that a relationship based on doing God's will overrode any relationship based on blood: informed that members of his family were present and wished to see him, he asked, "Who are my mother and brethren?" His reply made it clear that the most powerful and lasting relationship occurred between those who did the will of God (Mark 3.31–35). Thus the preparation of the soul to be with God after death was presented as the ultimate priority and criterion of judgment, a notion that drove right to the heart of a vision of humankind in which the good of the *domus* or the *civitas* was paramount (Rouche 1987b, 548–549; Brown 1988, 1–16).

The history of the individual was seen to illustrate the application of the agenda of creation as adjusted by the Fall and the coming of Christ. Each began Christian life with the ritual of baptism, an act that introduced one into the Christian community and removed the essential damage resulting from original sin. The Christian could belong to any group in society, but from the point of view of the effect of baptism all were equal before God. The end of life was followed by a judgment in which all choices would be examined and their eternal consequences weighed. Between baptism and judgment was the period when the individual was expected to follow the teaching of Christ, teaching that included control of all appetites; the sex drive was one of them. Here Christianity introduced or supported important changes of expectation in Roman society, changes that not only affected the development of the individual, but also had important consequences in society itself. The Christian could choose between the married and the celibate state, and for those who chose marriage there were new rules regarding the individual, the couple, and the wider community. Later in the life course, further choice became possible: widowhood or candidacy for clerical office could require a decision to discontinue an active sexual life. Ideally, decisions were to be made in terms of the ultimate good of which Christ spoke, eternal life.

The impact of this ideology on the late Roman Empire has been much discussed (Gaudemet 1977, 139–179). That world was undergoing rapid political and social change. No doubt profound shifts in the composition of the population, the economy, and other aspects of society contributed to what occurred, but the impact of Christian ideas cannot be ignored. That new ideology, expressed by the best minds of the age and in a manner to reach all levels of society, was in place by the end of the fourth century (Brown 1987, 251). Its adoption was evidently facilitated by other ideals and trends that were already operative in society, ideals that supported, even explicated those of the nascent Church (Hickey 1986, 1–11; Brown 1987, 247–251, 297–311, 1988, 17–25). But the slow evolution of attitudes to sexuality and to the married and celibate states in the West during the last two centuries of the empire is generally seen as at least in part due to the influence of the Christian understanding of humankind sketched above. This not only touched individual decisions but also found expression in the *Codex Theodosianus* (438) and in the novels of the next generation.

Just as the patristic period drew to an end, and in part the cause of this diminution of Christian reflection, western Europe was subjected to a series of invasions that injected new peoples into the population, especially into the dominant classes. Whether the Christian ideology, now shorn of its most successful exponents, was able to affect this group and continue to exert its influence on the older population and, if such were the case, how it did so, are serious problems. By the beginning of the sixth century the Ostrogothic kingdom had been established in Italy. Toward the middle of the century the peninsula was subjected to the scouring of the Byzantine wars and then, when it was almost powerless, to the last major invasion, that of the Lombards. Their rather tense relationship with the Church would endure into the middle years of the eighth century, when Carolingian power appeared on the scene. By looking at the documentation extant from the two hundred and fifty years bracketed by the arrival of the Ostrogothic and the Carolingian armies in Italy, it will be possible to learn something of the moral guidance and ecclesiastical and civil legislation that show to what extent the Christian ideology, described above, continued to be presented to the peoples of the peninsula.[2] There is, of

---

2. Compared with the literature of the age of the Fathers, it is inferior in quality and quantity. There are, however, a few collections of sermons, papal and episcopal letters, important liturgical documents, several collections of canon law, especially the *Dionysiana* assembled at Rome shortly after 500, and a remarkable group of monastic rules for both men and women. During the earlier

course, another dimension to the matter, that of the implementation of these ideals in the lives of the population. This difficult task will not be undertaken in a systematic way, though an attempt is made to suggest something of its impact on the lives of individuals and on domestic institutions.

The aspects of the Christian ideology that touched human sexuality continued to be taught at the pastoral level in Italy during the period under examination. There seems, however, to have been little of that development of theory, and reflection on the meaning and purpose of sexual powers, characteristic of the patristic era. Sexuality was to be realized principally in two forms, namely, the married and the celibate life. The latter, practiced in institutions that supported and protected it, was new and was to be important in its consequences. In the forms they assumed, both marriage and celibacy required adjustments to the traditional understanding and realization of the family, adjustments that became more evident as the Middle Ages progressed and that can be seen as operative in Italian society as described in several of the chapters that follow.

SEXUALITY

The documentation that survives from the sixth and seventh centuries gives some access to teaching on human sexuality and to guidance in its functioning. Sometimes these sources provide information that pertained to the external forum and its regulations. Occasionally an episcopal letter or a sermon shows community action on the matter in question.

One notion, fundamental to the understanding of sexuality, was the ancient one that sexual activity and contact with the divine are incompatible. Strict logic might have required that to be fully Christian a believer had to be celibate. But there was another principle, one that recognized the imperious quality of the sexual urge and provided for it, either throughout life or at certain periods along the life course. This was the notion of marriage as a means (*remedium*) of satisfying sexual desire. Its importance had been set out by Saint Paul in his discussion of the celibate life (1 Cor. 7.1–9). Having received considerable development in the writings of the Fathers, this notion was to remain an important element in reflections on the married and celibate states by medieval

---

part of the period in question, Provence was part of the empire of Theoderic the Ostrogoth. Not only were its ecclesiastical leaders among the most active of the time in preaching, writing, and issuing conciliar statutes, but also they were in close relation to Rome (Turner 1916, 236–247). For this reason, it has been deemed suitable to include their writings in this discussion.

theologians (Sheehan 1988, 467). The degree of self-restraint that was required was seen as a function of the approach to the sacred that the individual sought. Thus attempts were made to ensure that bishops, priests, and deacons, because of their frequent contact with things divine, lived a celibate life. Those whose contacts were occasional, however, were allowed marriage but were urged to become celibate at those moments when contact with divine things occurred. It was in this context that the parable of the seed yielding one hundred-, sixty-, and thirtyfold came to be interpreted. Each yield was good; each was of different value. The virginal and the Christian married life were expressed by the hundredfold and the thirtyfold, respectively. The sixtyfold was reserved to those between the extremes, who came to a life of celibacy after a time when they enjoyed the lesser good of marriage (Beck 1950, 223–224).

Thus the text from a Council of Carthage (419), which was widely read in Europe in the *Dionysiana* (*PL* 67.187, 191), the important canonical collection made at Rome early in the sixth century, required those who touched the mysteries to live a continent life.[3] The periodic abstinence required of those not in major orders is well illustrated in the writings of Caesarius of Arles. The late-fifth-century *Statuta ecclesiae antiquae* required those whose marriage had been blessed to refrain from consummating their union during their first night together (c. 101, Munier 1960, 100).[4] Caesarius went further, urging that their abstinence honor the model of Tobias and endure for three nights. He also mentioned a custom of the Church of Arles, according to which new brides "should not presume" to appear in church for thirty days after their wedding, and suggested that husbands follow their example (Beck 1950, 232–233). Those who were married were expected to avoid sexual union when important religious events were to take place. Thus married catechumens were to refrain from sexual activity before and after they received baptism, and all were expected to refrain during great feasts. Pope Gregory I (590–604), asked whether it was permissible to bathe on Sunday, said that bathing was in order so long as it was not preparatory to making love (Gregory 1982, 991). Both Caesarius and Gregory mentioned the personal problems, such as deformities in their children, that beset those who failed to abstain as required (Beck 1950, 234–235; *PL* 77.200–202). The penitent, too, was expected to live as a celibate,

---

3. That sexual union rather than marriage stood in the way of contact with the divine was underlined in a letter ascribed to Pope Pelagius I (556–561): a cleric who married a widow whose first union had not been consummated was not considered to have married bigamously and therefore was not bound by the impediment (Vogel 1977, 424).

4. The *Statuta ecclesiae antiquae* was a private collection of regulations that was compiled in Provence during the last quarter of the fifth century of which there is a substantial Italian manuscript tradition.

though Pope Leo (440–461) allowed that a dispensation could be given to those whose self-control was judged impossible without marriage (for example, the young), a decision that was included in the *Dionysiana* (*PL* 67.290).

Marriage, then, was seen as a lightning rod whereby sexual energy was discharged.[5] Yet writers of the time were well aware that the permitted use of marriage did not solve all problems. It was successful only for those who were self-controlled. Both Bishop Caesarius and Pope Gregory emphasized the necessity to avoid evil thoughts (Caesarius 1937–1941, 1.1.193; *PL* 77.109, 76.200–201). On several occasions Gregory pointed out the connection between gluttony and sexual appetite: "when the belly is extended, lust is aroused" (*PL* 77.81). Sermons and episcopal letters returned again and again to the dangers of heterosocial relationships. This was seen as especially significant for the clergy and for those celibate men and women living in the world or in monasteries. They were given not only general advice but also precise directions in letters that discussed the dangers of self-deception as well as other less worthy motives. It was all too evident that innocent contacts followed by the play of imagination could lead to masturbation, fornication, or in the case of clerics required to live in continence, a return to an active sexual life with their spouses.[6] The special danger in associating with lower-class women was explicitly stated in this context.[7] The *Regula Magistri* instructed monks to observe personal modesty, for the sexual stimulation from touching their own bodies could easily lead to heterosexual desire and its consequences (Vogüé 1964–1965,2.30–32). An extreme solution to sexual craving, occasionally referred to, was castration. Although a bishop who had been castrated by "barbarians" was not held responsible by a canon of the Council of Nicea, which allowed him to continue his ministry, self-mutilation was clearly forbidden. Pope Gelasius (492–496) taught that clergy would lose their official function and that laymen would do penance, positions reinforced by earlier law and repeated in the *Dionysiana* (*PL* 67.143–144, 147, 307).

That the preference for the celibate life was not always based on a choice between goods, but instead resulted from a tendency to despise the sexual

5. Thus the behavior of those accused of homosexuality or bestiality was judged to be less worthy of excuse if they were married (*PL* 67.154).

6. Gregory's *Dialogues* are especially rich in examples of both wise and foolish behavior in these regards: see the tale of Andrew, bishop of Fondi, and that of the priest of Norcia who, as he died, refused the ministrations of the wife he had avoided for forty years with the words: "Go away from me woman. The fire is still flickering" (*PL* 77.229–231, 336–337).

7. A similar notion is in *Edictum Theodorici regis* 62 (Bluhme 1875–1889, 158–159), which does not view sexual relations with a woman of the lowest class as adultery. See Sheehan 1988, 467–471.

aspect of humankind in general and marriage in particular, was to be expected. The Christian community sometimes provided a place for men and women with these or similar attitudes (Hickey 1986, 15). But this was not acceptable: the *Dionysiana* brought to Western eyes the powerful condemnation of the Council of Gangra (c. 345), which anathematized those who sought the virginal life not because it was good and holy, but because they looked on marriage with horror.[8] Yet though Church thinkers opposed such an extreme, they also agreed that human sexuality contained the disorder that resulted from the original sin of the first couple and should not be exercised without serious purpose. This attitude must be understood as the background to the teaching on the two states of life in which the Christian ideology was realized, the married and the celibate.

THE MARRIED STATE

One of the recurring patterns in the history of Christianity in ages marked by Manichaean thought has been the tendency to emphasize a positive view of marriage, and even to produce significant theological exploration of the institution. The Western Church of the sixth century had just come through a period of such dualist thinking; there are indications that it was judged important to insist that Christians should not contemn marriage. Thus in the prologue to the *Statuta ecclesiae antiquae* the matters on which a candidate for the episcopacy was to be examined included whether he despised marriage and forbade second unions (Munier 1960, 77, 112). A century later in his *Moralia,* Pope Gregory made it clear that he considered such an attitude to be heresy (*PL* 75.1125). Yet another facet of his judgment of marriage in its day-to-day realization is expressed in the *Dialogues.* After narrating the difficult choice for the continent life made by Galla, the widowed daughter of Symmachus, Gregory remarked that whereas spiritual marriage often begins with suffering and leads to the joys of heaven, earthly marriage begins with joy but ends in sorrow (*PL* 77.340).

In theological terms, marriage had long been presented as a sacred relationship symbolizing the union of Christ and the Church. Yet this understanding, stated once again by Pope Leo in his letter to Rusticus of Narbonne and repeated in the *Dionysiana* (*PL* 67.288–289), must have been hard to maintain in the face of canons of the Council of Laodicea, also made available in the *Dionysiana,* urging Christians to behave discreetly at marriage banquets, sug-

---

8. The council was reacting to the extreme asceticism of Eustathius of Sebaste (c. 300–c. 377), which provoked a local crisis in central Asia Minor. Included in the *Dionysiana* (*PL* 67.157–160), it became widely known in the West.

gesting that the clergy leave early, and prohibiting marriage celebration during the Lenten season (*PL* 67.165). Another development, however, reached closer to the comprehension of the laity and was to receive an ever greater importance as the Middle Ages unfolded, namely, the custom of giving public expression to the union of a couple in a religious ritual. Korbinian Ritzer and Cyrille Vogel have discussed this development in detail. For the present purpose it is sufficient to note that the blessing of the couple appeared in Rome in the fourth century and that by the middle of the sixth century the wedding was associated with the Eucharist itself, with blessing, prayer, and preface proper to the occasion (Ritzer 1970, 222–246; Vogel 1977, 421–426). This location of the marriage within an increasingly Christian ritual was not required—in some cases was not permitted—but combined with the growing precision as to the times when it was suitably performed, represents an important turning in the presentation of the very delicate teaching that marriage was a good, a symbol of immense dignity, and a means to sanctification, and at the same time contained tendencies that were uncontrolled and not worthy of God. Thus a use of ritual to reconcile seemingly opposite attitudes was developed in Italy in the period under consideration.[9]

However important the notion of marriage as an acceptable institution for the satisfying of sexual desire, its prime purpose was viewed as the begetting of children. Caesarius of Arles went so far as to state in one of his sermons that this purpose was expressed in the *tabulae nuptiales* (Beck 1950, 229). In his discussion of marriage in the *Pastoral Care,* Pope Gregory underlined this purpose of marriage as well (*PL* 77.102). Such an understanding was one with which civil society would agree.[10] The points of disagreement between the Christian ideology and the worlds it confronted were areas in which dispute had begun well before the period of interest, namely, the qualities of marriage and, closely related to these qualities, the persons for whom marriage was permitted.

Christian marriage was to be monogamous, exclusive, and permanent. Roman law, expressed in the Theodosian Code, and barbarian law as well had much to say about the adultery of the wife and, though considerably less, of the husband. In the context of Roman law the concubine was always a possibility. Although Christian teachers allowed that, under certain conditions, a con-

9. A further indication of this point: clergy were expected to have their marriages blessed (Vogel 1977, 424–425).

10. See *Edictum Theodorici regis* 36 (Bluhme 1875–1889, 154), and *Cod. Just.* 5.5.6; cf. Rouche 1987b, 548–549.

cubine could become a wife, she was forbidden to the married man.[11] The sermons of Caesarius of Arles reveal the scale of the problem and the vigor with which this bishop at least tried to deal with it. He makes it clear that some of his flock boasted and joked about their conquests, whereas others, perhaps with a wry reference to the remedium, pointed out that during their frequent separations from their wives on government affairs or business of their own no other mode of sexual release was available. Then there were soldiers who saw women as part of the booty of their trade (Beck 1950, 237–238).[12] Caesarius frequently confronted the double standard by which his hearers lived. He upbraided the men of his congregation for their inconsistency in expecting the same virtue in their wives that they destroyed in other women. Pointing out that at Rome men who maintained a mistress before marriage were not allowed the blessing of their new union, Caesarius imposed the practice on his own congregation. In the end, he hoped that the good example of some of his hearers would move the others to self-restraint (Beck 1950, 230–232). The *Dionysiana* recalled both the teaching of the Council of Ancyra (314) that husband as well as wife was subject to penance for adultery, and that of Pope Innocent, who frankly admitted that a husband could more easily accuse his wife than she could accuse him, but insisted that adultery by either sex was equally condemned (*PL* 67.247).

Pertaining as it did to the external forum, the question of the permanence of marriage was a more obvious point of tension in society. Christian thinking on the matter probably played a role in the publication of Constantine's constitution of 331, which established a not inconsiderable limitation of divorce (*Cod. Theod.* 3.16.1). The year after the publication of his code, in a novel (12, Mommsen and Meyer 1905, 2:29) that found a place in several of the barbarian codes as well as that of Justinian, Theodosius pointed out that for the good of children it should not be easy to dissolve a marriage. But civil law was reluctant to go further and forbid divorce (Hickey 1987, 55–58). The Christian communities had to be content with the moral pressure that they could bring to bear on their members. The *Dionysiana* quoted Pope Leo's judgment that marriage after divorce was adultery and included the rule and interesting suggestion of the Council of Carthage that when spouses dismiss each other they should be required to remain single or reconcile, adding that the civil law ought to

---

11. On the apparent dispute between the positions of Augustine and Caesarius on the possibility of a concubine becoming a wife, see Beck 1950, 226–228.

12. On opposition to his sermons and the lengths to which Caesarius went to ensure that his flock remained and listened—including locking the church door—see Beck 1950, 142, 265–266.

cooperate (*PL* 67.247–248, 215–216).Several Gallic councils of the sixth century returned to this question, and one of them, the Council of Agde (506), indicated that on some occasions a marriage could properly be dissolved. The text continues with a casual remark that was heavy with the future implying that it was for the bishops to make such a decision (c. 25, Munier 1963, 204; Beck 1950, 228; Sheehan 1988, 458).

A special problem, witness to the troubles of the age, was the second marriage of the woman whose spouse had been carried into captivity. The *Dionysiana* (*PL* 57.296–297) included a series of directions from Pope Leo to Bishop Nicetas of Aquileia: if the husband was presumed dead, the woman was allowed to marry again, but should the husband return, the command of Christ "What therefore God has joined together, let not man put asunder" was to be enforced. The woman would be required to return to her original husband. Secondary parts of the decretal confirmed that this was not always an easy solution.[13]

When marriage was approached by those free to enter the relationship, many obstacles presented themselves. Two of these, the seriousness of which would play important roles in the degree of endogamy in medieval European society, are especially important to the present discussion: impediments resulting from an earlier marriage and those from relationship within unacceptable degrees. The previous discussion indicates the seriousness of the opposition to divorce by Christian leaders. Inasmuch as this opposition was effective, it involved the limitation of an individual's freedom to seek elsewhere for the wealth and children that were so important to the maintenance of family fortunes (Goody 1983, 31–33, 188–189). Given the frequency of divorce among the visible classes of Roman and barbarian society, the consequences of a limitation of the practice would have been of major proportions. Pressure toward achieving that end was essentially a moral one until those great confrontations between popes and bishops on one side and major political figures on the other, during the Carolingian period, caused an important shift in attitudes.

There were also unions deemed unacceptable because of blood or spiritual relationships. This rather surprising development in the Christian teaching on marriage was to be one of the principal forces moving European families toward a wider degree of exogamy. The beginnings were of limited application and, indeed, rather cautious. Canon 2 of the Council of Neocaesaria (314) forbade a woman's marriage to her husband's brother, and a late-fourth-

---

13. These regulations were quoted in extenso in the *Responsiones* of Pope Stephen III during his visit to Gaul in 752 (Mansi 1759–1798, 12:562).

century oriental collection, the *Apostolic Canons,* denied ordination to anyone who married his wife's sister or his brother's daughter but did not mention its application to the marriages of the laity; both texts were brought to western Europe by the *Dionysiana (PL* 67.155, 143). Several imperial constitutions of the fourth century assembled in the *Codex Theodosianus* (3.12.1–4) applied restrictions in this area. More precise prohibitions and their extension were worked out in the Gallic councils of the sixth and seventh centuries against heavy opposition and only gradually found expression in the laws of the region (Rouche 1987a, 857–861). The degree to which the papacy was involved in the process, let alone the extent to which the results were intended to apply to Italy, is difficult to ascertain.

It was in the eighth century, toward the end of the period of the present study, that an important series of Roman statements on relationship began. The first was in a council of Pope Gregory II, held at Rome, probably in 721. Among canons touching freedom to marry, several forbade union with a brother's wife, a niece, a mother-in-law, a daughter-in-law, or a first cousin.[14] Then, after these precise prohibitions, a more general canon forbade marriage with any relative or wife of a relative (c. 9, *PL* 67.343). There is no indication how far through the parentela this prohibition was intended to apply.[15] Why it was deemed necessary to state the individual prohibitions of the earlier canons is unclear. One might conclude that the rule of c. 9 was intended as counsel rather than a strict prohibition, but the addition of a penalty, a most serious penalty in fact, stands in the way of this conclusion. Five years later, in a letter to Saint Boniface, the pope adopted a somewhat different approach: pointing out that marriage was forbidden within the fourth degree, he expressed the preference that those aware of relationship of any kind should not marry (Boniface 1916, 45). In this case there was no mention of anathema. Uncertainty on the matter was removed in 732 when Pope Gregory III informed Boniface that the prohibitions extended to the seventh degree (Boniface 1916, 51). This large increase of forbidden degrees must have posed many problems for Boniface. By 735 he had become aware of the *Libellus responsionum,* a letter to Augustine of Canterbury ascribed to Gregory I that somewhat hesitatingly permitted marriage of second cousins (Meyvaert 1971, 15–33). In spite of various inquiries he was unable to find confirmation of the texts in the Roman chancery, and Pope Zachary finally replied in 742 that the information was erroneous (Boniface

14. In a Roman council of 743, Pope Zachary stated that these regulations, which his council reaffirmed, were intended to apply to Italy (Werminghoff 1906, 19–20).

15. In Rothair's publication of the Lombard law in 643, the parentela was defined as consisting of seven degrees (152, Bluhme 1868, 35).

1916, 57, 90; Werminghoff 1906, 20). This exchange not only indicates resistance to the extended prohibition based on consanguinity and affinity, but also shows that there was an earlier ruling, thought to be of papal origin, that Boniface at least would have liked to see retained. An indication of the pressure that the papacy was applying in this area at the time is seen in a 723 law of Liutprand, king of the Lombards: marriage to the wife of a cousin was forbidden, and Liutprand explained the change by stating that the bishop of Rome had urged him to impose it (34.4, Bluhme 1868, 123–124). Liutprand's legislation also included the prohibition of marriage to spiritual relatives, that is, to a godchild or to the child's mother and between the godparents' child and the godchild (34.5, Bluhme 1868, 124). Condemnation of marriage between sponsor and mother of the child had already appeared in the Roman council of 721 (c. 4, *PL* 67.343; Lynch 1986, 234–242; Goody 1983, 197–199). Saint Boniface's correspondence after 735, strongly stating his objection to a Roman rule that seemed to stand in the way of reinforcing the spiritual bond established by baptism, suggests that the prohibition was recent. Thus in the period that saw a major increase of pressure to seek marriage partners outside the kin, regulations began to limit the reinforcement of spiritual kinship by marriage as well.[16] These limitations of the choice of marriage partner were to be of major importance, for they imposed significant restrictions on family strategies in the eighth century and thereafter.

THE CELIBATE STATE

The Church's teaching on marriage was essentially a comment on and a criticism of the institution found at the center of all the societies it met throughout the Mediterranean basin and beyond. Based on the Church's conception of humankind described above, it sought to adjust, improve, and occasionally to change one or another aspect of marriage, but essentially the institution remained as before. The teaching on celibacy, however, was new; personally and socially it represented a major change in the understanding of the possibilities for an adult life. There were virtually no models. Between the late third and the fifth century many social forms were developed to support those who chose to live the celibate life; sometimes the results were chaotic. But gradually order was applied and the celibates became organized for the most part around the local church or in a monastery, those two divine households of which the Master of the Rule wrote.

16. For an important general discussion of the historiography of spiritual relationships, see Lynch 1986, 32–80.

Great effort was made to ensure that the higher clergy of the local church was celibate. Since many of them were already married, this rule, if implemented, required that they live apart from their wives. It is likely that many clergy suffered this loss because they wished to enjoy clerical office. The degree to which they saw celibacy as a good in itself is difficult to measure. The endless problems that conciliar canons and episcopal letters tell us about make it clear that the teaching was difficult to implement. There is much evidence that, in the centuries here discussed, the married clergy living as celibates was in decline.

Also attached to the local church were three groups of celibate women: widows, deaconesses, and dedicated virgins (Turner 1931, 316–351; Daniélou 1960, 70–96). The enrolled widows of 1 Timothy 5.9 were the first group for whom celibacy was a requirement. They seem to have quickly assumed a role as assistants in such rituals as the baptism of women and are known to have instructed neophytes as well. The deaconess, as her name implied, was ordained for service. Whether celibacy was required of her at the beginning is not clear. Her function tended to be similar to that of the widows, and in fact, her role in the Western church was never an important one (Martimort 1982, 197–217). The dedicated virgins did not have a public role in the Church like their sisters the widows and deaconesses, but the future lay with them. All three classes of women received official recognition by the Church, expressed by rituals of reception and benediction. The virgin was a special case in the sense that her commitment was capable of several degrees. But if she did choose to receive official recognition, by the fourth century there was a ritual whereby the bishop blessed or gave her the veil, symbolic of her status, and by the middle of the sixth century, the ceremony found its place in the Eucharist (Metz 1954, 96–100, 138–160). This development is parallel both in time and in form to that sacralization of marriage noted above. In the fifth century it was already customary to consider this dedication permanent in ideal at least, under the image of marriage to Christ. Clearly the same ideology that sought to move society to accept the permanence of the marriage bond was at play here. Domestic arrangements for the support of dedicated virgins varied. Many continued to live with their families. Early on in the movement, however, there was a tendency to seek some form of common life. It might have been nothing more than the occasional gathering for instruction and prayer, but by the end of the fourth century in Egypt, Syria, and Cappadocia, the monastery for women had become the milieu to which many of those who wished to live a virginal life turned.

It was precisely in the region and at the beginning of the age presently being discussed that a remarkable period of monastic development occurred; women's monastic communities found a place in it. These years saw not only

Caesarius of Arles's publication of the first rule explicitly written for women (Caesarius 1988, 68–69), but also the composition of the *Regula Magistri* and the *Rule* of Saint Benedict. These texts were to have major influence on later rules and on monasticism as an institution throughout the Middle Ages and beyond. They also shed light on aspects of the development that are of special importance here.

In his *Life* of Anthony of Egypt, Athanasius describes the beginning of the saint's vocation not as a call to chastity but as a withdrawal from the world and its preoccupations with family and wealth (*PG* 26.835–978). Celibacy was involved, of course, but only as one element in the decision to leave all and follow Christ, a pattern similar to the process whereby Francis of Assisi found his vocation. Rules like the *Regula virginum* of Caesarius or that of Eugippius, with their incorporation of the *Rule* of Saint Augustine, are noticeably preoccupied with protection of the chastity of members and show a certain tension in this regard (Caesarius 1988, 44–45; Eugippius 1976). The rule Caesarius wrote for men and the rules of the Master and of Saint Benedict give a different impression. They were intended to create a place where men and women could grow in the love of Christ, a school of the Lord's service, as Benedict would express it. Concerned with those who seek to leave the world, they are designed to make clear to the monk that he has done so and to prevent the world from pursuing him into his place of withdrawal. This was achieved in part by the physical design of the monastery: it contained within itself much that was required—garden, mill, and so on—allowing members to live there without going beyond the walls. The development of rules of cloister in the *Regula virginum* was similarly intended to keep visits by outsiders to a minimum (Caesarius 1988, 70–84).

The ritual by which a candidate joined a monastery was clearly intended to impress upon him or her a complete separation from an earlier form of life and entry into a new one (Constable 1987, 783–796). By putting aside secular garb and assuming monastic dress, the candidate recognized that henceforth all the necessities for the physical support of life would be supplied by the head of the new household that he or she had entered. The different quality of the new life was enhanced also by the degree of ritualization in prayer, dining, conversation, and work.

The rules establish that members of a monastery were expected to cut family ties and to resist the endless attraction of family wealth (Borias 1977). It was understood that this was not easily achieved: Caesarius reminded the nuns of Saint Jean of Arles that they should not let family considerations influence their choice of superior (Caesarius 1988, 440–442), and when Benedict warned his monks not to defend one another, he added that the prohibition applied even if they were closely related by blood (69, Benedict 1971–1972, 2:64–67). The monastic communities described in the writings of the period, groups in which many men and women are known to have lived the celibate life, thus exhibited the qualities of inclusivity and exclusivity that are characteristic of vital communities in a time of major change. The monastery was presented as a society complete in every way but the power of reproduction, providing all the needs of its members, a society that recognized the necessity of excluding pressure even from the families that gave birth to its members and might seek to lead them to withdraw from their original ideals.

Italian monasticism would pass into northern Europe in the seventh century. Though not without many problems, as the register of Gregory the Great illustrates so well,[17] the movement was to be one of the Church's principal instruments in its pastoral, instructional, and missionary roles for the next five hundred years.

Examining the history of the family in central and northern Italy during the first three centuries of the Middle Ages in the context of the influence of Christian ideology suggests certain conclusions. First, there are good reasons for thinking that the effort to spread the Christian conception of sexuality and marriage and of the value of the celibate life, which had been stated in the early Church, was continued among older as well as new peoples of Italy during this period of major disturbance. At this stage of research, the impact of this teaching on the stability and fertility of the basic family unit cannot be gauged; much work remains to be done in this regard. Second, the gradual involvement of the Church in establishing the limits of relationships within which valid marriage was allowed proved to be very important, in terms of not only the choice of marriage partner but also kinship and family strategy. The immediate practical consequences—the acceptance of a more exogamous type of kinship and the survival or disappearance of families—remain to be tested, but the long-term influence, as indicated in several of the chapters that follow, is evident. Finally, the development of that other type of family, the monastery, proved to be rich in innovation and full of promise for the centuries that lay ahead.

17. Almost one-quarter of the letters in his register are concerned with monastic problems (Jenal 1986, 147–157).

Chapter 10

JULIUS KIRSHNER

Materials for a Gilded Cage: Non-Dotal Assets in Florence, 1300–1500

Dowries customarily accompanied brides into marriage in late medieval Italy. In commercial and financial centers like Florence, husbands typically received dowries in the form of cash payments or their equivalents, such as credits in the city's public debt (Monte Comune), which were easily converted into cash. Under the prevailing system of the *jus commune*—the common body of legal rules, regulations, and juristic doctrines developed primarily from Justinian's *Corpus juris civilis*—ownership and management of a dowry temporarily passed to the husband during marriage. He could invest, mortgage, and convert a dowry into other property as he saw fit, unless he forfeited his legal right to do so in a special dotal pact. As the expressed purpose of the dowry was to sustain the burdens of marriage, a husband was expected to apply income from dotal property to support his wife and their common household. Upon receipt of a dowry, it was customary for a husband, together with his father or other members of his family, to acknowledge joint liability for the dowry in a *confessio dotis* in the presence of witnesses and the notary redacting the document. A husband was legally obligated, and could even be compelled

The following abbreviations are used: ASF (Archivio di Stato di Firenze); BNF (Biblioteca Nazionale di Firenze); MC (Monte Comune); NA (Notarile Antecosimiano); CS (Carte Strozziane); and SMN (Santa Maria Nuova). All the archival documents and manuscripts cited below, unless indicated otherwise, are found in the Archivio di Stato di Firenze. I have converted all dates into modern style. The Florentine year began on 25 March, so that dates falling between 1 January and 24 March are one year behind the modern year. I want to express my appreciation to Thomas Kuehn for his helpful comments and for obtaining on my behalf a host of archival references.

by judicial authorities, to return to his wife an amount equivalent to the dowry he had received should it be manifest that he was verging on insolvency. In the event of his predecease, property belonging to the husband, to those assuming joint liability with him, and to all their heirs was necessarily secured for restitution of the dowry. If the wife predeceased her husband and there were no surviving children from their marriage, her husband was entitled under local municipal statutes (*jus proprium*) to a part or even all of the dowry. The statutes of Pisa, Siena, Arezzo, and Pistoia awarded such husbands one-half the dowry, the statutes of Montepulciano and Lucca a generous two-thirds (on condition that the wife died at least one year after having been introduced into her husband's household), whereas the statutes of Florence were even more generous, granting husbands the whole dowry (Kirshner n.d.).

Besides the dowry, a Florentine wife might come with, or acquire during marriage by gift, bequest, or descent, assets classified as non-dotal.[1] According to medieval jurists, non-dotal assets were of two types. One type was called parapherna, or paraphernalia, items beyond a dowry (*res extra dotem*). More specifically, parapherna were defined in a mid-fourteenth-century legal opinion as "those movable goods which the wife brings to the husband's household especially for her own use and the common use of herself and her husband."[2] As found in Roman and medieval Italian jurisprudence, the term *parapherna* generally designated a trousseau, the personal accouterments accompanying the bride into the husband's household, although any real and personal property she inherited or acquired by other means during marriage might also be designated as parapherna. The other type, *bona non dotalia,* generally consisted of assets belonging to the wife that she did *not* bring into her husband's household. In Florence, however, in stark contrast to both Roman law and the jus commune, the successive statutory codifications (1325, 1355, and 1415) omitted specific reference to parapherna.[3] Non-dotal assets were encompassed by the single category of bona non dotalia. These local statutes mirrored practice: the thousands of confessiones dotium and dozens of family account

1. On non-dotal assets in late Roman law, see Gerner 1954 and the review essay of the book by Wolff (1955), as well as García Garrido 1982, 28–40, 146–149; in the jus commune before 1300, see Bellomo 1961, 131–142.

2. "Bona parafernalia, et hec sunt bona mobilia que uxor defert in domum mariti maxime ratione sui proprii usus vel causa communis sui et viri." My translation, from an opinion rendered by Francesco di Bici degli Albergotti on a dispute that occurred in the *distretto* of Florence sometime after 1350. For an edition of Albergotti's opinion and a related opinion by Baldo degli Ubaldi, see Kirshner and Pluss 1979 (quotation on 74).

3. *Statuti* [1325] 1910–1921, vol. 2, *Statuto del podesia dell'anno 1325,* fol. 111, lib. 2, rub. 35 (*De eo quod uxor alicuius acquisverit*); ASF Statuti di Firenze, Podestà [1355], n. 18, fol. 152v, lib. 2, rub. 39; *Statuta* [1415] 1778–1781, vol. 1, fol. 161, lib. 2, rub. 65.

books and diaries (*ricordanʒe*) I have examined for this period fail to provide a single example of movable goods (*res mobiles*) that accompanied the Florentine bride to her husband's house at the beginning of marriage being designated as parapherna.[4] In Florence as in other Tuscan cities, Roman parapherna had been largely supplanted by its functional counterpart, *corredo, doni,* or *donora,*[5] comprising the bride's personal belongings, lingerie, and ceremonial dress and amounting to roughly 11 percent of a typical dowry accompanying well-to-do Florentine brides in the fourteenth and fifteenth centuries (Klapisch-Zuber 1988b). But unlike Roman parapherna, it cannot be emphasized too strongly, the Florentine bride's donora were given, received, and treated by notaries, jurists, and legislators as dotal property rather than non-dotal assets. The bride might also receive from her family on the day she was sent to her husband's household supplementary personal items and pocket money designated as non-dotal gifts, or *sopradonora.* Although these gifts were never called parapherna by their donors, they were regarded as such by medieval jurists.[6]

It is reasonably certain that non-dotal assets did not play the instrumental role that dowries did in shaping the matrimonial and patrimonial strategies of Florentine families; nor did non-dotal assets share with dowries the dubious distinction of becoming the focus of the many disputes that pitted many family members against one another. True, some abstract significance has been attributed by historians of medieval jurisprudence to non-dotal assets, reflecting the attention such assets have been accorded by jurists and legislators (Bellomo 1961, 131–142). The role of non-dotal assets in the domestic economy and in the devolution of patrimony in late medieval Italy, however, has yet to be studied by social or legal historians, for fairly obvious reasons. Foremost is that we are much less informed about non-dotal assets than we are about dowries, for which we have abundant archival information. At the same time, historians of law have operated on the assumption that once women were dowered they were legally excluded from succession to the paternal estate under both the jus commune and jus proprium (Mayali 1987). Thus they have embraced the comfortable simplicity that what assets, if any, wives might receive beyond the

4. Nor is the term *parapherna* found in Genoese notarial records (Epstein 1984, 250 n. 11). In Milan, on the other hand, *parapherna* was used to designate personal effects brought by wives to their husbands at the beginning of marriage (Caso 1981).

5. *Corredo* was commonly used in confessiones dotium drafted in Florence before the mid-fourteenth century. In confessiones dotium of the fifteenth century *donora* had all but replaced *corredo* as the designation for the bride's personal articles.

6. Lena di Bernardo Sassetti brought her husband a 700-florin dowry, 630 in cash and 70 in donora. When she arrived in his household on 12 May 1384, she came with additional personal items worth approximately 60 florins; see the ricordi of Paolo di Alessandro Sassetti, cs, ser. 21, 4, fols. 70, 74v, 143: "Cose date ala Lena in donora e in sopradonora quando [a] dì xii magio anno mccclxxxiiii n'andò a marito nel nome di dio e di buona ventura."

dowry must have been incidental and inconsequential. For their part, social historians are quick to point out that there was no shortage of medieval Italian women who received testamentary bequests, but they fail to note the practical consequences arising from the legal distinction between dotal and non-dotal assets and the ways in which such distinctions may have affected patrimonial strategies (Cohn 1989). To be fair, dotal assets are easier to identify than non-dotal assets, not least because the former were customarily classified as such. The technical classifications, paraphernalia and bona non dotalia, which were second nature to professional jurists, were almost never used as labels by the parties conveying non-dotal assets. The terminological problem facing historians in deciding whether the wife's goods should be considered dotal or non-dotal has also bedeviled anthropological investigations of property accompanying Mediterranean women into marriage (Davis 1977, 181–184). The problem is compounded by the vagaries of scribal habits. Notaries were inconsistent in providing the marital status of women mentioned in the documents they drew up, thus leaving to us the necessary sleuthing to establish whether a woman acquiring or conveying assets should be classified as unmarried, married, or widowed. The operative reality of the wife's property was less tidy, and therefore more problematic, than our historiography has hitherto led us to believe.

Far from intending to remedy past omissions by presenting a comprehensive account of non-dotal assets in Florence, the scope of this chapter is modest. It presents preliminary research findings that suggest the legal, material, and symbolic significance of non-dotal assets and their fruits in fourteenth- and fifteenth-century Florence. It considers first the legal regulations governing their disposition both during and on dissolution of marriage; second, the actual arrangements by which non-dotal assets were created, acquired, and encumbered; and third, their disposition on the husband's predecease. The ascendancy of the husband's legal capacity to control non-dotal assets and the corresponding attenuation of the wife's capacity to hold separate property are placed in the foreground throughout. In the end, my aim is to raise methodological questions and to stimulate discussion rather than to reach firm conclusions about a subject whose content remains to be clarified and whose boundaries remain to be demarcated.

Under the jus commune, a cardinal distinction between dotal and paraphernal assets was that ownership of the latter was vested in the wife during marriage. If, as the jurists observed, it was customary for the wife to place paraphernal goods in the husband's custody,[7] was she constrained to do so as a

7. Note, however, Antonio Strozzi's elliptical comment: "Et licet dicat quod in bonis parafer-

matter of law? Francesco Albergotti (d. 1376) insisted, in what became a *locus classicus,* that the wife was under no such legal compulsion: "Sometimes the wife gives over the management of these paraphernal goods to the husband, and then she is seen to have conceded tacit administration and rightful use of them; and sometimes she reserves management to herself, and the husband has no rightful claim to them" (Kirshner and Pluss, 74). In a related opinion on the same case, the prominent Perugian jurist Baldo degli Ubaldi (d. 1400) affirmed that the husband managed parapherna but did not establish whether the wife's consent, tacit or express, was necessary (Kirshner and Pluss, 76); yet his commentary on the *Codex* clearly indicated that her consent was indeed required. He stated unequivocally that the husband could not administer parapherna against his wife's wishes and that she, as *domina,* could reclaim parapherna during marriage.[8] As far as can be discerned, every jurist from the thirteenth century on affirmed that should his wife expressly forbid him the right of administration, the husband could not meddle with her administration of parapherna.[9] Unlike dotal assets, then, the husband's use of parapherna depended on his wife's consent.[10]

With his wife's consent, her husband could exploit the fruits and revenues accruing from *bona immobilia* treated as parapherna so long as they benefited them jointly. His obligation to return such fruits or their equivalent to the wife or her heirs on termination of the marriage was conditional. If the wife or her heirs established that the husband had received these fruits with his wife's consent, it became a question of what portion of them had been expended and what portion was extant. All extant fruits had to be returned to the wife. If the fruits had been consumed, it then became a question of whether they were produced by "industria" or "natura." Fruits produced by industria were characterized as those derived from the husband's purposeful activity, that is, his labor and management. Included under this classification were the fruits of olive groves, vineyards, and arable fields. In remuneration for the risks attendant on his management, the husband was granted a portion of the fruits produced by

---

nalibus que com[m]uniter tradant viro, forte dicendem totum contrarium" (cs, ser. 3a, 41, vol. 6, fol. 183).

　　8. Ubaldi 1498 (to *Cod.* 5.14.8, *Hac lege,* and to *Cod.* 5.12.29, *Ubi ad huc*).

　　9. Accursius 1569, 723ab (to *Cod.* 5.14.8); Odofredus 1552, 280a (to *Cod.* 5.14.8, n. 1): "Et in lege ista dicitur, quod maritus in rebus paraphernalibus mulieris sue, nullam habet communionem uxore prohibente: licet de rigore iuris videretur, quod ex quo mulier committit personam suam viro, quod res suas deberet committere. Tamen de equitate dicendum est, licet uxor committit personam suam, res paraphernales non committit. Unde in rebus paraphernalibus maritus nihil habet facere uxore prohibente"; Bartolomeo da Saliceto 1515, 25va (to *Cod.* 5.14.8).

　　10. "Unde requiratur consensus uxoris, prout est quando uxor tradit viro bona parafernalia . . ." (Antonio Strozzi, cs, ser. 3a, 41, vol. 6, fol. 183).

his own labor. He was thus under no obligation to compensate his wife for any such fruits consumed during marriage. Nor was he obligated to compensate her for the consumption of a moderate (*modicum*) amount of "natural" fruits. If the amount of natural fruits consumed was characterized as large, however, then compensation was mandatory. A husband seizing paraphernal fruits against his wife's wishes, or employing them solely for his own benefit or self-enrichment, was required to indemnify his wife or her heirs.[11]

In theory, the wife who allowed her husband to administer parapherna could demand, and even sue for, their return at any time during the marriage. In the same breath, the jurists took for granted that the husband, as legitimate and actual head of the household, would ordinarily take charge of any movables his wife brought into his household; if she knowingly and without objecting allowed him to receive and manage paraphernal fruits, her consent was to be presumed.[12] That is why the wife was admonished to possess valid legal instruments itemizing her personal belongings that were not included in the dowry as well as attesting that she had received consent from her husband to bring them into his house. Otherwise, to prove that they did not belong to her husband would be difficult, and they would be unrecoverable by the wife or her heirs at the termination of the marriage.[13] The husband, under the jus commune, exercised control at his own risk. If parapherna were dissipated or declined in value as the result of a husband's profligacy or mismanagement, his wife or her heirs could demand compensation from his estate.

Bona non dotalia, to which the wife retained the dual right of ownership and administration, generally consisted of assets the wife did not bring into her husband's household. In principle, they were for the wife's own use but could

11. In addition to the reference cited in note 2, see Bartolo da Sassoferrato 1570–1571a, 176b (to *Cod.* 5.14.11, *Simulier*), 1570–1571a, 138va (to *Dig.* 35.2.90, *Si heres*); Alberico da Rosciate 1586, 261v–262 (to *Cod.* 5.14.11); Ubaldi 1548, 119 (to *Cod.* 5.14.11); and Tartagni 1548, 47v (cons. 42).

12. This logic underlay a Bolognese statute of 1357; Archivio di Stato di Bologna, Statuti, n. 12, fol. 114r–114v, lib. 5, rub. 30 (*De dotibus restituendis et ipsarum parte lucranda et fructibus rerum parafrenalium*): "Preterea statuimus quod si quis receperit fructus vel redditus quoscunque ex bonis parafrenalibus uxoris sue voluntate uxoris non possit ipsa, vel eius heres, ipsos fructus vel redditus petere vel extimationem ipsorum que voluntas semper presumatur, nisi voluntas contraria legiptime probaretur." To the question, "nunquid bona constante matrimonio uxore pervenuta, si uxore sciente, patiente et non contradicente maritus per nonnullos annos fructus et redditus percepit, dicantur parafernalia et in paraferna conversa," Raffaele Raimondi answered, "puto quod sic." Concurring opinions were written by Prosdocimo Conti, Giovanni Francesco Capodilista, Giovanni da Imola, and Paolo di Castro (Raimondi 1576, 53v–54, cons. 105).

13. Baldo to *Dig.* 23.3.9.2, *Si ego Seiae* § *Dotis autem causa* (1498). Statutes like those of Bergamo translated this presumption into communal law: "Item quod si aliqua mulier, maritum habens, habeat aliquas possessiones vel bona cuiuscumque condictionis presumantur et intelligantur esse mariti, nisi probetur vel hostendatur ad eam pervenisse ex successione, donatione vel legato" (Storti Storchi 1986, 192, collatio x, rub. 3).

be enjoyed by the husband with his wife's express consent. Although the rules established by jurists for the disposition and restitution of paraphernal fruits and revenues were extended to bona non dotalia,[14] there is evidence (see below) that husbands were able to exercise control over all non-dotal assets and fruits during marriage, with or without their wives' consent, in disregard of legal niceties. Since the average age of Florentine husbands entering a first marriage tended to be thirty-two years, whereas the average age of their brides was eighteen (Herlihy and Klapisch-Zuber 1978, 205–207; Kirshner and Molho 1978, 431–433), it is hardly surprising that senior husbands sought control of all non-dotal assets and fruits, and younger brides had little choice but to entrust them to their spouses. Here it is worth making a comparative observation about the behavior of wealthy Roman matrons who could always divorce their overbearing husbands and Florentine wives who could not. According to Richard Saller, "the women's property often gave Roman husbands an incentive to be attentive to their wives' wishes" (1988, 408–409). Arguably, some Florentine husbands chronically in debt may have found it necessary to placate their wives, who for reasons suggested below maintained independent control over non-dotal assets. Yet there is scant evidence that Florentine wives from upper-echelon families enjoyed the same leverage attributed to affluent Roman wives by virtue of the dowry that accompanied them into marriage or the non-dotal assets at their discretion.

Ascertaining whether a wife had in fact given her husband consent to administer or even to alienate non-dotal assets was a recurrent issue facing medieval jurists. Speaking broadly, the attitude they brought to such disputes was paternalistic, and they were inclined to be as protective of women as they were of minors, or of anyone who suffered legal disabilities because of her or his "essential fragility." As a wife was regarded as a gullible and submissive creature to be kept in a perpetual state of trembling and fear (*in tremore e in paura* [Certaldo 1945, 105 n. 126]), in all things a legal dependent of her husband, it was easy for jurists to demonstrate a priori that she was incapable of freely given consent to her husband. On the issue of the husband's administration of

---

14. As Albergotti opined: "Quedam sunt bona mulieris neque dotalia neque parafernalia, veluti ea que sunt extra dotem et extra ea que uxor in viri domum inducit. Et ista differunt ab utraque specie predictorum, quia vir in istis non habet dominium ut in dotalibus habet neque administrationem ex tacita seu presumpta voluntate uxoris" (Kirshner and Pluss, 74). Paraphrasing Albergotti's opinion, Antonio Strozzi made clear that bona non dotalia, unlike parapherna, did not accompany the wife into the husband's household. Regarding parapherna, "ista consistunt in bonis mobilibus que uxor portat secum in domum viri, ratione sui vel com[m]unis usus"; and bona non dotalia, "quedam alia bona habet mulier, que non sunt inducta in domum, sed sunt propria ipsius uxoris et in illis maritus nullam habet administrationem" (CS, ser. 3a, 41, vol. 6, fol. 182).

non-dotal goods, it must be presumed that he acted *contra voluntatem uxoris,* Francesco Albergotti alleged, unless there were palpable and positive proof to the contrary. His allegation takes its force from further presumptions on the nature of women and the mutual obligations between phallocratic husbands and submissive wives:

> The second presumption proceeds from the very nature of women, because a woman is the most avaricious of the species. . . . It is unnatural to suppose that she would want to bestow the non-dotal goods on her husband, since as a general rule beings act according to their own nature and their accustomed and common habits. . . . The third presumption proceeds from the proper relationship of persons, for while it is fitting for husbands to support their wives from their own goods and from the fruits of dotal goods, it is not fitting for husbands to be fed and supported by wives. . . . The fourth consideration proceeds from the joining of persons and its defining quality, namely that between husband and wife there is a joining which is linked to deference on the wife's part, and there arises as a consequence of that docility the presumption of dissent or forced assent. (Kirshner and Pluss, 75)

Paternalism aside, the statutes of Florence granted the husband direct control over all non-dotal assets, with one glaring exception (discussed below). What accounts for this divergence between the jus commune and Florentine law? It was not a consequence of that all-purpose causal agent of late medieval history, the Black Death, which first struck Florence in the spring of 1348; the Florentine statutes granting husbands control had been promulgated twenty-three years earlier, in 1325. Unquestionably the calamities wrought by the Black Death and subsequent plagues had a sweeping effect on the general devolution of patrimonial property and the restitution of dotal and non-dotal assets in Florence (Falsini 1971, 437–482); nevertheless, apart from minor verbal modifications, the anteplague statutes regulating dotal assets were repeated in the postplague redaction of 1355. Although the statutes give no clue for the rationale justifying divergence from the jus commune, it is conceivable that they were designed to make fully lawful husbands' de facto control of non-dotal assets. If so, the period before 1325 should not be viewed as a golden age during which wives had unfettered authority over their own property and acted as autonomous agents. Even if this surmise is correct, the question is begged: beyond the issue of direct control, what stirred Florentine lawmakers to respond favorably to the husband's demand to administer non-dotal assets? The statutes were primarily aimed, I believe, at placing non-dotal revenues at his disposal in order to alleviate mounting financial burdens owing to expenses attendant on marriage and the struggle to maintain and enhance status in a world of intense social competition (Hughes 1983; Klapisch-Zuber 1985).

What was happening in Florence was hardly remarkable: it conformed to a wider pattern in which legislators across northern and central Italy were granting husbands broad control over all the wife's assets, non-dotal as well as dotal (Bellomo 1961, 139–142; Ercole 1908; Rinaldi 1909, 192; Storti Storchi 1980, 548).[15]

Paradoxically, the Florentine statutes of 1325 and 1355 regulating the disposition of non-dotal assets during marriage were flawed by a contradiction. At variance with the jus commune, by allowing the husband use and administration of property acquired by his wife during marriage, even against her wishes, they yet upheld the jus commune in that they did not encompass all non-dotal assets. The statutes reserved to the wife use and administration of property bequeathed by her parents and her maternal and paternal kin, except where her husband was expressly conceded the right of usufruct in the bequest. As the bulk of non-dotal assets acquired by Florentine wives derived from testamentary bequests made by parents and other kin, the proviso sharply blunted the general thrust of the statute to enhance the husband's claim to non-dotal assets. It would be a gross misreading of the statutes, however, to interpret the proviso as an attempt to empower wives by granting them control over their own patrimonies. And it is unlikely that the proviso could have been, or even was meant to be, strictly enforced against husbands who seized control of their wives' non-dotal assets, whatever their source. Its ostensible purpose was precautionary: to safeguard the wife's patrimonial property from seizure by creditors for debts incurred by her husband. Under the statutes suit could be brought by anyone acting on behalf of the wife, and in any place, for the purpose of protecting such non-dotal assets against all the husband's creditors (*contra omnes creditores viri*). In principle, at least, the husband's creditors, rather than the husband himself, stood to lose most from the statutes.

The responsibility for reconciling a statute at odds with itself fell to the jurists. The muddle that threatened to render the statutes inoperable was addressed by the jurist Angelo degli Ubaldi (d. 1400), who sought to demonstrate that the statutes were intended to benefit the husband (1551, cons. 42, 31vb–32a). He presented a hypothetical case in which the rent from two houses that had been bequeathed to a woman by her mother was appropriated by her

15. For Savona, see Balletto 1971, 2:183–184, lib.6, rub. 8 (*Quod aliquis non possit petere ultra sortem pro extradotibus*), which makes no distinction between parapherna and *bona extra dotalia:* for a Trevisan statute of 1385, see Betto 1986, 381–382, rub. 3 (*De dotibus mulierum et fructibus rerum parafernalium earum*): "Et quod de omnibus bonis, quecunque et undecunque habuerit uxor, fructus habere debeat et lucrari maritus constante matrimonio sicut fructus rei dotalis, et huic statuto per pactum aliquod vel modo aliquo renunciari non possit"; for Feltre, see *Statutorum* [1439] 1749, 200, lib. 2, rub. 70 (*Qualiter maritus lucretur fructus bonorum uxoris quomodo sibi spectantium*); for Forlì, see *Statuta* [1504] 1616, 215, rub. 43 (*Quod fructus bonorum uxoris sint mariti*).

husband, who was not defunct. Two questions arose from this model situation. Did the husband have a right to acquire and enjoy the rent? Could his heirs be compelled to restore the rent to his widow? In spite of the contradictory nature of the statutes, Angelo insisted that the overarching intent of the legislators was to place non-dotal assets and their fruits at the disposition of the husband. At the same time he admitted that in reserving to the wife control over bequests of non-dotal assets, the legislators had prudently avoided adding insult to the injury already inflicted by the death of her kin. His solution—granting the husband usufruct regarding bequests received by the wife from the paternal side, while granting usufruct over maternal bequests to the wife—was a compromise. Since in the case at hand the rent derived from houses bequeathed by the wife's mother, her husband was not entitled to use them, and consequently his heirs could be compelled to make restitution to the wife.

Angelo's attempt to make the statutes internally consistent and operable was hardly satisfactory. It failed both to eradicate the fundamental contradiction that made legislatorial intent difficult to determine and to answer the arguments from the jus commune that could be called forth to support the wife's claims. That the jurists in charge of revising the statutes in 1415 settled the matter once and for all by deleting the provision reserving to the wife control of paternal and maternal bequests was no accident. They also tightened the husband's grip on non-dotal assets by prohibiting a wife from alienating such assets without her husband's consent. From 1415 on, a husband could confidently claim that communal law gave him an unqualified usufruct of all the assets acquired by his wife during marriage. The husband's victory on the terrain of statutory law did not mean that he invariably gained control of non-dotal assets in practice, however. Room was left for donors and testators to deny the husband control of non-dotal property by attaching a stipulation to their gifts and bequests that would reserve usufruct to the wife exclusively. Numerous instances of such encumbrances between 1300 and 1500 testify to their enduring popularity and their perceived efficacy in safeguarding non-dotal assets. According to the jurist Alessandro Bencivenni, moreover, who wrote a commentary on the statutes of 1415, a wife required her husband's consent to alienate non-dotal assets only if they came to her during marriage and if her husband enjoyed usufruct. When non-dotal assets were acquired before marriage or a husband had no right of usufruct, his wife had a presumptive right under the jus commune to dispose of them as she wished.[16] A

16. BNF, MSS, II, IV, 435, fol. 49, gl. *et mulier in ipsa talia bona:* "Si qua fuissent acquisita uxori constante matrimonio et in quibus vir habet ususfructum; alioquin remanet libera facultas mulieri prout de iure communi conceditur." Note that neither the statute of 1415 itself nor Bencivenni's gloss indicates the source of the non-dotal assets. Note further that Bencivenni states that the assets "were acquired for the wife *(uxori)* during marriage," not by the wife *(uxore)* herself.

husband could also be denied usufruct if he had driven his wife from his house, subjected her to physical abuse, or squandered his own assets. In addition, his wife retained the remedy of having suit brought against any of her husband's creditors, to avert seizure of non-dotal assets or to demand restitution of assets already seized.

At the husband's predecease, his wife could demand restoration of not only her non-dotal assets but also the fruits from those assets not consumed during the marriage. At the wife's predecease, such remaining fruits were recoverable by her heirs. The husband's claim to non-dotal assets at his wife's predecease was defined for the first time in the statutes of 1325, carried forward in the redaction of 1355, and fortified in the redaction of 1415. If she died having made and left a will, her husband succeeded to at least one-third of the non-dotal assets, in the absence of surviving children or "other descendants." Alternatively, if she died intestate, his succession to the one-third was automatic, with or without surviving children or descendants. In both cases, the remaining two-thirds went to her closest living kin.[17] These statutes were diametrically opposed to the jus commune, which had made the wife's property-owning capacity the salient feature of non-dotal assets. They ran afoul of the teachings of canonists and theologians who defended the wife's right to dispose of non-dotal assets as she wished, in particular for the purpose of pious donations and bequests (Antoninus of Florence [1389–1459] 1581–1582, P. II, t. 1, c. 15 § 1). The Florentine statutes were also at variance with the statutes of cities like Lucca, where "a wife may make a will respecting paraphernal goods which she may dispose as she pleases, even without the consent of her husband."[18]

Although no justification was provided for the innovation that made the Florentine husband part successor to his wife's non-dotal assets, it was a bold

---

17. ASF, Statuti di Firenze, Podestà [1355], n. 18, fol. 168v, lib. 2, rub. 74 (*Quale succedat in dote et in aliis bonis uxoris premortue*); *Statuta* [1415], 1778–1781, 1:223, lib. 2, rub. 129: "In aliis vero bonis uxoris predictae non dotalibus si testata decesserit, vir succedat saltem in tertia parte bonorum non extante aliquo filio, vel filia, vel aliis descendentibus ex eis. Si vero intestata decesserit succedat vir in tertia parte bonorum non dotalium. Et in residuo ipsorum bonorum succedat proximior in gradu ipsi uxori . . ." According to Alessandro Bencivenni, her surviving children had no remedy if their mother had donated paraphernal assets to the Church, but reserved their fruits to herself, and then bequeathed to her husband the right to collect up to one-third of the fruits after her death (BNF, MSS, II, IV, 435, fol. 70v, gl. *in uxore predicta*).

18. Should she die intestate, however, her heirs possessed a presumptive claim to one-fourth of her paraphernal goods: Archivio di Stato di Lucca, Statuti del Comune di Lucca (1362), no. 6, lib. 4, rub. 120 (*De muliere defuncta in matrimonio*): "Et similiter testari possit de bonis parafrenalibus in quibus possit disponere eciam sine consensu mariti prout voluerit; dum tamen nulla mulier nupta vel vidua in sua ultima voluntate vel eciam in infirmitate sua possit de suis bonis alienare seu iudicare, quin heredes eius ab intestato succedentes eciam pater, ascendentes et descendentes habeant quartam partem bonorum eius."

extension of the legislation that had given husbands usufruct of non-dotal fruits during marriage.

Legal commentaries, opinions, and statutes leave the impression that non-dotal assets formed a substantial part of the patrimony of Florentine wives (*bona mulieris*). Our ability to test the validity of this impression is, however, handicapped by skewed sources. The sparse number of ricordanze kept by women unfortunately furnish only limited details on the administration and destiny of the gifts and bequests they may have received.[19] Married women, unlike widows who acted as the heads of fiscal households, were legally incapable of submitting separate tax declarations (*catasti*), thus impeding us from taking full account of their own assets and debts. True, husbands were bound by communal law to report in their own tax declarations real estate, goods, and monies acquired by their wives during marriage or by both spouses jointly, but these declarations unquestionably underreported their wives' non-dotal assets. Such assets acquired by wives before marriage were exempt from taxation, and therefore not reportable to the officials of the catasto.[20] In addition, married couples sought to evade taxes by not reporting inheritances that wives accepted after having moved into their husbands' households. This tactic was censured in an enactment of 1456, which ordered that estates inherited by married women must be included in their husbands' tax declarations.[21] Finally, in marked contrast to the husband's vocal acknowledgment in thousands of confessiones dotium of the receipt of the dowry and the terms applying to his management of it, his silence concerning non-dotal assets was mandated by the civil law prohibition against interspousal gifts (Dumont 1928), which prevented him from formally acknowledging the receipt of any assets from his wife during marriage. What follows is intended to lay out some of the ways in which non-dotal assets were created and conveyed and the sorts of conditions attached to them. Information on non-dotal assets is largely gleaned from wills, instruments conveying gifts (*donationes*), and the registers of Florence's public debt.

A husband created non-dotal assets when he made a gift to his wife in contemplation of his death (*donatio mortis causa*). Unlike a gift between spouses

19. Notable exceptions are the ricordi of the widow Alessandra Macinghi Strozzi, cs, 5th ser., 15, and those of Selvaggia di Bartolomeo Gianfigliazzi, widow of Filippo Strozzi, ibid., 55, 56, 60, 61.

20. *Statuta* [1415], 1778–1781, 1:342–343, lib. 4, rub. 23 (*Quod uxor non cogatur solvere libram, praestantiam vel aliquod onus vivente viro*): "si qua vero bona pervinissent ad ipsam mulierem nuptam constante matrimonio, iure haereditario, vel alio iure, pro dictis bonis, quae sic ad eam devinissent, non gaudeant benefitio praesentis statuti, sed talia bona transeant ad dictam mulierem cum onere suo durante dicto matrimonio."

21. Provvisioni-Registri, 147, fols. 44v–45 (29 Apr. 1456).

made inter vivos, a gift mortis causa was permitted under the jus commune. Since it was revocable and became fully effective only on the donor's death, a donatio mortis causa closely resembled a legacy (Vismara 1962, 761ff.; Abouçaya 1966, 378–431). The donatio mortis causa was an attractive option in situations where donors wished to avoid subjecting property to the constraints of testate succession and potential litigation attendant on non-testate succession. Arrangements that reserved to the donor continued use and enjoyment of the assets donated (*donatio reservato usufructu*) were especially favored. Cristoforo di Francesco Buongiovanni of Gagliano, a citizen of Florence, donated farmland with a house to his wife, but he reserved usufruct to himself during his lifetime.[22] So did the widow Lippa di Puccio, who with the consent of her guardian in 1371 gave usufruct to half of a house with all its appurtenances to her married granddaughter, Agnese. Two conditions were attached to the donation. First, the property was for Agnese's sole and separate possession; her husband was not to acquire any rights to the donation. Second, Lippa prohibited her granddaughter from alienating the property, which on Agnese's death would pass to the hospital of Santa Maria Nuova.[23] Sometimes non-dotal assets were created by children who donated property to their nonwidowed mothers. This was a practicable tactic for making property available to one's father, while at the same time shielding the property from his creditors.[24]

More frequently, the gifts awarded to married daughters, granddaughters, and sisters were conveyed before the donor's death.[25] A large percentage of premortem gifts must have been intended to supplement dowries. There are numerous examples of this practice in the registers of the Monte Comune. In 1457 Luca di Giovanni Carnesecchi provided his married daughter Ginevra with a life annuity by transferring to her his right to collect interest on *monte*

22. NA, 6207 fols. 280–281 (28 Nov. 1460). Further examples are found in NA, 195, fols. 77v–78 (8 July 1341), fol. 210v (18 June 1348).

23. NA, 205, fol. 51–51v (9 Mar. 1371); Kuehn 1981, 138.

24. See the donation of the widow Filippa di Ruggeri, whose mother would receive on the daughter's predecease Filippa's dowry worth 420 florins (NA, 205, fols. 12v–13 [8 June 1353]), and the donation of Giovanni di Antonio, whose stepmother would receive on the donor's predecease his claim for the balance due on the sale of several properties (ibid., 7046, no foliation [1 Oct. 1432]).

25. For premortem gifts made in the fourteenth century, see NA, 7414, fol. 88r–88v (29 July 1316), 195, fols. 25v–28 (30 May 1339), fol. 68v (7 Aug. 1345), 7417, fol. 11 (8 June 1344), fol. 55r–55v (7 Feb. 1346), fol. 65 (1 May 1347), fol. 70v (23 Aug. 1347), 1200, fol. 68 (21 Jan. 1371); for the fifteenth century, see ibid., 13288, no foliation (6 Aug. 1445), 6252, fol. 169 (17 Mar. 1455), 14713, fols. 99v–100 (30 Dec. 1465), 14722, fols. 70v–71 (17 Oct. 1485), 14723, fol. 16v (4 July 1487).

credits with a face value of 350 florins.[26] In the same year, Orlando di Guccio de' Medici conferred on each of his married daughters—Cilia, wife of Francesco di Giovanni Guicciardini, and Caterina, wife of Antonio di Francesco Boscoli—the right to collect interest (*paghe*) on monte credits with a face value of 300 florins for the duration of their respective lives.[27] The credits were actually worth much less; their market value in this period fluctuated—sometimes violently—between 15 and 30 percent of par value (Conti 1984, 34). The promised rate of interest, which was 3.375 percent in 1457, fell to 3 percent in 1478, and the real rate of interest was in fact lower, if one takes into account the frequent and lengthy delays of interest payments on monte credits. In spite of such uncertainties, which made monte credits a speculative investment at best, there were several advantages that made them attractive to potential investors. Because of their broad availability, monte credits were utilized as collateral in myriad credit transactions.[28] They were used to pay premiums for the funding of dowries in the city's Dowry Fund (Monte delle doti). Claims to both overdue and future interest payable on monte credits had value, as they could be discounted or applied by citizens to the payment of their taxes.[29] Regrettably, the monte registers seldom divulge the nature of the transaction (sale, payment of a debt, premium for credit, and so on) or the exigencies triggering the transfer to third parties of claims to paghe held by wives.[30]

Under the Florentine statutes women, even if they were legally emancipated, could not enter into legal acts without permission of a guardian (*cum consensu mundualdi*) whom, it must be stressed, they were free to appoint. As Thomas Kuehn (1982a) has shown, Florentine wives tended to designate as guardians their own husbands, a finding applicable to wives transferring non-dotal assets to third parties. Margherita di Albertaccio Ricasoli, for instance, received permission from her husband-guardian Saladino di Matteo Adimari to

26. MC, 2599, fol. 143: "Che monna Ginevra, donna d'Antonio di Filippo Nicholi, pigli le paghe durante la sua vita."

27. MC, 2599, fol. 194v. Orlando also made identical donations to his two unmarried daughters, Lena and Alessandra.

28. Anthony Molho and I are completing a study of the Monte delle doti that examines these practices in detail.

29. On these practices, which stimulated much of the speculative activity in monte credits at the end of the fifteenth century, see Molho 1987.

30. Bartolomea, wife of Guiliano di Matteo Pezzati, for example, held 594 florins in monte credits; she transferred her claim to collect interest on a parcel of credits (300 florins) between 1 Sept. 1454 and August 1458 (MC, 2599, fol. 34). Lorenza di Bernardo di Miniato, wife of Giovanni di Francesco di ser Andrea, who held 2,018 florins in monte credits, transferred to Simone d'Antonio Canigiani her claim to paghe on 200 florins in credits, from 1 Sept. 1456 forward (ibid., fol. 152v).

divide into separate shares thirty-five rental properties that she possessed jointly (*in simul*) with Niccolai di Lorenzo Soderini.[31] When a wife transferred her monte credits to third parties, she often did so with her husband's active involvement as well as his permission. Giovanna, wife of Bernardo di Guccio Adimari, on receiving permission (*licenza*) from her husband to transfer her credits, appointed him as her legal representative (*procuratore*) to carry out the transaction.[32] When a wife transferred credits with the permission and legal representation of someone other than her husband, she usually relied on her husband's kinsmen, a notary, or even her parish priest.[33] Procurators were most evident in transfers of relatively large blocks of non-dotal credits. Occasionally a wife's credits were transferred without any notation of her having received permission from either her husband or anyone else.[34] Can we conclude in the absence of such permission that she was acting in violation of formal rules and independently of her husband's wishes, or of any man's wishes? It is possible that she had acquired the credits under terms that gave her the right to dispose of them as she wished, which would explain why her husband's permission was not required. But other, equally plausible reasons may help to explain the apparent absence of male permission. For one thing, the wife may have acted with her husband's tacit consent; for another, permission to transfer credits, at least in the ledgers of the Monte, was recorded inconsistently. Furthermore, in accordance with Florentine legal practice, a guardian's permission could legitimately be granted *after* a transaction was executed. Although the guardian's belated permission, as far as I can discern, was usually not recorded in the Monte's ledgers, it was subsequently added to the separate instrument effecting the transfer. This was neither mere surplusage nor an empty formality. Without the solemnity of the guardian's permission the transfer would remain legally invalid, making the party to whom the credits were transferred liable for their return. In sum, the evidence is

31. NA, 1843, fols. 89–90v (23 Feb. 1464).

32. MC, 1802, fól. 115v (19 Mar. 1366). Similarly, Mattea received consent from her husband, Girigoro di Lorenzo, to trade 355 florins in credits and appointed him as procurator to carry out the transaction (ibid., 1319, fol. 62 [8 Feb. 1372]).

33. MC, 1802, fol. 23 (17 Dec. 1365): "Monna Margherita, moglie di messer Lapo da Chastiglionchio, quartiere Santa Croce, a Guido di Tribaldo da Chastiglionchio, detto quartiere, fiorini 380 del'uno tre, per licenza del piovano Antonio de' Chavalcanti suo procuratore"; ibid., 1319, fol. 173 (21 May 1376): "Monna Dianora, moglie di Niccholò di ser Franciesco e figlia di Nastagio Buccelli, quartiere Santo Spirito, a monna Piera . . . di licenza di Lorenzo di ser Francesco suo procuratore."

34. Lisabetta, wife of Giovanni di messer Iacopo, transferred credits without her husband's consent (MC, 1802, fol. 67v, 10 June 1366): "Monna Lisabetta, figliuola fu di Gherardo Corbizzi e moglie di Giovanni di messer Iacopo, quartiere Santa Croce, a messer Donato Gherucci Barbadoro, quartiere Santo Spirito, fiorini 150 di monte vecchio."

too porous to support the assertion that Florentine women acting without a guardian supply "a graphic illustration of female self-determination" (Rosenthal 1989, 377).

The evidence is in fact overwhelming that Florentine wives customarily designated their husbands as recipients of interest payable on non-dotal monte credits they had acquired during marriage. Next to the credits registered under the name of Giovanna di Giovencho di Giuliano de' Medici, for example, the scribe noted that "Matteo di Aghostino, a doublet-maker and her husband, takes the interest during marriage."[35] Wives could also assign their husbands the right of temporary possession, use, and enjoyment of real properties they received as gifts.[36] Occasionally, wife and husband shared a right to the credits or to the interest, or to both together.[37] Joint ownership or joint usufructuary rights were primarily, though not exclusively, limited to monte credits. Sandro di Benedetto of Prato, a citizen of Florence, gave all his real property and monte credits to both his sister Maria and her husband.[38] The instances of non-dotal assets possessed jointly by husband and wife only faintly resemble community-property arrangements found elsewhere in medieval Italy and Europe (Zordan 1966; Hilaire 1973; Donahue 1980). There is no indication whether these assets were treated as true common marital property (*bona provenientia communiter de bonis viri et mulieris*) over which the wife had as much control as the husband. The procedural disabilities circumscribing Florentine wives meant that in most instances such joint assets would be subject to the husband's administration. Whether they were subject to the testamentary disposition of the first-dying spouse or to the testamentary power of the wife, since the assets came from her kin, is not certain. What remains beyond doubt

35. "Che Matteo di Aghostino farsettaio suo marito pigli le paghe durante il matrimonio"; MC, 2601, fol. 120 (year 1456), 2599, fol. 111v. Giovanna's credits had a face value of 410 florins.

36. NA, 5346 (5 June 1473), fol. 360r–360v. Here Pasqua di Giovanni assigned her husband, Bartolomeo di Paolo di Meo, a life-usufruct to properties in and around Florence that she had received as gifts. She accomplished this by appointing him as her legal representative.

37. Poltrone di messer Luigi Cavalcanti and his wife, Margherita, were listed as joint owners of credits (MC, 2559, fol. 199v); Nanna di Filippo Arrigucci was listed as the sole owner of monte credits with a face value of 703 florins, but she and her husband, Bencivenni di Parente di Michele, shared in the right to collect interest: "Che lla detta e Bencivenni suo marito e ognuno intero pigli le paghe" (ibid., fol. 188); Lapo di Giovanni and his wife, Alessandra, were listed as joint owners of credits with a face value of 250 florins, but it was stipulated "che Lapo detto durante il matrimonio pigli le paghe" (ibid., fol. 140).

38. NA, 10188, fol. 17r–17v (8 May 1473). See also the testament of Gello di Maso Gelli, who left several rural properties to be possessed jointly by his nephew, his nephew's wife, and his own wife (SMN, 70, fol. 4 [19 Apr. 1409]), and the testament of India di Marco Salviati, widow of Giovanni di Piero Baroncelli, who left seven-twelfths of a farm worth 300 florins to Mariotto, an illegitimate son of her father-in-law, and his wife (NA, 10185, fol. 64v [19 Dec. 1463]).

is the rarity of the phenomenon of assets held jointly by spouses, which confirms that, in harmony with Roman law, the respective patrimonies of wife and husband continued to be reckoned as distinct legal entities.

Premortem gifts to married women were conveyed under varying circumstances. A father ritually provided a gift (*praemium emancipationis*) on the occasion of his married daughter's legal emancipation. For complex reasons, this practice was less common in Florence after 1430 (Kuehn 1982b). He might also convey to a married daughter title to properties that he wished to shield from creditors and the communal fisc. Above all, in exchange for their future care, elderly widows and widowers would bestow gifts on their sons, but lacking sons or male heirs, they would turn to their closest female kin. At the age of seventy-nine, the widow Agnola del maestro Ficino gave all her possessions (worth about 660 florins) to her niece Lessandra di Daniello Ficino, the wife of Biagio Buonaccorsi, with whose family Agnola was living (Buonaccorsi 1976, 176). The gift represented a financial contribution to the household in which Agnola would spend her last days in peace and comfort. Such gifts regularly came with stipulations spelling out the recipient's obligations. On condition that they provide her 20 florins a year, the widow Bartolomea di Francesco Lottini conveyed to her married daughter, to her son, and to another person dotal rights and properties she had received as a legacy from her husband, Giovanni di Piero Foresi.[39] The link between care in old age and intergenerational settlements and premortem gifts was common in late medieval society and remains so in Mediterranean society (Davis 1977, 187; Brettel, chapter 18 this volume). If storytellers like Giovanni Sercambi (1348–1424) of Lucca can be believed, however, encumbered gifts did not guarantee the recipient's attentive care. Sercambi devoted a novella to a rich Venetian merchant, Lord Sovranzo, who divided 30,000 ducats among his three married daughters, in return for which he would live with each daughter and her husband for a month at a time. His daughters and sons-in-law turned out to be ingrates, treating him miserably, but through cunning he was able to take advantage of their greed to teach them (and Sercambi's audience) a harsh lesson in parental retribution (Sercambi 1972, 1:326–333, nov. 57).

The principal means for the conveyance of non-dotal assets to married women were testamentary bequests, many of which reserved to the wife usufruct during marriage. Ser Bartolo di ser Chermontieri, a resident of the parish of San Felice in Piazza, left his married daughter Chiara a vineyard of un-

---

39. NA, 10185, fols. 81v–82v (23 Dec. 1463). Bartolomea's daughter Tita, married to Piero di Tommaso Deti, was one of the recipients. In another case, Andrea di Piero of Pontassieve donated half of his movable assets and his share of real assets held in common with his brother to his two daughters, one of whom was married; ibid., 10181, fol. 78r–78v (18 Feb. 1457).

disclosed value, the right to which she could "hold, sell, exchange, and do with whatever she wished." The bequest expressly denied her husband any legal interest (*jus*) in the disposition of the property.[40] Niccolò da Uzzano left his married daughter Bonda 1,500 florins beyond her dowry to be paid within one year after his death. In addition, he bequeathed to her all his monte credits and movable property, providing an estimated yearly income of 50 florins that would terminate with her death, after which assets would be transmitted to the infirmary of Santa Croce.[41] In his will of 13 July 1479, Giovanni Amici left his daughter Brigida a dowry of 1,000 florins—938 florins payable by the Dowry Fund and 62 florins in cash—and a trousseau whose value as to be determined by her mother. He also bequeathed a farm with all its appurtenances in the Upper Valdarno, stipulating that the property was solely intended for Brigida's use during her lifetime and that it was not to be included in her dowry. Immediately after having consummated her marriage, Brigida was enjoined under the terms of the second bequest to pay the friars at the Convent of Santa Maria Novella 20 lire annually to support a service in memory of her father.[42]

Married as well as unmarried women also received non-dotal assets when the heads of distintegrating conjugal households with no available male heirs named them universal heirs.[43] If E. A. Wrigley's calculations on the fertility

40. NA, 7414, fol. 26 (18 July 1313). For additional examples of bequests that denied the beneficiary's husband any interest in non-dotal assets, see Sapori 1938, 102; SMN, 67, fol. 106v (5 Oct. 1383), fol. 142v (30 June 1383), fol. 168v (5 Aug. 1384); NA, 16841, fols. 39–41 (4 May 1477), 6752, fol. 55r–55v (3 Apr. 1493).

41. NA, 9041, fols. 168–175 (27 Dec. 1430, with codicils of 4 Mar. and 7 Apr. 1431). It was customary for a wife to receive a life-usufruct of income-producing properties that reverted to a religious institution upon her death. See Orlandi 1960, 147–148; and MC, 2601, fol. 234, where the right to collect interest payable on monte credits with a face value of 200 florins registered under the name of Spedale di Santa Maria Nuova di Firenze, belonged to Chosa di Iacopo Cafferelli and her husband, Zanobi di Cristoforo Maggiolini, during their lifetimes; the same terms applied to Tancia di Giovanni di Pagolo and her husband, Bernardo di Iachopo Canacci (ibid., fol. 235).

42. SMN, 70, fol. 385v. For a similar bequest, see the testament of Francesco di ser Filippo of San Miniato, which named his sister, the wife of a Florentine citizen, universal heir and enjoined her to fund a mass and an annual service "pro anima testatoris" (NA, 16841, insert 4, fols. 74–75v [28 Aug. 1503]).

43. NA, 205, fol. 80 (23 Sept. 1378): testament of Giovanni di Neri, who named his married daughter Antonia universal heir; SMN, 67, fol. 132v (17 July 1383): testament of Nicholosa, widow of ser Iachopo of Fucecchio, a Florentine citizen, who named her married daughters Bartolomea and Andrea universal heirs; ASF, Archivio della Gherardesca, n. 55 (19 Apr. 1421): testament of the widow Margherita di Benedetto Peruzzi, who named her sister Taddea universal heir; NA, 3373, fol. 195-v (17 Oct. 1431): testament of the widower Ricciardo di Domenico Cambini, who named his married daughter universal heir; ibid., 16795, no foliation (10 Apr. 1476): testament of the widower Vermiglio di Sandro di Giovanni, who named his married niece universal heir; ibid., 14718, fol. 146v (27 Jan. 1477): testament of the widow Francesca di Matteo di Stefano Scolari, who named her daughter Alessandra, wife of Andrea di Francesca Zati,

patterns of stationary preindustrial populations are applied to Florence, about 20 percent of all Florentine couples would have produced only daughters (Wrigley 1978). The naming of daughters, sisters, and other married female kin as universal heirs thus represented a last-ditch effort to find a haven for patrimonial property. In this connection, did women in Florence show a stronger inclination than men to make bequests to their married female kin, as has been asserted for patrician women in Renaissance Venice? (Chojnacki 1974, 190). This question cannot at present be answered satisfactorily. My impression is that Florentine women bequeathing as well as donating assets to married women were preponderantly widows without surviving male heirs. As heads of fiscal households, they were more likely to distribute their assets among their female kin than wives, who remained subordinate to their husbands. Antonia di Antonio of Panzano, a citizen of Florence, divided her estate, including a shop in the city, real property in the *contado,* and monte credits with a face value of 3,350 florins, among her three married granddaughters.[44] The widow Maddalena di Salvestro Serristori provided legacies, ranging from 25 to 50 florins, to her four married sisters-in-law.[45] Giovanna di Michele of Terranuova left two houses to her married daughter, Antonia, with this conventional proviso: if Antonia died without legitimate heirs, the legacy would then revert to her mother's brothers.[46] Finally, the right to collect interest on 25 florins of monte credits belonging to the widow Alessandra di Nanni of Ponte a Grignano would pass after her death to her daughter, Agnola, and after Agnola's death the credits would revert to the commune.[47]

Admittedly, wills may tell us more about the intention to convey assets than about their actual conveyance; beneficiaries obviously would not receive anything if they were removed from subsequent codicils and wills or if they

---

universal heir; ibid., 10194, fols. 228–229 (10 July 1486): testament of the widow Caterina di Giovanni Marrazani, who named her married daughter Iacoba universal heir; ibid., 14724, fol. 128v (23 Apr. 1491): testament of the widow Lorenza di Poggio Bracciolini, who named her daughter Vaggia, wife of Giovanni Cavalcanti, universal heir.

44. NA, 682, fols. 67–68 (11 Jan. 1426). Her granddaughter Bartolomea was married to Matteo di Domenico Corsi; Francesca to Alamanno di Silvestro de' Medici; Ginevra to Piero di Maffeo Tedaldi. The widow Bartolmea di Iacopo di Lippo left her married sister, Piera, 20 florins (ibid., 12523, fol. 46v [15 June 1416]). Likewise, the widow Zanobia di Marco left her married relative Domenica di Olivia "usufructum et redditum" of "plures petias terrarum" (ibid., fol. 53v [21 May 1416]).

45. NA, 14719, fol. 166 (11 Sept. 1480).

46. NA, 683, fols. 143–144v (13 June 1429). Similarly, Giovanni di Pagolo Morelli in his testament of 1430 left his daughter Mea, the wife of Antonio di Luca da Filicaia, usufructuary rights to the income of monte credits with a face value of 500 florins. Should Mea die without legitimate and natural heirs, the credits would then revert to Giovanni's own heirs (Pandimiglio 1981, 175).

47. MC, 2599, fol. 1v.

predeceased testators. Breathing a sigh of relief, Tribaldo di Amerigo de' Rossi recorded how his mother's legacy intended for his married sister Alessandra was short-circuited by her death: "I record how monna Piera, on 6 July 1492, left and gave her daughter Alessandra, and wife of Piero Repetti, 100 florins from her own dowry should Alessandra have children with Piero, and Piera concealed her bequest from me. Alessandra died without heirs, and had she died with heirs we would have been ruined."[48] Beneficiaries might also be denied bequests due to insufficient assets in the estates of testators, the result of large business debts, tax arrears, or the prior distribution of assets through premortem gifts (Herlihy 1987). Bequests might not be executed owing to the machinations of heirs who sought to keep the estates for themselves (Chabot 1988, 294–295). Antonio di Filippo Macinghi (the half-brother of Alessandra Macinghi Strozzi), who died without heirs, left his property to his married sisters with whom he had resided (Morton 1980, 260). The will, however, was contested by Antonio's uncles (Macinghi-Strozzi 1877, 204–205, 220). Such were likely the circumstances that prompted Francesco Guicciardini to take the precaution of demanding collateral to secure a purchase of several farms from two married sisters who had inherited them, "because," he explained, "in fact the sisters possessed only the name of heir" (Guicciardini 1981, 111). Caution, therefore, was well-advised in transactions whose fulfillment was contingent on a future inheritance; and it must still be exercised by historians charting the devolution of property from generation to generation largely on the basis of wills.

Having registered that caveat, I would point out that wills, notably those of husbands, constitute a valuable and hitherto untapped source of information for the critical issue of who controlled non-dotal assets during marriage. A husband's will manifested his intention to restore to his wife the non-dotal assets that she received, but which he controlled, during marriage. In his will Sandro di Giovanni Biliotti restored to his wife, Ginevra di Zanobi Fei, her dowry and "117 florins which," he said, "passed into the testator's hands from Ginevra's own goods, namely monte credits with a face value of 200 florins, which he sold."[49] Beyond restoring her dowry of 1,200 florins, Bernardo di

---

48. BNF, MSS, II, II, 357, fol. 74v: "Richordo chome monna Piera sopradetta, a dì 6 di luglio 1492, lasciò e donò al' Alesandra sua figliuola, dona di Piero Repetti, fiorini 100 dela dote sua s'ela aveva figliuoli di detto Piero, e lasciogliela di naschoso a me; morì la detta Alessandra sanza 'rede, che se moriva chon 'rede stavamo disfatti." It is not entirely clear from the wording of the passage whether the bequest was made by a codicil or a donatio mortis causa.

49. NA, 14661; fols. 258r–258v (16 May 1424): "Item eidem legavit florenos auri centum decemseptem quos dixit sibi testatori pervenisse de bonis dicte domine Ginevre, videlicet de florenis auri ducentis scriptis super monte et quos vendidit." In his will of 1445, Niccolò di Antonio Cardi provided for the return of his wife's non-dotal goods in the following manner: "Et ultra dictas

Giovanni Portinari left his wife, Gita di Iacopo Ardinghelli, 200 florins as compensation for the goods, things, and property rights that belonged to her, but which, as he had previously acknowledged in a written obligation (*scritta*) and now again in his will, passed into his hands.⁵⁰ Filippo di Giovanni dell' Antella provided his wife, Maria di Stefano Bartolini, the following bequests: 20 large florins that he owed her for reasons not disclosed here, 100 large florins that she had inherited from her mother, but which were now in his possession (*in mano dello testatore*), and 200 large florins, the sale price he received for monte credits with a face value of 458 florins and paying 7 percent interest, which had belonged to Maria. Each bequest (*legatum creditoris,* in legal jargon) was made in recognition of an obligation that Filippo had duly recorded in his account books.⁵¹

Not infrequently, husband-testators acknowledged that they had acquired non-dotal assets by accepting a legacy on their wives' behalf; they also acknowledged appropriating such assets to their own use and beneficial enjoyment (*in suam utilitatem convertit*). Barna di Luca Alberti, in his will of 4 May 1390, acknowledged that he had collected and appropriated to his own use the fruits, monies, and rents from the properties that his wife, Agostina, had inherited *ex successione paterna vel materna.* The total amount of such proceeds was to be restored to his wife, less 100 florins he had provided to round out the dowry of her niece. On 16 October 1392, several years after Barna's death, Agostina received from her husband's estate 600 florins for the non-dotal proceeds Barna had consumed.⁵² In accordance with the wishes of Nanni di Manetto of San Miniato, his wife, Fiora, was to receive her dowry of 40 florins, plus 20 florins that he had formally acknowledged receiving on her behalf directly from the heirs of her first husband. Nanni had spent this sum, which he

---

suas dotes relinquo eidem de bonis meis florenos viginti auri, quos tam ab ea quam etiam ab altera persona pro ea confiteor habuisse recepisse tam in pecunia quam in aliis diversis rebus ultra dicta dotes" (BNF, Magl., XXIX, 193, fol. 72v).

50. SMN, 70, fol. 186 (29 July 1436): "Et ultra dictos florenos mille ducentos dicte domine legavit et sibi dari et restitui voluit florenos ducentos auri, quos dixit ipsum habuisse et ad eius manus pervenisse de bonis, rebus et iuribus ad ipsam dominam pertinentibus et expectantibus, de quibus florenis ducentis dixit ipsum fecisse quamdam scriptam privatam sua manu."

51. NA, 15852, fols. 103–104 (25 Oct. 1513). Maria's monte dowry, which her husband began collecting in 1471, amounted to 1,200 florins (MC, 3737, fol. 13).

52. Agostina's dowry of 678 florins had been restored on 13 June 1390, almost immediately after Barna's death (SMN, 67, fol. 310r–310v). Similarly, Francesco di Lorenzo Manelli of San Iacopo sopra Arno, in his will of 31 Jan. 1455, acknowledged that he had collected and appropriated to his own use the interest due on monte credits with a face value of 100 florins, which his father-in-law had bequeathed to his wife. In consideration, the total amount of interest he had collected was to be restored to his wife, Margherita di Alberto di Zanobi (NA, 19075, fols. 307–308).

characterized as his wife's own money (*propria pecunia*), to purchase properties that provided him with revenue.[53]

Clauses containing an acknowledgment of the receipt and appropriation of non-dotal assets protected a wife by recognizing her as a legitimate creditor. In effect, they were the functional equivalent of a confessio dotium, which, under the jus commune, the husband was constrained from executing during marriage. Admitting that one should be on the lookout for fraud as the motivation for such testamentary confessions, Raffaele Raimondi (1576, 20, cons. 2, n. 1) went on to advise that they should be construed as valid, so long as the husband is reputed to be honest and his wife swears that his confession is true factually. Should the husband's heirs refuse to restore non-dotal assets by claiming that they belonged to the husband, or refuse to restore the revenues they produced by claiming that the husband had applied them to the common benefit of his family, the wife or her heirs, acting as creditors of the deceased, could introduce the will to prove otherwise. By the same token, in fixing the amount of his debt the husband sought to shield his estate and his heirs against exaggerated or even fraudulent claims.[54]

To sum up, bona non dotalia was a legal construct that served to unify diverse types of property belonging to a married woman into a single conceptually cohesive phenomenon. Although a minority of adept Florentines may have understood the formalistic mumbo jumbo surrounding the distinctions between dotal and non-dotal assets, it doubtless perplexed, or eluded entirely, the large majority. If we could ask them to characterize in their own words bona non dotalia—what I have redescribed as non-dotal assets—how would they have responded? I doubt that they would have qualified the bona they conveyed

---

53. NA, 13498, fol. 109v (12 Feb. 1437): "Et ultra dictos florenos auri quadraginta ab ea nomine dicte dotis receptos et confessatos eidem uxori sue legavit et reliquit et sibi restitui voluit, iussit et mandavit florenos auri viginti quos a dicta domina Fiore uxore sua fuit confessus in alia parte habuisse et recepisse de ipsius propria pecunia sibi domine Fiori restituita ab heredibus quondam Pieri Cambii olim primi eius mariti et pro eisdem heredibus ab Antonio olim ser Donati de Sancto Miniato predicto, quos florenos auri viginti receptos ab ea et pro ea et a quibus supra dixit et confessus fuit expendisse et de eis emisse quasdam possessiones et petias terrarum et ipsos et dictarum terrarum ususfructum et redditus in sui testatoris utilitatem convertisse."

54. Such concerns were behind the legacy intended for Selvaggia, the wife of Francesco di Geri. In addition to her 250-florin dowry, Francesco left her 300 florins and a bed with an estimated value of 50 florins (*secundum bonam et pinguem extimationem*) as full compensation for the monies and goods that had been left to Selvaggia by her grandmother and other relatives, but which Francesco had appropriated to his own use. Under the terms of the legacy, Selvaggia would be obligated to release her husband's heirs from, and to agree not to bring suit for (*pactum de ulterius aliquid non petendo*), any further payment regarding the said monies and goods (SMN, 67, fol. 16 [9 Nov. 1378]).

or promised to convey with the addition of non dotalia. The documents I have
examined suggest that they thought of themselves as simply providing gifts
and bequests to married women for any number of socially prescribed reasons,
among which were: to supplement the dowries of daughters, granddaughters,
nieces, or sisters during marriage; to supply them with a stream of income so
they might live honorably during their widowhood; to compensate family
members for the care of aged parents and kinfolk; to ensure that patrimonial
assets would be transmitted to the last surviving kin; and to protect assets from
creditors and the fisc. For the large majority of Florentines with wealth, the
provision of such gifts and legacies was a "self-evident activity" marking the
emotional bonds between married women and their original families.

How widespread was this self-evident activity in fourteenth- and fifteenth-
century Florence and other comparable cities? Systematic archival research
should permit us to detail the sources and makeup of non-dotal assets and to
estimate what proportion of wives in Florence and elsewhere in northern and
central Italy were likely to receive them. It should also furnish data to analyze
the extent to which kinship, gender, number of surviving children, stage in the
developmental cycle, and not least, level of wealth impinged on the decision to
donate and bequeath non-dotal assets to married women. Other issues that
demand investigation are the relative contribution of income earned from non-
dotal assets to the financial support of the wife's family and the husband's
utilization of these assets as collateral in business transactions. Finally, the
records of religious societies, monasteries, convents, and churches should yield
data on the transformation of non-dotal assets into pious gifts and bequests.

As legal historians have repeatedly observed and as feminist historians have
lamented, the wife's formal loss of authority over non-dotal assets was a victory
for patriarchy, which attenuated the proprietary capacity of women in central
and northern Italy during the late Middle Ages and the Renaissance (Guerra
Medici 1986). Unlike their counterparts in northwestern Portugal, for example,
where wives could retain rights over their own property and dispose of it
without marital authorization, wives in Italy would not regain the right to
dispose of non-dotal assets freely and without first obtaining their husband's
consent until 1919 (Leicht 1960, 219–222). After recognizing Italian women's
deterior conditio, we should remember that Florentine legislators and jurists
made a resolute effort to protect the wife's patrimony from husbands who were
incompetent, improvident, or scoundrels; that the regulations and remedies
they instituted to safeguard the wife's claim to her dowry and non-dotal assets,
though perhaps ineffective in curbing husbands hell-bent on consuming her
property and defrauding her heirs, were enforced by the court of the podestà
(Kirshner 1985); that her kin encumbered non-dotal assets to deter husbands

from exhausting them in payment of their own debts, hoping thereby to save female beneficiaries from the disgrace of destitution; that husbands themselves, through testamentary confessions, sought to ensure on their predecease restoration of the non-dotal assets they had enjoyed during marriage. Patriarchy's victory was thus undeniably tempered by paternalism. Nevertheless, circumscribed by both patriarchy and paternalism, non-dotal assets were just more materials for the construction of the Florentine wife's gilded cage.

Chapter 11

CHRISTIANE KLAPISCH-ZUBER

Kinship and Politics in Fourteenth-Century Florence

In fourteenth-century Tuscany the kinship groups called houses (*case*) were well defined, including only the male descendants of a particular ancestor, who was not always well-known. They did not have a fixed organization, however, or a clearly hierarchical internal structure. In all cases their identity was expressed by a hereditary and collective name, and they commanded strategic landholdings and joint revenues, shared by the family members, or *consorti*. Such houses were nonetheless diversified into lines or branches (*lati*), within which individuals exercised successional strategies with regard to their own possessions (Violante 1977, 1981; Commarosano 1977; Hughes 1976; Kent 1977; Goody 1983, app. 1:222–239; Herlihy 1985; Lansing 1985, chap. 2).

Awareness of belonging to a *parentela* can be broken down in two ways. First, it resided in the feeling, shared by all eventual cousins, of having in common an infinitely fragmentable heritage, for example, in the name they all bore or in an interest in the family's urban fortress. Second, this awareness depended on an evaluation of the distance separating an individual from his agnatic kin, a distance that determined his position and his rights.

With rights came duties, for acknowledgment of kinship entailed obligations. Kinship imposed solidarity in the defense of each individual's reputation, the accumulated result of which was collective honor. When public power asserted its right to repress crime and public offenses, it did so by coming to terms with such lineage-based solidarity groups, but it also made use of them. By turning the solidarity of such groups to work against them, the Italian communes, Florence in particular, took control of the violence that was an institutional part of kinship groups of the governing class and a daily occurrence among them. As the Comune—the communal government—gradually came to understand the weapons it held, it put pressure on familial groups in various ways; in part by citing, to varying degrees, the judicial responsibility of the agnatic relatives of a culprit; in part by deliberately seeking to break up family groups by divining hidden fractures within them.

MEASURING KINSHIP

By what scale was close kinship to be measured? To judge the genealogical distance between cousins, families could use either the canonical method of reckoning or its civil counterpart, Roman law. As is known, the Roman method doubled the canonical count, defining first cousins as related in the fourth degree, whereas the Church counted only two degrees. Thus the Lateran Council of 1215 set the fourth degree as the limit beyond which marriage to a consanguinean was permitted, but the civil equivalent was the eighth degree (Esmein 1929–1935; Schwartzenberg 1960, 641, 644; Besta 1933, 21–22; Pertile 1893, 56–57).[1]

It would seem important, then, to define *degrees* accurately, which is not always the case. Examining the circumstances in which the method of reckoning is explicit is also worthwhile. During the last years of the twelfth century, for example, when one group of Florentines, acting as consortes, joined to form a *società delle torri* ("tower association"), they followed the canonical method to define their kinship as they outlined the instances in which they owed one another armed assistance and mutual support. In this particular case the associates took pains to be specific regarding consorts with close cognatic relatives who could be implicated in a quarrel with an associate (Santini 1895, 524).[2] In this circumstance, the consort would not have to make his relative's quarrel his own and would be exempted from the obligation to solidarity that normally existed between consorts. Most relatives of the man in question would thus be excused from the obligation of vendetta and self-defense, an obligation that would pertain to the eighth degree if kinship were defined according to civil law. I cite this text for another reason as well: its lay utilization, in situations involving affines and maternal relatives, of the Church's

1. Although the principles of both systems are well known, as is the debate that opposed them until the twelfth century, historians of law have given only marginal consideration to their enforcement during the late Middle Ages. Antonio Pertile, however, emphasizes the prevalence of the canonical reckoning in Italian statutory law.

2. "Item nos sotii qui nunc sumus vel in antea erimus inter nos de [personis nostris] alii alios adiuvabimus de nostris discordiis excepto de [proximo parente] qui sit michi coniunctus in quarto gradu secundum computationem canonum ex parte mea vel uxoris mee" (1180).

method of reckoning, which unambiguously insisted on the bilateral nature of kinship.

Contemporaries did not always indicate their method of reckoning, however, and in practice the laity—both the authorities and citizens—were often less explicit than our 1180 consorts. In the period that most interests us here, the fourteenth and fifteenth centuries, the division between the two methods of reckoning kinship is much less clear than it might seem, even in statutory texts.

Indeed, communal legislation, at least after the late thirteenth century, apparently reckoned kinship by the civil method when its object did not involve the matrimonial matters that the Church reserved to its own jurisdiction, when the case was not a direct consequence of a prohibition or a decision coming from the ecclesiastical authorities (for example, in cases of sumptuary law or sexual conduct), or when matrilinear kinship was not involved. The Ordinances of Justice (1293–1295) (Salvemini [1899] 1966) and legislation contemporary to them or introduced subsequently into the city statutes clearly calculated kinship by the civil method, particularly when a legislative text set up the basis of fiscal, judicial, or political solidarities between consanguineans—solidarities that operated exclusively in the male line in Florence. The Roman civil method of reckoning, which was particularly geared to the measurement of distance between agnates and to distinguishing precedence among heirs, had an assured place in a Tuscan society keen on genealogy and patrilineage.

In contrast to situations that directly or indirectly involved patrimony and the transmission of social identity, a 1365 law aimed at sodomy branded as suspect any adult found in suspicious circumstances with a boy under eighteen who was not "of his kin, family, or stock, or not otherwise related to him in some other way up to the third canonical degree."[3] Here the consanguineous relationship that justifies the proximity to a young relative would quite normally be appropriate to either line, and the ecclesiastical reckoning is used. Similarly, in 1366 the municipal councils decreed that priors in office could no longer force anyone to accept a compromise in litigation that opposed the litigant to one of the priors or to "a consort of consanguineous relatives in the male line, or to a close kin or affine" of one of the priors or of the standard-bearer of justice, "up to and including the fourth degree, as understood in canon law."[4] This amounted to recognition that families and political entities

3. "De parentela, familia seu de stirpe eiusdem vel eidem alio modo coniunctus usque ad tertium gradum intelligendo gradum secundum ius canonicum." *Provvisioni Registri* (hereafter cited as *PR*) 52, fol. 28r-v, 2 Apr. 1365. All archival references are to holdings in the Archivio di Stato di Firenze. All dates are given in common style.

4. "Seu cum aliquo consorte vel coniuncto per lineam masculinam, seu usque in quartum gradum inclusive secundum iura canonica intellectum actinente parente seu affine alicuius ex ipsis dominis prioribus." *PR* 54, fol. 72r, 19 Nov. 1366.

used affines and allies as well as patrilinear relatives to effect political pressure. To offer a third example, in 1377 the same councils published a decision that the close relatives (*attinentes*) of a certain spendthrift, whom the same relatives considered not quite sane, could prevent him from alienating his possessions unless he had the consent of "three of his agnatic or cognatic kin, up to and including the fourth degree according to canon law."[5] Here, as in the guardianship of orphan minors, maternal kin participated in the preservation of the wealth of an irresponsible relative.

The patrilinear bias typical of familial practice and family organization in Florence clearly did not do away with a sense that parents on the wife's side had a role to play. What is remarkable is that such kinship seems to have been reckoned only by the same method that determined the legality of the couple on which the kinship was based.

When they spoke of their family affairs, lay people generally proved punctilious in their count of the degrees that separated them from their cousins, but were often vague about the method of reckoning used. One example of this sort of imprecision, which may be innocent or may be calculating, permits an evaluation of the skill of social agents in manipulating definitions of kinship in their own interest. In June 1349, Messer Giovanni di Messer Alamanno Gherardini, who belonged to the group of "noble and powerful" families known as magnates, appealed to the communal government for a legal separation from his kin, pleading that he, along with his brother and a nephew, were isolated within their lineage and even within their branch of the lineage. Their closest cousins, they declared, were "distant at the ninth degree from Messer Giovanni and at the tenth from his sons and his nephew." Separation was warranted, they argued, "because in truth, not only could the sons and the nephews of Messer Giovanni legally contract marriage with any member of the lineage (casa) of the Gherardini but also because, as Messer Giovanni is closer by one degree to all the other member of the case Gherardini than his sons or his nephew, it would be impossible to forbid him to contract a marriage with any person born or to be born in the said casa Gherardini."[6]

This ninth degree, whether civil or canonical, clearly fell beyond the matrimonial limit of the fourth canonical degree. It is noteworthy, however, that the writer of the appeal does not specify the method of reckoning used. Preserving

---

5. "De consensu expresso interveniente trium ex suis agnatis seu congnatis . . . usque in quartum gradum secundum jura canonica intellectum." *PR* 65, fol. 224v, 4 Dec. 1377.

6. "Cum re vera nedum filii et nepos dicti domini Johannis possent licite matrimonium contraere cum quocumque alio de domo de Gherardinis set etiam ipse dominus Johannes qui est proximior eis aliis de dicta domo de G. uno gradu quam sint dicti filii et nepos domini Johannis non prohiberentur [sic] matrimonium contraere cum quocumque alio nato de domo de G. vel qui in antea nasceretur." *Balie* 4, fol. 4r, 29 June 1349.

the ambiguity might have been to his advantage, since his distance from his nearest kin seemed to him an argument apt to persuade the government to grant him legal separation from them. I prefer to believe, however, that he was perfectly aware of the usual procedures of communal offices and neglected to specify a detail that seemed to him self-evident because the case, by definition, dealt with agnatic kin. Messer Giovanni undoubtedly used the civil method of reckoning kinship: it is highly improbable that he could reconstitute both lines of filiation to the ninth or tenth common ancestor, as implied in the canonical method. In Tuscany, genealogical memory often went back four or five generations to a common ancestor, but only exceptionally would memory include anterior generations, who at best were represented only by a string of names.

A text of this sort reveals what a member of a great Florentine lineage knew about the Church's matrimonial prohibitions, at least in the domain of patrilinear consanguinity. But such knowledge, if we accept Messer Giovanni's arguments, had as a corollary an awareness of belonging to an exogamous lineage—to a casa—since he proposes to reduce this casa to the group of consanguineous relatives who could not intermarry.[7] For him, the inverse would be equally true: logically, once the canonical limit of the fourth degree was exceeded, kinship could be recognized as null and a new lineage could be created. In practice things did not work out this way, at least not automatically. Many urban lineages continued to group under the same name (an indisputable sign of their unity) cousins distant by more than four canonical degrees who nonetheless avoided intermarriage. As a kinship group, the urban lineage of the upper classes seems to have been spontaneous in its observance of rules of exogamy that were less permissive than the matrimonial prohibitions for consanguineans taught by the Church. Once more we note that patrilinearity penetrated deeply both judicial models and the daily practice of the urban lineages of Florence.

Is this observation valid for families that did not belong to the Florentine ruling classes? I will limit my remarks on this largely unexplored topic to a few comments based on the documentary evidence. Such indications suggest, first,

---

7. At the same date and in the same circumstances, members of one branch of the Squarcialupi family evoked the distance separating them from their cousins descended from Messer Albertino, a distance great enough "to allow them for a long time to contract matrimony with them" ("quegli del lato di messer Albertino sono tanto di lungi in grado che più tempo fa che potavamo fare parentado insieme") (*Balie* 4, fols. 36r–37v, 1 Sept. 1349). The same opinion is expressed by Bartolo and Francesco Adimari: "I nomi e gradi degli uomini de la decta casa e lati de la decta casa sono tanti e sì di lungi in grado con noi che noi no' li saperemo contare, ma tanto di vero vi diciamo e facciamo manifesto che con tucti potremo fare parentadi, e che niuno è nella decta casa che con noi sia strecto in sept[im]o grado." In other words, they declare that although they could marry those cousins, they do not. *Balie* 4, fol. 28v, 25 Aug. 1349.

that cognatic characteristics were much clearer in the structure of kinship groups or coresident households in the rural areas of Tuscany, and second, that perhaps during the fifteenth century judicial practice began to recognize cognatic links in the Florentine family.

Legislative texts dealing with judicial responsibilities in rural areas show that Tuscan peasants felt much closer to matrilinear relatives than the members of urban patriciate families did or could. In 1357, for example, the municipal councils decreed that someone who lived in the *contado* and who participated in the suit of one not related to him patrilinearly could be considered a magnate and, consequently, be subject to the exceptional juridical procedures reserved to this category.[8] The communal government later made a concerted effort to control peasant *consorterie,* the excesses of which came to light in some of the measures against them.[9] A 1371 law severely prohibited excessive violence of such peasant consorterie of ten or more members against the owner of the land they worked or any member of his entourage. The Florentine legislators specified that the ties of kinship among these probably coresident rustics were to be understood as including the female line, something almost inconceivable in Florence itself in the consorteria (which was defined by transmission in the male line alone) or in the residence group (in which all males were of the same blood).[10]

During the fifteenth century, a new awareness of the solidity and tangibility of links with maternal kin may have arisen among the Florentine ruling classes. In 1452 a law aimed at nepotism barred from certain offices individuals related to those who would fall under their control. *Cognati* and matrilinear kin to the fourth degree were included in this ruling, along with patrilinear kin, but the innovation was so startling that the scribe's pen faltered and he needed a second try to write the word *feminine* correctly.[11]

Variations in the method of reckoning kinship and in the categories of

8. On these procedures, see discussion below. The law of 1357 ("Nullus de comitatu praesumat tenere ad unam et eamdem brigam, hodium seu inimicitiam cum aliquo sibi non coniuncto per lineam masculinam") is in *PR* 44, fol. 64r, 19 Feb. 1357. See Dorini 1923, 128.

9. In 1388 a Florentine merchant, Tieri di Domenico Tieri, entered claims against his father's murderers: one against the "famiglia et consorteria," consisting of twenty men of an age to bear arms, of a lime burner, Bartolo Casini, from Santa Maria Impruneta, and the other against a "famiglia et consorteria" commonly called "la famiglia di que' da Foglia," which included six adult men. The councils decided in Tieri's favor. *PR* 77, fols. 248v–249r, 12 Dec. 1388.

10. "Eo etiam declarato quod . . . consorteria et familia intelligatur constare et constet non solum ex coniuntis per lineam maschulinam, set etiam ex coniuntis per lineam femininam, et licet non essent coniunti per lineam maschulinam." *PR* 59, fol. 103v, 12 Sept. 1371.

11. "Vel etiam qui essent coniuncti per lineam [femini]nam infra quartum gradum aut cognatus alicuius de dicto officio." The portion of the word *femininam* between brackets was canceled and rewritten. *PR* 143, fol. 170v, 19 June 1452.

relatives subject to it suggest several observations and questions. Was the civil
method of reckoning used to deal with problems involving agnatic kinship only
in Florence (if indeed such a specialization existed)? Or was this also true of
statutory legislation of other communes in northern and central Italy? It seems
plausible that the diffusion of civil law reckoning followed the peregrinations of
the class of jurists, judges, notaries, and *podestà* formed at the school of Bologna
who circulated from one commune to another from the thirteenth century
onward. We need to assess more precisely what this specialization signified in
terms of the contemporary conception of kinship.

The tendency to consider kinship "by the male line" as a whole and without
fixing limits is repeatedly countered by a more restricted definition, never
exceeding the fourth canonical degree, of relatives on the maternal side. For
cognati and relatives by alliance, the Church's reckoning was used and the
limits it set were respected. Inversely, consorts tend to be defined as all *conjuncti
per lineam masculinam*—that is, all individuals for whom memory preserved
even a vague consciousness of common patrilinear kinship. Was this true for
strata of the population other than the upper classes of Florentine society? I
shall return to this problem to compare texts originating in different social
spheres that give reasons for repudiating certain kinship ties.

The texts cited earlier raise another question. We have seen how certain
Florentines, to justify their request to separate one group of consanguineans
from the trunk family and set it up as an autonomous lineage, alleged not only
familial distance but also the possibility of marrying cousins. Do the arguments
of these men indicate a more widespread awareness of the implications for
kinship practices of the decrees of 1215 that fixed the prohibition to marry kin
at the fourth canonical degree (equivalent to the seventh degree in the civil
reckoning given in Roman law concerning agnatic relatives)? To put the question differently, did this new definition facilitate the splitting up of important
lineages by making it both possible and logical to recognize that agnatic
solidarity broke down roughly at the same point that permission to marry
appeared?

Another aspect of the problem—one that I can only indicate here, not
solve—concerns the role that Roman law played in the crystallization of the
urban patrilinear lineage. Can one assume that the method of reckoning
favored by Roman law contributed to the triumph and persistence of agnatic
bonds within kinship groups? Whatever term Florentines used to designate
these groups (*casa, schiatta, famiglia,* and so on), they recognized transmission
in the male line as their constitutive principle. Was awareness of this principle
strengthened by being formalized in civil reckoning?

THE EXTENSION OF KINSHIP

Thus there was great flexibility in the criteria employed for defining kinship, and even for a definition of the extent of kinship itself. Did public agencies concertedly encourage the enlargement or restriction of the kinship groups they dealt with, and in so doing redefine the moral and social obligations entailed in membership in a kinship group?

In the mid-fourteenth century, justice by and large remained in the hands of the offended party or victim and his family. Seeking an equal or superior counteroffense, negotiating adequate compensation for the damages incurred, reestablishing the honor of both parties, and restoring peace were all family matters over which public power had little hold and in which it intervened only marginally (Köhler and Degli Azzi-Vitelleschi 1909; Enriques Agnoletti, 1933, 90–223; Dorini 1923). The steps toward a gradual lessening of the chain of violence are well known, but other aspects of the question concerning the influence the communal government exerted on kinship groups, exploiting the very solidarity that resulted, in theory, from common blood, are less well known.

In its efforts to keep and restore public order, the Comune conceived of and applied the pressures it brought to bear on contending parties differentially. The common law in theory applied to everyone, but included in its principles, procedures, and penalties exemptions or important exceptions for certain categories of citizens and subjects. The so-called magnates (*magnati*) occupied the first rank among such citizens.

The common folk—the *popolari*—both great and small (*grassi* and *minuti*) retained the right to avenge a blood crime within limits that communal justice gradually sought to impose or narrow. The bounds of the *vindicta competens* were tightened as the persons allowed to participate in and the circumstances permitting vendetta were more precisely defined. In this way, the Comune limited the cases of legitimate exercise of private vengeance, reserving to itself, around 1300, jurisdiction over minor aggressions that left no trace, such as simple blows and insults. It required that the revenge suit the offense; it reduced the lapse of time within which vengeance could take place; it considered as aggravating circumstances the exploitation of situations ideally suited to assassination such as festivities in which people went about the streets masked; it forbade vendetta in reaction to vendetta. Finally, and this is of special interest here, it attempted to define the nature and limit the number of the avengers and their potential victims. The Statute of the Captain of 1322 reiterates that the office of the executor of justice could compel enemies to make peace only after the vendetta required for a homicide or a severe wound had been carried out (Santini 1886, 163; Dorini 1933). The Statute of the Podestà of 1325 defining those exempt from pursuit still included relatives to the fourth degree among the potential accomplices of a victim turned avenger, who could thus act with impunity (Caggese 1921, 278).[12] The statutes of 1415 continued to recognize that members of the family consortium and their followers could participate in acts of vengeance. Limits were set earlier concerning the possible victims of vendetta. If the initial offender was still living, vengeance taken on any of his relatives was forbidden. If he was dead, however, a vindicta competens could be carried out against one of his *congiunti,* descendants, or male agnates of any degree, and a law of August 1331 exonerated the accomplices of the avenger, who was permitted revenge on any of the perpetrator's agnatic relatives, from his closest to his most distant kin.[13]

Florentine annals, public and private, offer many accounts of violence regulated by the law. Among the vendettas executed by populars (popolari), one might cite the well-known story of revenges taken by the Velluti family, solid merchant-class burghers. In 1295, twenty-eight years after a Manelli murdered Ghino Velluti, two of his brothers, a nephew (the son of a first cousin), and a maternal relative (an uncle or a cousin) killed the nephew of the murderer. The second Velluti vendetta, in 1334, avenged a murder that had occurred twenty-three years earlier. This time, two nephews (the son and grandson of first cousins) and an "intimate friend," the neighborhood baker, were persuaded by the victim's closest kin, whose responsibility the vendetta should have been, to do the deed. Things went badly, however, and far from achieving their goal, they were overtaken by their enemies and the baker lost his life (Velluti 1914, 11–15, 62–70; Del Lungo 1886; La Roncière 1977, 246). The case demonstrates one of the strategies of the vendetta: the avengers sought to strike a close relative of the offender who they knew had been sentenced for another offense and could thus be attacked with impunity. The same sort of calculation is visible in another vendetta described in the Velluti chronicle, which demonstrates how private persons who took justice into their own hands used weak

12. Following the example of Pope Alexander II, theologians explained the canonical method of reckoning by the need to count two persons at the same degree when dealing with marriage, which of course served to unite two individuals. Roman law was instead concerned with succession, and thus needed to enumerate each individual separately in order to establish the hierarchy of respective positions among heirs; see "Consanguinité," in *Dictionnaire de droit canonique* 4:235.

13. The law "De puniendo qui studiose percusserit aliquem" was added at the end of the statute of 1325, bk. 3, rubr. 45 (Caggese 1921, 207–212; see also Santini 1895, 164). The prohibition against attacking any relatives of the culprit as long as he was alive is in the Statute of the Podestà, bk. 3, rubr. 126, entitled "De puniendo qui fecerit vindictam nisi in principalem personam." Caggese 1921, 278.

points in public law to avoid even the not overly severe legal limitations imposed on the right of vengeance (Velluti 1914, 67, 77).

At the end of the process by which the communal government changed the normal course of vendetta and *nimicizia mortale* by imposing laws that countermanded or paralleled private initiative, state justice would acquire a monopoly of jurisdiction over violence. It was henceforth the government that triggered repressive action, set the amount of the retribution, punished the guilty party or parties in both body and property, and maintained a public peace that no longer depended on the private peace agreed to by the parties concerned (Elias 1978–1982).

This entire evolution put increasing stress on the principle of the individual's responsibility for his crime, even outside the specific domain of the vendetta. As early as the thirteenth century, only the close relatives of populars who tasted communal justice when they broke the laws shared in the penalties. Indeed, if the father, son, or even the brother of the guilty party had to contribute to the damages, it was because they happened to share their purse or their cook pot with him. In theory, the fine or the punishment imposed was personal (Statuto del Podestà, 1325, bk. 3, rubr. 64, in Caggese 1921, 226), and only a few exceptional crimes—bankruptcy, heresy, breaking a sworn peace, and political offenses (Salvemini [1899] 1966, 116 nn. 87–94)—extended responsibility and penal consequences for the crime to near relatives (Statuto del Capitano, 1322, bk. 2, rubr. 33–40, in Caggese 1910, 115–118; Kirshner 1985, 256–303).

One group of citizens, the magnates, who in the late thirteenth century were stigmatized as violent and little concerned with the common good, were not covered by this communal legislation. After 1293, because they were accused of using violence to impose their own interests, certain houses of the great, referred to by name, were placed under the jurisdiction of the Ordinances of Justice, which curtailed their political rights and subjected them to special judicial procedures. In the 1280s and the 1290s, regulations systematically obliged them to put up a security bond, a mechanism designed to prevent eventual delinquents from having recourse to violence against one another or, even more important, against the populars, and from disturbing public order with their private wars (Salvemini [1899] 1966). As practiced in the last two decades of the thirteenth century and during the fourteenth (Cavalca 1967–1968; Becker 1965), this security bond was not only a preventive measure—as such, close kin contributed to its payment—but a repressive one as well when fines were paid out of the bond, thus directly implicating close kin in the punishment.

Who were the relatives endangered by the misconduct of a magnate? This was a sensitive point in the actions taken by the government of the people—the Popolo—in view of controlling the "powerful," as is clear from the varying responses to the problem. From 1286 on, if a magnate refused to put up the required security bond and to pay the penalties prompted by his refusal, both the sentence and posting the bond reverted to his father or his brother—that is, they fell within the second civil degree of kinship. In 1293, this limit was extended to the second and third civil degrees, which meant that a paternal uncle was held responsible for a nephew or a grandfather for his grandson. Even worse, from that date on, such measures concerned not only failure to post the bond but the criminal penalty as well. During the first half of the fourteenth century, the limit was extended still further, to the fourth degree. A variety of measures brought the limit back to the third degree of kinship during the government of the duke of Athens (1342–1343), that of the Fourteen that followed his downfall (August 1343), and the popular government that in turn brought down the Fourteen (September-October 1343). In June 1349, however, the limit was set at the sixth degree.[14] In 1351, the limit was finally returned to the third degree or, in the absence of third-degree kin, to the fourth.[15] The statutes of 1409 once more reiterated that "relatives of magnates are held responsible only in the male line up to and including the fourth civil degree."[16] In the first third of the fifteenth century, then, the last of the magnates continued to bear the judicial consequences of their extended genealogical solidarities.

During the entire long period that the Ordinances of Justice remained in effect, the notion obtained that birth from a common stock had tangible effects, measurable in practice, on the behavior of that particular category of "noble" and "powerful" individuals. Because their houses were welded together by a solidarity presumed to be broader and more active than that of ordinary families and because their power and arrogance thrived on such cohesion, the popular government dominated by the Arti (the guilds) concluded that they should be made to drink the brew of kinship to the dregs—that is, that their family attachments should work against them by forcing them to accept all the ensuing consequences. In reality, the measures creating exceptions to the application of common law were in evident contradiction to the principles of Roman law that inspired the development of communal justice. The paradox is that public power and its jurists should have employed such measures to assure

---

14. *PR* 36, fol. 95v, 29 May 1349, fols. 95v–105v, 12 June 1349. The discussions of the commission that decided it can be found in *Consulte e Pratiche* 1, fols. 6r–7r.

15. *PR* 39, fol. 7r, 17 Aug. 1351, 42, fol. 34r, 10 Apr. 1355.

16. *Statuti del Comune* 23, fol. 434r.

the triumph of a notion of justice contrary to the coresponsibility that such measures implied. An understanding of this paradoxical situation affords a better grasp of the meanders of Florentine politics concerning this particular group of families, but more important, it illuminates the slow elaboration of a state justice, a key factor in the genesis of the modern state.

The application to the populars of measures specifically designed to strike at the magnates—in other words, the diversion of exceptional procedures inherited from the bloody political confrontations of the thirteenth century—helped to empty this statute of its original meaning by making it an arsenal of all-purpose measures, among them the expression of state power. Indeed, the status of magnate was not strictly reserved to the families whose names figured on the official list in the city statutes, drawn up and, in theory, closed in 1295. From the early fourteenth century on, the communal government authorized collective or individual attributions of the status of magnate to one or more populars. In 1323, for example, common citizens who joined with a group of magnates to plot against the government of the Popolo were prosecuted along with their magnate associates and received the same penalties as they, in application of the Ordinances of Justice.[17] An important step was taken in 1352, when "peaceful" common citizens petitioned the government to have the overly arrogant and violent among their numbers, whom they accused of committing atrocious or abominable crimes, declared magnates.[18] The legislation of those years was reactivated in the 1370s, and the problem of the transfer of populars to the category of magnates became a crucial topic in political debate during that decade (Brucker 1962, 129–130, 261–262, 321–324, 359–360).[19] As we have seen, from 1357 on, this change of status affected people in the contado who engaged in actions of private justice to which they were not bound by patrilinear family ties, and from 1371 on, it applied also to members of a rural consorteria guilty of aggression against a Florentine.[20] Change of status could also strike those whose only major crime was fiscal delinquency. In

17. *PR* 20, fol. 27r-v, 30 Sept. 1323.

18. *PR* 39, fol. 192r, 27 Aug. 1352. Measures for the enforcement of the law were taken on 3 Dec. 1352 (*PR* 40 fols. 27v–28r); the procedures to be followed and the list of crimes justifying the magnatization of a popular were more precisely defined on 27 Sept. 1356 (*PR* 43, fol. 151r-v) and repeated on 19 Jan. 1377 (Brucker 1962, 323 and n. 101).

19. A law of 27 Jan. 1372 protected those who petitioned for a popular to be declared a magnate and accelerated the process (*PR* 59, fols. 210v–211r). The law was the first of a series of measures aimed at members of important popular lineages: Ridolfi, Albizzi, Strozzi, Brancacci, Medici. The reaction against "ineptam et absurdam practicam que inolevit circa observantiam reformationis . . . de faciendo magnates et supermagnates cives florentinos et comitatinos et districtuales" is best expressed on 3 June 1378. *PR* 66, fol. 33r.

20. *PR* 44, fol. 64r, 19 Feb. 1357, 59, fol. 103v, 12 Sept. 1371.

1364, recalcitrant taxpayers with delinquent accounts going back three years found themselves classified as magnates, and in the mid-fourteenth century an analogous measure covered citizens unwilling to pay the *novina* tax.[21]

This legislation often seemed to hesitate before full utilization of the weapon of magnatization, and it seldom systematically extended the coresponsibility of relatives typical of the magnates to those we might call neomagnates. In 1323, for example, the sons and descendants of a father judged guilty of intrigue were to be treated as he was, but unlike magnates by birth, "neither their consorts nor their consanguineans" faced penalties.[22] In 1352, criminals only and not their descendants could be declared magnates, and close kin of a fiscal delinquent living under his roof would not face exclusion from municipal offices, as he did.[23] The Statute of the Podestà compiled in 1409, however, maintained traces of laws originating in the last third of the fourteenth century that associated male-line kinship with qualifying a popular as a magnate. These laws are not numerous, and they pertain to the *conjuncti* of murderers who had executed their crime on the square before the communal palace; those of political exiles who violated their confinement; the consanguinei of a rural murderer of a citizen; the members of a peasant consorteria who offended a Florentine; and the descendants of anyone who might assault a member of a governmental body.[24]

There was thus a certain prudence in unspecific measures applying to some categories of criminals and their kin. When its enemies were more clearly defined, the popular government put greater pressure on the relatives of a criminal classified as a magnate. Several individual measures, for the most part aimed at political opponents, show that once the Comune had designated someone a magnate, it often sought either to include his kin in its judgment, with or without their assent, or attempted to separate the culprit from his family. The feeling that some popular lineages or some of their members were more powerful and more of a danger to public order and the safety of peace-loving merchants than the families listed as magnati at the end of the thirteenth century lies behind many of the transfers of status. Giovanni Villani gives an account of the objections that greeted the *popularitas* accorded to a number of impoverished and downgraded magnate families in 1325. Some grumbled that

21. *PR* 52, fol. 21r, 13 Sept. 1364; *Balie* 25, fol. 63r, 5 Dec. 1434.

22. *PR* 20, fol. 27r-v, 30 Sept. 1323. The exemption of the relatives of populars "commictentes aliquem tractatum contra commune florentinum," inscribed on the register of the Parte Guelfa, can be found in *PR* 71, fol. 58r-v, 19 June 1382.

23. *PR* 39, fol. 192r, 27 Aug. 1352, 52, fol. 62r, 14 Nov. 1364.

24. *Statuti del Comune* 23, "Nova collatio de Ordinamentis Justicie," fols. 418r–440r, in particular rubr. 33, 34, 36 bis, 38.

transferring some of the great families of populars to the rank of magnate would have been more advisable (Brucker 1962, 129–130).[25]

The Strozzi family provides a good example of the mistrust that a popular lineage of major notables could evoke. In 1381, Nofri di Pagnozzo Strozzi was declared a magnate when he was tried for repeated violent acts against both men and women and, more specifically, for having recently attacked a *popolano* (Jones 1956, 183–205). Six years later, his brother Pagnozzino assaulted a standard-bearer of the companies, who died of his wounds ten days later. Pagnozzino, his brother Nofri (for the second time), and all their sons and descendants were declared magnates, along with the entire Strozzi lineage, and the two brothers alone were declared rebels. All the Strozzis, with the exception of a few individuals who managed to be declared exempt, were henceforth to be considered magnates, unless one of them should kill or turn in the culprits within three years. Furthermore, the victim (who had not yet died at the time of the decree) and his close kin (brothers, sons, and descendants) were to be permitted to wreak vengeance on the culprits, their sons, their descendants, and their agnates "whatever their degree of kinship." Furthermore, the Strozzis were prohibited from countervendetta and were obliged to grant peace to the avengers (Brucker 1971, 111–116). When the avengers attacked a servant who was employed by one of the Strozzis exempted from the condemnations and thus not a legitimate target, the entire Strozzi clan immediately rallied behind the victim and mounted a counterattack (Brucker 1971, 114–115, 1977, 19–20, 34, 85). Five years later, in Pisa, the vendetta was fulfilled on Pagnozzino's son, and the Comune interceded with the Pisan government to request that it recognize the legitimacy of an act duly authorized by revenge procedures (Brucker 1971, 116).

This case demonstrates what the communal authorities expected from magnatization—to involve the kin of the culprit in repressive action. Transferring a family to magnate status meant exposing it to heavier sentences and more expeditious judicial procedures. Above all, it meant holding the family collectively responsible for the fulfillment of justice, if not for the crime itself.

The Strozzi affair also reveals that the relatives who had been implicated could show contradictory responses. Some who had better connections among the governing bodies maneuvered to get a personal exemption from the collective sentence. But when, against their will, they became embroiled in a vendetta, they closed ranks with the others of the lineage, in spite of deep internal

---

25. "Per certi fu lodato, ma per molti biasimato, però che delle schiatte de popolani possenti, et oltragiosi erano degni di mettere tra grandi per bene di popolo." Villani 1537, bk. 9, chap. 288, fol. 176r.

divisions within the family, to brave a common enemy (Jones 1956, 188–189). Others attempted to separate themselves from their house of birth permanently and to assert their autonomy. The Strozzi case is a practical illustration of the real effects of public pressure on the cohesion of kinship groups.

DISSOCIATED RELATIVES

When the communal government forcibly implicated the kin of a guilty party—temporarily, at least—it probably had a greater long-term aim. That is, the government hoped to break up the lineage and goad some members of the family group into dissociating themselves from the sentenced person, which would amount to recognition of the supremacy of the public covenant over birthright solidarities. This is the essence of the Strozzi affair, and the same intention seems visible behind a series of legislative measures, at first sight heterogeneous, that applied to various categories of citizens: magnates, magnates become populars, magnates become supermagnates, neomagnates (populars become magnates), and populars who remained so. All these laws had the explicit goal of breaking up lineages and aiding the formation of smaller and less powerful kinship groups. Unlike the magnatization procedures, which widened the coresponsibility of agnatic kin for purposes of repression, these measures aimed at preventing violence on the part of family groups strong in numbers and financial or political power. They were also intended to discourage the making of a common cause between a more restricted kinship group and some family hothead.

In the 1340s a series of laws proposed two different policies regarding the magnates, between which the Comune vacillated: either magnates were to be integrated with the *popolo* and included within the purview of the common law, or they were to be incited to separate from their kinship groups and found autonomous lineages. In either case, however, a new idea was surfacing: to carry out such a decision, the bonds of lineage had to be repudiated, along with the solidarities they presumed and the signs of their permanence. Furthermore, it was up to the Comune—to the state—to record a decision of this sort, thereby guaranteeing the validity of the separation.

In October 1343 a number of lineages and some isolated individuals, more than five hundred persons in all, who had been magnates were transferred to popular status. When a part of the family retained magnate status, the government required that the new populars give up their former armorial insignia, adopt new ones, and renounce all solidarity with their ex-consorts.[26] In 1349

26. "Omnia latera et singulares persone laterum . . . non possint tenere ad eamdem brigham,

the communal government offered magnates the possibility of abandoning their lineages and founding new houses, which would remove their obligation to be "a una pace e a una briga" (at the same peace and the same quarrel) with their blood relatives. The new casa would still belong to the juridical group of the magnates, but the legal solidarities pertaining to this category of citizens would be required only among members of the same house, ancient or newly created. The repudiation was official and formal, requiring a solemn declaration before a commission of twelve populars, who were responsible also for attributing a new name and armorial device to the divided magnates who opted for leaving their *domos, agnationes et stirpes* (Klapisch-Zuber 1988a, 1214–1215, 1219–1220).[27] Two aspects of this procedure need to be stressed: first, the commitment required of the divided kin much resembled a formal abjuration of inherited kinship; second, the Comune did not reserve the right to abolish kinship, but acted on the forms of familial groups that resulted from the separation. A joint declaration of the candidate or candidates and the state was needed to nullify the obligations between patrilateral kin and to create a new lineage: the candidates had to express the intention to no longer consider consanguineous relatives as kin; the Comune consecrated the separation and guaranteed its effects from that time on.

During the latter fourteenth century both policies were put into practice; under the first, magnates turned populars and, by extension, populars turned magnates, and under the second, citizens, whatever their judicial and political status, chose to distance themselves from their kin or were forced by law to do so. In both cases, the legislation concerning members of the popolo apparently was inspired by the measures previously drawn up for the magnates.

The most noteworthy texts concerning magnates turned populars date from 1361. It was then that the Comune stipulated (and the measure applied retroactively as well) that the magnates granted popularitas must come before a government notary and solemnly swear to renounce their kinship bonds and all solidarity with relations who remained magnates. In addition, they were to register the name and the armorial insignia they intended to adopt, so that they could be clearly distinguished from their former consorts.[28] The law remained

---

hodium seu inimicitiam cum aliis de eadem domo de qua erant remanentibus in numero magnatum nec possint . . . facere . . . aliquam offensionem ad vindictam . . . alicui offensioni . . . facte vel fiende contra aliquem qui remaneret magnas de dicta sua domo seu casato. . . . Item quod etiam debeant predicti portare et ferre diversa arma seu signa armorum ab armis et signis domus et casati de qua fuissent." *Capitoli, Registri, Protocolli* 4, fol. 61r-v.

27. *PR* 36, fols. 103v–105r, 12 June 1349; "Contra magnates divisos," *PR* 37, fols. 99r–100v, 17 Feb. 1350.

28. *PR* 49, fol. 1r-v, 11 Aug. 1361. The renunciation concerned the "consorterie et agnationi

in effect to the end of the fifteenth century. Its practical implications for subsequent relations between consorts remain problematic: although many of the new populars continued to participate, along with their ex-consorts who remained magnates, in the rights and obligations of the consorteria to which they had belonged until they declared their independence, the Comune clearly stood as a guarantee of the change of family identity and the obliteration of the kinship relationship.

Magnates convicted of criminal acts were subjected to further constraints in the 1350s. In 1355, shortly after application of the Ordinances of Justice was to some extent mitigated,[29] major criminals among the magnates were obliged to sever all ties with their kin by moving their residences to urban neighborhoods or rural parishes where they had no relatives. Their families were forbidden to assist or advise them.[30] As of 1371, magnates who had been sentenced not only had to change residence but also lost the benefits of the lighter application of the Ordinances of Justice that had been in effect since April 1355.[31] This category of magnates became known as supermagnates. Thus cut off from the moral and material support of their *prossimani* (near relatives), the culprits were gradually dispossessed of their identities. In May 1372, a law stripped them of the right to bear the arms of their lineages and reiterated the prohibition on relatives from offering them counsel or assistance.[32]

Equivalent dispositions were taken against the criminals among the populars who had been transferred to magnate status. Like the supermagnates, they were obliged to change their names, their armorial insignia, and their residences to avoid being confused with their kinfolk.[33] In fact, even when the law did not oblige them to do so, the popular relatives of a disreputable person or a sentenced criminal seem to have felt more comfortable once they renounced

---

omnium et singulorum suorum consortum seu coniunctorum per lineam masculinam magnatum." Thereafter it was prohibited "quoquo modo aliquam seu aliquas iniurias vel offensas factas seu que fierent alicui ex dictis suis consortibus seu coniunctis magnati ad iniuriam aliqualiter revocare nec inde vindictam facere," and so forth. Changing the family name and armorial insignia was not necessary if the person granted popularitas was the last member of his own lineage to benefit from it (in which case he was permitted to keep his old name) or if the entire lineage became popular.

29. *PR* 42, fols. 33r–34v, 10 Apr. 1355.

30. The fine was set at one thousand lire for relatives helping "in aliquam . . . brigam, guerram, hodium seu inimicitiam." *PR* 42, fol. 113r-v, 21 Aug. 1355.

31. *PR* 59, fols. 102v–103v, 12 Sept. 1371. One of the major innovations in April 1355 was to limit coresponsibility to kin to the third degree under Roman law.

32. *PR* 60, fols. 16r–17v, 30 May 1372.

33. This can be seen in the notarized document of 7 Feb. 1374 by which Lando di Antonio Albizzi, made a magnate in April 1373, took Antonii as his name and chose new insignia and a new place of residence, the parish of Santa Maria Novella. *Manoscritti* 439, unpaginated.

their kinship connection with him. Some fifty renouncements of kinship ties of this sort, legalized by a decision of the municipal councils, remain from the latter half of the fourteenth century. Only a few appeals refer to a sentenced person made a magnate;[34] many, however, appear to be related to a judicial action taken against a consorte, and almost all reveal a fear that the reprehensible actions, political, commercial, or moral, of the black sheep might create a storm of troubles for his relatives. Most of these renouncements of kinship (the instigators and the victims of which need further study) attest to the prudence of families anxious to shield themselves from the possible consequences of the financial bankruptcy or moral misdeeds of a relative.

Finally, a few divisions within important popular lineages followed the scenario inaugurated in 1349 for the magnates. The members of the Albizzi clan who became the Alessandri family in 1372, or those of the Bardi family who took the name of Larioni in 1452 (nearly all the Bardis were populars at the time) went through the same formalities as the magnates who split off from their clans in 1349.[35] They renounced their consorteria before a notary, and they gave up their names and arms to adopt new ones.[36] Nonetheless, a radical rupture with the identity that a lineage had in common was rarely necessary for populars, as most of them did not have names sufficiently well known to merit changing, and some had no family name at all.[37]

Without more advanced genealogical research (a nearly impossible project where humbler families are concerned), guessing at the fractures that might have authorized a request for division from one's kin is difficult. All applicants spoke of consorts (or of a consort), but few referred to the precise kinship ties between them.[38] For the purposes of this discussion, it is nonetheless helpful to attempt to clarify the nature of these bonds to go beyond simple analysis of the articulations, the vocabulary, and the rhetorical effects of these discourses on kinship and its disappointments. The best I can do, for the moment, is to of-

34. The new magnates, like the older ones, had to come before the Podestà once a year to post their bonds and swear their oaths. In 1381, for instance, we can identify some of them, like Salvestro and Guasparre Brancacci, who had also been involved in renouncements of kinship ties. *Atti del Podestà* 2977, not paginated.

35. For the Albizzis, *PR* 60, fol. 108v, 19 Nov. 1372; for the Bardis, *PR* 143, fol. 209r, 23 July 1452.

36. The Larioni are the only family, to my knowledge, who also renounced the rights of patronage of their former consorteria.

37. Two out of every three populars involved in a suit for division from their consorts bore a family name, often very obscure; one out of three had no family name.

38. Where family ties were given more explicitly, humbler people seem to have been concerned with very near relatives—brothers, first cousins, or uncles and nephews—whereas members of more important popular lineages who sought to expel a renegade cousin were more loosely related and perhaps even belonged to different branches of the lineage.

fer a few provisional remarks about texts that formalize an end to agnatic bonds.

The separation *per viam legis* from a relative whose behavior caused problems occurred only after his consorts had repeatedly urged him to mend his ways; the petitioners emphasize how long they attempted to do so. When all their efforts proved of no avail, they threw up their hands and turned to the communal government to sanction the decision henceforth to have nothing to do with him, since the enforcement of familial justice had failed. Dissociation generally involved a declaration by the petitioners that they would no longer take upon themselves offenses against the repudiated consort, which implied swearing to keep peace with his enemies and refusing vendetta. The *grandi* who instituted this procedure still speak of "mortal hatred," "quarrel," and "war" (*odium mortale, briga, guerra*), but humbler folk at most renounced the obligation to support relatives against people who have offended them. The government, for its part, cut more boldly into the kinship network, decreeing, at the request of any group of petitioners, that "all kinship or consorteria that exists or has existed with the aforementioned D. and Gi. is eliminated and ended, as if the said D. and Gi. never belonged and had never belonged to the same house, stock, family, or stem to which F. and G. and other aforementioned [parties], with their descendants, have belonged or will belong."[39] At times, the city government merely added legal force to an agreement drawn up in private between the persons concerned.[40] In reality, communal ratification covered a variety of forms of division. The Comune's endorsement of the rejection and expulsion of a black sheep by a group of consanguineans implied that it shared their judgment of his moral worth.[41] To the contrary, an individual's demand for separation from his consorts—good or bad, true or false—had no such

39. "Et quod omnis parentela seu consorteria que sit vel esset cum ipsis Ducio et Giannotto sit sublata et finita . . . ac si ipsi D. et G. vel aliquis eorum nunquam fuissent seu essent de ea domo et agnatione casato seu stirpe de qua fuerunt seu erunt predicti Franciscus, Gerius et alii predicti [Risaliti] et eorum posteri" (*PR* 43, fol. 98r-v, 9 June 1356). Another common formula is: "Et insuper vigore presentis provisionis omnis parentela consorteria agnatio seu cognatio que esset inter N. . . . ex una parte et quoscumque alios eorum agnatos cognatos seu coniunctos per lineam masculinam ex parte altera intelligatur esse et sit finita et sublata." Division of the Canigiani family, *PR* 51, fol. 60r, 21 Nov. 1363.

40. For example, in the agreement between the notary ser Vermiglio di ser Franchino Vermigli and his three "nepotes et consortes . . . qui tenent vitam aliam." They agreed before a notary to renounce their consorteria, but prefer that the Comune ratify and abolish their kinship bonds. *PR* 56, fols. 159v–160r, 23 Feb. 1369.

41. A similar characterization of the rejected relative is implied in the request of five members of the Nobili family, who "nollent in eorum grege hominem talis conditionis." *PR* 84, fols. 162r–163r, 27 Aug. 1395.

clear-cut implications.[42] Nonetheless, intervention of the Comune at the demand of a private citizen, like its intercession in favor of the magnates in 1349, proclaimed the dissolution of kinship bonds that had become unbearable or dangerous to some of the persons involved—a dissolution that could have full effect in the law courts and in successional distributions only with communal sanction.

When the Comune applied to the populars, offender or not, dispositions that it had taken regarding the magnates, it appeared to consider the bonds of extended kinship equally valid for both groups. This was patently untrue, however. The family connections to which the communal government ascribed so much weight where populars were concerned were restored by its repressive action, though somewhat artificially and, more important, always provisionally. Such premises gave unity to the legislative arsenal the government was constituting with the aim of stifling private violence and of reserving to the public power the right of punishment for such violence.

The dissuasive or repressive effect of bracketing popolari and magnati consisted in forcibly overcoming individual resistance by applying to populars kinship bonds more far-reaching than they actually were. The effect of the communal government on kinship did not stop there, however. The state assumed the power not only to set the boundaries of practical kinship but also to eliminate kinship, "as if" it had never existed. Here, like in the fiction of new "native" citizens, who were "as if" born of Florentine blood and sprung from Florentine soil, art imitated nature (Riesenberg 1974; Kirshner 1974, 1976). The decisions taken by the government "separate and divide the concerned parties from their kin as if they had never been consorti or agnates of the same stock."

In my opinion, the Comune's incursions into the realm of the definition and the signs of kinship were innovations. To give them their full significance, we would need to compare them with other public strategies, also elaborated in the latter fourteenth century, regarding birth and, somewhat later, marriage. Was it by chance that as the Comune gained increasing control over the limits and the definition of birth kinship, it also produced legislation dealing with the rights that birth conveyed in citizenship? Or that it increasingly endorsed legitimations certified by Palatine authority and, on its own behalf, granted privileges

42. Some requests do not even give the name of the rejected relative (*PR* 57, fol. 211r-v, 6 Apr. 1370). There are as many claims, generally collective, for division by expelling an individual as there are requests from an individual for separation from the group of his consorts.

of legitimation enabling an illegitimate child to be considered "as if" he were wellborn, and hence eligible to inherit? Through all this legislative activity, the government of the city-state seems to have played an increasing role in the civil implications of birth; a role parallel to, though quite distinct from, the one that the Church assumed in sacramental matters.

The example of Florence in the second half of the fourteenth century can be said to clarify an important stage in the long history of kinship groups forced to come to terms with nascent public power. When families and lineages were obliged to accede that public power controlled not only their rights and traditional behavior but also their very definition, they gradually came to recognize the state as the guarantor of their identity and their perpetuity.

Translated by Lydia G. Cochrane

Chapter 12

EVA CANTARELLA

Homicides of Honor: The Development of Italian Adultery Law over Two Millennia

The *lex Julia de adulteriis* was a milestone in the history of family relations and Roman sexual ethics (Mommsen 1955, 688–699; Mayer-Maly 1964; Daube 1972, 373; Galinski 1981–1982; Richlin 1981; Raditsa 1980). By approving this law, Rome affirmed the principle that female sexual behavior was of public interest and regulated it with great severity. Until then the sexual relationships of women who belonged to a *familia* were considered a private matter. The lex Julia established that an illicit sexual relationship was an offense open to public trial at the request of any male citizen and punishable by *relegatio in insulam* (exile to an island) for both members of the adulterous couple and by the payment of fines levied from their patrimonial wealth.[1]

Furthermore, when it used the word *adulterium*, the lex Julia did not refer solely to adulterium in the strict sense of sexual relations between a married man or woman and anyone other than his or her spouse or between a male citizen, even unmarried, and someone else's wife. In the text of the law adulterium covered *stuprum* as well, a term that was defined as any sexual relations of or with a virgin or a widow (*Dig.* 48.5.6.1, Papinian). Thus the lex Julia established that, with the explicit exception of relations with prostitutes and between persons cohabiting as husband and wife, all extramarital sexual rela-

1. *Pauli Sent.* 2.26. The patrimonial penalty for a woman was confiscation of one-third of her property and one-half of her dowry. The penalty for the man was confiscation of one-half of his property. In 326, under Constantinus (*Cod. Theod.* 11.36.4), adultery became punishable with death, inflicted by the *poena cullei*, closing the adulterers in a sack with a dog, a cock, a viper, and an ape and throwing the sack into the nearest river or sea.

tions were crimes to be punished by a special standing court (*quaestio perpetua*), which continued to function until the age of the Severans. After the *quaestio de adulteriis* disappeared, adulterium was punished by a trial known as *cognitio extra ordinem,* and as such was judged by the emperor or by an imperial official.

With the lex Julia, then, the punishment of adulterium (in the broader sense) passed from the private to the public sphere. There were exceptions to this rule, however, which regarded adultery in the strict sense and sought to establish special rules reconciling the new principle, in which the crime concerned the entire state, and the old, where it concerned only the father and the husband of the adulteress (Volterra 1930; Daube 1956; Thomas 1961; Ankum 1985, 1987).

First, a distinction was made between the *jus accusandi jure mariti vel patris* (the right of accusation by right of husband or father) and the *jus accusandi jure extranei* (the right of accusation by right of a third party) (Volterra 1928). The jus accusandi jure extranei, possessed by all citizens, could be exercised only if the husband and the father of the adulteress had not made the *accusatio* reserved to them in the sixty days following the divorce, which had to precede the accusation.[2] The husband took precedence over the father in making the accusatio adulterii (*Dig.* 48.5.2.8, 48.5.3, Ulpian). Second, the husband and the father of the adulteress had the *jus occidendi*—the right to kill—only in certain circumstances. In other words, the law restricted the right to kill traditionally granted the father and the husband rather than totally abrogating it.

If we are to understand why Augustus limited the right to kill adulterous women and to comprehend the basis of continued consent to such killing, we need to look briefly at the norms preceding the lex Julia. Until 18 B.C., the right of a father to kill his daughter (whether this right was exercised frequently is not of interest here) was founded on *patria potestas* (paternal power); a man's right to kill his wife was founded on the personal power called *manus,* which was identical in substance to the patria potestas. The wife was subject to manus if she had been brought into the familia of her husband by a marriage cum manu, and according to the rules of the *jus civile* the husband possessed manus only if he was *sui juris* (under his own legal power). The husband still in his father's power (*filiusfamilias*) thus had no legal power over his wife, who from a legal viewpoint was joined to her husband by a fraternal relationship. According to law, the wife in manu was loco filiae (in the position of a daughter) with

2. Reservation to the husband and the father of the right of accusation is stated in *Dig.* 48.5.15.2 (Scaevola); *Dig.* 48.5.12.6 (Papinian); *Dig.* 4.4.37.1 (Tryphoninus); *Dig.* 48.5.4.1 (Ulpian); *Dig.* 48.5.16 pr. (Ulpian); *Collatio legum romanarum et mosaicarum,* 4.4.1 (Paulus); and *Cod. Just.* 9.9.6 (A.D. 223, A. Severus). That a person other than the husband and the father could not accuse the adulteress unless she had been divorced is stated in *Dig.* 48.5.12.10 (Papinian); *Dig.* 48.5.27 pr. (Ulpian); and *Cod. Just.* 9.9.1 (A.D. 226, when a Severus confirmed the rule).

regard to her husband if he was a *paterfamilias,* but she was like a sister to him if he was a filiusfamilias (Gaius, *Inst.* 1.114, 115b, 118). In theory, then, if the husband was a filiusfamilias, the right of manus belonged to his paterfamilias, but it seems that in practice the exercise of this power (including the right to kill) was delegated to the husband-filius (Volterra 1966; Guarino 1967).

During this period the right to kill, whether of the pater or the husband, was unlimited. Cato said of the husband in his *De dote:* "If you had taken your wife in adultery, you would kill her with impunity without legal judgment; if you were committing adultery or about to do so, she dare not lay a finger on you, nor is it legal" (Aulus Gellius, *Attic Nights* 10.23.5). A satire by Horace illustrated the equally unlimited impunity for killing the wife's paramour (an impunity founded on social recognition of the right to take revenge). Among various forms of vengeance a husband could take, Horace mentions death by flogging (*Sat.* 1.2.41–42). A passage in the *Digest* shows that jurists had questioned the legality of such revenge and had concluded, Galba alone dissenting, that it was lawful (*Dig.* 48.5.46). The lex Julia, however, notably restricted the jus occidendi of both the father and the husband.

According to the lex Julia, a father could kill his daughter and her lover with impunity only if the following conditions were fulfilled:

1. The father had to be sui juris, his daughter had to be in his legal power, and he had to be her natural father. In other words, only the natural father who was a paterfamilias could kill the adulterers (*Dig.* 48.5.22).

2. The pater had to surprise the daughter when she was engaging in illicit sexual activities, and he had to kill her and her lover immediately (*Dig.* 48.5.24 pr.). Ulpian says that the pater must kill the adulterers "by one blow and one attack, with equal anger against both" (*Dig.* 48.5.24.4)—in other words, in a fit of rage caused by the discovery of the illicit relationship.

3. The law that made paternal impunity dependent on killing the daughter is confirmed by the *Collatio legum romanarum et mosaicarum* 4.2.6–7. In a passage of Ulpian we are told that this provision was established in the hope that the father, in order to spare his daughter, would not kill the lover (*Dig.* 48.5.23.4). Aside from seeking to curb revenge taking, the lex Julia thus imposed a notable restriction on the exercise of the powers of patria potestas by insisting that the father must kill immediately on discovering the illicit relationship and in a fit of rage. This last limitation of patria potestas was basically new and had nothing to do with the right to punish, which by its nature could be exercised in any state of mind, not exclusively when prey to anger.

4. The daughter had to be caught in the act in her father's house or her husband's house and not elsewhere. The reason for this rule was that adultery committed in the house of the father or the husband constituted a major insult

(*major injuria*) (*Dig.* 48.5.24.2). Thus once again the lex Julia established a new criterion, offense against honor, as a condition of impunity that differed from the exercise of the patria potestas.

These rules applied only if the daughter was adulterous in the strict sense— that is, if she was married. This was an important innovation because it denied the paterfamilias the right to kill an unmarried daughter guilty of stuprum; a right he formerly possessed (whether it was ever exercised or not).

Jurists debated this last provision, asking, for example, whether the father and the husband had the right to kill a *filia ignominiosa* or a wife married *contra legem*. The jurist Macer concluded in the first half of the third century that "it is more correct to say that the right of killing belongs to those who can bring an accusation by the right of the father or of the husband" (*Dig.* 48.5.25.3, Macer). Since only a married woman's father had this right, it followed that an unmarried daughter, even if ignominiosa, could no longer be killed. Perhaps the discussion arose because the text of the law was ambiguous; perhaps because not all jurists welcomed so drastic a limitation of the patria potestas. Still, the law was favorably received in juridical circles, reconfirming that the basis of the right to kill an adulterous daughter fell outside of patria potestas.

The *Collatio legum romanarum et mosaicarum* (drawn up between the late fourth century and the early fifth century A.D.), which also contains legal rules subsequent to the lex Julia, states that the father may kill his married daughter even if the daughter has been transferred into the manus of her husband (4.2.3), the father is not a paterfamilias (4.2.2), and the daughter is under her own legal power (4.2.4). With the passage of time, juridical interpretation of the paternal jus occidendi thus clearly abolished the remaining traces of its former nature as an empowering act in the lex Julia, which stipulated that if the natural father was to kill with impunity, he had to be a paterfamilias.

In the centuries following the lex Julia, paternal impunity was increasingly founded on the new criteria introduced by Augustus—the emotional turmoil (*dolor*) of the father who discovers his daughter's adultery and his desire and duty to punish the offense (injuria) to the family honor. This new basis allowed the pater to kill his daughter even when patria potestas no longer included the power of life and death.[3]

Under the lex Julia the husband could no longer kill his wife. Furthermore, he could kill her lover with impunity only if he surprised him in his own (the

---

3. Some years ago my analysis of Augustan rules on the paternal jus occidendi was different. In 1976 I thought that in the lex Julia this jus was still strongly based on the patria potestas and that its transformation into homicide for reasons of honor occurred in later jurisprudence. See Cantarella 1976.

husband's) house and only if the lover was a slave, an *infamis,* or disreputable person (gladiator, *bestiarius,* dancer, singer, pimp, prostitute, or condemned on a public charge) or a freedman of the husband, the wife, or close relatives of either (*Dig.* 48.5.25; *Coll. leg. rom. et mos.* 4.3.2–4; *Pauli Sent.* 2.26.4.5). If he killed his wife, the husband was treated as a murderer (*Dig.* 48.5.23.4, 48.5.25 pr.; *Coll. leg. rom. et mos.* 4.3.1., 4.10.1, 4.12.13). Ulpian explains why a husband should not be allowed to kill his wife (or other adulterer): "It is granted to the father and not to the husband to kill the woman and any adulterer, because most often a father's sense of affectionate duty (*pietas*) takes counsel for his children; on the other hand, the heat and violent impulse of a husband readily making a judgment was to be restrained" (*Dig.* 48.5.23.4).

The husband was denied the right to kill his wife not because marriage by the Augustan age had come to be mainly sine manu; it was denied him because it was thought that the husband would find controlling his anger more difficult than the father would and because the pater could be induced to spare his daughter. The passage referring to paternal pietas and the father's willingness to spare his adulterous daughter is not entirely convincing, however. This is not to deny that such pietas existed, or to assert that fathers inexorably exercised their jus occidendi. In fact, the imperial decrees concerning specific cases in which a woman was killed refer as a rule to women killed by their husbands, not their fathers.[4] My point is that the law on which Ulpian comments was singular: while permitting the father to kill his adulterous daughter, Augustus made his impunity for killing her lover dependent on killing the daughter. The most reasonable explanation of this provision (which might even have induced the father to kill his daughter rather than spare her) is that Augustus wanted to eliminate adultery as a pretext to justify murders committed for personal or political reasons. The paternal pietas on which Augustus counted (in Ulpian's interpretation) was thus shown toward an innocent daughter. If so, the rule does not enable us to compare the father's dolor with the husband's emotions. Nonetheless, the general thrust of the passage from Ulpian is that a husband was restrained from killing his wife not because he lacked personal power over her, but because his wife's adultery was such an intolerable offense that he would otherwise certainly kill her.

These were, very briefly, the provisions of the lex Julia concerning the husband's impunity, which was also dependent on certain conditions. Within three days, the husband had to notify the magistrate with jurisdiction in the territory of the killing and where it had occurred. If he failed to do so, he could

---

4. The decisions of Antoninus and Commodus are quoted in *Dig.* 48.5.39.8, and *Coll. leg. rom. et mos.* 4.6.3, and the decision of A. Severus in *Cod. Just.* 9.9.4.

be tried for murder (*Pauli Sent.* 2.26.6; *Coll. leg. rom. et mos.* 4.3.5). Furthermore, after he killed her lover, the husband had to divorce his wife. If he failed to repudiate her he could be accused of pimping.[5]

Thus Augustus imposed considerable limits on the impunity of the husband with regard to killing his wife and her lover. In the course of time, however, these limitations lapsed, and the husband was permitted to kill both his wife and her lover, to kill a lover of any social rank, to kill him no matter where the adultery had been committed, and to do so even if the couple had not been caught in the act.

The first step in this direction was taken in the second century by the emperor Antoninus Pius, followed by Marcus Aurelius and Commodus, who established that the husband who killed his adulterous wife should be punished less severely than a common murderer because it "is very difficult [for him] to moderate his *justus dolor*" (*Dig.* 48.5.39.8). The sentence was hard labor for life if he was of lower social status and relegation or exile to an island if he was of higher status (*honestior*). This development culminated in 506 under Alaric II with the *lex Romana Visigothorum,* which established that the husband who killed his wife was guaranteed complete impunity (*Pauli Sent.* 2.27.1). Since the same provision appears in the *lex Visigothorum* (3.4.4), in dictating the rules for Roman citizens living in Visigoth territory, Alaric II may have been guided by Germanic tradition. Killing an adulterous wife was, in fact, considered lawful not only in the lex Romana Visigothorum but also in the Rotari *Edictum* (chap. 212). Whatever its origin (it may also have applied under the vulgar Roman law), around the mid-fifth century the rule was introduced into the imperial legislation and was applied to the entire empire by a Novella of Majorian referred to in the *lex Romana Burgundionum* (chap. 25).

Marcus Aurelius and Commodus also established less severe punishment for a husband who killed his wife's lover, even if the established conditions of place and person were not met (*Coll. leg. rom. et mos.* 4.3.6), and Alexander Severus ordained between 213 and 223 that this punishment be exile: "Although a homicide has been committed, nevertheless, since night and dolor justus mitigate the deed, he can be given exile" (*Cod. Just.* 9.9.4).

Once stated, the provision was reconfirmed on several occasions. It appears in the epitomes of the lex Romana Visigothorum (*Epitome Aegidii* and *Epitome Codicis Guepherbitani*), but also in the *lex Raetica Curiensis* (also called *Utinensis*), which regulated the relations between Roman citizens in the Francoman state between the eighth and ninth centuries.

---

5. *Dig.* 48.5.25.1; *Coll. leg. rom. et mos.* 4.12.7 = *Pauli Sent.* 2.26.7. The rule was confirmed in A.D. 199 by Severus and Antoninus, who specify that a man who fails to divorce a wife only suspected of adultery cannot be considered a pander (*Cod. Just.* 9.9.2).

Finally, Justinian issued new rules concerning the husband's right to kill his wife's lover. In the Novella 117 (chap. 15), the emperor established that if a husband suspected that his wife was unfaithful, he must send her presumed accomplice three written warnings signed by three trustworthy witnesses. After these warnings he could kill the man with impunity, whether he surprised him in the lover's house, in his own house, in a tavern, or in a house in the suburbs. By imposing the obligation of the three warnings the emperor limited the husband's powers only in appearance. In reality, the Novella increased the number of places where the wife's lover could be killed, and it justified the killing even if the adulterous couple was not caught in the act and without regard to the legal and social status of the lover.

The Greek expression Justinian uses to describe the situation in which the presumed adulterer could be killed (*syntynchnonta,* translated into Latin as *convenientem suae uxori*) can have a much broader meaning than "to have sexual relations"; it can mean also "to meet" or "to be with." The concept of justus dolor by now granted the husband considerable freedom to kill for the sake of honor. Although less extensive than his former right of revenge, the laws guaranteed the husband impunity if he killed his wife's lover, no matter who he was or where the deed was done, and he no longer had to catch the adulterers in the act. The only limitation to the exercise of the husband's very ample right was sending three preliminary warnings.

The provisions of the lex Julia and of the modifications through juridical interpretation and imperial edicts show that the new principle of justus dolor introduced by Augustus to justify the jus occidendi was not only very different from the principles on which this right had previously been founded but also more extensive. In fact, a single juridical criterion could justify killing a daughter or a wife (which previously had involved the exercise of personal power) and killing her accomplice (which had previously been considered legitimate vendetta).

This principle could serve to justify killings other than the ones Augustus allowed, however. The concept of justus dolor was clear enough, but the definition of the acts that gave rise to dolor and of the persons whose dolor was justus was obviously open to interpretation. The concept had already been subject to interpretation during the centuries between Augustus and Justinian, which led to an extension of the jus occidendi. In the centuries of the *jus comune* (and into the modern age), its interpretation was to be extended still further, and the justus dolor was to justify many more sorts of killing than those permitted by Roman law.

In dealing with the problem of the jus occidendi in the centuries of the renewed theoretical study and practical application of Roman law, my purpose is to

demonstrate the persistence of an ideology and a family code of honor. Consequently, I do not treat the intricate problem of the value of Roman law as jus
comune or its relation with ecclesiastical law or with the other sources of law,
general or particular, territorial or personal, that obtained in various lands. The
system of the sources of law in these centuries is the subject of ongoing debate
that involves the very conception of the jus comune. Although medieval jurisprudence opposed this law (considered as the law of the universal systems, of
empire and church) to the *jus proprium* of particular systems, today scholars tend
to consider the jus comune as a whole—that is, as a result of the interweaving
of the two universal systems and the *diversa jura propria* (territorial rights of the
monarchies, major principalities, and free city-states, plus the personal rights
of the feudal orders, corporations and guilds, and privileged bodies) (Astuti
1978).

In reality, the contrast between the jus comune and the jura propria is
essentially theoretical. This contrast is based on the formation of monarchies
superiorem non recognoscentes (that is, those that did not recognize the supremacy
of the emperor) and the rise of the free city-states. Although formally subject to
the empire, they acquired a de facto independence that led to a reversal of the
relation between the jus comune and the jus proprium, wherein the common
law was applied only as a subsidiary law. My intent is to demonstrate the
survival of an ideology that remained unchanged through the centuries in spite
of political vicissitudes and social and economic change. I thus leave to one side
the enormous problem of the place that Roman law occupied among the many
sources of law in different times and circumstances.

What counts here is that in the complex juridical system that emerged at the
beginning of the twelfth century and persisted for another seven centuries or
so, jurists differed in their conception of the jus comune, in their evaluation of
the relative weight of its constituent elements—custom (*consuetudo*) and equity
(*aequitas*) included—and thus with regard to the role of Roman law. Nevertheless, a common thread seems to run through the centuries and the various
interpretations to reveal a broad and shared acceptance of the concept of
homicide of honor. The jurists' works consistently base justification of an act of
this sort on the lex Julia. Although their interpretations vary from case to case,
they always extended the right to kill (obviously according to time and
circumstances).

I am not concerned here with the so-called jura propria, which by and large
also considerably extended impunity. The statutes of some Italian communes,
for example, granted the right to kill an adulterous wife not only to her husband
but also to her father-in-law and to her son, and they also allowed a father to kill
an unmarried daughter. The Statute of Verona, in particular, established the

impunity of a man who killed "anyone speaking with bad intent with a wife, a daughter-in-law, a daughter, or a sister." In the *Constitutiones regni Siciliae* we read that "if a husband has caught his wife in the very act of adultery, he will be permitted to kill the adulterer as well as the wife without any delay." If the wife was not caught in the act, however, the husband could do no more than cut off her nose.[6]

The jura propria differ greatly, and untangling what comes from Roman law and what comes from other sources is extremely difficult. The Sicilian constitutions, for example, contain not only elements from Roman law but also from Byzantine law, Franco-Lombard law, Norman law, Arab law, and customary Sicilian law. The specific punishment of cutting off the wife's nose seems to be a Byzantine inheritance. Unknown in Roman law, it was established in 740 by the *Ecloga* of Leo III Isauricus (*Ecloga* 17.27 in *Ius graeco-romanum* 1962). In the sixteenth century, however, Giovanni Nevizzano d'Asti recalled that in the diocese of Turin a nobleman cut off his adulterous wife's nose so that, deformed, she would find no more lovers. He states that this was the practice in Flanders (Nevizzanus Astensis 1573, 2:86). Clearly, the intermingling of traditions makes it difficult to analyze the multiple components of the various jura propria. Even if it were possible, however, there would be little point in listing all the rules concerning crimes of honor contained in the innumerable legislative provisions of the various communes and kingdoms, much less in tracing exceptions according to personal or social status. Since my concern is to trace the juridical principle, I shall return to the juridical works and the judicial decisions they inspired.

Although space does not permit examination of canon law, it is worth noting that it did not grant immunity to homicide for the sake of honor and that Thomas Aquinas gave the arguments for and against immunity in his *Summa theologica* (5.60.1.304f.). One of the arguments in favor was that since divine law had ordained the lapidation of the adulteress, the husband who killed his wife was not committing a sin because he was carrying out divine law. Furthermore, it was the husband's duty to correct his wife, and correction implied inflicting a just penalty for wrongdoing. Since the punishment for adultery was death, the husband could thus kill his wife. One of the contrary arguments was that because the Church is not bound by earthly laws, a member of the Church need not apply the law that condemns the adulteress to death. Furthermore,

---

6. *Statutorum magnificae civitatis Veronae libri V,* ed. I. P. Cominius (Venice, 1797), bk. 3, par. 40. The rule does not appear in the text for the year 1276, in the texts of the fifteenth century, or in the edition of the year 1561. See also *Constitutiones regni Siciliae,* ed. Jean-Louis Alphonse Huillard-Bréholles, in *Historia diplomatica Federici Secundi,* 4.I (Paris, 1854), bk. 3, pars. 47, 74.

husband and wife must be judged by the same standards, so if the wife may not kill her adulterous husband, the husband should not be permitted to kill his wife. Thomas also recalls that secular law excuses the husband's act by the "violent excitation" that gripped him, a consideration that did not oblige the Church either to exempt the uxoricide from eternal punishment or to adapt ecclesiastical judgments to secular rules (Roberti 1957, 335 and bibliography). In other words, the Church obviously could not take the justus dolor into account. This did not stop jurists from continuing to value it highly or to interpret in the most favorable light anyone who killed *honoris causa*.

Augustus's law recognized the jus occidendi only when the adulterers were caught in the act, and Pomponius interpreted *ipsa turpidine* to mean *in ipsis rebus Veneris* ("in the very act of love"). Papinian had explained that the expression corresponded to a Greek phrase used in the laws of Dracon and Solon that established the limits of the jus occidendi in Greece in the seventh and sixth centuries B.C. (*Dig.* 48.5.24). Bartolus, however, had already asserted that adultery was considered proved if the adulterers were surprised during the *praeparatoria Veneris,* and that kisses could be counted among these praeparatoria (Bartolus 1590). According to Accursius, in ipsis rebus Veneris would include "in bed with her or kissing her warmly," and he explains that *apparatus* (provisions) and *colloquia* (conversations) were praeparatoria as well (*Dig.* 48.5.24). The jurists had made the need to be caught in the act obsolete. That their interpretation was excessively broad was pointed out by such major jurists of the sixteenth and seventeenth centuries as Tiberius Decianus and Antonius Matthaeus. Although there was disagreement over how broadly to interpret the phrase *res Veneris,* the attitude toward a person who killed while in the grip of justus dolor remained unchanged.

This attitude is revealed by the interpretation of the Novella 117 of Justinian, which stipulated that the husband must send his wife's lover three written warnings before killing him. In 1551 this rule was included in the treatise *De maleficiis* of Angelus Aretinus de Gambilionibus (1551, fol. 71, par. "Chi hai adulterato la mia donna," n. 2), but Giovanni Nevizzano d'Asti informs us that it was opposed by "doctors" who drafted a model ridiculing the warning: "I, Martinus de Cornigliano, in these letters announce, call to witness, and declare publicly to you, Tristano de Bravis, that I hold you suspected of adultery with my wife. And since you have nothing to do with her against my will, in the future [you must] stop meeting with her and speaking with her: If you should dare to attempt it, I announce, call to witness, and declare publicly to you in these letters that I will use against you remedies and means of enforcement granted to me by law" (Nevizzanus Astensis 1573, bk. 1, par. 102, p. 67). The irony directed toward the husband who is issuing the three warnings is clear from the name given to him, Martinus de Cornigliano, an obvious allusion to *cornutus* (cuckold), a term of insult found in later works of jurisprudence as well and still used in Italy to ridicule the husbands of unfaithful wives. Social conscience evidently passed unfavorable judgment on husbands who hesitated to take the law into their own hands. Contempt for a man who denounced his adulterous wife, thus rendering his shame public, is confirmed by Julius Clarus Alexandrinus in a treatise on criminal law published in 1583 (Clarus 1583). Husbands, Clarus observes, did not dare denounce their wives before the courts for fear of the perpetual infamy that would be their lot, thanks to "an evil custom."[7] This evil custom that seemed so obvious to Clarus is clarified by Marianus Socinus Junior: judges usually derided men who made accusations of adultery (Socinus 1561, vol. 2, cons. 34, n. 9). The risk of ridicule was so great that, according to Felinus Sandeus, wise husbands would do well to "keep their horns in their breasts" to save their faces (*cornua portare in pectore, et factum in fronte*) (Sandeus 1547, comm. in chap. 2, *Dilectus* 10.5.2, *De calumnis*, n. 9). In short, the wise husband had only two options: to follow Sandeus's advice or to take the law into his own hands.

A century after Julius Clarus, the treatise *De aequitate* of the Milanese senator Julius Caesar Calvinus shows that nothing had changed. According to Calvinus, the rules established by the Roman emperors conformed to the criteria of *aequitas,* since both "the force of honor" and the *injuria* that adultery caused were great. Quite obviously, Calvinus's very broad interpretation of the Roman rules gives lesser importance to the need to defend one's honor than to the killer's state of uncontrollable emotion. Unlike Decianus and Matthaeus, Calvinus agrees with Bartolus on catching the adulterers in the act: kisses were an unmistakable proof of adultery (Calvinus 1675, 1.57).

The Milan senate went even further, however. It no longer even required that the husband, after warning his wife's presumed lover not to see her again, discover him with the wife. As proved by a sentence passed on 26 April 1588, the husband's honor was offended simply by his being thought to have been betrayed. Togninus Gamendus had warned Menghinus Dentonus not to frequent his wife. When the two men met on the street, Menghinus insulted Togninus, saying among other things that Togninus was a billygoat (*hircus*). For this Togninus killed him. The senate decreed that this was not a normal homicide but a homicide honoris causa.[8] The Milanese court was in fact very

---

7. Clarus 1583, par. 3, *adulterium,* versic., *sed. quaero.* On Julius Clarus's work, see Massetto, 1979a, 1979b.
8. Togninus was sentenced to *triennio remigare* (three years of galley duty). Many senators, however, considered this penalty too harsh.

lenient toward husbands and acquitted them even for killing their wives, following a practice that jurists from Bartolo onward had disapproved.

Decianus, whose authority was unquestioned, confirmed that the imperial constitutions permitted application of a less severe punishment to an uxoricide, but not acquittal. Furthermore, to explain why the husband was not granted the same impunity as the father, he cites the explanation Papinian had given: paternal pietas would hold back the father's hand, which would limit the number of homicides. In Decianus, however, this explanation is clearly a pretext, since he states that a father whose paternal pietas prevented him from killing his daughter could commission a third party to do the deed, in which case neither of the two was punishable (Decianus 1593, 1.9.38, 25).

After remarking that the impunity granted to the uxoricide was not prescribed by law but conformed to the principles of aequitas, Calvinus poses the question of whether granting impunity to someone who commissioned a third party to perform the killing was right. He declares that the *communis conclusio* was that it was (Calvinus 1675, 1.58.6, 29–30). The communis conclusio Calvinus refers to, however, did not confine concession of this right to the father (as in Decianus): the husband also could kill through a third party. Calvinus justifies the impunity of the agent (as well as of the husband) by referring to a rescript of Alexander Severus. In reality, however, the reference is not very pertinent. Alexander Severus speaks of the case of a certain Gracchus, who one night killed his wife's lover with the aid of his son (*Cod. Just.* 9.9.1), a scenario considerably different from a husband's use of a hired assassin. Calvinus's justification of total impunity in this instance is not at all convincing. The ideology that inspired both the senate's judgments and Calvinus's opinions is clearly revealed, however, in his comment on sentences awarded by Milanese judges. Murders carried out by a father and a husband even some time after they discovered the relationship of their daughter or wife were considered partially justified and therefore required less severe punishment. Calvinus comments on this practice, which completely left out any evaluation of the killer's rage (dolor), "This judgment is generally embraced as the more equitable by the most excellent Milanese senate, which generally attaches as much weight as possible to honoris causa" (Calvinus 1675, 1.58.31–33, 13–14). Thus it was no coincidence that homicide, theoretically justified as the expression of an uncontrollable justus dolor, came to be commonly defined as "for the sake of honor." Defense of honor was a social duty, a duty on which Calvinus even theorizes. In his opinion, husbands who ran to the law courts instead of taking the law into their own hands were behaving basely, in a manner unworthy of real men. They were cornuti. That this was not merely Calvinus's personal opinion but a widely accepted ideology emerges clearly from what he has to say about the attitude of the judges. Confirming the comments of Julius Clarus and Felinus Sandeus, Calvinus observes that the Milanese senators ridiculed accusations of adultery and mocked husbands who denounced their wives (Calvinus 1675, 1.58.11–12).

The conviction that the betrayed husband was duty bound to kill his adulterous wife, and not just her accomplice, is clear. This idea was certainly not confined to Milan. Antonius Matthaeus confirms that uxoricides for the sake of honor were generally acquitted and that a husband's failure to take the law into his own hands brought social opprobrium. This jurist, following the principles of the Church, considered the ideology and the practice unacceptable, and he denounces both as lamentable. In 1644 in *De criminibus,* Matthaeus reminds students at the University of Pavia, to whom the treatise is dedicated, that those who kill honoris causa may be acquitted by the law, but no "in the forum of conscience." He adds that those who "today make use of that right"—Italians, Spaniards, and Germans—and who allow a husband to kill his wife should be reminded of that fact. The practice, Matthaeus states, is blameworthy enough, but the mores of Neapolitans who not only approve killing the wife but also consider the husband who spares her a pander (*pro lenone*) are even more reprehensible (Matthaeus [1644] 1803, 3.3.19).

Justus dolor ultimately justified a good many more homicides than Augustus intended, but even when the killer's emotional state was left out of consideration, impunity was always derived, in theory, from Roman law. Once jurists and judges began to give more weight to defense of honor than to an expression of an uncontrollable dolor, the values that had inspired Augustus's legislation continued to be reflected both in popular sexual morality and in that morality as it was recognized and protected by the law. Reinforced by continual juridical approval, the idea that family honor was linked to female sexual behavior persisted unchanged even into the eighteenth century. Neither the debates on the nature of the family nor criticism of the relation between the family and the state had any effect on it (D'Amelio 1965; Bellomo 1967; Ungari 1974). Around 1763, Cesare Beccaria wrote: "Such pernicious and unauthorized injustices have been approved even by the most enlightened men and practiced in the freest republics because society has been considered as a union of families rather than as a union of individuals" (Beccaria 1965, par. 39). Enlightenment critics sought to diminish the power of the father, placing their hopes for the renewal of society in a proposed codification that, by written regulation of all social relations, would eliminate positions of privilege (Vismara 1988, 71). The great codifications were not drawn up until the nineteenth century, and debate on paternal (or marital) powers did not question crimes of honor any more than they did the "naturalness" of female inferiority, which in fact was even confirmed during the French Revolution. The Comité de Législa-tion, having declared the equality of the sexes in 1793, affirmed in 1796 that "natural order" called for the supremacy of the husband, and the legitimacy of homicide honoris causa—which was not limited to the exercise of personal power—was unquestioned. Jean-Jacques de Cambacérès's third draft of the Civil Code (Year III) nonetheless established that female adultery was no longer punishable and that parents would hold power over their children jointly (a certain reduction of male powers).

The revolutionary model of the family (if one can speak of such a model or unified concept) was, in any event, short-lived. With the fall of Robespierre in 1795 the wind shifted, and Napoleonic legislation reaffirmed the old principles (Levy 1974). In his introduction to the Civil Code of 1806, J.-E. Portalis declares that the recent revolutionary theories were just "the principles of certain individuals" and that the time-honored principles were "the spirit of the ages" (Vismara 1988, 83). Thus female adultery reverted to being a crime in the *Code pénal* (1810, art. 336), and honor was recognized as grounds for complete immunity for a husband who killed his wife and her lover if they were caught in the act inside his house (art. 324).

Legislation went a different way in Italy in the nineteenth century, however. Whereas Italian law established that the motive of honor was only an extenuat-ing circumstance, not a reason for total impunity, it extended both the number of persons who could benefit from this circumstance and the number of victims whose death honoris causa could be considered less serious. Furthermore, this extension introduced two important innovations. First, the extenuating circum-stance applied not only to the husband but also to a wife who killed her philandering husband. Second, the motive of honor was recognized as an extenuating circumstance in relationships other than that of husband and wife, such as father and daughter, mother and daughter, brother and sister, and sister and sister, even when the woman in question was unmarried. The Sardo-Italian code of 1859 and the code of the Neapolitan Provinces of 1861 established that homicide would be punished by imprisonment rather than death, not only if one spouse killed the other and his or her lover but also if the crime was "committed by the parents and in their house on the person of the daughter or the accomplice or of both in the moment of surprising them in the act of illicit relations or adultery."[9]

The first code after the unification of Italy (Codice Zanardelli, 1890, art.

---

9. In both legislations the rule is in art. 561. The same rule is in the Code Ticinensis, art. 294, par. 1. Other legislators limited the impunity to the marriage relationship, however (see Parma legislation, art. 351).

377) extended the right to defend family honor to all male ascendants (not just the father) and to the brother and sister of the adulterous person. In 1930 this provision passed almost unchanged into the Codice Rocco (art. 587), which, moreover, no longer required that the lovers be caught in the act in the husband's house but extended recognition of extenuating circumstances to a person who killed "in the moment when he discovered" the illicit relationship.[10] The courts interpreted this extenuating circumstance to apply to someone who discovered the illicit relationship by opening a letter or listening to a telephone conversation (Casalinuovo 1939; Caraccioli 1960).

At first sight, the innovations introduced into the Italian codes seem sweeping enough to suggest a change in the concept of family honor, according to which men, no longer sole guardians of that honor, could also offend it by their behavior. In fact, however, this was not the case.

The extension of extenuating circumstances to the wife merits separate discussion because it differed greatly from the benefits offered a mother or a sister. To see it as a first indication of a tendency to establish some small measure of equality in relations between spouses, and in the right to mutual fidelity in particular, is tempting. This tendency (not to be found in Napoleonic legislation, which punished only female adultery) appears in Austrian legislation. The Austrian code of 1811 (which was preceded by the *Editto Giuseppino* of 1784 and included in the Lombard-Venetian code of 1816) established male adultery as a crime (art. 247). Italian post-unification codes (and some pre-unification law codes) had established sanctions for unfaithful husbands, although the treatment reserved for them was different. The husband risked punishment only if he "kept a concubine in the conjugal house or notoriously elsewhere."[11]

These new tendencies might lead one to think that allowing the extenuating circumstance of the motive of honor to the wife reflected the notion that the husband, too, was held to respect the conjugal bond. If that was how popular opinion saw the matter, however, the jurists had other ideas. According to the most authoritative criminal lawyers, it was appropriate to extend this benefit to the wife not because she had even a limited right to her husband's fidelity, but in consideration of her emotions and sentiments. In Giulio Crivellari's commentary on the Codice Zanardelli (the most complete and authoritative commentary), we read that the *causa d'onore* was conceded to the wife not because the

---

10. In the new code, however, the word *father* replaced the word *ascendant*.

11. Codice Zanardelli, arts. 353 and 354; Codice Rocco, arts. 559 and 560 (abolished in 1969). The penalization of the husband's adultery already appeared in the Tuscan penal code (1859, art. 292).

husband's adultery might harm the family, or because it was politically oppor-
tune to penalize male adultery, but because "of the offense to *her* honor and to
the *affections of her heart*" (my emphasis).[12]

The ministerial report on the project for the Codice Rocco confirms that the
wife who killed her husband could be defended in part because "it was not to be
excluded" that she might "poignantly feel the offense to *her* honor and to *her*
sentiments of affection" (my emphasis).[13] Thus the wife reacted to a personal
offense, not to an offense to the family. The family was still offended only by the
illicit sexual behavior of its female members. This is demonstrated by the
extension of the motive of honor to the mother (Sardo-Italian code and code of
the Neapolitan Provinces) or the sister of an adulterous woman (Codice Zanardelli and Codice Rocco). They could kill a daughter or a sister (married or
unmarried), but not a son or a brother. In other words, they could defend the
family honor if the illicit sexual activities of another female family member cast
doubt on their own respectability. Rather than recognizing their dignity as
individuals, the extension to mother and sister of the benefit of the motive of
honor inscribed the subordination of females to male values in the law code.
Paradoxically, while they were recognized as possible and legitimate vin-
dicators of family honor, women found the new principles affirming the equal
dignity of the sexes turned against them. Instead of confirming this equal
dignity, the mitigation of the penalty for killing "for the sake of honor" to
which they were entitled incorporated their subordination to male ideology
into the letter of the law. Finally, Crivellari's commentary regarding the extension of the motive of honor to the killer of an unmarried daughter or sister
states that "the offense to the family honor is greater in the case of an unmarried woman than in that of a married woman already separated from the
family" (Crivellari 1896, 7:964).

This brief survey, although limited to salient points in Italian legal history,
should illustrate the survival of an ideology and of a concept of family honor
that remained almost unchanged for twenty centuries and was used by medieval and modern law to justify a large number of murders by appealing to a
juridical principle formulated by Augustus. Homicide for honor's sake was
removed from the Italian penal code only ten years ago, in 1981. In some
regions, the concept of family honor still makes an occasional appearance, and
vestiges of a code of honor exist in the vulgar use of the term *cornuto* as an
insult—though never applied to women.

---

12. Crivellari 1896, 7:954. The opinion referred to in the text was that of the scholar Carrara.
13. *Relazione ministeriale al progetto di codice penale,* in *Lavori preparatori del codice penale e del codice
di procedure penale,* vol. 5, pt. 2 (Rome: Ministero delle Giustizia e degli Affari di Culto, 1929), 388.

THE MODERN PERIOD

DAVID I. KERTZER

Introduction to Part Three

Modern Italy has become a burial ground for many of the most ambitious, and well-known, theories of household and marriage systems proposed by historians, sociologists, and demographers. Scholars who tried to generalize about a single western European family type were confronted with evidence that their model—typically based on the English family—could not be reconciled with the kinds of family forms found in Italy. When such scholars attempted to redress this problem by distinguishing between Italy's presumed "Mediterranean" family pattern and the classic northwestern European pattern, they soon found that the historical evidence for such a Mediterranean pattern was weak (see Kertzer 1991 for a review of some of these problems).

What we find in modern Italy raises serious questions about the whole effort to generalize a single demographic and family system for large geographical areas, even when we confine ourselves to a relatively limited historical period, such as the eighteenth or nineteenth century. Yet it is just this diversity which is most intriguing, for it raises crucial questions: what does account for particular family patterns and what exactly are the mechanisms accounting for change?

Four of the six chapters that follow are written by anthropologists, although we begin with chapters by a sociologist and a historical demographer. The work of the anthropologists is notable in that their historical, archival research is typically complemented by ethnographic research in the areas being studied. They go back and forth between the contemporary situation and the historical patterns unearthed through archival methods and, in some cases, oral history. Note that the oral historical record is not simply taken as basic data for characterizing the past, but also is treated as a text that must be examined for what it tells us about the culture of the present. Contemporary culture symbolically expropriates the past in ways that may only tenuously be related to what actually transpired.

The first three chapters of this section focus on household formation systems. These chapters demonstrate how previous characterizations of household processes in Italy (and Mediterranean Europe more generally) have been flawed and put forth new ways of looking at them. In this regard, Marzio Barbagli proposes a new typology, one that distinguishes three different, distinctive patterns of household formation in eighteenth- and nineteenth-century Italy. Luigi Tittarelli examines the workings of one of these—the system associated with sharecroppers in central Italy—and how individual family strategies affected marital patterns. William Douglass, returning to his earlier well-known argument that southern Italy cannot be seen simply as an area of nuclear-family systems, considers data from four communities in the Molise to bolster his argument that multiple-family households were the ideal in the mid-eighteenth century. His chapter provides evidence of the problems of pigeonholing family forms in Italy, suggesting geographical gradations in the family forms found on the peninsula.

The transformation of family processes over time is one of the primary focuses of this book, and Anthony Galt's chapter is especially noteworthy for examining such change in the context of a single community over a two-century period. We know from the work of John Davis (1973) and others that in portions of Italy, as elsewhere in southern Europe (see Brettell chapter 18), daughters were provided with houses as a form of dowry at marriage. This had wide-ranging social repercussions, including the creation of clusters of houses populated by matrilaterally related families. Galt shows how such a system was transformed during the nineteenth century in a community near Bari into a system where men, not women, were provided with houses at marriage. He links this historical transformation in family behavior to ecological and political economic changes during those decades.

Increasing concern for the impact of gender relations on family processes is evident among both historians and anthropologists, and Sylvia Junko Yanagisako's chapter provides a provocative example of how cultural constructs affecting family life are mediated by gender. Focusing on the recent past, Yanagisako shows just how complex the process of negotiation over the distribution of goods is within families, and how tenuous is the link between the formal legal system (the courts) and the actual process of property transfer. This provides a nice temporal counterpoint to some of the studies of antiquity found in Part One of this book; it also suggests the enduring importance to both historians and anthropologists of the problematic link between juridical norms and actual behavior in family law.

Finally, we conclude the volume by placing Italian family history in the broader perspective of Mediterranean Europe through a focus on inheritance systems. Caroline Brettell's analysis takes issue with previous generalizations about the relation of inheritance systems to household and marriage systems. She also shows why the terms historians and anthropologists have used in their analyses—in particular the key concept of dowry—confuse historical analysis by lumping together different customs that have different causes and effects. It is an appropriate way to end this book, since our emphasis has been on overcoming the simplifications that have plagued European family history. By demonstrating the geographical and temporal complexities of family patterns and by identifying concepts and methods that allow us to deal with these complexities, we can move forward in plotting the course of family history and make sense of the forces that have influenced it.

Chapter 13

MARZIO BARBAGLI

Three Household Formation Systems in Eighteenth- and Nineteenth-Century Italy

To understand household formation patterns in past times and to analyze the connections between age at marriage, postnuptial residence patterns, and the structure of domestic groups, one must necessarily start from the hypotheses put forth by John Hajnal in two studies published twenty years apart (1965, 1983). In his earlier study Hajnal affirmed that at the end of the nineteenth century the model of matrimony in the countries of Europe to the west of an imaginary line running roughly from Leningrad to Trieste was "unique or almost unique in the world" (1965, 101). The distinctive characteristics of what he called a "marriage pattern" were that people of both sexes married late (men at age twenty-six or older; women at twenty-three or older) and that a large proportion of the population (from 10 to 15 percent) never married. The outstanding feature of the model was late age at marriage for women. Hajnal showed that this matrimonial pattern was typical of many European lands in the eighteenth century as well, and he hypothesized that it emerged in the sixteenth century, at a moment when age at marriage was rising in those countries. Other countries had always had a matrimonial model that Hajnal calls "non-European," in which nearly everyone married and married early (the mean age at marriage for women, for example, was under twenty-one).

Hajnal also in his 1965 study advanced interesting hypotheses on the connection between age at marriage and household formation patterns. He states

An earlier version of this chapter was presented at the First Spanish-Portuguese-Italian Conference on Historical Demography in Barcelona in April 1987 and was published in Barbagli 1988.

that early marriage occurred in societies in which domestic groups were large and complex, where the young couple could be "part of a larger unit" such as the "joint family." Late marriage occurred in societies in which neolocal residence after marriage was the rule and the nuclear family predominated. When this was the case, it was necessary "for a man to defer marriage until he could establish an independent livelihood adequate to support a family." In other words, if men marry late it is because "they cannot 'afford' to marry young"; they must "wait until they have a livelihood, a farmer until he acquires land, an apprentice till he finishes his apprenticeship" (1965, 133). Late marriage also existed, however, in regions where the stem family predominated—that is, the family in which land passed on to a single heir and patrilocal residence after marriage was the rule.

Hajnal's study has had a great influence on historical demographical studies and on the history of the family during the past twenty years, notably on the work of the Cambridge Group, who heeded his insistence on the role of marriage in historical demographic systems. Two members of the Cambridge Group, E. A. Wrigley and Roger S. Schofield (1981), have shown in a monumental study that the most important variable in any explanation of population shifts in England between the mid-sixteenth century and the mid-nineteenth century was not the death rate, but the marriage rate. According to their study, population growth usually created a decline in real wages, which then induced people to marry relatively late, consequently reducing the birth rate. Demographic stagnation had the opposite effect: real wages rose, which set off an increase in the standard of living, favoring marriage and increasing the birth rate. Thus in a system of "low demographic pressure" such as England, the marriage rate worked as a thermostat to regulate the balance between economic development and population growth.

Hajnal's hypothesis of a connection between age at marriage and family structure has also had important effects. It was in fact adopted, in somewhat revised and corrected form, by Peter Laslett (1977), who affirmed that the "western family" had four interdependent traits: a nuclear structure, a late age at marriage for women, a relatively small age gap between spouses, and the presence of servants in the household. According to Laslett, late marriage was typical of regions in which neolocal residence was the rule and the nuclear family (rather than the stem family) predominated.

During the past ten years several important studies have furnished data and new information regarding matrimonial models and household formation patterns. Above all, such studies have shown that, Hajnal to the contrary, the European model existed in England before the sixteenth century; indeed, as early as the thirteenth century (Smith 1983; Hallam 1985). In contrast, David

Herlihy and Christiane Klapisch-Zuber's massive study (1978; English trans. 1985) showed that the European model of matrimony had not yet touched Florentine Tuscany of the fifteenth century. Men who lived in towns and cities married later (around age 30) than those who lived in the country (twenty-five). Women, however, married very early, not only in the Florentine *contado* immediately surrounding the city but in the urban centers as well (between fifteen and twenty).

These and other studies of family structure in Italy and France led Laslett (1983) to revise his initial hypotheses and to offer a typology contrasting the countries of northern Europe with the Mediterranean countries. The nuclear family and neolocal residence after marriage predominated in northern Europe; the multiple family was more typical of Mediterranean lands. Age at marriage, which was linked to residence rules and the prevailing family type, also differed in the two zones. The more widespread neolocalism was in a given area, the more probable late first marriage was, though this was truer for women than for men. According to Laslett, in northern Europe women's age at marriage was always over twenty-two, even reaching thirty years, whereas in Mediterranean lands it remained under twenty.

Hajnal himself (1983) returned to the question to compare two contrasting household formation systems in preindustrial societies. The first system, typical of many lands in northwestern Europe (the Scandinavian countries, the British Isles, the Low Countries, northern France, and German-speaking lands), was based on three rules. First, both men and women married fairly late (men at age twenty-six or older, women at twenty-three or older). Second, the married couple set up their own household creating a nuclear family. They might live in the husband's parents' house as a stem family, but only if the older couple retired. In any event, when the man married he became head of the new family. Third, before marrying, a large number of young people spent several years out of the family house in the service of another household. Servants amounted to at least 6 percent, and more typically 10 percent, of the total population.

The second type of family formation, typical in many other countries, Asiatic lands in particular, was based on totally different rules. For one thing, marriage was relatively early, especially for women (by age twenty-six for men and by twenty-one for women). Second, the new couple joined a family that included an older couple (usually of the husband's kin). Thus the husband did not become head of household upon marrying. Finally, to enter service in someone else's household before marriage was not customary.

In his second study, then, Hajnal developed, articulated, and documented a theory, barely touched on in his 1965 study, on the connection between age at marriage, residence rules after marriage, and family structure, linking those traits to the institution of domestic service. The "circulation of servants" among households was, according to Hajnal, an essential characteristic of the system of family formation in northwest European lands. That circulation made late marriage possible, because service "provided a function for young unmarried adults" (1983, 70, 71). The period spent in service—the time between leaving the family home and marriage—was a particular stage in the life cycle of young people of both sexes. From another point of view, the use of farmhands in northwestern Europe allowed farm families to remain nuclear. Adjusting the number of available hands to the needs of the farmhold offered flexibility, obviating the family's need to combine with other nuclei among their kin (Kussmaul 1981; Smith 1981a).

Robert Rowland (1983, 1986), in a meticulous and convincing analysis of the available data, has shown that Hajnal's and Laslett's typologies are inadequate to describe and account for familial and matrimonial systems on the Iberian peninsula. Can the same be said of Italy? Is it true that in past centuries Italian women married young and that patrilocal residence in complex households was the rule after marriage, as Laslett has maintained? More generally, after analysis of the Italian data can one establish a strict connection between neolocal residence, late marriage, and the custom of domestic service, or conversely, between early marriage and living in a joint household after marriage (as Hajnal posits)? What were the principal modes of family formation in Italy, and what territorial variations do they show?

AGE AT MARRIAGE

"In spite of its importance," Lorenzo Del Panta and Massimo Livi Bacci wrote in 1980, "nuptiality still remains an unknown, still to be revealed." It cannot be said that the situation is very different today. Although interesting studies have been published in recent years and have provided us with new data, the available information is still fragmentary and inadequate.

The most striking aspect of the available data is the enormous variation in behavior reflected (Barbagli 1988). In the eighteenth century—in Venice, for example—there are instances of delayed marriage when men married at thirty or thirty-one and women at twenty-nine. At the other end of the scale, in some areas of southern Italy men married as early as age twenty-three and women at age twenty.

In spite of this wide variation, some areas show relative homogeneity. One of these is certainly Apulia (the region for which we have the most abundant data), where the mean age at marriage for women in the sixteenth and seventeenth centuries was always under twenty and in some areas under fifteen (Barbagli 1988).

An examination of localities in Apulia for which data over a number of years are available shows that in general the mean age at marriage for women increased from the seventeenth to the eighteenth century, at times even by two or three years (as in Leporano or Taurisano). Even in the eighteenth century, however, Apulian women continued to marry early.

Scarce as they are, the data available indicate that in some parts of Sicily, Calabria, and Campania women (on occasion, men as well) tended to marry young. In Eboli and San Cipriano, for example, women married very young—at twenty or under—in both the seventeenth and eighteenth centuries. In other parts of Campania, however, age at marriage for women was considerably higher, at times reaching and even exceeding twenty-five. The situation was different in the north. In rural Piedmont and Lombardy in the early nineteenth century the mean age at marriage for men was about twenty-seven; for women, about twenty-two. In rural Emilia and Tuscany women's age at marriage was considerably higher, even in the eighteenth century—as high as twenty-five in many areas, and in some instances twenty-seven. In the province of Grosseto women married much younger, but this exception was due to a high death rate, which encouraged taking "full advantage, in the presence of such precarious conditions, of the woman's reproductive period" (Del Panta 1984, 67). Age at marriage for men was particularly high in rural Tuscany, around twenty-nine to thirty.

Richard Smith's thesis (1979, 81–82) that a model that had held firm for three centuries persisted in eighteenth-century Tuscany thus fails to be confirmed by the data. The best historical data series that we have (on the Prato contado) clearly demonstrates that as early as the mid-seventeenth century the marriage model that Hajnal called "non-European" no longer existed. In 1678 the mean age at marriage for women was over twenty-three, and a century later it was over twenty-five (Della Pina 1986). Age at marriage for men also rose sharply, from twenty-four toward the end of the fifteenth century to almost thirty in the mid-seventeenth century.

In mid-nineteenth-century Italy there were still significant differences in age at marriage between one area and another. The regions in which women married the latest were the Marches, Umbria, and Tuscany; women married earliest in Sicily and Basilicata. Age at marriage for men was lower in Basilicata, Sicily, Calabria, and Apulia than in the central and northern regions. Early in the twentieth century researchers studying the condition of peasants in the southern provinces remarked on this difference. In this report on Basilicata and Calabria, Francesco Nitti wrote: "The ancient customs still pertain in great part, despite the passage of time and emigration. Weddings are still early. Women quite often marry before reaching majority; men as soon as they reach it" (1910, 180). Writing on the agricultural population of Basilicata, Eugenio Azimonti remarks that "women generally marry from 16 to 21 years of age; men from 20 to 25" (1909, 154). Oreste Bordiga wrote in his report on Campania that in the agricultural strata of that region women married between 16 and 22 and "the great majority" of men "between 24 and 25" (1909, 532). He adds, "it is not infrequent, however, that someone, in love with some girl, will marry her before he is 20 so that he will not have to wait until after he has done military service."

PERSONAL SERVICE

In northern Italian cities during the sixteenth century, one-third to one-half of men and nearly one third of women spent at least several years in the service of others. In rural areas the number of people who entered into service was lower, but still appreciable: 20 percent of men and 10 percent of women (Barbagli 1988, 234–236). As in northern Europe, going into domestic service in these regions of Italy was simply a stage in a young person's life cycle, generally before marriage. The situation changed radically in Italian cities and towns during the seventeenth and eighteenth centuries, however. The number of persons in service fell, and domestic service increasingly became a female occupation (Tittarelli 1985; Arru 1987).

Service persisted in country areas, however. In the early eighteenth century, servants in the rural areas surrounding Reggio Emilia made up around 7 percent of the population (Moretti 1989). In rural areas around Pisa during the same period, servants accounted for 11 percent of the population (Doveri 1987b), and between 30 and 40 percent of households included a farmhand. As in the preceding centuries, agricultural servants were almost exclusively males between the ages of ten and twenty. In fact, in the Pisan countryside in 1720 a good 41 percent of males between fifteen and nineteen years of age were in service. They usually came from families of agricultural laborers—*braccianti*— and often from broken or denuded nuclear families made up of a widow and children. Their service began when they were young—between the ages of eleven and twelve—and lasted an average of eight years.

Once again, the regions of southern Italy show a completely different picture. In mid-eighteenth-century Chieti few people went into service in the cities and towns and even fewer in rural areas (Forlini 1983–1984). In Turi, in Apulia, only 1.4 percent of all households had one or more servants both in

1781 and in 1855 (Da Molin 1987). Similar data exist for Paceco, in Sicily, in the seventeenth and eighteenth centuries (Benigno 1985).

We need to turn to data from the 1921 population census, however, for a more detailed picture of the differences between the various regions of Italy. They show that in Sicily and throughout southern Italy, including Lazio, the number of agricultural households with farmhands was extremely low (see table 13.1). The largest numbers of agricultural servants were in Sardinia and the Trentino.

HOUSEHOLD FORMATION SYSTEMS

These data, combined with information on household structure (Barbagli 1988), enable us to test Laslett's and Hajnal's interpretations. It is immediately

TABLE 13.1

Households and Agricultural Households with
One Male Servant in Italy in 1921,
by Region

Region	Households (%)	Agricultural Households (%)
Piedmont	1.73	3.88
Liguria	0.55	2.32
Lombardy	0.48	1.35
Trentino–Alto Adige	6.17	11.89
Veneto	0.57	1.23
Venezia Giulia	1.54	4.15
Emilia-Romagna	2.46	5.02
Tuscany	1.06	2.68
Marches	1.88	3.63
Umbria	1.35	2.42
Lazio	0.36	0.98
Abruzzi and Molise	0.42	0.61
Campania	0.25	0.59
Apulia	0.24	0.43
Basilicata	0.27	0.39
Calabria	0.33	0.53
Sicily	0.28	0.59
Sardinia	4.07	7.49

Source: Istituto Centrale di Statistica, *Censimento generale della popolazione* (Rome 1921).

apparent that Laslett's typology of traditional European forms of domestic organization is totally inadequate. To classify Italy in past times as a country characterized only by early marriage for women and by the predominance of the complex household is impossible. If one thing emerges clearly from all the data we have examined, it is that Italy, unlike other European countries, has always had multiple systems of household formation, not just one system.

Can Hajnal's typology be used to describe and analyze these multiple systems? Yes and no, but I would have to add immediately, more no than yes. Without question, the two systems of household formation described by Hajnal are found in Italy. Tuscany in the fifteenth century offers an excellent example of Hajnal's second system of household formation, characterized by early marriage for women and the creation of complex domestic aggregates. Furthermore, this system long pertained to the aristocracy and the bourgeoisie of central and northern Italy and probably to the same groups in the south of Italy. On the other hand, cities and towns in central and northern Italy in the eighteenth and nineteenth centuries offer good examples of the first system, based on neolocal residence and late marriage for both spouses. As we shall see, the same system also can be found in Sardinia.

Apart from these cases, however, Hajnal's typology is of little help in analyzing Italian household formation systems. First of all, the data we have examined raise a number of doubts concerning the connection proposed by Hajnal between family structure and the institution of domestic service. Although it is true that, at least in certain regions and in specific historical periods, in Italy entering into service "provided a function to young unmarried adults," in only one region—Sardinia—did domestic service coexist with neolocal residence after marriage. As we shall see, before Sardinians married and set up their own households, they tended to spend a certain number of years in service. Nor does Hajnal's scheme apply to all other regions of Italy. In rural areas throughout the south, neolocal residence and the nuclear family predominated, but domestic service was unknown. Where sharecropping was most typically practiced (Emilia, Tuscany, the Marches, Umbria), "circulation of servants" was ample, but complex households and patrilocal residence were the rule.

The data prompt even greater doubts concerning the relation Hajnal proposes between age at marriage and postnuptial residence. Except for Tuscany in the fifteenth and perhaps the sixteenth century and the aristocracy until the mid-seventeenth century, the idea of a strict connection between early marriage and the incorporation of the young couple into a joint household is not confirmed by the empirical documentation. Richard Smith (1979, 1981b) has indeed pointed to Tuscany in the eighteenth and nineteenth centuries as one area where the second household formation system proposed by Hajnal predominated. On closer examination, however, in Tuscany during those centuries the custom of going to live after marriage in a multiple household (extended either vertically or horizontally) coexisted not with early marriage but with late marriage for both women and men. Furthermore, with the exception of Tuscany, the available data show that the regions in which the complex family was most prevalent (the Marches and Umbria) were precisely those in which women's age at marriage was highest.

As if this were not enough, the variations over time of age at marriage and of family structures differ completely from what we should expect from Hajnal's description. In rural areas in central and northern Italy between the fifteenth century and the nineteenth century household structures increased in complexity, whereas the age at marriage for women rose.

Even the hypothesis of a strict connection between the rule of neolocal residence and age at marriage fails to be confirmed by the documentation gathered. As we have seen, neolocal residence and the nuclear family have always been widespread in southern Italy; nevertheless, the women of those areas (on occasion the men as well) married young.

How did young couples go about setting up their own households? Analyzing the system of household formation in Basilicata and Campania, Nitti wrote: "To girls who go to a husband it is customary for parents to allot a small dowry packet: bed, clothing, linens. The better off also have a bit of money or some real estate. To men who marry parents usually allot an advance on the inheritance, often reserving enjoyment of the interest for the donor" (1910, 180). Obviously, this could happen only if the family owned something that could be transmitted to their children. In Basilicata, Azimonti observes, the males in families of *coloni e massarotti* (tenant farmers) often received "some piece of land as an advance on their inheritance" (1909, 154). Different arrangements were made in other cases. Nonetheless, people married young, and went to live by themselves after marriage. Bordiga wrote, speaking about Campania:

> In the agricultural class, it very rarely happens that the young man receives from the father an advance on the inheritance. If they are farm laborers, the young man sets up his own household, partly with his own money, partly with his wife's money, partly [by incurring] debts, and he creates a new household right away. In the class of small-scale tenant farmers, sharecroppers, and the like, division in the paternal family is even aided by the fact that these farmers only rarely have any capital of their own, thus—now in particular—they find a little land to cultivate right away (1909, 532).

Thus during the eighteenth and the first half of the nineteenth century, there were a number of systems for household formation in Italy. Of the three main ones, the first, patrilocal residence and late marriage, predominated in rural central and northern Italy. We can distinguish two secondary types within this system, however. One was typical of rural Piedmont, Liguria, and Lombardy, where the tendency to late marriage was coupled with the presence of the stem family; the other was widespread in rural areas in the rest of central and northern Italy, where late marriage was linked with multiple households (horizontal as well as vertical). Determining whether or to what degree the practice of service influenced age at marriage is impossible. Available data for the Pisan countryside in the early eighteenth century (Doveri 1987b), however, indicate that any influence of the sort was weaker than in northern Europe.

The second system—neolocal residence and early marriage for women—was the prevalent system in southern Italy. The third—neolocal residence and late marriage for both women and men—was the dominant pattern in the cities and towns of central and northern Italy and in Sardinia.

THE STEM FAMILY AND SMALL-SCALE
PEASANT LANDOWNERSHIP

The census data on the population of Italy collected in 1881 are the only source for the nineteenth century that permits analysis of a territorial entity smaller than the province—namely, the *circondario,* or administrative district.[1] Examination of the fifty-one circondari of Piedmont, Liguria, and Lombardy reveals that age at marriage for men and women has interesting connections both with the numbers of people who never married and with social stratification in rural areas.

Notable differences can be seen in mean age at marriage in these circondari. Men married no earlier than age twenty-five and no later than thirty. The range was even greater among women, with some circondari showing a mean age at marriage of only twenty-one years, and other districts one as high as twenty-seven.

The greater the proportion of farmers who owned or rented their land in the overall agricultural population, the later marriage was for both men and women

1. The data in tables 13.2, 13.3, and 13.4 were drawn from analysis of the 196 circondari defined for the purposes of the 1881 population census, which includes all provinces except those formerly under Austrian rule (the Veneto and Mantua). I have excluded provincial capitals from my analysis, subtracting the population of those communes from their respective districts. Age at marriage was calculated using the method followed by John Hajnal. Figures for celibacy, male and female, were obtained by taking one-half of the totals for the percentage of unmarried men and women in the age cohorts forty-five to forty-nine and fifty to fifty-four. Percentages for agricultural laborers, sharecroppers, and other agricultural categories were calculated on the basis of all males engaged in agriculture.

and the higher the celibacy rates were for both sexes. This ratio is high for the fifty-one circondari of Piedmont, Liguria, and Lombardy, and even higher if we consider only the first two regions (table 13.2).

Such data indicate that in these areas small-scale landownership and land tenancy favored late marriage, the formation of stem families, and definitive celibacy. We can hypothesize schematically how the system worked: to avoid dividing their holdings into overly small plots, peasants tended to leave farms to one of their male offspring, often the eldest, who ultimately married (in general, fairly late) and brought his bride into his parents' house, thus forming a stem family. The other siblings left the paternal house in search of other work and often married late, whereas some never married.

THE AGRICULTURAL CLASSES IN CENTRAL AND NORTHERN ITALY

In Tuscany in past centuries (certainly in the fifteenth century), *mezzadria* (sharecropping) favored both first and second marriages (Herlihy and Klapisch-Zuber 1978, 411). Men and women from sharecropper families all married and married young. When they were widowed they remarried. The situation in the early nineteenth century was quite different, however. Widows were less likely to remarry in regions in which sharecropping was widespread and the complex household predominated: the Marches, Umbria, Tuscany, and Emilia (Livi Bacci 1981). The mean age at marriage in these regions was in general somewhat higher than in other parts of Italy.

TABLE 13.2

Correlation Coefficients between Age at Marriage, Celibacy, and Social Stratification in 1881 in Piedmont, Liguria, and Lombardy

	Age at Marriage		Celibate	
	Male	*Female*	*Male*	*Female*
percentage of male agricultural laborers	−.18	.02	−.16	−.22
percentage of male farmer landowners and tenant farmers	.44	.30	.45	.52
	(.64)	(.53)	(.67)	(.66)

Note: The figures in parentheses represent the values of the correlation coefficients for the twenty-eight circondari of Piedmont and Liguria alone.

What explanation can be offered for these changes in the matrimonial model in regions where sharecropping was practiced? An interesting recent study by Giuliana Biagioli (1986) offers a partial answer, at least concerning first marriages. According to Biagioli, the mezzadria system underwent profound transformations at the end of the eighteenth century. An overabundant supply of prospective sharecroppers (due to population growth and an inadequate increase in the number of farmholds) had weakened the sharecroppers' bargaining position. As a result, sharecropping families lost their "traditional autonomy in the cultivation of the *podere*" by accepting increasingly unfavorable contracts, which not only obliged them to work harder but also allowed landlords to exercise severe controls over their tenants' private lives, including marital decisions. In response to this situation and to counter the danger of becoming agricultural laborers, the sharecroppers slowly changed their matrimonial habits. The number of unmarried men and women increased because "the presence of more productive units in the place of merely consumer units" was for them a "last defence against the risk of expulsion from the *podere*" (Biagioli 1986, 66).

Support for this hypothesis comes from several sources. First, in the nineteenth century, a number of scholars and other observers noted that mezzadria hindered or delayed marriage. According to Gino Capponi (Bowring 1838, 44), "farmers . . . wary and calculating, make few imprudent marriages. Confined to a small plot of land, they limit their families to the size of their holding." Carlo Mazzini, the author of the report on Tuscany for the Inchiesta Agraria Jacini, noted that in sharecropper families *capocciato*—headship—"fell to the bachelor." Mazzini adds: "Generally, if all the sons are unmarried at the death of the father, the eldest has the choice of marrying or taking over as head of household. In the first case, headship passes to the second in order of age, [who is then] forbidden to take a wife."

Domenico Spadoni (1899, 39–41) had similar things to say of the Marches toward the end of the century. He notes: "For the countryman's family, and especially the sharecropper's, a male is an important economic value because he represents a unit in the labor force—and of capital—the size, structure, and development of which are to be regulated according to the needs of the tenant lands. For this reason," he continues, "the young man does not normally get married before his thirtieth birthday." When the family included many women and children and the ratio of hands to mouths was unfavorable, the young man could not marry, because "family finances did not allow it and the landlord would not permit it." If the family included younger male siblings, one of them, usually the oldest, could marry. The others either resigned themselves to bachelorhood or had to wait their turn, according to the principle *maritu a chi troa e moglie a chi tocca* (a husband for whoever finds one and a wife for the one whose turn it is).

Marco Della Pina (1986, 1987) offers equally important arguments to support Biagioli's interpretation. He shows that in the country areas around Prato in 1646 the children in sharecropping families married as young and as consistently as they had a century and a half earlier, women at a mean age of twenty and men at twenty-five. Definitive celibacy was unknown. The situation began to change in the next thirty years, when mean age at marriage for women rose to twenty-two years and for men to twenty-nine. This tendency continued in the following century, and by 1786 women on average married at twenty-six and men as late as thirty-three. Celibacy reached enormous proportions. Among sharecropper families 30 percent of men and 18 percent of women were unmarried at the age of fifty. During the same period—as we have seen—such households became more complex, extending horizontally, however.

According to Della Pina, several factors contributed to these changes. From the mid-seventeenth century, as the population grew in rural areas around Prato, existing farms became inadequate to support the enlarged sharecropper households. In this situation, the "surplus" sharecroppers were faced with the prospect of downward social mobility, that is, having to abandon their podere and become agricultural laborers (*braccianti*). To avoid this, sharecroppers needed to pursue a strategy that would improve the balance between the composition of the family and the size of the farmhold and thus maintain a positive ratio between hands and mouths. Following this strategy led to increasingly delayed marriage, to a gradual rise in male celibacy, and to horizontal rather than vertical extension of the household (Della Pina 1986, 1987).

Indirect proof of these tendencies comes from the contrast between the eighteenth-century household formations of sharecroppers and those of farm laborers. First, the mezzadri generally inclined toward patrilocal residence after marriage, whereas the braccianti followed the neolocal pattern. Second, sharecroppers married much later than farm laborers. More precisely, this was true of men in the rural areas around Prato, where the mean age at marriage of male sharecroppers was thirty-one and that of agricultural laborers twenty-eight (Della Pina 1986). Celibacy was much more common among sharecroppers than among laborers as well, although the women of the two groups married at the same age (about twenty-five).

Differences of this sort existed elsewhere than in the Prato countryside during the eighteenth century. There were variations (lesser ones, however) between age at marriage for male sharecroppers and that for agricultural laborers in the Pisan hills in 1895, and in such Tuscan localities as San Casciano and Bagni San Giuliano, also during the nineteenth century (Doveri 1987a;

Rettaroli 1987). As in Prato, age at marriage for women in these areas was the same for both sharecropper and laborer families.

What about outside Tuscany, in other regions in which mezzadria was practiced? Sharecroppers in the Marches and in Emilia, following the pattern of patrilocal residence after marriage, lived in multiple households, whereas agricultural laborers set up independent households. With respect to age at marriage, however, the research to date shows no appreciable difference between sharecroppers and laborers outside Tuscany. In the mid-nineteenth century, men and women from mezzadri and braccianti families in Jesi, in the Marches, married at approximately the same age (Rettaroli 1987). Around Bologna and Reggio Emilia the age at marriage for male agricultural laborers was even slightly higher than for sharecroppers. Landowning farmers near Bologna married the latest of all (men and women both) (Angeli 1987), probably because sons delayed marriage until they could take over the farmhold from their fathers.

The census data on the population of Italy gathered in 1881 offer some confirmation of these findings, but they also raise a number of new questions that cannot be answered satisfactorily. There were a total of fifty circondari in Emilia-Romagna, Tuscany, Umbria, and the Marches. Excluding provincial capitals, the population of these circondari was largely agricultural, with sharecroppers typically making up a fairly high proportion of the total, although that proportion (like that of other agricultural categories) varied significantly from one circondario to another. In some districts—Ancona, Arezzo, Rocca San Casciano, Macerata, and Montepulciano, for example—more than 60 percent of males in agriculture were sharecroppers, whereas in other districts (Comacchio, Ferrara, and Grosseto) mezzadri accounted for fewer than 5 percent of males in agriculture.

If we take the circondario as our unit of analysis, then, we find that the higher the proportion of sharecroppers in the agricultural population, the higher age at marriage was for both men and women. Nevertheless, the correlation between these two variables is fairly weak. Celibacy correlates better with social stratification variables. The number of unmarried women between forty-five and fifty-five years of age rises as the fraction of agricultural laborers declines and, consequently, as the fraction of other agricultural categories rises. The ratio of celibates to sharecroppers in the agricultural population is less conclusive (table 13.3). Obviously, these results cannot be interpreted in terms of changes in the sharecropping system alone.

SICILY AND SARDINIA: CONTRASTING MODELS

Comparing the situation in Italy's two great islands not only confirms the inadequacy of Hajnal's and Laslett's schemata but also permits a closer look at

TABLE 13.3

Correlation Coefficients between Age at Marriage, Celibacy,
and Social Stratification in 1881 in Emilia-Romagna, Tuscany,
the Marches, and Umbria

	Age at Marriage		Celibate	
	Male	*Female*	*Male*	*Female*
percentage of male agricultural laborers	−.17	−.24	−.24	−.61
percentage of male sharecroppers	.26	.22	.27	.31
percentage of male sharecroppers, farmer landowners, and tenant farmers	.12	.23	.30	.51

the second and third systems of household formation in Italy. As in many other areas of southern Italy, neolocal residence after marriage was the rule in both Sicily and Sardinia. They differed greatly, however, regarding the other two crucial aspects of household formation: age at marriage and the custom of domestic service. This is clear from the relations between age at marriage, celibacy (both male and female), and social stratification, which are reversed from one region to the other (see table 13.4). The differences become clearer when we turn to other sources.

For centuries Sicilian women (perhaps men as well) apparently married young. Fragmentary data indicate that in the fifteenth century age at marriage for women in Sicily ranged from twelve to eighteen years (Bresc 1986, 702). During the eighteenth century, travelers to Italy from other European countries were struck particularly by the exceptionally early age at which Sicilians married. "Sicilian ladies," Patrick Brydone observed in 1773, "marry at thirteen or fourteen, and are sometimes grandmothers before they are thirty." Joseph Hager, a German traveler, made similar observations twenty-five years later. According to other foreign travelers in the eighteenth century, both women and men married young in Sicily (Tuzet 1955, 451). During the same period, moreover, the poet and abbot Giovanni Meli (1884, 87, 88) lashed out in his poem "L'invettiva" at the men of his island for their "haste" to wed and their refusal to wait until they were of an appropriate age and had a "shining purse" (that is, enough money): "Lads, have we perhaps used up all the women? The world is not dead; there are still some left. There's a flock of them at the breast. Fast a bit; what urgency have you? What's your hurry? A little

TABLE 13.4

Correlation Coefficients between Age at Marriage, Celibacy, and Social
Stratification in the Administrative Districts of Sicily and Sardinia in 1881

	Age at Marriage		Celibacy	
	Male	Female	Male	Female
Sicily				
percentage of male agricultural laborers	.54	.34	.18	.19
percentage of farmer landowners and tenant farmers	−.45	−.37	−.48	−.56
Sardinia				
percentage of male agricultural laborers	.80	−.48	−.40	−.67
percentage of farmer landowners and tenant farmers	.32	.03	.63	.92

Note: Sicily had twenty-four administrative districts (circondari); Sardinia had nine.

time and things will go better, no one will restrain you or tell you no." He returned to the charge: "And you, little birds, grow up a little, and in the right time and place the bargain will be struck. Every bird makes a nest; many need this comfort: but first you wait for the appropriate age, and when your purse is shining, do the same and you will be wise."

The situation was totally different in Sardinia. At the same period that Meli was writing his "L'invettiva," Carlo Felice Leprotti in a report to the king of Sardinia asserted that the most important "immediate moral cause" for the "depopulation" of the island was the "scarceness of marriages." Leprotti observes: "Weddings are extremely rare, or they are put off until the time when girls have become less suitable and less fertile. How important this is for population is in itself obvious." Sardinian women, according to Leprotti, did not marry before the age of twenty-five. "Which means that since Sardinian women reach puberty rather early than late, due to the warmth of the climate, it follows that at twenty-five they could already be called on the old side as regards generation, with unspeakable harm to propagation" (1966, 106). During those same years, Antonio Bongino expressed similar conclusions in an official report. "The natural tendency of the Sardinian," he wrote, "does not incline him to toil but rather he prefers idleness; he eats frugally and dresses roughly, so that little suffices for his sustenance. Thus it is that he is very poor, and in view of his poverty he is disinclined to matrimony" (1966, 224).

Such descriptions as well as the available data indicate that in Sicily the pattern of neolocal residence included early marriage for women (and perhaps, in certain areas, relatively early marriage for men). In Sardinia, to the contrary, neolocal residence combined with late marriage for both women and men. In a Sicilian town such as Paceco, for example, extended households were nearly nonexistent during the seventeenth and eighteenth centuries, and women married between the ages of sixteen and nineteen and men around twenty-one or twenty-two (Benigno 1985). The same was true of another Sicilian city, Noto, in the mid-seventeenth century (Benigno 1988).

The situation changed in part during the nineteenth and early twentieth centuries, though not for women. In the first decade after the unification of Italy, 29 percent of Sicilian women still married when under twenty years of age, according to a study of population changes for 1875 (Direzione Generale della Statistica 1878). Some were almost children—under the age of fifteen—when they married. This occurred in other regions of Italy as well, but of all Italian women married under the age of fifteen after 1870, nearly 45 percent were Sicilian (Somogyi 1965, 352). In some parts of Sicily—the province of Catania, for example—the mean age at first marriage for women was twenty (Rettaroli 1987). Sicilian men married on average at twenty-six—which certainly cannot be called early, even if it was lower than in some regions of central and northern Italy or in Sardinia.

Giovanni Lorenzoni accurately described household formation rules in Sicily in the early twentieth century: "A son begins to think about marriage when he has done military service, or, if he is exempt from it, around twenty-five years of age. The preferred age for a man is considered to be twenty-eight years; for women, eighteen." He adds, "It is rare that young married couples cohabit with the parents and parents-in-law. As a rule when a son marries he leaves home" (1910, 464).

In Sardinia, to the contrary, the pattern of neolocal residence accompanied a high age at marriage for both men and women, as is confirmed in several recent historical studies (Anatra and Puggioni 1973; Day 1983, 1986). This was also the conclusion reached at the beginning of this century by Francesco Coletti, who observes that in Sardinia "every individual who takes a wife leaves the paternal house and sets up a family; creates a hearth of his own." He notes, however, that "the relative lateness of marriages is striking" (1908, 94, 96). Indeed, Sardinia showed the highest age at marriage, for both men and women, of all regions of Italy.

Sicily and Sardinia probably also differed considerably concerning the custom of domestic service. Our knowledge of the subject is limited, since we lack systematic studies, but various sources indicate that domestic service, as a distinct stage in the life course, was more widespread in Sardinia than in Sicily. Noble and bourgeois Sicilian households had servants, of course, but servants were less common in other households, among agricultural families in particular (Benigno 1985). In Sardinia, to the contrary, *servitù rustica,* to use Francesco Salaris's expression (1895, 71), was more widespread and probably had a significance for household formation.

Antonio Bongino, writing in the eighteenth century, observed that in Sardinia:

> Custom has decreed that no one marries unless the men are first provided with oxen and various pieces of equipment useful for agriculture, and the women with the bed and other domestic furnishings and utensils. The poor, finding no one to help them, have no other means for procuring the capital necessary to the furnishing of the aforesaid things, except that of offering their servile labors for recompense, so that, since a number of years are needed in order to accomplish this, they are not in a position to contract matrimony until around the age of thirty, thus they lose in servile exercise the time most propitious to generation (1966, 244).

A century later Francesco Salaris wrote at some length analyzing servitù rustica in his report for the Inchiesta Agraria Jacini. Salaris points out that the number of servants varied according to the amount of land under cultivation and in relation to the phase of development of the employer family. "When the peasant landowner has sons able to do agricultural labor," he wrote, "the number of servants is limited in relation to their number" (1895, 42).

Some division of labor and a certain hierarchy existed even within servitù rustica. A "more important" (*maggiore*) servant called a *socio,* for example, coordinated and oversaw the work of the other servants. A younger servant called *boinargiu* cared for the draft animals, and another called *carradori* drove the carts and wagons. There might also be other servants who did "domestic" work. All these persons slept in the landowner's house and ate there, on occasion "at the same table" as the owner. "The sons of these landowners," Salaris writes, "are mingled with the servants, and they sleep fully dressed on a mat in the kitchen on winter nights and in the open air during the spring and summer" (1895, 42).

At least some servants remained in service until they married. "Servants," Salaris observes, "also do not marry unless they have first—thanks to the strictest savings—acquired or built a house. It is considered dishonorable to lead a wife to a house that is not the husband's; and it is custom—founded on reason—that dictates that the husband will provide for the house and the wife will furnish it" (1895, 71).

Thus in Sardinia the rules for household formation were very similar to

those of northern European lands: both men and women married late; after the
wedding they lived on their own; a considerable proportion of the young (at
least among the lower strata of society) spent several years as servants in other
people's households. In Sicily, to the contrary, as well as in much of southern
Italy, there were patterns that do not fit the models suggested by Hajnal and
Laslett. Neolocal residence was the rule in Sicily, but marriage (at least for
women) was earlier and the custom of going into service before marriage was
not widespread.

How can we explain this difference? Why should the pattern of neolocal
residence coincide with early marriage in one case and with late marriage in the
other? There is no easy answer to these questions. Some scholars have sought a
structural explanation for late marriage in Sardinia; others have emphasized
cultural factors. In the eighteenth century, Bongino attributed late marriage to
poverty and Leprotti blamed it on "avarice, the most tyrannical of human
vices" (1966, 105). Early in the nineteenth century, Lodovico Baille stressed the
importance of the "lack of security in life, in reputation, and in material
wealth." When these "three sacred properties are not secure and respected,"
Baille continued, "there is not, nor can there be, happiness; without happiness,
there are no marriages; without marriage there is no population" (1967, 275).

In the early twentieth century Coletti also offered a predominantly cultural
explanation for late marriage in his analysis of the rules of household formation
in Sardinia. In order to understand these rules, he claims, we need to begin with
two traits particular to Sardinians, the first of which was the "individualistic
sentiment" that "pervaded every fiber" of the Sardinian man. This sentiment
explained why "the Sardinian who takes a wife leaves the paternal house and
creates a new one for himself, even to the point of abandoning his old mother,
even [when she is] alone." The second character trait was a "sense of prudence
and ponderance," particularly accentuated in Sardinia because universal poverty and lack of strong class differences had reduced the Sardinians' ambition,
subdued their restlessness, and favored instead a sort of "passive acquiescence." Prudence and gravity also dictated the Sardinians' decisions where
marriage was concerned, and Coletti was persuaded that, unlike other regions,
in Sardinia "someone who does not feel he has the energy and the means to
found a family does not take the first step; does not marry. And those who do
want to marry do not follow the first impulse of their senses . . . but are able to
wait until they can in good conscience undertake the burdens and the responsibilities of a family of their own" (1908, 97–100).

Explanations of this sort are useful for ascertaining men's age at marriage,
but not women's, which provides, as we have seen, the greatest difference
between Sicily and Sardinia. In his 1965 study Hajnal observed that women's

age at marriage is the variable most difficult to account for. More recently, Rowland (1983) has maintained that if Hajnal's and Laslett's models are inapplicable to the Iberian peninsula, it is because they are based on the assumption that men and women had the same roles and responsibilities in the creation of the economic conditions that made the formation of a new household possible. Where this was indeed the case, as in the lands of "companionate marriage" of northern Europe, the pattern of neolocal residence could coexist with late marriage for women as well as men. In the areas in which the age gap between the sexes was greater and the duties and responsibilities of the spouses were different (as on the Iberian peninsula), the connection between neolocal residence pattern and age at marriage for women does not hold. Thus Rowland concludes that "the determinants of the mean age at which women married are more cultural than economic and demographic."

Rowland's interpretive scheme may also explain why Sardinia is different from Sicily and all the other southern regions. Why should women have married later in Sardinia than in the other areas of southern Italy? Two centuries ago Leprotti (1966, 105) offered a most interesting response to that question:

> Since in nearly all the civilized lands of Europe, and particularly in France, it is the custom that the maidens who go to husband take with them, beyond the dowry, a notable packet [of goods], so that thereby the same can more easily bear the weights of marriage, thus fathers on similar occasions are accustomed to provide them with the same in order to place them sooner. In Sardinia, to the contrary, they [the spouses] are constrained to make it up themselves, nor may they marry before having prepared it. Now, since the hours spared from the day that they can use in this labor are few, it happens that very many years and the most precious, when they are still young, are spent fruitless and infertile.

Thus if women married late in Sardinia, unlike other regions, it was not merely because couples followed the pattern of neolocal residence after marriage and set up their own households. Above all it was because, unlike other regions, the responsibility for creating the economic conditions required to form a new family fell on the shoulders of the women as well as of the men.

Furthermore, various studies clearly indicate that the age gap between spouses was less in Sardinia than in the rest of southern Italy. In particular, studies in juridical history have shown that women in Sardinia were accorded "a dignity and a juridical position not easily found in other regions" (Vismara 1971, 184). In fact, for a long period of time, two contrasting marriage patterns coexisted in Sardinia. "Marriage *a sa sardisca*" was characterized by common property among spouses. Marriage *a sa pisanisca* (Pisan style), however, was based instead on the dowry system typical in other regions of Italy and was practiced in Sardinia only by families from other places of origin, for example, by the great Genoese, Tuscan, and Catalan families settled on the island (Day 1986). Whether the Sardinian pattern represented a generalized, universal community of property (Roberti 1908), or whether the goods brought into the household by the husband and by the wife remained separate and only wealth acquired during marriage was considered common property (Cortese 1964; Marongiu 1975, 1981) has been debated at length. The second hypothesis is probably closer to the truth, but it is still undeniable that the rule for both matrimony and succession in Sardinia tended, much more than in other regions, toward equality between husband and wife.

The system of inheritance typical in Sardinia was quite different from the dominant one in other parts of Italy, where the laws stipulated that male offspring only (as a group or one of them) had a right to inherit from the father, whereas daughters could only hope for a dowry out of the estate. In Sardinia, however, and as early as the Middle Ages, daughters had the same rights as sons to the paternal estate.

As the historian of jurisprudence Giulio Vismara has written, in Sardinian marriages the wife could be party to contracts and could obligate or alienate her own property, either "with the consent of her husband or even without that consent, provided that she was seconded by three relatives and could prove the need for the act to the *podestà* and the Consiglio maggiore. . . . In contrast, in marriage of the dowry rule, the dowry goods were inalienable; the wife could in no way obligate herself, whether she had her husband's consent or no, and all the obligations she contracted were null" (1971, 188). This state of things, which existed during the Middle Ages, remained in effect for a long time. As late as 1827 the code promulgated for the kingdom of Sardinia by Carlo Felice Leprotti provided for common property (community of gain and of acquisitions) between spouses, stipulating that in case of the dissolution of the marriage the goods be divided equally between the husband and the wife.[2]

Translated by Lydia G. Cochrane

2. In Sardinia, according to Anna Oppo, "the married woman continued throughout her life to be identified and known by her father's last name (1983, 65). As John Day (1983) remarks, crimes of honor, which can be seen as a sign of the intense submission of women, were fewer in Sardinia than in Sicily.

Chapter 14

LUIGI TITTARELLI

Choosing a Spouse among Nineteenth-Century Central Italian Sharecroppers

To what extent can the now canonical models for family formation systems explain or interpret past reality, in particular in European lands during the eighteenth and nineteenth centuries? Robert Rowland (1983, 1987), working in Spain, and Marzio Barbagli (1988) in Italy have now demonstrated that neither John Hajnal's (1983) influential marriage models nor Peter Laslett's (1983) well-known typology adequately account for the diversity of forms found in Southern Europe. Barbagli's own distinctions of various family forms in different parts of Italy may be found in his contribution to this volume.

Other authors have noted that systems of family formation cannot be limited to generalized territorial models, and a variety of factors—economic, but also political, juridical, ecological, and cultural—have been seen as determinant to diversification in marriage patterns (Kertzer and Brettell 1987). As Gladys Quale notes, "No marriage system develops in isolation from other elements in people's lives" (1988, 3), and the systems of marriage that have been described appear conditioned by the demographic situations in which they operated. Thus we need to take all these elements into account, along with psychological, social, economic, and political factors, if we wish to understand the functioning and the underlying cultural explanation for systems of marriage in human societies (Quale 1988, 13). Francesco Benigno takes a similar position, and he urges reconsideration of the very concept of a "system of family formation," not on the basis of residence patterns alone but as deter-

This chapter was originally prompted by an earlier version of the chapter by Marzio Barbagli in this volume.

mined by economic, social, and demographic factors as well (1989, 187). In particular, Benigno argues that age at marriage as one of the constituent variables of a "model of nuptiality" must be considered not "by itself" but as one element in a general "demographic system"—in certain instances, for example, in its connection with death rates (1989, 176).

With all this in mind, I propose not so much to verify once more that the classical models are inappropriate to certain situations in Italy as to show the ample range of marriage patterns in an environment defined as rural and predominantly sharecropping; an environment into which diversification is introduced by socioeconomic stratification (even beyond the dichotomy of sharecroppers and day laborers) and by models of settlement (thickly populated agglomerations or scattered houses) and is governed by powerful spatial and cultural restraints.

THE RESEARCH SITES

The data presented here concern marriages celebrated in two distinct population groups during nearly coinciding periods of the mid-nineteenth century. The first set includes marriages contracted in the period 1835–1860 in five parishes in the Perugian *contado* situated to the east and northeast of Perugia, now the chief city of Umbria, which at the time was part of the Pontifical States. The five parishes—Ponte Felcino, Bosco, Civitella d'Arno, Colombella, and Pieve Pagliaccia—lie almost entirely on the left bank of the Tiber River at a distance from Perugia that varies from about five to about twenty kilometers. Ponte Felcino is the parish closest to Perugia and is cut in two by the river. Colombella (to the northeast) and Civitella d'Arno (to the east) are the most distant from the city. Pieve Pagliaccia lies to the northeast and Bosco to the east.

Toward the beginning of the period under examination the combined population of the five parishes was nearly 1,500, and it rose to around 1,900 by 1860. The most thickly populated parish was Ponte Felcino, with almost one-third of the overall population. Bosco and Colombella each accounted for approximately 19 percent of the total population; Civitella d'Arno and Pieve Pagliaccia for approximately 13 percent each. Not only was Ponte Felcino the most populous parish, but 60 percent of its inhabitants lived in the village center. The rest lived in the countryside on isolated *poderi* (farms) and *possessioni*—smaller farms commonly found in Umbria near a major town like Perugia where sharecroppers sometimes enjoyed more favorable conditions than those on *poderi*. On occasion, two or three farm families lived grouped together, forming a small hamlet. There were centers of habitation in the other four parishes as well, but of minimal demographic dimensions, with most of the parishioners living on their farms. The scattered population was made up largely of share-croppers, but some *casengoli* (agricultural laborers) also lived in isolated rural dwellings. Not only agricultural laborers but also artisans, small shopkeepers, and property owners lived in the village center of Ponte Felcino.

My decision to study this territory in this time period was determined by the availability of source materials; in particular, parish marriage registers and continuous series of ecclesiastical *stati delle anime* listing all members of the parish by name. In spite of the exceptional quantity of such parish lists in the archives in Perugia, it is not an easy task, even for the nineteenth century, to find sufficient materials concerning a large enough group of contiguous parishes. The general characteristics of such source materials are by now well-known.[1] The combined use of marriage registers and parish lists, however, greatly enlarges opportunities for the study of nuptiality and the family. The stati delle anime usually permit calculation of age at marriage, normally absent in marriage registers, and often provide information on the origins of the couple's families (size and type of family, occupation, and so on) and on residence after marriage.

The second group of marriages studied were celebrated between 1818 and 1860 in Cortona, a city of the Grand Duchy of Tuscany. Within the territories of the commune, which bordered the diocese of Perugia on its southeast side, sharecropping was clearly predominant, as it was around Perugia. The urban center of Cortona had a population of around 3,200 inhabitants in 1825; the population rose until 1840, but then dipped to 3,450 inhabitants in 1845; it rose again to nearly 3,900 in 1855. The population of the entire commune, city and country included, remained substantially the same, between 20,000 and 25,000. The city center was divided into four parishes: Santa Maria (the cathedral), San Cristoforo, San Filippo, and San Marco. We lack information on the populations of individual parishes because the archives do not contain parish stati delle anime, but from the number of marriages celebrated in each parish we can infer that slightly fewer than half of the city's inhabitants lived in the parish of Santa Maria, 30 percent in San Filippo, 15 percent in San Marco, and 10 percent in San Cristoforo. Although the prestige of the cathedral church may have attracted marriages from other urban parishes, the priests of the parishes of the spouses were loath to permit the celebration of their parishioners' marriages elsewhere because of the offerings weddings brought to the individual church.

1. The topic was first treated in depth and with reference to all of Italy in an ample collective publication (CISP 1972–1974). Many authors subsequently have made local surveys, one for the diocese of Perugia (Leti and Tittarelli 1976).

The Cortona sources give somewhat less information than the Perugia documents, but they, too, are exceptionally rich. In fact, each marriage was registered twice, since the parish priest entered marriages in his own parish register as well as (after 1818) in the record books of the Ufficio di Stato Civile of the grand duchy. The grand duchy required not only the information then noted in parish registers (name and place of residence, marital status, parish of each spouse, and the witnesses' names) but also the age and occupation of each spouse. With time and by imitation, the parish registers regularly included the same information. Obviously, the Cortona sources do not permit the more thorough analysis that comparison of the marriage registers and parish lists provides for the Perugia parishes, given that there is little or no information in them on the original families of the spouses.

NUPTIALITY

During the period 1835–1860, 312 weddings were celebrated in the five Perugia parishes, giving an average of 12 per year. The late 1830s were years of poor harvests due to bad weather, and hence unfavorable for weddings, as were the years 1848–1850 because of political disturbances (Tittarelli 1977, 67). The 1850s, however, show a notable upswing. The annual mean nuptiality rate for the entire period shows homogeneous figures for the four parishes with scattered settlement and a nearly exclusively sharecropping population, ranging from 6.4 per thousand in Colombella to 6.8 per thousand in Civitella d'Arno. In Ponte Felcino, where 60 percent of the population lived in the *villa* (the village center) and were not sharecroppers, the rate was notably higher, 8.1 per thousand.

In Cortona from 1818 to 1860, 1,022 marriages were celebrated, giving an average of nearly 24 per year. Marriages in Cortona declined noticeably around 1840, probably in connection with the food shortages of those years. Instead of rising after 1850, nuptiality in the city declined between 1850 and 1860, in contrast to rural areas in the communal territory, which show a rise similar to that in the country areas near Perugia. The lower nuptiality rate among the urban population was probably due to repeated cholera epidemics, the gravest of which occurred in 1854–1856 (Del Panta 1980, 229–230). Nuptiality rates, which have been calculated from the scarce data available for the entire population, show a decline over time from more than 8 per thousand around 1830 to slightly more than 6 per thousand in the crisis years after 1850. The mean annual rate for the entire period was approximately 6.7 per thousand.

The distribution of marriages in the calendar year, another important temporal aspect, shows the classic pattern, with highest density in February and in the autumn. Few marriages were celebrated during the Church's prohibited times (Advent and Lent) or during months reputed to be unpropitious, either for religious reasons (May was the month of the Virgin Mary) or because of the practical demands of seasonal agricultural labor. May began the season of heavy field work, which culminated with harvesting and threshing the grain during June and July, months in which marriages were celebrated only exceptionally. Nonetheless, seasonal fluctuation in Ponte Felcino was notably less than in the other four parishes of the Perugia countryside, and the reasons for it were moral (respect for the prohibited times) rather than economic. Ponte Felcino did not experience the typical concentration of sharecroppers' weddings in periods of lighter field work and higher availability of cash, for example, in the autumn after Saint Martin's Day (11 November), when accounts with the landlord were settled, or in the winter after Advent.

REMARRIAGE

In the Perugia parishes, nearly 93 percent of all marriages were unions between previously unmarried men and women. Remarriage was rare among men (only 6 percent of bridegrooms are identified as widowers) and even rarer among women (2 percent of brides are listed as widows). In other words, the few widowers who did remarry for the most part wed previously unmarried women; the union of a widow and a widower accounts for only 1 percent of all marriages.

This extremely low figure for remarriages is not reflected within the city limits of Cortona, where 75 percent of all marriages (for the entire period) united previously unmarried men and women—a figure that rose over time, from 71 percent of marriages in the years 1818–1830 to 76 percent for 1845–1860. Male Cortonans were three times more likely to remarry than rural Perugians: in Cortona 20 percent of bridegrooms were widows compared with 6 percent in the rural parishes near Perugia. Women in Cortona were five times more likely to remarry than their counterparts in the Perugia parishes (11 percent of widow brides compared with 2 percent). Unions of bachelors and widows or of widowers and widows each account for 5 percent of total marriages in Cortona, as opposed to only 1 percent in the territory of Perugia; marriages between widowers and previously unmarried women represent 14 percent of the total in Cortona and 5 percent in the Perugia parishes. The tendency of Cortona citizens to remarry weakened with time, however, and was more marked among men than among women.

These data seem to demonstrate that the rural environment of sharecropping, where a majority of families were large and plurinuclear in structure (multiple families), did not encourage the remarriage of widowers and even less of widows, especially those who were young and had small children. Family solidarity and women's greater capacity for overcoming certain of the negative consequences of widowhood were factors, but other considerations pertained as well. The remarriage of a widower would have brought the share-cropper family an extra pair of hands (the bride's, in almost all cases not previously married), but she would soon produce other mouths to feed. A bachelor sharecropper (or even a widower) who brought a widow into the house as his bride would normally take in her children as well. In both cases, the ironclad rule applied of keeping the number of hands and mouths in the family in the best possible balance with the size and nature of the farm. This balance was the founding principle of a strategy for conserving the existing relationship with the landowner—that is, for the family's remaining on the farm. Such a strategy was particularly important in the mid-nineteenth century, when land was subject to continually increasing pressure, thanks to a demographic rise coupled with what amounted to stagnation (for the greater part of the century) in the number of available farms and in the selection of crops grown and the available agrarian technology.

In the cities and towns most families were nuclear and consequently smaller and less fully articulated than sharecroppers' families. Once the momentary solidarity that kin and neighborhood could offer the widower or widow had elapsed, pressure to remarry was greater than in rural areas.

AGE AT MARRIAGE

The mean age at marriage in the country parishes near Perugia was twenty-eight for men and twenty-five for women, with an average age gap between spouses of about three years.[2] These data, which are taken from 269 marriages for which the age of both spouses is known, refer exclusively to marriages between previously unmarried men and women. In 15 marriages between widowers and previously unmarried women whose ages are known, the brides were on average thirty years old and their husbands forty-two.

In Ponte Felcino, the only parish in which brides and bridegrooms not from sharecropper families were numerous enough to take into consideration, mean age at marriage for men among the casengoli was somewhat lower than for

2. Age at marriage for couples in the five rural parishes near Perugia has been derived from the listings of status animarum; that of couples in Cortona from marriage registers. In both cases the data are to be taken as approximate but fairly accurate, since errors in age reporting are known to have been minimal for younger people (Galmacci and Tittarelli 1982).

sharecroppers, but women's age at marriage was the same in both categories. If we consider couples of homogeneous occupational status (from two sharecropper families or two casengolo families), however, we note that the average age gap between casengolo couples was only one year (mean age at marriage for males in this group was three years less than for sharecropper men). Several individuals are listed as "living in their own house," a notation that may indicate a higher socioeconomic condition than that of sharecroppers, let alone day workers or farmhands, and include small property owners, artisans, and shopkeepers. In this group the age gap rises to four years because of a lower than average age at marriage for women. In short, given that the overall mean age at marriage was twenty-eight years for men and twenty-five for women, the only groups who varied notably from these figures were (1) male casengoli who married women of their own occupational category, in which case age at marriage was two years lower than the average; and (2) women "living in their own house" who married within that category, who were one year younger than the average.

In Cortona mean age at marriage for bachelors was just under twenty-nine; for previously unmarried women, twenty-six. Men's age at marriage rose slightly with time; women's declined slightly. Considering that these figures are calculated from the age at marriage of all previously unmarried men (including whose who married widows) and women, if restricted to unions between unmarried males and females the age at marriage would certainly have been somewhat lower. Thus we can conclude that there was little significant difference in mean age at marriage between Cortona and the Perugia parishes.

MARRIAGE BY BRIDEGROOM'S PLACE OF ORIGIN

The distribution of marriages according to the bride's and bridegroom's places of origin—more accurately, according to their families' residences of origin—is examined here according to three categories: close territorial endogamy (where the man and the woman were from the same parish); extended endogamy (the man and the woman were from the same general area, the five Perugia country parishes or the city of Cortona); and exogamy (the husband came from a parish outside the two areas under consideration). In the mid-nineteenth century, as in preceding centuries and until recent memory, marriages were normally celebrated and registered in the parish of the bride.

Within the city of Cortona 40 percent of marriages followed the pattern of close endogamy; 35 percent that of extended endogamy; and 25 percent that of territorial exogamy, where a woman from an urban parish married an outsider. In the five parishes near Perugia close endogamy characterized 145 of the 308 marriages for which the place of origin of each spouse is known, giving a figure of 47 percent of all marriages. Extended endogamy was the case for 14 percent of couples, and 38.6 percent of marriages were exogamous. At Ponte Felcino intraparish marriages were nearly twice as frequent as in the other smaller parishes, representing 63 percent of the total. Moreover, out of 77 marriages in which both spouses belonged to the parish of Ponte Felcino, 64 percent involved a bride and bridegroom who both lived in the village center and 25 percent involved a bride and bridegroom who were both from the rural part of the parish.

From a territorial point of view, proximity seems to have been the most important element in choice of a mate, not only in terms of actual distance but also in terms of ease of communication. Perhaps, however, it is simply easier to measure than such considerations as membership in families who cultivated farms that belonged to the same landlord but were situated in different parishes. Inhabitants of a particular Perugia parish tended to marry either someone from another Perugia parish, or someone from a parish on the nearby rural periphery. The proportion of marriages with outsiders from a maximum distance of ten kilometers in all exogamous marriages varies from 64 percent for Bosco to 90 percent for Pieve Pagliaccia. For the most part, such marriages were contracted between women in the five parishes and men from parishes outside the five that were closer.

This description is a direct outcome of the decision to examine these particular areas based on available documentary sources rather than on criteria that take into account such factors as geographic and economic homogeneity, an approach that might have brought us closer to the true situation and perhaps produced more interesting results. Nevertheless, some conclusions can be drawn. Close endogamy was more common in the Perugia parishes, whereas extended endogamy was more typical in Cortona. This is even more the case if we consider that 60 percent of exogamous marriages in Cortona (which account for 25 percent of all marriages) consisted in the union of a townswoman and a man from the commune's rural surroundings. Where matrimonial relations were concerned, the parish was more closed in a rural area than in the town, whereas the town, as a collection of parishes, was in turn a more closed space than a group of contiguous rural parishes, at least in the group examined here.

SPOUSES BY TYPE OF FAMILY OF ORIGIN

It has been ascertained, at least for the eighteenth and nineteenth centuries, that there was a high proportion of multiple families among sharecroppers.[3] In

3. Family typology here follows Laslett 1972, 31.

areas predominantly cultivated by sharecroppers, however, the nuclear family was the most prevalent type among agricultural day laborers.[4] Study of the distribution of marriages according to the type of the bride's and the bridegroom's family of origin thus gives results that closely parallel those on occupational homogamy. This means, of course, that once again Ponte Felcino stands out from the other four Perugian rural parishes.

In the other four parishes, the proportion of brides from multiple families— more accurately, from families that at the time of the wedding were in a multiple-family phase—varied from 56 percent to 67 percent (see Papa 1985, 58–64). The figure for brides from nuclear families was always lower, varying from 20 percent to 33 percent. Bridegrooms show less variation: according to the parish, from 36 percent to 52 percent of men came from multiple families; around one-third in every parish came from nuclear families. The marriages in which both spouses belonged to multiple families varied from 20 percent in Colombella to 40 percent in Civitella d'Arno. The proportion of marriages between a bride from a multiple family and a bridegroom from a nuclear family in the same two parishes reached, respectively, 26 percent and 20 percent.

That more sharecropper bridegrooms than brides belonged to a nuclear family may signify that the man initiated marriage as a way to strengthen his family of origin, a necessity typical of the phase of greatest contraction of sharecropper families (the nuclear phase). Conversely, brides were more readily available in expanding sharecropper families (the multiple phase).

Among Ponte Felcino couples from the village center, two-thirds of the brides and more than one-half of the bridegrooms came from nuclear families. Similar figures exist for marriages between women from the village center and outsiders. Furthermore, 35 percent of marriages involved spouses who both came from nuclear families, and in only 10 percent of marriages did both come from multiple families. In other matrimonial combinations (both spouses from the rural part of the parish; a country bride and an outsider bridegroom), the figures for persons from multiple families and from nuclear families are more balanced, both around 40 percent for brides. Bridegrooms show more diversification and include a certain number of men of unknown profession. Only 5 percent of marriages between inhabitants of the rural part of Ponte Felcino parish involved individuals who were both from a nuclear family, and 21 percent involved spouses who both came from multiple families.

There is further confirmation of the connection between the occupation of sharecropping and multiple-family type (or the multiple phase of family development) in the family of origin—and between agricultural day laborers and the

4. See Barbagli 1988, 547–548, and the authors cited therein, for example, Biagioli 1986 and Della Pina 1987. See also Tittarelli 1980.

nuclear type. In the four parishes, Ponte Felcino excluded, two-thirds of share-cropper brides came from multiple families, and only one-fifth from nuclear families. Nearly all casengolo brides and bridegrooms came from nuclear families. Once again Ponte Felcino stands apart: 45 percent of brides from sharecropping backgrounds belonged to multiple families and 40 percent to nuclear families, and two-thirds of the brides from families of other occupational status came from nuclear families. Of casengolo bridegrooms 70 percent came from nuclear families. Among sharecropper bridegrooms and those whose families "lived in their own house," the figures for those from multiple families and those from nuclear families are closer: respectively, 43 percent and 34 percent among sharecropper families and 37 percent and 43 percent among the others. The notable presence of bridegrooms and brides of nuclear share-cropper families in the parish of Ponte Felcino can be explained by the large number of possessioni, smaller farmholds requiring fewer hands, rather than poderi.

POSTMARITAL RESIDENCE PATTERNS

In all the parishes near Perugia patrilocal postmarital residence predomi-nated. In other words, the new couple became part of the husband's family of origin. This was true in proportions ranging from 69 percent of marriages in Civitella d'Arno to 88 percent in Bosco. This time, Ponte Felcino is no exception: in 73 percent of marriages the new couple chose (or accepted) patrilocal residence; among couples both from the village center the figure is 75 percent. Figures for neolocal couples are fairly consistent in four of the five Perugian parishes, ranging from a low of 15 percent of marriages in Pieve Pagliaccia to 20 percent in Ponte Felcino. In Bosco no neolocal couples appear. Only eleven couples joined the bride's family of origin, four of them in Ponte Felcino. The predominance of patrilocal residence is linked to the large number of share-cropper families in this area and, consequently, to the high number of multiple families.

To summarize, men only rarely left their sharecropper family of origin, but leaving home was normal for women. Women usually left one sharecropper family to join another, but more often than men they left their sharecropper family to form a neolocal family, nearly always with a casengolo.

Given that most new couples found a place within the husband's family of origin, what modifications of family type resulted? The entry of the new couple into a multiple family only enlarged its plurinuclear structure. For families that had been nuclear or extended it prompted transition to a multiple phase. In Bosco, for example, the families of forty-three couples were patrilocal after marriage. Fifteen of the men came from families that had been nuclear and nine from extended families; after marriage all but one of these families became multiple. In Civitella d'Arno, before marriages resulting in patrilocal residence only 58 percent of the man's family of origin were multiple; all were multiple afterward. For Colombella the corresponding figures are 29 percent and 94 percent; for Pieve Pagliaccia, 48 percent and 76 percent.

Ponte Felcino shows similar results concerning patrilocal couples: 28 percent of the families of origin for men were multiple before marriage and 86 percent afterward. Considering only couples who were both from the village center, the comparable figures are 27 percent before marriage and 89 percent after. Moreover, for the most part only nuclear families were transformed in this manner, since men's families of origin of the extended type accounted for just 26 percent of marriages in Colombella and as little as 15 percent in Ponte Felcino.

On the basis of the localities studied here we can state that in the mid-nineteenth century the rate of marriages celebrated—the nuptiality rate—was higher in urban centers than in rural areas, which confirms accepted judgments. In the countryside, however, the nuptiality rate was not uniform, but rather was higher among a more concentrated population (as in Ponte Felcino) than among a scattered population (as in the other four Perugia parishes). In other words, nuptiality was low in a strictly sharecropping environment where farms were isolated, but in the country towns, inhabited by a population that was rural but for the most part not responsible for a sharecropped farm (that is, a population of agricultural day laborers, artisans, small householders and landowners), nuptiality was as high as in the city.

Mean age at marriage for both men and women was generally high in town and country alike, but in the country casengolo bridegrooms were younger than their sharecropper counterparts, particularly when the couple was homogamous occupationally (or, more accurately, when their socioeconomic status was the same). Brides from better-off families of origin ("living in their own house") tended to form occupationally homogamous couples, and they were younger than the rule. Furthermore, economic and social status undoubtedly influenced their age at marriage more than residence in population centers.

High levels of territorial endogamy testify to an extremely circumscribed marriage market limited primarily by distance and facility of communication, but further restricted by occupational constraints (that is, social constraints deriving from the economic status connected with the spouses' activities in their families of origin). This can be seen in the frequency of marriages between men and women of casengolo families in Ponte Felcino.

In the rural areas around Perugia patrilocal residence for new couples was clearly the predominant mode. This contributed to the dominance of the plurinuclear (multiple) family, in particular, by prompting the shift of a good number of men's families of origin from a nuclear phase (more rarely, an extended phase) to a multiple phase of family development.

These conclusions seem to confirm Barbagli's claim that in nineteenth-century Italy there were a number of systems of family formation, not just the three identified as typical of Italy. In fact, the system considered typical of central and northern rural areas in Italy (high age at marriage, patrilocal residence, complex family structure) is reflected accurately in the rural parishes near Perugia, with a scattered population and a strong prevalence of sharecroppers, but only partially (age at marriage was lower) in the country towns of the same rural areas where agricultural laborers and people of other socioeconomic categories lived. Thus this system was typical only for sharecroppers, not for the entire non-urban population. At closer inspection, in fact, it was typical only of the sharecroppers who lived on a podere, because sharecroppers who farmed the smaller possessioni were less likely to have a multiple family. Furthermore, a restricted occupation group seems to offer another exception to the same typical system: couples of casengolo origin in Ponte Felcino were characterized not only by lower age at marriage for men but also, in many instances, by neolocal residence after marriage. At this point we can state that diversity among the various systems of family formation was not territorial, nor was it linked to any generic division of the population into urban and rural. At least in rural areas, diversity depended on the activity of the family of origin, or rather, on the economic and social status connected with its occupation, and on its residence pattern.

As for more deep-seated motives for matrimonial behavior, if there was a strategy behind the marriages of inhabitants of the Perugia contado, in most cases it aimed at safeguarding the economic and social status that the family had achieved. A sharecropper family content with what it could produce from the podere that it farmed worked first to keep the farm by maintaining an equilibrium of hands to mouths as time passed and the family was subjected to a variety of demographic events. Second, the family worked to keep a similar balance between family size and makeup and the size and agricultural characteristics of the land farmed. When the family had a surplus of hands—the most common situation in the nineteenth century (Biagioli 1986)—young men were discouraged from marrying and young women encouraged, although with dubious success, given the scarcity of men interested in marriage (thus explaining the high age at marriage). When hands were scarce, male marriage was favored, and if the family lacked males (not often the case, given the high fertility rates), women were encouraged to marry a man who would join her household of origin. A momentary surplus of family members was resolved by sending very young males out of the family to work as *garzoni;* a momentary scarcity, by taking farmhands into the household, preferably from other sharecropper families with too many children, but also from a casengolo family or the foundling home. An urgent need to marry off a daughter or to find a wife for a young male might induce a sharecropper family to accept a spouse of inferior condition (a casengolo or casengola, a garzone or *serva,* an *alunno* or *alunna*). When marriage could be put off no longer, the family that had gained more hands and could soon expect to have more mouths to feed might decide on the expulsion of one of its couples (usually the youngest), who would then have to seek a small podere to farm or a yet smaller possessione or to work for others as agricultural day laborers.

Of course there were sharecroppers who were dissatisfied with the living they made from the podere they cultivated. They could put themselves on the market for a larger or a better farm and, in the meantime, improve their labor force through the marriage of a family member. The sequence could also be reversed: the family might discover that it had a surplus of labor after a marriage or as children grew up, and rather than expelling a family member or a conjugal unit, it might look for a bigger and more profitable farm. That was a risky decision, however, because the market showed an overall surplus of sharecropper labor in relation to a nearly stagnant number of tenant farms.

In every case, however, in its search for the best solution the family used and cultivated kinship ties established by earlier matrimonial exchanges and ties of solidarity determined by proximity to or by living and working with other farm families in a large farmhold. There were not many of these *tenute,* as they were called in Umbria (*fattorie* in Tuscany), in the lands around Perugia. More typically, the great proprietors, clerical and lay, owned widely scattered lands, often quite far from one another.

The casengoli pursued a goal of simple survival, except when an opportunity arose to better their condition through marriage with a member of a sharecropper family (preferably not one of the poorest), an artisan, a small landholder, and so on. When a casengolo founded a family (and, as we have seen, the couple went to live on its own more often than sharecropper newlyweds), his principal concern was to keep down the number of children who lived in the household. His sporadic labor and his low income would otherwise be inadequate to raise them. Casengolo families were not only predominantly nuclear but also much smaller in size than sharecropper families (composed on average of four family members, as compared to eight; Tittarelli 1984, table 9). To that end various expedients were used, among them, abandoning newborn children to the institutions of public aid.

These, in brief, were families' matrimonial aims. They undoubtedly worked counter, however, to a number of constraints of a territorial, economic, social, and cultural nature; constraints that combined to form the prevailing mentality where marriage was concerned.

Although the territory within which young people could seek a mate was limited by the difficulties of communication, it was also restricted by local loyalties. Even in living memory, young men in small towns and villages everywhere considered local girls to be their special preserve and opposed (even with violence) their engagement to outsiders. At the most, traditional lines of exchange were acceptable, but only when they worked both ways. On occasion, traditional rivalries could be subordinated to the opportunities and advantages offered by a large farmhold touching more than one parish and worked by several families. Also, the proprietor of the farm exercised a firm control over nineteenth-century sharecropper families. Contracts increasingly concerned not only the head of the sharecropper family but all family members, imposing limits on family size and on the movements of family members, including marriage, at first implicitly, but toward the end of the century even explicitly (Papa 1987, 198–200).

Agricultural day workers were poorer than sharecroppers and their status more precarious; in addition, the figure of the casengolo was subject to long-standing negative prejudice. He was considered lazy and thievish, so that if a sharecropper needed a farmhand he tended to seek first among other share-croppers before taking on a casengolo lad. Only in cases of dire necessity would a young person of sharecropper family be permitted to marry someone from a casengolo family.

In country towns like Ponte Felcino, family status was a strong considera-tion in matrimonial exchanges, and the search for a mate occurred primarily within homogeneous socioeconomic groups, even the ones with few members, such as those who "lived in their own houses" and the casengoli. Moreover, over and above strictly economic considerations and in spite of the close proximity of the town center to rural part of the parish, the *paesani* of the town avoided marriage with "peasants."

The choice of a mate was undoubtedly also determined by other charac-teristics—physical suitability, aesthetic qualities, morals, and sentiment—but it is impossible to evaluate their respective weight or their relation to the more constraining ties. If a sharecropper family urgently needed a woman and could offer only an old man or a disabled or particularly unattractive male, it would certainly be willing to accept any woman in good health who was a good worker. A casengola would be preferable to a widow from a sharecropper family who had small children. Similarly, if a family decided to pare down its size by marrying off a woman who was no longer young or appealing, it would not be too particular about the qualities of the prospective husband. The same was true of a widow with small children, and if a woman had been "talked about," finding a husband would not be easy and she could permit herself few pretensions. A particularly attractive young woman had a special advantage, but other considerations were primary. Sentiment, sexual attraction, and love were certainly not unknown in the rural world, but little room was left for them in a society that was repressive on all levels and even more so among the unlettered and poorer classes. At best, they created some elbowroom within decisions that were social and familial rather than individual. Marital decisions were made by the family—by the head of household or the dominant conjugal nucleus—and they were based on the family's circumstances at that particular time, not on the wishes of the person involved. This is not to say that individual desires were uniformly and deliberately ignored (although I tend toward pessimism in this regard). In general, families probably intended to take preferences into account. They acted according to their needs, however.

Moreover, interpersonal relations and relations between conjugal nuclei within the family (large sharecropper families, for example) followed the same pattern. Affective ties between parents and their children did not have priority over need when a son had to be persuaded or constrained to contract a marriage he may not have wanted. Good relations between the multiple nuclei in a household did not prevent one of the nuclei leaving the family when necessary. Conversely, bad relations between members of one family nucleus and another (mother-in-law and daughter-in-law; the wife of the head of household and a sister-in-law; brothers) led to the breakup of the larger family only when it did not compromise good relations with the owner of the farm.

Matrimonial choices and family structures were subject to strong constraints of an economic, social, and cultural nature. These constraints shaped family strategy. Personal choice thus operated only within the restricted space that society and family left to the individual.

Translated by Lydia G. Cochrane

Chapter 15

WILLIAM A. DOUGLASS

The Joint-Family Household in Eighteenth-Century Southern Italian Society

In an article published some years ago (Douglass 1980), I argued that the multiple-family household, and particularly its patrilineally extended joint-family form whereby adult sons continue to reside with their father after marriage, was the cultural ideal in the southern Italian town of Agnone (located in the Molise region). I based this conclusion on anthropological fieldwork, surveys, and archival research conducted in the early 1970s, as well as on an analysis of a 1970 detailed household census and of a tax roll (*onciario*) compiled for the town by authorities of the kingdom of Naples in 1753. The findings of this study, comparing for the years 1753 and 1970 all households in Agnone containing one or more conjugal units, are presented in table 15.1.[1]

My contention was that, despite its low incidence, the joint-family household was perceived by the actors themselves to be the basic social unit of Agnone society.[2] To be sure, my informants were aware, indeed acutely so, that the patrilineally extended, patriarchal joint-family household seemed anachronistic in the modern world and was therefore disappearing. Many, however, including young adults of both sexes, regarded its passing with nostalgia and a

---

1. I have excluded the categories of "solitaries" and "no family" households included in Peter Laslett's widely employed classificatory scheme (1972, 31).

2. Before its twentieth-century decline (6,481 persons in 1970), Agnone was a servicing center of considerable importance (Douglass 1984, 45–47, 74–79). In the seventeenth century it was the largest town in the Molise, and in 1871 its 11,073 residents made it the second-largest town in the province (Istituto Centrale di Statistica 1967, 124–125). There are three discernible broad social distinctions within Agnone society past and present—peasants, artisans, and professionals—and all three included joint-family households. For the economic rationales underlying the multiple-family household in each of Agnone's social classes, see Douglass 1980, 343–348.

TABLE 15.1

Agnone Family Structure: 1753 and 1970
Compared

	1753 Households		1970 Households	
Family Form	N	%	N	%
Nuclear	479	63.4	1,203	75.9
Stem	190	25.2	268	16.9
Joint	86	11.4	114	7.2
Total	755	100.0	1,585	100.0

Sources: Onciario dell'università della città di Agnone, 1753, copy in Biblioteca La Banca di Agnone; *Censimento di Agnone,* 1971, copy in Archivio Comunale di Agnone.

sense of loss. Nor were our discussions entirely retrospective since joint-family households accounted for 7.2 percent of those in the population at the time of the study. Related cultural patterns, such as late marriage and attendant delayed social adulthood, with corresponding financial dependence of celibate adult males on their parents, were still quite palpable. Other aspects, such as arranged marriages, were gone but remained in the recollections of elderly Agnonesi. My informants' perception that the joint-family-household pattern was waning rather than waxing led me to conclude that it was more characteristic of past than present times.[3] Its higher incidence in 1753 seemed to support this interpretation.

There remained, however, the enigma posed by the low statistical incidence of the joint-family household form over time. Given this, could one contend that it was the culturally preferred form? I argued that in actuality the incidence of joint-family households in 1753 Agnone was not low given the eighteenth-century demographic variables that militated against its formation. To demonstrate, I employed both marital records, to establish mean age at first marriage for males,[4] and mortality records, to determine life expectancy for adult males

3. For a discussion of the reasons for this twentieth-century decline in the incidence of joint-family households in Agnone, see Douglass 1980, 352–354.

4. It should be noted that the mean age at marriage figures in my 1980 article for both sexes (males 26.92 years and females 24.54 years) were generated from nineteenth-century sources and therefore differ slightly from those presented in this chapter. They do not, however, change materially the demographic argument.

who had attained marriageable age. I then projected the "best case" scenario, wherein a man fathered two offspring in his first two years of marriage, both of whom were males, survived to marriageable age, married, and continued to reside with their parents (the minimal conditions for creating a patrilineally extended joint-family household). Even under such ideal circumstances a man would be fifty-seven years of age before becoming the patriarch of a joint-family household, whereas his life expectancy was only fifty-three. I concluded that there were clear demographic impediments to formation of the ideal household type, which might account for its low statistical incidence. Since peoples' lives do not conform strictly to statistical norms, however, a number of households in each generation attained and thereby sustained the ideal.

The original study was flawed in two obvious ways. First, the data were derived exclusively from a single community, which meant, of course, that the analysis rested solely on a sample of one. In this chapter I have included comparative mid-eighteenth-century onciario data for three other communities in the Molise. Although still falling short of statistical significance, this at least enhances somewhat the diagnostic power of the argument. Second, the treatment was essentially synchronic. That is, although I compared eighteenth- and twentieth-century censuses, each was a synchronic slice through time. Process could only be inferred through an internal analysis of the corpus rather than demonstrated by means of record linkage over a temporal sequence.

Since preparing the 1980 article I have located and analyzed a rich data base for a part of Agnone's eighteenth-century population. The archive of the parish church of San Emidio, largest of Agnone's seven parishes, contains nine *stato delle anime,* or *status animarum,* registers detailing the composition of every household on an annual basis over a thirty-five-year period (1769–1803). This new evidence permits precise tracking of changes (births, deaths, and marriages; entries and exits) within a large sample of households over an extensive time frame, thereby facilitating insight into the actual, rather than the imputed, processes of household formation. Data concerning associated demographic issues (for example, age at marriage, incidence of celibacy, widowhood and its consequences) also can be discussed in terms of the life-course approach within the family history literature.

CROSS-SECTIONAL ANALYSIS OF EIGHTEENTH-CENTURY HOUSEHOLD FORM IN THE MOLISE

Gérard Delille, in his seminal study, correlates different demographic patterns with distinctive ecological features of the southern Italian countryside. In particular he contrasts the predominantly monocultural, large-estate, grain-growing agricultural communities of the plains with the small-plot, mixed-agricultural regime of the more mountainous areas (Delille 1985, 171–172). In this regard all four of the Molisan communities selected for analysis would be of the second variety. They do, however, display internal ecological differences.

In Agnone the town nucleus is situated 850 meters above sea level, or at about the dividing line between pastoralism and plow agriculture in this part of southern Europe. In the lower parts of the municipality the agricultural system is devoted to the Mediterranean crop trilogy of wheat, grapes, and olives, whereas in the upper reaches the emphasis is on pastoralism. During the eighteenth century two-thirds of Agnone's population engaged in agriculture on their own small plots or as day laborers and sharecroppers on the holdings of local and absentee landlords.

The three other Molisan communities in my sample are overwhelmingly agricultural in their economic makeup. Two are within Agnone's hinterland of satellite villages. Pescopennataro, located at 1,190 meters above sea level, depends almost exclusively on animal husbandry involving winter transhu mance to the Apulian plain, supplemented by the seasonal labor of those men who migrate to cities on the plains where they work as stonemasons in the winter months. In Pietrabbondante, 1,027 meters above sea level, agriculture is more mixed, with the Mediterranean crop trilogy present in the lower reaches, and some animal husbandry. The third community, Cantalupo nel Sannio, 587 meters above sea level, is a considerable distance from Agnone and outside its sphere of influence. Lying in the hilly rather than the mountainous part of the Molise, it is favored agriculturally in terms of both climate and topography.

The family forms discernible within the households of the four communities are presented in table 15.2. Several methodological notes are in order. In contrast to table 15.1, which includes only households with at least one con-jugal unit present, I have added the categories "solitaries" and "no family" (coresident unmarried siblings). I have, however, excluded individual priests who were listed as a separate entity and therefore possibly residing alone as solitaries. I have not distinguished simple families from what the Laslett classi-ficatory schemata designates as extended ones.[5] Rather, a married couple, their children, and coresident unmarried sibling(s) are treated as nuclear. Con-versely, a married couple and their offspring who are coresident with a wid-owed parent (and possibly unmarried siblings) are classified as a stem family. But a married head of household and his offspring who live with a widowed sibling and his or her offspring are listed as a joint household. Finally, even

5. Were we to make this distinction the incidence of extended families would increase considerably.

TABLE 15.2
Comparative Family and Household Structure in Four Communities of the Molise

Household Type	Agnone[a] (N = 861)	Pescopennataro (N = 157)	Pietrabbondante (N = 133)	Cantalupo nel Sannio (N = 229)
Solitaries	23 (2.7%)	5 (3.2%)	2 (1.5%)	9 (3.9%)
No family	15 (1.7%)	1 (0.6%)	4 (3.0%)	8 (3.5%)
Nuclear family	544 (63.2%)	67 (42.7%)	94 (70.7%)	143 (62.5%)
Stem family	189 (21.9%)	28 (17.8%)	22 (16.5%)	31 (13.5%)
Joint family	90 (10.5%)	56 (35.7%)	11 (8.3%)	38 (16.6%)

[a]In the previously published calculations for Agnone reproduced in table 15.1 I treated a household with a married male and his widowed brother (or extensions through a deceased brother to celibate collateral kinsmen) as lateral extensions of a nuclear family and, for statistical purposes, nuclear. In recalculating the data I treated them as joint families. Hence the small discrepancy in the figure for joint families in the two listings (86 in my 1980 article versus 90 in the present one).
Sources: Onciario listings for Agnone, Pescopennataro, Pietrabbondante, and Cantalupo nel Sannio in the Fondo Catasti Onciario, Archivio di Stato di Napoli.

though I distinguish the stem-family household statistically, I do not suggest that it was regarded as a significant cultural construct by the actors themselves.[6] Instead, I would argue that it was one phase in the formation of the culturally valued joint-family household.

A perusal of table 15.2 suggests that Agnone was far from unique in the Molise in possessing a double-digit incidence of fully elaborated joint-family households. Indeed, that in the mountainous community of Pescopennataro was three and one-half times as great and in the lowland community of Cantalupo nel Sannio half again that of Agnone. Only Pietrabbondante had a slightly lower frequency of joint-family households.

LONGITUDINAL ANALYSIS OF HOUSEHOLD FORM IN AGNONE

The stato delle anime records, a series of nine linked parish rolls listing the inhabitants of Agnone's largest parish of San Emidio annually from 1769 to

6. Italy may not, however, be entirely devoid of the stem-family-household system. Marzio Barbagli (this volume) suggests that the form may exist in the Piedmont, Liguria, and Lombardy.

TABLE 15.3
Agnone Cross-sectional Household Data in 1769, 1780, 1790, and 1803

Family Form	1769 N	1769 %	1780 N	1780 %	1790 N	1790 %	1803 N	1803 %
Solitaries	29	7.6	13	3.9	12	3.7	7	2.2
No family	14	3.6	5	1.5	6	1.9	7	2.2
Nuclear	225	58.9	145	43.6	135	41.6	162	50.3
Extended: one married couple; one or more unmarried siblings of head of household	12	3.1	16	4.8	14	4.3	17	5.3
Stem lineal: one or both parents; one married offspring	24	6.3	31	9.3	34	10.5	29	9.0
Stem lineal and lateral: one or both parents; one married offsprng; one or more unmarried offspring	48	12.6	67	20.1	49	15.1	37	11.5
Joint lineal: one or both parents; two or more of their married offspring	8	2.1	17	5.1	28	8.7	14	4.3
Joint lineal and lateral: one or both parents; two or more married offspring; one or more unmarried offspring	11	2.9	19	5.7	21	6.5	26	8.1
Joint lateral (a): two or more married siblings	6	1.6	10	3.0	9	2.8	8	2.5
Joint lateral (b): two or more married siblings; one or more unmarried siblings	5	1.3	10	3.0	16	4.9	15	4.6
Totals	382	100.0	333	100.0	324	100.0	322	100.0

1803, allow detailed analysis of household formation and dissolution over a thirty-five-year period. The first register lists 382 households[7] in the year 1769 containing a total of 1,828 inhabitants, for a mean size of 4.8 persons per unit.

A cross-sectional view of households at four points over the 1769–1803 period is presented in table 15.3. Some households forms increased over the period, for example, when former joint-family households divided into two or more units as married brothers ceased to coreside. The registers are explicit on this point, giving each new household a separate entry. Decreases resulted

7. The summary page in the register cites 383 households, but this appears to be a compiler's error.

from households "dying out," the fate of almost all solitaries, and from migration. Neither in-migration nor out-migration is treated in the analysis. Therefore, the household statistics for any year after 1769 do not parallel the population of the parish. For our purposes there was a decline, but in terms of numbers of both households and inhabitants, the parish in fact increased in size over the 1769–1803 period.

Of the original 382 households in 1769, 247 are observable over the entire thirty-five-year period and can be identified in their most elaborated form. Thus we find that only 15, or 6.1 percent of all households in the sample, failed to elaborate beyond the nuclear family, whereas 128, or fully 51.8 percent (categories 7 through 10), attained joint-family status. In 7 of the 128 joint-family arrangements extension was effected by other than strict adherence to the patrilineal rule. That is, in four instances a married only son lived with his married sister. In three households lacking any male offspring two sisters married and lived together. Even here, however, the male bias is apparent, since in two of those three households the sisters married brothers.

Of particular interest are the 119 households (the nuclear-, extended-, and

TABLE 15.4

Most Elaborated Form Attained by the Households Observable throughout the 1769–1803 Period

Family Form	N	%
1. Solitaries	—	—
2. No family	—	—
3. Nuclear	15	6.1
4. Extended: one married couple; one or more unmarried siblings of head of household	9	3.6
5. Stem lineal: one or both parents; one married offspring	31	12.6
6. Stem lineal and lateral: one or both parents; one married offspring; one or more unmarried offspring	64	25.9
7. Joint lineal: one or both parents; two or more of their married offspring	34	13.8
8. Joint lineal and lateral: one or both parents; two or more married offspring	77	31.2
9. Joint lateral (a): two or more married siblings	8	3.2
10. Joint lateral (b): two or more married siblings; one or more unmarried siblings	9	3.6
Total	247	100.0

TABLE 15.5

Reasons for Failure to Achieve Full Joint-Family Extension
in Nuclear- and Stem-Family Households

| | Households | |
Reason	N	%
1. There were no male offspring in a particular generation	13	10.9
2. There was a single male offspring in a particular generation	53	44.5
3. The potential male heirs remained celibate by choice or circumstance	34	28.6
4. The potential male heirs married out or effected a schism in the household	19	16.0
Total	119	100.0

all stem-family forms) that failed to achieve full joint-family elaboration (see table 15.5). Given that full extension required the presence and marriage of two or more male siblings in each generation, in 66 cases, or 55.4 percent of the total (categories 1 and 2 aggregated), realization of the joint-family household ideal was thwarted on biological grounds. Extension was precluded by some degree of choice in 53 cases, or 44.6 percent of the total (categories 3 and 4 aggregated).[8] In only 19, or 16 percent, of the households (category 4) did two or more male siblings marry but fail to coreside.

In sum, of the 247 households that can be traced throughout the 1769–1803 period, 128 (51.8 percent) attained the joint-family ideal at some point in their development cycle; 66, or 26.7 percent of the total, were precluded on biological grounds from doing so. In only 21.5 percent (53) was there an element of choice in the failure to effect full extension, and 19 of these households, or 7.7 percent of the 247 household total, consisted of two or more male siblings who married but subsequently failed to coreside. These results more than bear out the inferential analysis in my 1980 article, which concluded, on the grounds of ethnographic and historical evidence, that the patrilineally extended joint-family household was the social ideal in Agnone despite its low statistical frequency in cross-sectional censuses.

---

8. Determining from the records the extent to which male celibacy was an option (excepting clerics) is impossible. In some cases celibacy surely was imposed by physical or mental infirmity. For the purpose of this analysis, however, every celibate male is treated as if personal preference were involved.

LIFE-COURSE CONSIDERATIONS IN
EIGHTEENTH-CENTURY AGNONE

The life-course approach to family history is characterized by its proponents as an alternative to the foregoing structural analysis of household form
(Elder 1987, 186). Crucial to life-course analysis is the understanding of transitions in the lives of individual family members as they relate both to developments within the family and to those within the wider society that affect
individual careers and familial patterns (Hareven and Masaoka 1988, 272).

Before proceeding with the present analysis I should introduce a caveat.
Without doubt the most successful applications of the life-course approach
involve studies that address recent, and relatively short, time sequences. They
rest heavily on the capacity to elicit retrospective life-history information from
living informants. These self-reported attitudinal and interpretative data are
used to construct (or reconstruct) both the life expectations of the individual
and his or her perceptions of the wider social and cultural setting that give
meaning to life transitions within changing familial milieus.[9] Even so, and as
Glen Elder laments in reference to the well-studied twentieth-century American family, "we generally lack empirical evidence on the normative structuring
of life or family patterns" (Elder 1987, 182). Although this applies even to the
recent and contemporary scene, it can still be approached through the recollections of middle-aged and elderly informants; eliciting comparable contextual
data with which to interpret the extant statistical demographic record of an
eighteenth-century southern Italian town is qualitatively more difficult.

Keeping in mind such a limitation, John Hajnal (1983, 69) provides a framework with which to consider the eighteenth-century Agnone data. He develops
and contrasts the elements of a nuclear-family household system and those
common to the joint family. The nuclear family is characterized by late marriage for both sexes (over 26 years of age for men and over 23 years for women)
and postmarital autonomy of the married couple (neolocality). Servants are
present in many households since single young people are available. In the
joint-family household marriages are generally earlier (under 26 for men and
under 21 for women) and young couples begin life together in an established
household, usually the husband's (virilocality), under the authority of an older
couple. Such units eventually may contain several married couples and often

---

9. In a sense, then, the life-course family historian is most effective when adopting an
"anthropological" methodology. At this point, however, he or she buys into the dilemmas and
debates surrounding the relation between anthropology and history, and particularly the appropriateness of their respective methodologies in dealing with the remote past. Similarly, the
approach is vulnerable to criticisms within historian circles regarding the reliability of life-history
methodology.

split up into two or more households, each containing one or more couples. Hajnal finds that servants are rare in the joint-household system (1983, 98).

The eighteenth-century longitudinal data for Agnone can be examined in light of both Hajnal's household-formation rules and Delille's comparative data for other parts of the kingdom of Naples.[10]

Delille qualifies his discussion of mean age at first marriage for women. First, female marriage occurs much earlier in the monocultural plains regions of agricultural estates than in the mixed-crop, more mountainous, small-holding agrarian settings. Second, in both contexts females tended to marry earlier in the sixteenth and seventeenth centuries than in the eighteenth (Delille 1985, 192–193). We have noted that Agnone conforms ecologically to Delille's mixed-culture, mountainous, agrarian regime. If we compare Agnone with Delille's eighteenth-century data, the mean age at first marriage for women of 22.88 would place the town at the younger end of the spectrum of ecologically similar southern Italian communities, such as Agerola, where the mean age was 25.67. Only San Cipriano, with 20.65 years, reflects a younger female mean age at first marriage.

What might we say with respect to Hajnal's thesis? Is early marriage necessary to the successful formation of the joint-family household? Both the Agnone and other southern Italian data suggest that it may not be or, conversely, that the division between "early" and "late" marriage should be modified somewhat. For males in Agnone the age at first marriage of 25.85 years is right on the cusp between early and late marriage (26 years). For females, however, the 22.88 figure better approximates late marriage (23 years or older) than early marriage (21 or younger) in the Hajnal model. At the same time, it might be argued that in a virilocally biased marital system the mean age at marriage of males is more critical to household formation than that of its female members.

The prevalence of virilocality in the formation of Agnone's joint-family households was discussed earlier. The longitudinal data clearly suggest a pattern where sons married at home and daughters married out. Two related features are that marriage was expected for both sexes and that women who failed to marry appear to have been under considerable (although not inexorable) pressure to leave their natal household. Of 496 adult males in San Emidio who attained the age of thirty-five, 464, or 93.2 percent, married. The 32 celibate males included an undetermined number of Catholic priests.[11] Among

10. The full treatment of this data base, which would support comprehensive multivariate analysis, remains to be done.

11. Unlike the 1753 onciario, the stato delle anime records do not list occupations. It is therefore impossible to determine the number of clerics encompassed in this longitudinal analysis.

the 449 adult women who left their natal households for any reason (marriage, profession of religious vows, domestic service, migration, and so on) the mean age at departure was 23.1 years. Comparing this with the mean age of (in-marrying) women of 22.88 years, we suspect that young adult women were expected to leave their natal households. The rare exceptions were a spinster who continued to live with her married brothers or a childless widow who returned to her father's household.

Virilocality, of course, by definition places a premium on the generational continuity of a particular family line within a particular household. Delille describes in eloquent terms the emphasis on the *casa* and the way in which virilocal residence reinforces the patriline or *casali* (lineage) in southern Italian society (1985, 90–111). Such concerns appear to have been quite pronounced in eighteenth-century Agnone. The question then becomes how life's vagaries were dealt with in order to effect social continuity within the household in each generation? Stated differently, what exceptions provided flexibility to deal with real-world exigencies and thereby to reaffirm the logic of the rules?

Essential to the normal functioning of the virilocal joint-family-household system was the premise that a married couple would have at least two sons who survived to adulthood, married, and assumed postmarital residence in their father's household. As we have seen, however, certain biological, psychologi-cal, and social factors could work against the formation of the joint family in a particular generation within a given household (see table 15.5). Let us consider certain demographic anomalies faced by some of the households in the San Emidio sample, the life-course characteristics of persons within them who were key to their resolution, and their ultimate disposition.

First we might examine the situation of households lacking suitable male heirs. Within the logic of the system this called into question their ability to effect social continuity at all, let alone to realize the fully elaborated joint-family household in the generation in question. An obvious way to deal with this contingency was to permit one or more daughters to marry at home. Indeed, as noted earlier, in two of the three cases in which two daughters did so they married brothers, thereby reaffirming the patrilineal bias of the system. More commonly, however, one daughter would marry and thus provide the basis of a nuclear-, or at most extended-family, household for that generation. A straight-forward example is that of the Petitto family. Antonio and his wife, Angela, had four daughters and two sons. Their boy Donato died when he was two years old, and their eldest daughter, Cecilia, died at age eighteen. Daughters Prosede and Concezza, second and third in the family in terms of age order, married out at nineteen and eighteen years of age respectively in the same year (1778). This left Antonio and Angela (then ages fifty and forty-six) as heads of a nuclear-family household containing son Vincenzo (age ten) and Maria Orazia (age five). Thirteen years later Vincenzo died. In 1794 twenty-one-year-old Maria Orazia married Filippo, age twenty-six. She and Filippo resided with her elderly parents, forming a stem-family household.

Another variation of the theme was for an elder sister with juvenile siblings to marry and remain at home temporarily until her brothers were old enough to wed. Such was the case with twenty-year-old Maria Anna Di Ciocco, who married in 1797. Her husband, Giosue, moved into the household headed by her father Cristanziano, then fifty-seven years of age. Present in the household at the time were Rosa, Cristanziano's second wife, and Maria Anna's younger siblings from that marriage (four girls and two boys). Her two brothers at this juncture were five and two years of age respectively—almost a generation removed from marriageable age. Maria Anna's marriage was obviously the means of bridging this gap.

Equally interesting in the Di Ciocco case is the absence of other potential players. Cristanziano was widowed in 1776 at age thirty-five. The following year he married his second wife, Rosa, who in 1778 gave birth to Maria Anna. The infant was born into a household that contained her fifteen-year-old stepsister Lucia, her thirteen-year-old stepbrother Lonardo, and her father's twenty-one-year-old niece Maria Antonia. We do not know how Maria Antonia came to be in the household. She could have been the orphaned, siblingless remnant of a *frérèche* household in Cristanziano's generation. She may have been Cristanziano's sister's daughter, providing domestic service to the household. In any event, at age twenty-three she left. In 1787 Lucia, age twenty-four, also left. More intriguing is the case of Lonardo, who in 1795, two years before Maria Anna's marriage, left the household as well. His departure was not predictable within the logic of the system. He was thirty years old at the time, but only twelve years younger than his stepmother, Rosa, who was in turn fifteen years younger than Cristanziano. Was this a case of a younger second wife manipulating her older husband to the detriment of a fully mature stepson whose prospects were reduced because the household's resources were "warehoused" for the new wife's own male progeny? Did she make life impossible for Lonardo? We will never know for certain, but we could apply the same lifecourse speculation to similar anomalies in the Agnone data.

The system was also capable of grinding out its logic to the bitter end. Indeed, the solitaries were usually the last flicker of a doomed household's dying flame. Consider the luckless Giacoma. In 1772, when she was forty-six years of age, her only son, Mario (twenty-four years old), died and her daughter Euforia (age twenty-one) married out. In 1780 her second daughter, Anna, then twenty-eight, married out. Two years later daughters Santa (twenty-nine) and Maria (twenty-four) likewise married into other house-holds. Giacoma was then fifty-eight, and she resided alone for eight years until her death in 1791.

Certain comments may be made with respect to realization of the male aspect of the recruitment process. Some males did leave their natal household; witness Lonardo Di Ciocco. Unlike his circumstances, however, males were most likely to depart from "full" households. The prime consideration here is that patrilineal extension of households was finite, particularly in an urban setting totally lacking the frontierlike conditions that have favored such exten-sion elsewhere (compare Hammel 1972). In every generation the largest fami-lies provided candidates both for maintenance of the lineal joint-family ar-rangement and for formation of neolocal nuclear households.

Again, the life-course considerations of the players seem to have been prime factors in the decision to stay or go. There is, for example, the Gualdieri household. When first encountered in the 1769 stato delle anime, it consisted of Giuseppe (age fifty-eight), his wife, Domenica (fifty-two), their son Nazario (twenty-seven) and his wife Santa (twenty), their unmarried daughters Angela (eighteen) and Teodora (thirteen), and their son Nicola (ten). The following year Nazario and Santa had their first child, Giovanni. By the time Giovanni was a young adult he was the eldest sibling of two surviving sisters and two brothers. Meanwhile, in 1783 his twenty-four-year-old uncle, Nicola, married a woman his own age and brought her into the household. Over the next eleven years the couple had four children, after which Nicola's wife died and he immediately remarried (a union that by 1803 was to produce six children). In 1793 Giovanni, now twenty-three, married out of his natal household, which at the time contained fifteen members.

Individual males might therefore choose to leave a fully elaborated joint-family household. That solution for overcrowding, however, was not nearly as common (or as effective) as the departure of married couples and their off-spring. Indeed, it is clear from the Agnone data that the deaths of the elderly couple triggered the beginning of the end for the joint-family household. Stated differently, the bond that resulted in coresidence was inter- rather than intra-generational. Married sons stayed with their fathers rather than with their brothers.[12] Thus, although there were exceptions, the frérèche household de-void of a founding couple in the ascending generation was a rarity. As long as

---

12. Indeed, this is reflected in the naming system by which a man was expected to name his son after his father, and possibly a daughter as well (e.g., Giuseppe, son of Antonio and Santa, would name his firstborn son Antonio, his firstborn daughter Santa, and possibly his second daughter Antonia). Giuseppe was not expected to name his sons after his brothers.

one of the parents remained alive the unit tended to hold together; once both were deceased it was unlikely to endure for more than a couple of years.

In the interim, however, it was not uncommon for one or more married brothers to leave a particularly full household. Thus households with several male offspring in a generation rarely attained their maximum logical extension. If four brothers married, for example, they were unlikely to all live in one household, though they might do so briefly. That is, the youngest brother might begin his married life "at home" but then leave a year or two later after the birth of his first child.

Obviously, given the logic of the system, a household normally passed between the generations down a particular patriline. We have noted that in the absence of a male heir transmission in one generation might be through a daughter. Although this would alter the patronym associated with a casa it would not interrupt the bloodline. In some instances, however, social continuity could be effected in more byzantine fashion, for example, in the case of the Pietro Mastrostefano household. We first observe it in 1769 when Pietro (age unlisted) died, leaving Reparata (age twenty-seven) a widow and the single parent of two young daughters, Lucia (four years) and Giuseppa (one year), and pregnant with a son (Giuseppe). The following year Guiseppa died. In 1772 Reparata, at age thirty, married Domenico (age twenty-nine) and bore him three daughters: Maria, Saia, and Columba. Four years later Reparata's widowed mother, Rosa (age fifty-three years), joined the household. At age forty-one, Reparata died in 1783, leaving Domenico to care for his stepchildren, Lucia (nineteen) and Giuseppe (fifteen), and his natural daughters, Maria (eleven), Columba (eight), and Saia (four). Rosa then left the household (perhaps because of bad blood between her and her son-in-law). With a houseful (not to mention a handful), the widowed Domenico married the twenty-year-old Rosanna, who brought her two-year-old daughter, Concezza, into the household. Rosanna's age suggests that Concezza was likely illegitimate rather than orphaned.

Having provided Domenico with three children, Rosanna died in 1794, at age thirty. The following year the fifty-year-old Domenico married his third wife, Teodora (age twenty-four). At this point the twenty-six-year-old unmarried Giuseppe (son of the long-since-deceased Pietro and Reparata) left the household. Domenico and Teodora began a young family in a household that still contained Maria (age twenty-three) and Saia (fourteen), daughters of Domenico and Reparata, Concezza (eleven), daughter of Rosanna, and Giuseppe (seven), son of Domenico and Rosanna. By 1802 all the children except twenty-three-year-old Saia had either died or left the household. That year Teodora's widowed mother, Maria (age sixty-three), moved into the household of her son-in-law Domenico, a man only five years her junior.

What is interesting is that Pietro Mastrostefano's household passed to Domenico's patriline via Reparata's marriage to him. Because of the deaths and departures of all of Reparata's children with both Pietro and Domenico, however, the household ultimately passed into the hands of persons with whom the founding figure, Pietro, had no direct consanguineal or affinal link. It should be noted that reference is to the household's coresidential constitution and not necessarily to its legal disposition. Ownership of the dwelling may have stayed in Pietro's patriline, with Domenico and his successive wives living there as tenants. Pietro may himself have been a tenant of a third party. We have no way of knowing.

This case raises the question of widowhood. Reparata was a widow with small children for three years before she married Domenico, whereas Domenico subsequently married his second and third wives within a year of being widowed. In microcosm this is the pattern of widowhood and its consequences in eighteenth-century Agnone. That is, widows were slow to remarry if they did at all, whereas widowers were much more likely to remarry—and soon. Of 150 widows in the sample only 24, or 16 percent, remarried, and they were generally young widows with small children. Thus 9 of the 17 who were widowed before the age of thirty remarried. Conversely, 81 of the 159 widowers in the sample, or 57 percent, remarried. On the average they did so within two years of being widowed. Of the 49 men widowed by age forty, 46 remarried. The mean age when widowed of those who failed to remarry was sixty. The youngest was thirty-four, and only 16 of the 78 men in the non-remarrying sample were under age fifty when widowed.

The average age of males at second marriage was forty-one, whereas that of their wives was thirty. Widowers therefore tended to marry somewhat older women than the Agnone norm, both spinsters and young widows (who sometimes had their own young children). Young widows with children might provide the solution for households facing a succession crisis. The Ingratta household, for example, in 1791 was headed by Giuseppe (sixty-nine years) and his spouse, Vincenza (fifty-seven), coresiding with celibate sons Carmine (thirty-five) and Pietro (twenty-five). Vincenza died, leaving the three adult males to fend for themselves. Carmine, slow to marry up to that point and possibly a confirmed bachelor, immediately married the thirty-five-year-old widow Pasqua, who moved into the household with four children (the oldest age thirteen).

From the records we cannot determine Pasqua's circumstances before marrying Carmine Ingratta. She may have been widowed after she and her first husband departed a full household or in the aftermath of its dissolution following the death of his parents. A woman still in her active childbearing years, she may have been unwilling to accept a life of celibacy as a member of her deceased husband's household. It is always possible that she could not get along with her in-laws. In any event, her circumstances, although not unique, were unusual. Once a woman was widowed and one or more of her children reached adolescence, she was unlikely to ever remarry or to leave her deceased husband's household.

Under certain circumstances affinal ties could be activated to effect coresidence. There are three examples of daughters taking in their widowed mothers. And Margherita (fifty-two years), widowed head of her deceased husband's household, in 1773 took in her younger sister Nicoletta (forty-eight years). Nicoletta was either celibate or a childless widow. Although Margherita died shortly thereafter, Nicoletta remained, until her death at age seventy-two, a member of her married nephew's and, ultimately, married grandnephew's household.

Such examples of affinal extension seem to have corresponded to the personal needs of an individual rather than to those of a household. If the household's continuity or well-being was called into question, a solution within the patriline was more common. The apparently childless Bernardino Petillo (age fifty-five) and his wife, Domenica (fifty-three), for example, in 1777 brought into their household Bernardino's niece Lucia (twenty-eight), her husband, Pietro (twenty-eight), and their two children. By 1800 Bernardino, Domenica, and Pietro were all deceased, and Lucia was the widowed head of the household, which contained her four celibate children (the eldest age twenty-two).

Domestic servants could, theoretically, provide an additional source of at least short-term relief for households in demographic "crisis." Hajnal notes that servants are unusual in joint-family household systems, no more than 2 percent of the population (1983, 98). The Agnone data support this contention. The presence of a "stranger" in the household was extremely rare. Even then patronyms may mask the servant's kinship (for example, a father's sister's daughter, who would bear a different surname). Indeed, the domestic servants who were present in eighteenth-century Agnone appear to have been the exclusive prerogative of the wealthy. This conclusion is based on the 1753 onciario, where only a few professional households are listed as having domestic servants.

There are two lessons to be learned from the Agnone data. The first is that we must be sensitive to any incidence of household extension when analyzing population lists. In a sense the nuclear family may be regarded as a structural given whether or not it is also a social construct. That is, the near-human universal recourse to marriage and the coresidence of spouses with their off-spring meet the definitional requirements of the simple or nuclear family, an arrangement achieved quite comfortably by two young adults without refer-ence to the circumstances of their predecessors. The same may not be said of more elaborated forms such as the stem or joint family. In the stem family, one son or daughter must survive until marriageable age, contract marriage, and then opt (or be forced) to coreside with his or her parents. Under the joint-family arrangement, two or more offspring must survive, marry, and coreside with their aged parents. Both systems obviously are vulnerable to such demo-graphic factors as fertility rates, mean age at marriage, and life expectancy. In societies with short life expectancy a person might indeed be more likely to die than to survive long enough to become the patriarch or matriarch of a stem- or joint-family household.[13] Such considerations prompted Hajnal to state that "the joint-household systems did not normally produce a situation where the majority of households were joint at any one time, though there may have been joint-family household systems which have operated in that way. However, under a joint-household system, the majority of people were members of a joint household at some stage in their lives" (1983, 69). The longitudinal data for Agnone considered earlier certainly confirm this statement. Whether a particular family-household form constitutes a societal norm, then, is more an ethnographic and historical question than a statistical one.

The second lesson to be derived from the foregoing analysis is the hetero-geneity of family systems on the Italic peninsula. In the early years of family history studies Italy bedeviled attempts to extend to the Continent the sug-gestion, based on English evidence, that the nuclear-family household was the characteristic domestic unit of the European past. Similarly, the heterogeneity of the Italian evidence frustrated the subsequent attempt to discern a Mediterra-nean household system in counterdistinction to a northwest European one (Kertzer and Brettell 1987). Only recently, however, has the full complexity of Italian family systems become apparent. Just as Marzio Barbagli (this volume) finds critical differences between the nuclear-family households of Sicily and Sardinia, it seems clear that the joint-family-household system described for Agnone differs considerably from that found in the *mezzadria* or sharecropping regions of central and northern Italy.

David Kertzer (1989) describes a situation in Emilia characterized by the durable joint-family household, where married brothers continue to coreside

13. This point was made originally with reference to stem-family households by Berkner (1972) in his classic article on Austrian household formation.

well beyond the deaths of their parents. The underlying rationale is the need for labor. Under the sharecropping system the absentee landlord prefers a tenant family with several adult male members who farm the property most effectively. A household undergoing demographic constriction runs the risk of being dispossessed. Kertzer is therefore able to report an incidence of multiple-family households greater than 70 percent (1984, 5), one of the highest-known frequencies in the world. Carla Bianco (1988), analyzing the mezzadria system in a Tuscan community, reports that there are finite limits on a household's ability to expand given its available resource base. At a certain point fragmentation is likely to occur with one or more junior married sons leaving the household. This usually transpires well after the death of the patriarch or *capoccia,* however, and is seemingly not triggered by it. Bianco also reports that male celibacy and delayed marriages are common means of stabilizing an adult male labor force on the farm, thereby meeting the expectations of the absentee landlord.

Clearly, such a system differs from that described for Agnone, where there is little sharecropping, where the death of the patriarch initiates household fission, and where almost all males marry. It is therefore incumbent on the family historian to further elucidate the range of variation, the causes, and the dynamics of the several social forms that are currently considered under the rubric of the Italian joint-family-household system.

Chapter 16

ANTHONY H. GALT

Marital Property in an Apulian Town during the Eighteenth and Early Nineteenth Centuries

This chapter describes and accounts for change in marriage assigns and related considerations in an eighteenth- and early-nineteenth-century peasant cultural setting, Locorotondo in the province of Bari, Apulia. Primarily it concerns the transition from a marriage rule whereby peasant women received housing from their parents to the expectation that newly wed men be assigned family dwellings. Ethnographers who leaf the dusty pages of such documents as marriage contracts especially know that there was far more to social life than can be gleaned from a record keeper's pen scratchings; where documents are now silent, people expressed loud concern. Because of this, my documentary interpretations partially depend on immersion in ethnographic knowledge about more recent southern Italian cases, in particular twentieth-century Locorotondo. This chapter thus intends to demonstrate ethnohistorical methods as well as to contribute understandings about family formation.

The enthnohistorian William Fenton coined the term *upstreaming* to label the interpretation of the past using more recent materials.[1] Upstreaming rests on three premises: (1) major cultural patterns often tend to be stable over long

I should like to thank George Saunders for his comments, the organizers of and participants in the Bellagio conference, and the anonymous reader of this volume. I conducted ethnographic and archival research on Locorotondo during 1981–1982 and again during the summers of 1986 and 1989. I am grateful for funding from the National Science Foundation, the University of Wisconsin—Green Bay, and the National Endowment for the Humanities. I treat the town's development more fully in my book (Galt 1991), to which I refer the interested reader.

1. Fenton may have been influenced by Marc Bloch (1953, 47), who used a similar metaphor to argue for the use of present in the interpretation of the past.

periods, (2) it is best to proceed from what we know—from the more familiar—toward the less-known past, and (3) a good test of sources and inferences about a past society consists of an ethnological sense about societies in general (Fenton, 1949, 236).

Following these premises heuristically, we can presume that some major family formation strategies have remained stable in Apulia over several hundred years, and that some have changed. Going upstream must allow for a shifting stream bed. Therefore, we must attempt to understand the direction of those shifts from a general understanding of southern Italian and local historical context, which should help determine what we can safely project from the ethnographic present into the past. Second, in dealing with the less literate in the Italian past—the peasants and lower-ranking townspeople—we face the problem that social class and regional prejudices often prevented understanding of subaltern populations by the elite record makers. The test of ethnological verisimilitude helps here. Fenton's third premise also suggests the use of the method called ethnographic analogy—the careful use of what is known from recent sources about cultural patterns of covariance to make inferences about the past. Having only scraps of evidence about illiterates in past Italian society, we must rely extensively on inference to understand their cultural systems. Some ethnographic generalizations are beginning to be discernible for southern Italy, and if such generalizations are reasonable, they can be used in conjunction with historical documents to ask questions and make inferences about the past.

Locorotondo, with a population of approximately 11,000, crests a hill in the southeastern end of the province of Bari on the edge of a plateau, the Murgia dei Trulli, which overlooks the Adriatic coast. This town and those neighboring are particularly interesting for two reasons: they lie in the heart of the famous zone of *trulli,* or cone-roofed rural houses, and they exhibit high proportions of small-holder viticulture coupled with an unusual pattern of peasant residence in the countryside. Elsewhere in southern Italy, especially in Apulia, the agrotown is much more common, and few peasants permanently live in the countryside.

Emphyteusis contracts were key in the development of this unusual pattern. Through these perpetual-lease contracts that stipulated transformation of land into vineyards, land began to diffuse into small proprietor hands as early as the late seventeenth century. The last decade of the eighteenth century and the first four decades of the nineteenth witnessed a significant expansion of land division, formation of small-holder properties, and movement of peasants from within the town walls into rural residence. From around 37 percent of the total population in 1811 (ACL-SP 1810–1811), rural residence expanded to 66 percent by the mid-nineteenth century. Those who took up such residence specialized in raising grapes for the wine market alongside subsistence crops. The thin rocky soils in the karst landscape, coupled with low rainfall that was immediately absorbed into deep underground water courses, forced many gentlemen who owned larger pieces of land to divide their properties. By doing so they realized steady emphyteutical rents from peasants, who labored extensively to transform the land into vineyards. This process continued throughout the nineteenth century, inspired again in the 1870s by the demand for Italian wine created by the death of vineyards in France because of phylloxera.[2] Division continued until the 1950s, although sale to returning emigrants with savings replaced emphyteusis in the early twentieth century. Peasants could expect land to become available on the market and attached strong values to "making a step ahead," as one old informant put it, in property acquisition for their children. By the mid-nineteenth century almost the entire peasant population of the town lived in the countryside in rural hamlets, and the town population consisted of gentlemen (who continued to own medium-sized estates surrounded by peasant small holdings), a few professionals and merchants, and various artisans.

CAPITOLI MATRIMONIALI

My interest in these patterns necessitated documentary research involving questions of family as well as ethnographic and oral history interviewing. The marriage contracts, or *capitoli matrimoniali,* I collected to compare with listings of households and property holders in three cross-sectional documents—the *catasto onciario* (ASB-CO 1749), the *catasto provvisorio* (ASB-CP 1816), and the census (*statistica*) of 1811 (ACL-SP 1810–1811), date from the mid-eighteenth and early nineteenth centuries. Tracing marital property usages farther is difficult because as early as the 1820s marriage contracts among peasants are rarely represented in the notarial contracts. I have notes describing 20 contracts for the decade before the eighteenth-century cadastre (1739–1749), 72 drawn up between 1755 and 1759, and 217 drafted during the decade preceding the Napoleonic census of 1811 (ASB-AN, various dates). Explaining the difference in numbers of contracts from these periods is difficult. Some mid-eighteenth-century contracts may be missing—there was no regulation about depositing

2. The pattern of emphyteusis and peasant transfer to the countryside began in Locorotondo in the late eighteenth century and was emulated in such neighboring towns as Martina Franca and Cisternino as the French phylloxera attack created enormous market demands for wine internationally.

them in a central archive. More to the point, not everyone had recourse to a notary. The mid-eighteenth-century data therefore represent only a small proportion of marriages, although various wealth levels are represented in the sample. The early-nineteenth-century data seem to record nearly all marriages during the decade in question (1801–1811). I also recorded a few contracts outside these two eras for comparative purposes.

Eighteenth-century notaries drew up marriage contracts in front of the bride and groom to be and their family representatives, often the parents and sometimes elder siblings or an uncle. Several witnesses, one representing a royal magistrate having jurisdiction over contracts, and often a priest or two, signed. The trip to the notary was the culmination of earlier oral agreements and negotiations. In the opening paragraphs the notary defined the parties to the contract and added that they would marry according to the commandments of God, the Holy Roman Catholic Church, and the decrees of the Council of Trent, but he set no precise marriage date. The notary referred to the prospective bride as a *vergine in cappillis,* a marriageable and virginal girl.[3] An itemized list of the bride's dotal goods was attached. Such a list for landowning peasants of the era typically included: a new wooden bed frame and straw mattress, three sheets, a fringed blue woolen blanket, three pillows and pillowcases, four blouses, three aprons, three skirts, three bodices, three tablecloths and three napkins, a shawl embroidered with silk, a veil, a new pine chest, a new bench, a new rolling pin, five pounds of copper with which to have a cauldron and a frying pan made, a pair of chains for hanging pots in the hearth, an iron spit, a cheese grater, and the bride—dressed "ordinarily."

A list of dotal buildings and land itemized according to surface area, cropping, and location generally followed. During this era brides usually brought houses to their marriages, at least the promise of part of a house, or perhaps rent for several years. If no house or lands were mentioned the bride's parents usually promised a sum to be given to the groom for the purchase of immovable goods *(beni stabili)*—a house or lands. The wording of some contracts makes clear that brides were expected to bring houses, for example, when parents declared that they would provide rent "instead of the house." In the 1755–1759 span of 72 contracts, exactly half assigned the bride a house, rights in a house, or a sum to be used specifically for housing. With a single exception these were town houses, not rural dwellings.

3. This term refers to the custom by which an unmarried woman wore her hair up until marriage. Whether this legal term was actually reflected in everyday dress in Locorotondo is difficult to say, but the custom did survive elsewhere in the south until the beginning of this century (Ungari 1970, 217).

Many contracts note that the items provided by the parents or guardians of the bride constituted a part of her eventual inheritance, and a few specify that she renounces any further claim on it. According to John Davis's suggestions about marriage property terminology for Mediterranean contexts (1977, 184), the *dote,* as the contracts label it, should then be considered as a "settlement." It is also clear that a system of partible inheritance prevailed among peasants, because efforts to balance the settlements of siblings crop up in the documents. Male and female siblings received land equally, and women received houses if possible. In receipt of the bride's settlement the groom promised to keep the dotal properties *salve e indenne* (preserved and undamaged) and to "make restitution or reassignment in every case of restitution and reassignment," which meant that they returned to the bride's family if she died childless. Although the 1749 cadastre recorded a married couple's property as pooled, a wife transmitted dotal property to her heirs. Their permission, and assent from a royal magistrate, was necessary to alienate dotal property.

These contracts stated that in contemplation of the marriage, the bride's representative assigned her dowry to the groom "according to the uses and customs of this land and Province of Bari in which people live by Lombard law."[4] But by the seventeenth century Lombard law had been superseded by the Prammatica "De Antefato" of 1617, which brought some uniformity to marital property usages in the kingdom of Naples, so this statement was mostly an empty formula (De Stefano 1979, 5). There may be a remote trace of the *morgengabe,* "morning gift" to the bride, which became her absolute property, in the groom's parents' assigns of jewelry and sometimes clothing to the bride, but no indication that these were bestowed after the wedding night in the old Lombard sense.[5] Notaries recorded these assigns separately after the itemization of her settlement, as given by the groom "for love," as "ornaments."

In a separate codicil the antefato, as defined in 1617, was assigned to the bride over the groom's eventual property. Legally it consisted of her widow's rights to usufruct over one-third of her husband's property, but this was never precisely stated in the contract. If she remarried, or if she had already been "kissed," the antefato was reduced to half that sum (Ungari 1970, 214). Upon her death, rights to the antefato reverted to her husband's line (Dibenedetto 1976, 210).[6]

---

4. "Secondo l'uso e consuetudine di questa terra, e Provincia di Bari, in cui si vive Iure Longobardarum."

5. Within the twentieth century, however, the mothers of the newlywed couple inspected the sheets for signs of the bride's lost virginity the morning after the wedding night. Lack of evidence could lead to annulment.

6. One notary always refers to the antefato using the old Lombard term *meffio,* but clearly the

In summary, to the marriage a bride brought her settlement, consisting of linens and utensils, a bed, a house (if possible), and lands. According to Gérard Delille's recent analysis, this pattern was typical during the early modern period for the Apulian region, and contrasted sharply with those in Campania, where women often received only trousseau and cash as marriage settlements (1985). In addition, the bride received gifts from the groom that were untied and were to remain her property, and widow's rights during her lifetime over part of his estate.

In some eighteenth-century contracts, the groom's parents or guardian provided part of his settlement at marriage.[7] In a few cases (one in the earlier series and five in the later), parents provided a temporary settlement with the stipulation that upon their deaths their children pool the immovable property again and redivide it. Several other contracts fully indicate a settlement, but only if the newly formed family decided to reside neolocally—the implication is that they were going to start married life in a patrilocal coresident household and participate in the farming of undivided family lands. The catasto onciario of 1749, however, which was a family census as well as a tax roll, recorded only four such households in the entire town; three consisted of a parental couple residing with a son and his wife and the other of three coresident brothers and their families.[8]

The groom's settlement typically consisted of land, rural buildings, and such capital as threshing floors, grape-crushing areas, and cisterns, plus agricultural tools. In only one of the 1739—1749 contracts did a groom bring urban property to the marriage. And in only one of the 72 contracts drafted between 1755 and 1759 did a father specify that he would build his son a house in the countryside (the custom to come, as we will see below). Richer peasants, who in addition to cultivating their own lands often sharecropped the local gentlemen's estates and husbanded their animals, sometimes provided sons with a few head of livestock and seed for the first year.

The large sample of early-nineteenth-century contracts reproduces, except for the clause about Lombard law, the general features of earlier counterparts. These chaotic times, however—late-eighteenth-century economic crises, the aftermath of 1799, the onset of the French Decade—clearly affected parents' ability to provide their children with dowries, especially those including

---

assign does not constitute a gift to the bride from the groom or his parents through her father, according to the original Lombard sense (ASB-AN 1734–1784).

7. Half of the contracts in the small 1739–1749 series contain this provision, but in the 1755–1759 series only 16 out of 72 specify the groom's settlement.

8. See Galt 1986 for an analysis of social structure in Locorotondo at mid-eighteenth century that is based on the catasto onciario and other documents.

houses. Many contracts promised the bride sums of money with which to buy immovable goods, but only to be paid to the marrying couple in yearly installments with interest. Beginning marriage with a house would have been impossible for most couples planning to reside within the town walls.

Clauses that suggested the possibility of extended family postmarital residence were rare. Among 217 contracts, only 23 indicated permanent or temporary rural coresidence with a parental head. (Others gave a widowed mother rights to reside with the couple, but her son or son-in-law would be the household head.) Of those multiple-family arrangements, 19 favored patrilocality, and only 4 suggested matrilocality. In each case the contract itemized what the couple would receive from the parents should they decide to form a separate household. One contract specified that patrilocal coresidence would last only until the following August fifteenth, after the harvest.

Expectations about housing were changing, probably reflecting the expansion of population from the town into the countryside in response to the possibility of improving land into vineyards. Thirty-one grooms received newly constructed or remodeled rural houses from their fathers. Fourteen brides received rural housing, but most of these probably had no brothers. Yet a greater proportion of brides (twenty-five) than grooms (ten) received town dwelling space. There seems to have been a trend toward providing males who would reside in the countryside with housing at marriage. This would become the norm as reported by twentieth-century rural informants.

That 136 contracts mention no housing suggests that renting had become much more common. In the 1811 census 41 percent of town households rented their dwelling space. Those who lived outside the walls—37 percent of the total—lived either in trulli they owned or on the larger estates as sharecropping *massari*. Rental of housing had increased by five times since 1749, when only 8 percent of the entire household population rented. Population had doubled over the sixty years that separate the two documents, and this, added to the economic crises of the last decade of the eighteenth century, had stressed the supply of housing and driven up costs. Construction in town must have been expensive; the contracts never refer to building a town house for a daughter. Contracts that formed rural marriages, however, often mention building a trullo for a son or adding space to the parental dwelling to form a new hearth.

MARRIAGE STRATEGIES

Property settlement at marriage is but part of a set of adaptive strategies having to do with the family cycle. The concept of adaptive strategy was elaborated by John Bennett (1976, 271–272), who argues that people in sociocultural systems evolve conscious plans of action for dealing with the constraints and opportunities of their social and natural environments and that sometimes those strategies become custom.[9] For the period considered, marriage settlement documents are the only surviving artifacts of strategies surrounding property transmission between parents and children, their continuing relationships, and the reproduction of households. These sets of strategies are intricately interrelated. Among small proprietor peasants we are likely to find such concerns tightly circumscribed by sets of rules and institutional constraints because vital wealth is involved. Pino Arlacchi (1980), who compares peasant families and social structure under three differing economic regimes in twentieth-century Calabria, suggests this strongly. His Cosentino peasantry, which historically consisted of small proprietors, had more elaborate and rigid rules about questions of courtship, mate selection, parental control over unmarried children, and marriage settlement than did the peasantries of the Crotonese area, who were rural proletarians, or those of the Piana di Gioia Tauro, an area of rampant entrepreneurial activity and constantly shifting fortunes. My work in Locorotondo and previous experience on the island of Pantelleria, another small-proprietor viticulturalist setting, point in the same direction.

Recent marital property strategies for Locorotondo may cast light upon the past. After 1960 the economy of the region of Apulia and of the *mezzogiorno* in general became less favorable for peasant farming. But before that, in an existence now locally thought of as traditional, the provisioning of newly forming household enterprises was a central life's purpose for small-proprietor parents. The ideal was to live in and to reproduce households that produced most of their own subsistence needs—olive oil, cheese, wine, wheat, fava beans, fruit, and a little meat, as well as fibers for weaving. Locorotondo specialized in viticulture, and each household aspired to market the bulk of the grapes it produced.

Peasant couples developed strategies about providing for their children, and the reputation of parents greatly depended on how well they accomplished this.[10] From the peasant's point of view, Locorotondo was an expanding universe in which for nearly two centuries the elite had been sloughing off poor, but improvable, land that could be captured into peasant small holdings.

Partible inheritance prevailed. Their eventual inheritances in part formed

9. See Ortner 1984, 157, for a similar description.
10. Such values persist, but as the overwhelming economic changes of the post–World War II era penetrated, new opportunities, contradictions, and problems arose.

marital property settlements for both men and women, and the parents of the groom hoped to provide a newly constructed house for the young couple. The ability to "systemize" children obviously was an accurate reflection of parental success at solving the problem of adequately expanding and managing the family patrimony. People respected the successful farmer, and providing family subsistence and profiting from growing grapes were highly desirable goals that defined honor along with questions of honesty and male and female sexual behavior. Although the trousseau was not publicly displayed, there was much gossip about whether the bride would receive the requisite number of *panni* (cloth items)—*panni sei* (a trousseau of six) was the norm among country women during the interwar years.

Marriage settlements, not to mention the cost of the wedding itself, required large amounts of property for each child. Parents planned years ahead to meet such exigencies. Several factors entered into this strategizing behavior. Amassing a daughter's *dote* and building a house for a son tended to delay marriage for most people until their mid-twenties, and this attenuated fertility. Even so, late-nineteenth and early-twentieth-century families produced a modal number of five or six children who survived the first few years, and living women now past childbearing years in the Locorotondese countryside most commonly produced two or three children. Rules were strict about marrying women off before their brothers, and people were expected to marry according to their age. Parents saw daughters as something as a liability; marrying them off well was more of a worry, especially because they were the passive partner during courtship. Also, the longer they remained unmarried the more concern there was about their potentially lost virginity and the consequent damage to family honor (however unlikely, given the care with which girls were watched). "Daughters are like checks," the local folk analogy goes, "the sooner you cash them the better!"

Although for a girl to sew and embroider the things in her trousseau took time, acquiring land and resources to build houses for males also took a long time. This was done with a master *trullaro*'s supervision, but also with family labor—brothers expected one another's help. For years before the marriage sons dutifully consigned their earnings (at hired vineyard work) to their father for this purpose and for acquiring land for marriage, if necessary. Girls, who often worked at seasonal migrant agricultural labor before their marriages, did likewise.

Because marriage could be dissolved only unsatisfactorily through legal separation and at the risk of family dishonor, and for reasons having to do with care of parents (detailed below), mate selection was extraordinarily important in Locorotondo. Betrothal was a serious step circumscribed by rigid expectations. Young people began the process by showing mutual interest, subtly expressed through glances and gestures from a distance, and young men approached young women slowly, over a matter of weeks. Parents and siblings became aware of this and activated networks of relatives and friends to find out about the spouses their children had in mind, and about their families. Parents were concerned that the partners their children chose be hard workers who would bring resources to the marriage. The parents of prospective grooms also concerned themselves with whether the future bride would take care of them in old age. Since property was all-important in marriage, young men and women from richer families were desirable catches. Mothers warned their sons about females desirous of an advantageous match who might purchase love magic from local sorcerers and administer it secretly to unsuspecting young men.

Families took engagement very seriously. For a woman there was little flexibility about breaking up, which would raise questions about her virginity. Betrothal meant that she could not, under any circumstances, talk casually to any other eligible man, and informants of both sexes related instances of relationships broken by young men because of seemingly innocent conversations. A woman who lost her fiancé had to face the distinct possibility that she would not marry, but a young man who broke it off with his finacée was not stigmatized. A young man who too casually considered leaving his betrothed, however, risked her curse or that of her mother, especially if there was any question about the fiancée's virginity. He also ran the risk that she might visit the local sorcerer and procure a spell to do him harm, or even cause his death.

Engagement was undertaken seriously by people in their early twenties and not easily broken. Parents and siblings consequently exercised great care about individual and family reputations before betrothal and talk about property transfers began. In particular, the brothers of marrying children were consulted because they had wide networks in the generation of the prospective fiancés and could provide good intelligence. The engagement period was typified by rules about visits and by tightly chaperoned contact between the couple. They exchanged customary gifts at holidays, and men visited their prospective in-laws' homes for dinner on Thursdays and Sundays.

Marital property transactions in Locorotondo (and I suspect elsewhere) concerned children's continuing relationships with their parents as much as the founding of new households. As children left home, so did their labor, and as children took over fields, the subsistence and income-generating base of the parental household diminished. Eventually parents grew old enough to require help, and later perhaps full care. The expectation in Locorotondo was that parental property be divided upon the marriage of the last remaining child. Thereafter children were to support their parents through *mantenemènte* (maintenance), which consisted of an allowance in foodstuffs—wheat, wine, olive oil, favas—to be provided periodically by each child. The parental house with all furnishings and farm equipment passed on under a rule of male ultimogeniture, which usually meant that the youngest son's dwelling initially consisted of rooms added to it, including a separate hearth. The youngest son and especially his wife provided care and companionship for the retired couple, at least until their ill health made this too burdensome. Lone parents, unable to look after themselves (notably men who did not take care of domestic chores), went *mési mési* (month by month) among their children of both sexes, circulating from one household to another.

For Locorotondese peasants the major connection between marital property arrangements and parental care was a strong sense of reciprocity. Parents believed that because they devoted their energies to their children's marriages, they deserved respect and care in old age. The worst violation of the local value system was for children to rupture that expectation, and supernatural consequences could befall them for so doing. Wronged parents might curse their children. Worse, God himself was believed to punish errant children not only with damnation but also with sickness or misfortune while they were alive, through retributive power known in dialect as *malapotènse de Diggje* (the harmful power of God). These sanctions, over and above social control exerted through gossip and internalized feelings of loyalty, thwarted temptations to abandon parents (or nowadays to institutionalize them).

CONFRONTING PAST AND PRESENT

I now come to the difficult task of interpreting the remnants of the deeper past through knowledge of the recent past. Comparing Locorotondo with other places indicates that not all southern Italian small proprietors have exactly the same ways, and common sense tells us that economic and social conditions changed between the early nineteenth century and the present and that such changes will be reflected in strategies.[11] A problem the documents present is whether the contracts that talk of coresidence between children and parents indicate a strategy of formation of long-term multiple-family enterprises, or temporary coresidence, or in fact a situation limited to youngest sons who will inherit the parental dwelling with its work and storage spaces, as is

11. There are, of course, other alternatives as well. Some southern Italian small proprietors, past and present, have adopted multiple-family coresidence strategies, for instance. See Mariuccia Giacomini's analysis of eighteenth-century Belmonte in Calabria (1981, 31–45) and William Douglass's discussion of Agnone in the Molise (1980, and in this volume).

now the case. The temporary coresidence hypothesis is attractive, at least for the mid-eighteenth century, because the catasto onciario is so vehement about defining only four hearths in the entire population of 626 households as those of multiple families. Of the approximately 10 percent of households for which early-nineteenth-century contracts mention coresidence, many may represent temporary situations ascribable to bad times. Parents must often have despaired of providing adequate housing for their children at the right moment; one father clearly specifies that his son and daughter-in-law will live with him for four years until a trullo can be constructed from stones taken from a ruined building acquired for the purpose (ASB-AN 1780–1838, 10 Apr. 1808). Thus I am reluctant to read the capitoli matrimoniali for either period as demonstrating a pattern of permanent coresidence between parents and children. The bulk of documents show a preference for neolocality, although marital residence often reflected a pattern of living close to family members.

My best hypothesis about interpersonal relationships between parents and children in the more distant past is that parents who had built something to manage and pass on exercised considerable authority over the lives of their children as laborers, and eventually as heirs to the family patrimony. My expectation, based on ethnographic analogy with the field locales I have studied and with Arlacchi's findings for Calabria, is that such parents demanded utmost obedience of children, about choice of mate and in the struggle devoted to the accumulation of marital property goods. I would certainly not be surprised to find the supernatural sanctions concerning obedience to, and loyalty toward, parents that I have described for the recent past. It is important to remember that such documents as marriage contracts and the agreements they represent could be circumscribed by illiterate folk with supernatural, as well as legal, sanction.

There are shreds of evidence for the custom of mantenemènte, or parental allowance, in the eighteenth century in a contract in which brothers assigned their mother all that was necessary for her subsistence for the rest of her life (ASB-AN 1683–1729, 9 Sept. 1725). In a later marriage contract a son agreed to support his father with six tomoli of grain and one and a half tomoli of fava beans annually (ASB-AN 1780–1838, 1 Mar. 1804). Otherwise, the capitoli matrimoniali have little to say about the care of parents, except where they are assigned lifetime rights to dwell in houses that are being passed on. In fact, the maintenance of parents beyond their retirement, before the introduction of old age and disability pensions, may have been less a question in this earlier period than in this century, because most parents probably did not survive as long.

Perhaps we can most profitably explore what we know was in the process of change in the observed past—the rule about who brought a house to marriage.

The documents indicate that generally, in the eighteenth and in part the early nineteenth century, parents provided peasant daughters with houses, if possible. Interviews with living informants in the Locorotondese countryside strongly established that today grooms provide housing, and as noted above, even during the first decade of the nineteenth century there was a trend among country-dwelling peasants toward male contribution of a trullo. There is no folk memory whatsoever about the earlier custom; the idea that brides customarily received houses surprised country informants, and they commented that in their memories this would have happened only in the absence of a male heir.

Here we can use ethnographic analogy to explore the change. In southern Italy there are towns where parents dower women with houses, and they allow us to speculate about what happened in Locorotondo armed with some ethnographic ammunition.[12] These cases currently seem to cluster in Basilicata and parts of Calabria, although our ethnographic map of such strategies is far from complete. According to Davis (1973), the fulfillment of this expectation in Pisticci in Basilicata results in loosely matrilocal neighborhoods in which ties between households are expressed through women. In most cases the maternal household passes to the youngest daughter, and other daughters tend to seek housing near parents if possible.[13] Many sisters are neighbors. Those families Davis describes as living in the countryside appear to be coresident groups composed of brothers and their wives, but not year-round. Each nuclear family component has a town house brought to the marriage by the woman, which it occupies during slack portions of the year (1973, 45–46). Country residence, however, seems to have a patrilocal aspect, even if it is only seasonal, which suggests that there might be some perceived strategic advantage to the pattern (see below).

The dowering of females with houses at marriage emphasizes female solidarity. Women are together all day in the neighborhood, men are dispersed in their fields or away on jobs (Davis 1973, 67–72). Neighboring kinswomen cooperate openly with one another, wander freely into one another's houses, watch one another's children, and share cooking ingredients, utensils, and resources. Groups of female kin who are neighbors have recognized identities

12. Besides the case discussed in detail below, other ethnographic hints about this custom come from Pitkin 1985, 21; Cornelisen 1976, 28; and Banfield 1958, 55.

13. Davis argues from cadastral data alone that this pattern represents a change from an early-nineteenth-century pattern by which only men inherited immovable property, and then only upon the death of their parents, and women received only a trousseau (Davis 1976). Although the original pattern Davis claims for Pisticci had wide distribution, as Delille has shown it remains hypothetical without corroborating evidence from marriage contracts, if they exist.

and common concerns about the honor of the constituent families and the potential dishonor of families in other female kin and neighborhood groups. They therefore attempt to monitor the behavior of ingroup members and criticize that of other groups. Daughters also care for their aged parents.

We can infer that neighbor relations were structured through female kin ties in Locorotondo during the eighteenth century for the same reasons they exist in Pisticci.[14] Delille's extensive study of kinship and residence in the mezzogiorno between the sixteenth and nineteenth centuries suggests that this was, in fact, the common pattern in Apulia, which was characterized by a population of day laborers, and that it contrasted with a patrilocal neighborhood pattern found among small proprietors in Campania (1985, 135—156). Even if Locorotondese parents could not for practical reasons keep their daughters as neighbors, the town was mostly contained within an elliptical walled space measuring about two hundred meters at its longest axis, and no woman would have been more than a few minutes away from her female kin. The movement of peasants into the countryside meant leaving this solidarity among neighboring female kin, and facing residence either in isolation or in a patrilocal rural enclave that emphasized brother and father ties.

Early-nineteenth-century marriage contracts refer to fathers building trulli for their sons adjacent to their own. Many rural hamlets, or *jazzèlere,* composed of clusters of families related through men (although the larger ones contained several such clusters), date from this period of expansion of country residence. The jazzeile contained essential spaces and equipment for agriculture—a threshing floor, a large cistern, sometimes a bread oven, a grape-crushing floor, and hearths for boiling down grape syrup that was used to fortify wine.[15] Residents owned and used common space according to rights, clearly defined both in property transmission documents and orally (if we can project oral historical evidence into the past), in a series of commonly understood but unwritten conventions about the use of resources.

Male cooperation in the jazzeile facilitated gaining a stake in the countryside through emphyteusis, which required the transformation of thin soiled land into vineyards over the space of ten years. Related men could more easily exchange heavy labor, just as brothers now help one another build houses for their marriages. My best estimates, from interviews with older peasant men, and those of historical economist Vincenzo Ricchioni (1958, tables 5 and 6)

14. To glimpse such neighborhoods through the 1816 cadastre, which inventories urban as well as rural property, unfortunately is difficult because wives' dotal property is lumped with that of their husbands for taxation purposes.

15. The components of these hamlets are itemized in various kinds of contracts surviving from the eighteenth and nineteenth centuries.

suggest that transforming a hectare of typical unimproved land into a vineyard, using only manual labor, took two to three thousand man-days. Vineyard surface area in Locorotondo had expanded by three times the mid-eighteenth-century figure by the time of the catasto provvisorio of 1816, and five times that figure by the mid-nineteenth century, to about 25 percent of the total communal land surface. By the early twentieth century, half the land surface of the commune was in vineyards. Peasants invested enormous amounts of family labor in this expansion.

Kinship and the presence of paternal authority also would have lessened the potential for arguments arising from the necessity to share the fixed capital existing in the jazzeile. In addition, during the tormented times of the late eighteenth and early nineteenth centuries and later, after 1860, when brigand bands roamed the Apulian countryside, the solidarity of males would have been important for protecting hamlets and their contents. Nor can we discount the probability that peasant housing in the Apulian countryside, unlikely without the emphyteusis strategy, was also facilitated through fatherly and brotherly cooperation in construction. The change to a father and son rule about endowing new peasant families with housing therefore was an adaptive strategy contingent on the opportunity to capture land through the labor-intensive process of emphyteusis, which in turn was best carried out through residence in the rural zones.

Perhaps more important, we can infer that the new strategy also concerned the legal question of the fate of a woman's dotal immovable properties if she died childless. Households established in the countryside were farm headquarters that included the important fixed capital items shared in the jazzeile, as well as stalls, vats, barrels, wine jars, storage areas, and lofts, all essential to the small-proprietor existence and associated with individual trulli. If we consider that the male was, both legally and practically, the agricultural manager and head of the household, it becomes apparent that for rural small proprietors, female dowering with housing could produce serious problems if a wife died without producing children. In that unhappy event, of course, marital property would return to the woman's parents or to their heirs, with the effect of abruptly depriving a man not only of his wife and her land and labor, but also of the necessary aspects of a farm and rights in a jazzeile. He would face the difficult problem of starting his enterprise again with only his own land. At a time when death in childbirth was a distinct possibility for a woman, this consideration must have been quite important in the agricultural adaptive strategies of peasant parents for their children. This factor might even explain why in Pisticci, where women still receive town houses, rural seasonal dwellings pass between generations patrilineally.

Other issues that are important to contemporary Locorotondese country people help us think about the past. In the female kin-oriented neighborhoods of the eighteenth century and before, primary care for aged parents was likely provided by their own daughters, who probably resided a few steps away, or indeed in the same dwelling. Daughters who moved to the countryside into a patrilocal enclave could no longer easily provide such care, and instead probably assisted their parents-in-law, as they do now. In fact, we can imagine the early-nineteenth-century transitional phase as one in which many women literally left their parents behind in town. This would have changed certain aspects of the mate selection process, because whereas parents previously could have expected care based on daughterly sentiment, those who adopted the rural adaptive strategy depended on the good graces of women not their kin. The need to scrutinize sons' marriage choices must have intensified.

Further, women who were without houses must have found themselves at a disadvantage on the marriage market, whereas those who did have houses, but perhaps little land, had a distinct advantage.[16] Once a substantial part of the Locorotondese peasantry had moved into the rural zones and men began to construct houses, the parents of peasant girls would have been relieved of this necessity. In strategizing their daughters' marriages, they probably thought increasingly about providing land to attract marriage partners. This, in turn, would have made emphyteusis an attractive opportunity, especially because once a daughter was dowered with land taken under such a contract, her husband assumed the annual rent and taxes on it, as well as the obligation to improve it.

Another likely outcome of the change concerned widowhood. Under the old system, if a woman received a house at marriage or managed to buy one with the money she received as a settlement, it remained in her hands until death or cession to a daughter, providing a measure of security. Under the newer rural adaptive strategy by which men brought houses, widows may have sometimes faced a degree of uncertainty about continued shelter after the death of their husbands. Sons from the dead husband's previous marriage could make certain claims on their father's property and perhaps contest their stepmother's antefato, which, after all, implied only an unspecified third of the deceased mate's wealth. Formerly, security about shelter rested on clear ownership, but under the new system it rested only on sentiment, the vagueness of contestable law, and probably the fear of an old woman's curse.

Fleshing out contracts like the capitoli matrimoniali through knowledge of more recent southern Italian peasant usages is a dangerous, almost archae-

16. Donald Pitkin, in his description of Stilo in Calabria, makes this point strongly (1985, 21).

ological, process of inference, to be sure. Making inferences about the past is more easily and securely done, however, on the basis of some knowledge about the lives of peasants in the recent past. That knowledge allows us to exercise our imaginations, but it also helps us to make inferences that have ethnographic verisimilitude and to exercise the anthroplogist's preference for holism. Similarly, when we project customs and behavior from the present of a place into the past we must do so with circumspection, a sound knowledge of local and national history, and with consideration for what might have changed. We can hope to discover better and richer sources of data, or even fragmentary indications, that will validate our hypothetical interpretations or lead us to reject them. Having considered what are likely to have been important strategical issues among such a population as the Locorotondese peasantry, we at least develop a sharper eye for clues in documents there and elsewhere.

ARCHIVAL SOURCES

ACL-SP (Archivio Comunale di Locorotondo).
> 1810–1811. Statistica della popolazione del Commune di Locorotondo formata in esecuzione degli ordini di S. E. il Signor Intendente, busta 71, fasc. 450.

ASB-AN (Archivio di Stato di Bari, Atti Notarili).
> 1683–1729. Acts of Not. G. Aprile.
> 1729–1780. Acts of Not. P. Aprile.
> 1734–1784. Acts of Not. G. Chialà.
> 1761–1796. Acts of Not. A. G. Chialà d'Aprile.
> 1777–1808. Acts of Not. F. G. Aprile.
> 1780–1838. Acts of Not. Giuseppe Convertini.
> 1797–1809. Acts of Not. G. M. Convertino.
> 1808–1811. Acts of Not. O. Trinchera.

ASB-CO (Archivio di Stato di Bari, Catasto Onciario).
> 1749. Locorotondo.

ASB-CP (Archivio di Stato di Bari, Catasto Provvisorio).
> 1816. Locorotondo.

Chapter 17

SYLVIA JUNKO YANAGISAKO

Capital and Gendered Interest
in Italian Family Firms

Early on in the course of my research on family firms in Como[1] an industry
official recounted to me an adage that purportedly summarized local knowledge about the rise and fall of family firms. "Il nonno fondò, i figli sviluppano, i
nipoti distruggono" (The grandfather founded [the firm], the sons develop it,
and the grandsons destroy it). The same adage was later repeated to me by
several firm owners. A minor, but notable, variation of the adage ends "i nipoti
mangiano." In other words, the grandfather founded [the firm], the sons develop it, and the grandsons eat it.

My translation of this adage is intentionally gendered. It could, after all, be
translated "the grandfather founded [the firm], the children develop it, and the
grandchildren destroy it," because the plural nouns *figli* and *nipoti* can include
both males and females. A gender-neutral translation, however, was ruled out
by the firm owners' interpretation of the adage.

The founder of the firm, the grandfather, is characterized as a self-made
man. The founder of a silk dyeing and printing firm whose son described him in
precisely these terms provides a paradigmatic case. This was a man who began
working in arduous laboring jobs at the age of nine, who acquired his vocation
through practical experience and by studying at night, and who worked long
hours and lived a frugal life while establishing a firm that flourished because of
his technical expertise and dedication.

1. In 1984 I began conducting ethnographic and ethnohistorical research on the transformation of family firms in the silk industry of Como during the nineteenth and twentieth centuries. I
interviewed the owner-managers of thirty of these firms, as well as many of their family members
and relatives. Since then I have increased my firm sample size to forty. I also interviewed industry
officials and collected archival materials on firms and the industry as a whole.

The founder's sons, in turn, are said to acquire their father's technical know-how and work discipline as a result of working by his side in the firm. Given the education their father's success affords them, and the business reputation and capital he has accumulated, these sons have even greater social and financial resources with which to expand the firm. By the third generation, however, so the story goes, the drive and self-discipline that enabled the grandfather to build the firm do not exist among his grandsons, who squander the firm's assets in ill-considered schemes and frivolous expenditures. The picture painted is more or less that of dilettante bourgeois youths who prefer sailing in the Bahamas to putting in the long hours needed to advance the firm.

Like all adages, this three-generational tale of firm succession has a moral. And, like all moral tales with any power, it leaves some things out. Quite obviously, it leaves out women. It is a tale of patrifilial succession in which one generation of men succeeds in carrying forward their father's project and the next fails. Exclusively concerned with male productive force and its dissipation over time, the adage represents an intriguing variation of what Carol Delaney (1986) has called a monogenetic theory of procreation, in which males alone supply the creative force that produces succeeding generations. It replicates in the profane world of business the cosmological model of male reproduction embodied in the sacred origin myths of Christianity.

That the son of a self-made man can himself be a self-made man may seem a conundrum. But the answer, at least according to the second-generation self-made men I interviewed, is simple. First, the father requires the son to learn everything from the most menial, unskilled tasks to the technical and managerial, thus making him work his way up the occupational hierarchy (*dalla gavetta*). Having provided him with this practical education, the father then leaves his son free to manage the firm. Given the rapidly changing nature of the industry and the market, the son inevitably finds himself on terrain unfamiliar to the father and so must make his own decisions and, thereby, make himself. In the next generation, however, the contradiction inherent in being the third generation in a lineage of self-made men results in failed reproduction; by then the grandsons of men who were the producers of capital have turned into their antithesis—namely, the consumers of capital.

To return to the question of what has been excluded from the moral tale of patrifilial succession conveyed by the adage: in addition to excluding women, the adage leaves out gender. For not only are there no women in this tale, but the motives, strategies, and actions of the men in it appear to operate and make sense in an ungendered social world—albeit, a homosocial one. The possibility of asking why a founder would want his sons to succeed him as head of the firm or why a son would want to make himself in his self-made father's image is denied given the self-evident character of men's desires and ambitions.

Finally, like most moral tales the adage leaves out history. The three generations of men struggle, succeed, accumulate, and finally dissipate their energies in a once-upon-a-time that is suspended above any particular historical context.

The analysis I undertake here adds women and gender to this story of firm succession. At the same time, it pulls the story out of an ahistorical, timeless cycle of intergenerational succession and situates it in a particular period of Italian capitalism. I hope to demonstrate that we can better understand the dynamics of Italian families—whether capitalist, peasant, or working class—if we treat family members' goals and strategies as the culturally specific, gendered interests and strategies of real people living and acting within a particular history of social and economic transformation. In the case at hand, I elucidate the transformation of women's and men's interests in capital accumulation in family firms in contemporary Italy.

Another problem in social theory and cultural interpretation motivates this analysis. This is one that has vexed feminist scholars from the moment we began to treat female subjects as social agents capable of acting in and upon social systems, and not simply constituted and constrained by them. As feminist scholars began to question Durkheimian assumptions about the unity of the desires and interests of members of collectivities ranging from domestic groups to social classes, some of the first concepts to fall suspect were those of family strategy and household strategy. Our recognition that women, among others, may not be as committed to the projects men or elders pursue and celebrate was linked to our reconceptualization of the family as a site of political contention and struggle. That women's complaints and attempts to wield power in families were often cast as petty squabbles with either insignificant or tragic consequences was interpreted as an ideological masking of the inherently political character of the relations and struggles that take place inside families (Collier 1974).

Feminist scholars, of course, were not the only ones politicizing the family. So were other social theorists who had become equally suspicious of Durkheimian collectivities. Pierre Bourdieu aptly summarized this sentiment well when he wrote that "from the undivided family up to the largest political units, the cohesion endlessly exalted by the mythological and genealogical ideology lasts no longer than the power relations capable of holding individual interests together" (Bourdieu 1977, 65).

Having unraveled the mythological and genealogical ideologies holding together collectivities, some anthropologists have taken Bourdieu's attack on structuralism and system-fetishizing objectivism as a mandate to pursue more actor-focused analyses of the ways people create systems, reproduce them, and transform them. The results of these attempts have often been disappointing, especially when the actors have been actresses. Too often, as in Bourdieu's analysis of Kabylian matrimonial strategies and social reproduction, the "structured dispositions" and interests of women are assumed rather than explicated. Bourdieu's view of Kabylian women as "less sensitive to symbolic profits and freer to pursue material profits" (1977, 62) is equivalent to claiming that women operate as instrumental actresses outside cultural systems of representation and meaning.[2] This poses the danger of replacing a mythological concept of collectivity with an equally mythological one of "practical, individual interest." Instead of focusing on how women pursue strategies designed to attain assumed goals and realize assumed interests in families, my concern is with understanding how women and men come to have particular interests, goals, and strategies that lead them to act in particular ways in particular historical circumstances. I do not take for granted what motivates either women or men; rather, I assume from the outset that people's desires and the concepts of self, interest, and self-interest out of which those desires are constucted are shaped as much within a particular historical dynamic as are the strategies people employ to attain them. This leads me to an analysis of the constitution of desires and strategies and their dialectical transformation in specific historical circumstances.

My approach studiously avoids a mechanistic model of the capitalist firm as an economic and political structure constrained by a universal logic of capitalism. To assume that capitalism operates the same way everywhere and for all time is to assume that the people who enact the relations that constitute capitalist firms operate as the same kind of social agents everywhere and for all time. Such an economic reductionist assumption is anathema to a cultural anthropologist. Instead I ask how contemporary Italian capitalist family firms are constituted as complex systems of relations of production, reproduction, nurturance, love, and power, along with the desires and strategies of their members, and how they change over time. I focus on the gender dimension of this system, because gender is central to the constitution of social actors and their desires in Italian family firms, as it is in most kinship systems (Yanagisako and Collier 1987).

2. See Yanagisako and Collier 1987 for a fuller critique of Bourdieu's analysis of Kabylian matrimonial strategies.

THE SILK INDUSTRY OF COMO

From its preindustrial beginning, the silk industry of Como has been characterized by a decentralized structure of production.[3] As in the early development of the northern European textile industry (Goody 1982), merchants functioned as the industry's entrepreneurs by taking on both supply and marketing functions. Rather than grouping the weavers together in factories, the merchants bought the thread and gave it to artisans to weave on their own looms. Even after the industrial transformation of the industry with the adoption of mechanical looms, production has continued to be highly decentralized. Today, there are few vertically integrated firms in the industry, and the vast majority of firms operate in only one phase of the production process. The twisting of the silk thread, its preparation for weaving, the dyeing, weaving, and printing of the fabric, the preparation of screens for printing, and the packaging and marketing of fabric all take place in different firms.[4] In this decentralized production structure, firms called converters put the production process in motion by deciding what kind of fabric should be produced and then ordering its weaving and dyeing and printing by other firms.

The industry is also characterized by the overwhelming predominance of local ownership by Como families. In 1985, out of the approximately four hundred firms in the industry, only one joint-stock company had been started by investors outside of Como and none were owned multinationally.[5]

The present discussion of family firms in this industry is restricted to those firms in my sample whose characteristics qualify them to speak to the adage about intergenerational succession. I focus on four firms that share the feature of standing at the brink of the third generation.[6] Through them we can scru-

---

3. Although it is called the *tessitura serica* industry, which literally means "silk-weaving," the term today refers to continuous-thread weaving. This includes the production of silk fabric destined for high fashion as well as artificial fabrics for ready-to-wear clothing manufacture.

4. Como has not produced any of its own raw silk since World War II and instead imports it from China.

5. In 1985 the industry employed about 13,000 workers in the province of Como, thus constituting its leading manufacturing industry. Although the total number of firms and employees in the industry had declined during the 1970s and 1980s, the size distribution of firms was fairly stable, with 68 percent having fewer than 10 workers, 18 percent having 11–50, and 14 percent having 51 or more. Total sales figures continued to increase in the 1980s—in 1981 the industry sold goods worth 950 million dollars, 600 million of which came from export sales (Piore and Sabel 1984, 312, quoting industry report).

6. These firms should not be considered representative of those in the industry or even of the forty firms in my sample. For one, they fall within the percentage of firms employing more than 50 workers; for another, their volume of production and earnings is also in the upper range. They do

tinize the moment when firms are poised between the sons who have expanded them and the grandsons who will purportedly destroy them.

A COHORT HISTORY OF FIRMS

All four firms were founded between 1925 and 1933, and in each of them one or more sons have succeeded their father as head of the firm. All four evolved from humble beginnings as dependent subcontracting firms relying heavily on the labor of family members to firms in which family members no longer work alongside their employees in the production process, but manage it.

Il nonno fondò. The founders of these firms, who were born between 1898 and 1907, came from peasant or petty bourgeois backgrounds, or from a mixture of the two. Giuseppe Pozzi,[7] who grew up in a sharecropping family in a small town outside the city of Como, had the kind of humble background typical of these founders. By the time he was nineteen, Pozzi had tired of farming and landed a position as assistant to the shop foreman in a firm that wove ties. He had barely completed elementary school, but during the four or five years he worked for the firm he attended night classes at the Setificio, the local state-operated textile school. In 1926, the owners of another firm, who had come to appreciate his skill in fixing and adjusting looms, loaned Pozzi twelve looms, some of which he in turn distributed among households in the nearby countryside. The firm owners supplied him with thread, prohibited him from using the looms to weave for any other firm, and paid him a set price for each meter of fabric produced. As a dependent subcontractor, Pozzi was in a sense little more than a shop foreman whose "shop" was dispersed throughout the countryside. He continued to function as a dependent subcontractor until the middle of the 1950s, by which time he was overseeing about a hundred looms.

The firm's early years were characterized by long working hours and what is sometimes these days called self-exploitation. By the early 1930s the self that Pozzi, like the other founders, was exploiting included a wife. All the founders married between 1931 and 1934—and given that the early years of marriage coincided with the early years of the firm, wives were a common source of unpaid family labor.

By the time their second children were born, most of the wives began phasing out of working in the firms; by the late 1930s they were no longer

---

not, however, include the largest firms owned and managed by long-standing bourgeois families. Nor do these four include the smallest subcontracting firms, which have not broken away from their dependence on larger firms.

7. Like the other personal names in this chapter, Giuseppe Pozzi is a pseudonym.

working at all. Many other relatives, however, continued to do so for a number of years, including the siblings both of the founders' wives and of the founders. Male relatives usually filled technical and semimanagerial jobs, whereas female relatives often were weavers and consequently at the bottom of the job hierarchy.[8]

I figli sviluppano. By the second half of the 1950s these firms were prospering, and by the early 1960s they were well into a period of growth and modernization in which a good deal was invested in state-of-the-art high-speed automatic looms and printing equipment, in constructing new factories and warehouses (in some cases on newly purchased land), and in remodeling office space. The majority of these improvements were self-financed through profits with the aid of low-interest government-sponsored loans.

At the same time, firms that had been dependent on one or two clients began buying their own equipment thus freeing themselves to work for a larger number of clients, which gave them more stability and also better placed them to negotiate the cost of their services. Others moved beyond subcontracting work and began to produce their own fabric. Giuseppe Pozzi's firm, for example, no longer wove fabric as a service for the larger firm that had given him a start, but instead bought thread, developed its own patterns, and sold the finished fabric to converters.

This period of growth and technological modernization coincided with the entry of sons, who often began working in the firm while still attending school. Most sons studied at the local technical high school, where they were trained in weaving or dyeing and printing; a few were geared toward the university, where they studied economics or political science. Meanwhile, their sisters, about whom I will have more to say later, were without exception trained to become schoolteachers or went on to study languages at the university. As sons became firmly established as their fathers' successors, other relatives tended to leave the firm—often on bad terms, particularly when they set up competing firms and took some of the business with them. By the early 1970s, what might earlier have appeared superficially to be an extended family firm revealed its true restricted character.

During the heated period of labor contestation in the early 1970s, Como's silk industry experienced much less disruption than the large factories in Turin, Milan, and Bologna. But labor militancy, strikes, and factory shutdowns did

---

8. It was also common for nephews and nieces of the founders and their wives to work in the firms—in some cases for only a couple of years before they moved into permanent occupations, in others for much longer periods in jobs that were evidently career commitments. Regardless of how long any relatives worked in their firms, founders and their sons uniformly declared to me that these relatives did not hold special positions or claims on the firm.

increase. These four firms escaped any serious disruption, but the experience convinced those who had been planning to expand production or to add another phase of production that it was advisable to limit the size of any factory and even to set up other factories as separate legal entities. Consequently, by the beginning of the 1980s none of these firms employed more than 110 workers, whereas in the early 1970s some had grown to include as many as 300. In the case of the Pozzi firm, decentralization in the 1970s entailed establishing former shop foremen with a small number of looms in a dependent subcontracting firm. Where once it had been the dependent subcontractor, now it was the parent firm. Moreover, the looms placed with their former employees were not outdated ones that had been supplanted by modern ones in the central factory. Rather, they were expensive state-of-the-art looms and equally productive as the ones at the central factory. The small number of workers (35) employed in the Pozzis' central factory was misleading, because their thirteen subcontracting firms employed a total of 280 workers.

The recession in the early 1980s brought about the closing of many firms, and the number of firms and employees declined as a consequence. But by 1985 the industry had rebounded, and since then it has been booming along with the rest of the Italian economy.

I nipoti distruggono? What then of the grandsons, the purported consumers and destroyers of the firm? Recall that the children of the founders were born in the 1930s and 1940s. Their marriages, in turn, were concentrated in the 1960s. The sons tended to marry women whose fathers were themselves firm owners, although not necessarily in the silk industry; the daughters tended to marry liberal professionals and salaried business managers rather than firm owners.

By 1985 the four founders had a combined total of thirty-five grandchildren—with a few on the way. The eldest cohort of these grandchildren had reached their early twenties, and some of the grandsons had begun working in the firms while continuing their educations. By the time grandsons entered the firms, the founders had long retired from any active management role; the founders of two of the firms had died.

In 1985 these two presented a telling pair of opposites concerning the dynamics of succession. The Pozzi firm showed great promise of being passed on to the third generation. Giuseppe Pozzi's two sons had taken over the management of the firm twelve years before his death, and the two eldest of their sons were preparing to enter the business by studying accounting and textile engineering. Giuseppe's only daughter, Caterina, had never married, and after she had used her university degree in languages to teach for more than a decade, her brothers convinced her to take over the accounting in the firm. Like her brothers, Caterina drew a salary from the firm, although hers was considerably smaller because, as her brothers explained, she had no family to support. She continued to live in the family home with her widowed mother until her death, and she was a doting aunt to her brothers' children. With all the Pozzi siblings involved in the management of the firm and all committed to its perpetuation by the next generation, which in effect meant the sons of the two brothers, the family did indeed appear in 1985, as the eldest brother characterized it, "un clan molto unito."

The Cavalli family, in contrast, was badly fractured. Critical differences between the Pozzis and the Cavallis, who owned firms of similar character and origin, appeared to be the size of their sibships and the occupations of the siblings. Of the eight children born to Angelo Cavalli and his wife, Maria, only the three eldest sons had entered the firm. The other two sons had become professionals—one a university professor and the other a lawyer; the three daughters, all housewives, were married respectively to a salaried business manager, a university professor, and an architect.

The eldest brothers had begun working in the firm in the late 1950s, and during the 1960s and 1970s they expanded tenfold the firm's productive capacity. By the early 1970s their father had handed over management of the firm entirely to them and had assumed a role of symbolic leadership. Around 1965, Angelo began transferring some of his shares in the firm to his three eldest sons, and in 1973 he worked out a system for giving them control of the entire firm. He had the firm's assets evaluated and divided this amount into eight equal parts, one for each of his children. He then "sold" the shares assigned to the children who had not entered the firm to the three eldest brothers. As one of them put it, however, the "payment" for these shares was deferred and all money remained in the firm, with the agreement that the other brothers and sisters would withdraw their money only after Angelo had died.

The "understanding," it should be emphasized, existed between Angelo and his eldest sons exclusively, because the other siblings were not told about it. As much as seven years after their father's death, the exact nature of that agreement was unclear to the younger siblings. What they did know was that their father had called all of them to a family meeting in 1982, where he announced that he had transferred his shares to his eldest sons and that upon his death these sons were obligated to compensate the other children for their shares. The eldest sons were also to pay their mother a regular stipend. Angelo had ended the meeting by urging his children not to withdraw their share of the capital out of the firm in the near future, because the firm would suffer. He had outlined a system by which his eldest sons would pay their younger siblings a fair interest rate for keeping their capital in the firm.

According to several of the children, their father had called this meeting at the insistence of their mother, who was concerned about the inequality of the existing financial arrangements. Signora Cavalli was particularly concerned about the financial well-being of the daughter married to the university professor.

A year after the meeting, Angelo Cavalli died, leaving no will and none of his instructions in writing. Confusion and disagreement as to the nature of the agreement quickly turned into an open breach when the eldest brothers informed their siblings that the firm could not afford to pay the promised interest that year. The other siblings became outraged when, in addition, they discovered that their mother had not been regularly receiving her stipend. They found it difficult to understand this shortage of funds when the elder brothers had recently enlarged the firm, invested in new equipment, and even bought out another firm. One of the elder brothers, Piero, who had borne the onerous duty of conveying the bad news to his siblings, was convinced that his mother had incited some of these siblings to protest and subsequently refused to speak to her.

The siblings outside the firm claimed they had no intention of demanding that the firm be divided equally among all of them, and they acknowledged the years of work their older brothers had put into managing the firm. But, they said, as things stood at the moment, they were too unequal. What was especially troubling to them was the obvious inequality in wealth between the elder brothers and themselves; in other words, between those in the firm and those outside it. Those in the firm lived in plush modern condominiums or large houses in the best residential areas on the outskirts of Como. Those outside the firm lived either in modest apartments or in the family home in the old city center.

The outside siblings' unhappiness with the inequality in wealth was exacerbated because they and their widowed mother had planned to use the first interest payments to renovate the family home, which was badly in need of repair. The eldest daughter and her husband, the university professor, occupied the third floor of the building, and the mother lived in the space originally occupied by the family on the first floor. Plans had been afoot to remodel other areas of the building so that two other children and their families could move in.

There was a second aspect to the inequality among siblings that grated particularly on the sisters whose children were close in age to those of the eldest brothers. In 1985 those children were in their late teens to mid-twenties, and most of them seemed destined for university degrees. But their equality of educational achievement was not matched in other aspects of their lives, at least not according to the sisters, who were angry that their brothers' children had been given such opportunities as studying English in the United States whereas their children had not. This inequality among the grandchildren was reported by the sisters to be upsetting to their mother as well.

The sisters and younger brothers were dismayed by their father's failure to leave a will. They could not understand how a man as conscientious and scrupulous as their father could have left his affairs in such a mess. They claimed they had no intention of litigating the matter and were quick to point out that none of them had consulted an attorney or solicited the opinion of a notary public as to their inheritance rights. This disclaimer, of course, glossed over the fact that one of the younger brothers was a lawyer. They did, however, mention that other "good Catholic families" in Como included children who worked in the firm and others who did not and that they had worked out an equitable division of their patrimony.

As for the two firms whose founders were still living in 1985, for the purposes of this discussion, two facts are significant. First, in both cases, the brothers who had taken over the firm claimed they had an understanding with their sisters about leaving their shares in the firm for a while—but the precise nature and stability of these agreements were unclear. Second, in both cases, the founders had not yet written wills.

Like Angelo Cavalli and Giuseppe Pozzi, these founders were not heeding the advice of financial consultants who publicly lamented that so many firm owners in Italy were dying intestate. As one of these consultants complained, he all too often had to inform heirs that their father had failed to consider how to bring about the orderly transmission of the firm patrimony to them. Those fathers who had considered the matter often procrastinated and in the end failed to make a decision. The consequences of such indecision, according to these business consultants, were unstable agreements among heirs, untenable forms of shared firm ownership and management, and fights within the family over the value of their shares—all of which led to the inevitable paralysis of the firm. Accordingly, in the autumn of 1985, the School of Business Management at Bocconi in Milan was offering a special seminar for entrepreneurs entitled "How to manage firm succession."

That men whose disciplined ambitions had achieved so much would fail to leave wills that might prove crucial to the future of their firms and families cries out for explanation. At the very least, this paradoxical end to the lives of self-made men adds an odd twist to our tale of male succession and thus opens up a critical space for an analysis of family members' gendered interests in capital accumulation. In the following sections, I undertake that analysis by asking where the interests of various family members lay in the stalemate that characterized the Cavalli family and firm in 1985—a stalemate that illustrates a conflict common today among family firms in Italy. A conflict that threatens to destroy firms even before grandsons can get their hands on them can tell us a great deal about the transformation of people's interests and the dynamics of capital accumulation in contemporary Italian family firms.

MEN'S GOALS, MEN'S INTERESTS

Men's interests appear at first glance to be easier to discern than women's, because the cultural legitimacy of their desires and schemes entitles men to boldly state them. To a man, fathers who head firms want one or more of their sons to succeed them. Indeed, succession by a son is such a strong goal that it is cited by many men as their primary reason for working so hard for so long to build a successful firm. Fathers without sons, in contrast, are inclined to sell their firms.

A father's commitment to passing his firm on to his sons has to be understood in relation to a dense system of meanings about the male self, its actualization through men's projects, its relation to the projects of other men, and its perpetuation through the lives of sons. Independence is a key symbol in this ideology of masculinity, and a close examination of its multiple meanings reveals a complex and contradictory set of interests, or "structured dispositions," among men.

Independence is something fathers say they want for both themselves and their sons. In the realm of work, being independent means being your own boss, being an employer rather than an employee (which in Italian is to be literally a *dipendente*). In the realm of the family, being independent means being the head of your own family (*il capo di famiglia*). Rooted as it is in the ideal of male parity and a disdain for any man subject to the authority of another man, this concept of independence embodies a problematic contradiction. For what seems attainable in an abstract model of male parity is not when it comes to relationships on the ground—or, rather, in families. Instead, one man's independence necessitates another man's dependence, because to retain his position as head of a family a man must have a family to head. Once his children grow up, his daughters are lost to him through marriage, for married women are said to come under the authority of their husbands, not their fathers. Fathers also are in danger of losing their authority over their sons, not through marriage but through employment. A son who works for someone else not only comes under another man's authority (his *padrone*), but he also has the financial means to be independent of his father. In contrast, a father whose sons take over his firm has given them the resources to remain independent of employers; in other words, he has given them the means of their independence. Such a father has the good fortune of having ensured his headship of an enduring family that includes his sons and, at the same time, having provided for their independence. Such a father, it could be said, has mediated the contradiction embodied in a male ideal of independence that requires the dependence of other men.

Unfortunately for fathers today the effectiveness of this mediation appears to have been subverted by a transformation in the meaning of *independence* in Italy. In the pre–World War II past, independence drew its meaning from an agrarian model of society in which the struggle of families to free themselves from the paternalism of landowners made sense of the paternalism in their families. More recently, a concept of personal independence more familiar to Americans has encroached upon the old one, peppering the speech of entrepreneurs and their sons with such English phrases as "self-made man." The bourgeois liberal celebration of the independence of individuals—in particular male individuals—from father as well as from *il signore* or *il padrone* has brought new power to the contradiction already lurking in the older commitment to the emancipation and actualization of the male self. Sons succeeding to the headship of family firms are proving themselves a receptive audience for these new meanings. Like most audiences of political discourse, they are not mere passive listeners, but active collaborators in the creation of an emergent discourse of male independence.

In spite of the potentially alarming new meanings of independence espoused by the younger generation, the strategy that a father committed to perpetuating his project through his sons should pursue would appear to be rather straightforward. Sons should be prepared to take over the business and daughters prepared to marry out. What daughters require is an education that endows them with the symbolic capital necessary to acquire a husband of the right class and, in the event they do not, with the credentials to become schoolteachers. The resistance of fathers to having daughters enter the firm is not surprising given dominant gender conceptions about women's emotionality, their poor technical skills, and their inability to confront the competitive world of business. But most important is the idea that women are controlled by men and, once they are married, by their husbands. Married daughters would represent a dangerous intrusion of outside interests into the firm.

WOMEN'S GOALS, WOMEN'S INTERESTS

Women's goals and strategies are more difficult to uncover, especially when the women interviewed are so articulate in what might be called the rhetoric of silence. Women commonly represent themselves as having no desires aside from wanting the best for their families. Rather than interpret this as merely the self-interested manipulation of an ideological misrepresentation of women by women, I suggest that we might get a lot farther if we take what women say at face value. This does not mean assuming that women have no desires, but rather assuming that their desires are shaped by dominant ideological representations of gender. As these representations emphasize women's responsibilities, we need to ask what women are made responsible for.

Quite obviously women are not responsible for the success of the firm, at least not directly. But they are responsible for their children's welfare and happiness and for keeping the family together. The tenaciousness of a mother's efforts to get the best for her children, even when that entails conflict with her husband, is a core cultural theme of the Italian family. As the emotional center of the family, mothers are responsible for the strength of its emotional bonds. That means she (and not her husband) is ultimately responsible for family unity.

The complementarity of the gendered division of responsibilities between husbands and wives appears to have created an ideological unity between the family and the firm, at least during the early years of marriage and parenthood. The husband's work in the firm is seen as providing the financial resources to feed the family and ensure its independence; the wife's work in the family provides the emotional resources to keep it together—in other words, to ensure its interdependence.

More recently, however, this ideological complementarity has come under considerable strain as a husband's responsibility for keeping the firm together conflicts with his wife's responsibility for keeping the family together. Indeed, the changing circumstances in which women strategize to keep the family together have led to the transformation of their interests and to a direct conflict with their husbands' interests. This transformation is the consequence of changes in the occupational and class structure of Italy and of changes in the inheritance rights of women.

With the imposition of the Napoleonic Code on northern Italy in 1808, equal division of the patrimony among all children regardless of gender became the law, if not the practice.[9] When Napoleon's empire collapsed in 1815, Austria again took over Venice and Lombardy. After struggling to suppress Italian resistance, the Austrians, whose inheritance codes struck a compromise

---

9. Article 745 of the Napoleonic Code required that daughters as well as sons share in inheritance. It also abolished primogeniture and made children by second marriages equal inheritors with those by the first (Mengoni 1961, 45). Testators with one child had to leave him or her at least half of the estate; if there were two children, at least two-thirds of the estate had to be divided equally between them; if three or more, three-quarters (Davis 1975, 142).

between the egalitarian principles of the Enlightenment and the values of a conservative ruling aristocracy, were less respectful than they previously had been of inheritance laws and customs that emphasized male inheritance, entail, and primogeniture (Davis 1975, 142). The civil code of unified Italy, promulgated in 1865, was modeled on the Napoleonic Code and governed Italian inheritance until the enactment of new family laws in 1975.[10]

The threat that daughters' jural rights to inheritance posed to their fathers' and brothers' interest in keeping the patrimony together appears to have been met in the past by a variety of customary practices among propertied families in northern Italy. In Como, until recently, the common practice was for fathers to give daughters their share of the inheritance in the form of a dowry. That the dowries and other premortem payments daughters of propertied families received even came close to the portion of the patrimony that was their legal due seems highly dubious. But daughters hardly had the resources, either political or material, to enforce their claims. Propertied men, whether landed aristocracy or bourgeoisie, after all, shared an interest in male inheritance and female dowry; and every daughter's husband was also a father's son. Daughters, too, had some stake in the undivided strength of their natal patrimony, for fathers and brothers were their only refuge from a failed marriage. Moreover, the continuing success of a woman's natal family was a source of symbolic capital that enhanced her position both in relation to her husband and in the community at large.

Widows shared their sons' interest in keeping the patrimony intact because the inheritance guaranteed them by law was limited to usufruct, not actual ownership. This entailed only the right to a stipend and to administer the property. Dependent as they were on sons to manage the property or business, widows had little interest in being strong advocates of their daughters' inheritance rights. Even today, widows who were raised in landowning or long-time capitalist families emphasize the value of an undivided patrimony and the perpetuation of their husbands' and fathers' projects.

But the widows and wives of the founders of the firms with which we have been concerned, it will be recalled, did not come from propertied families, and they do not declare a commitment to an aristocratic or bourgeois tradition that is not theirs. Instead, to a woman, they stress a commitment to equal inheritance by all children, whether sons or daughters, whether inside the firm or outside the firm. Indeed, their commitment to an equality among siblings disposes them to help those children they think need help the most. As a

---

10. The code was revised in April 1942, when the civil and commercial codes were joined, but inheritance provisions were not affected.

general rule, this means helping daughters who have fewer financial resources than sons, but it also means helping sons outside the firm. The wives of the two founders still living responded to their husbands ceding of shares to sons by ceding their shares to their daughters. We might wonder why the daughters in these families did not ask for their share of the patrimony at the time they married in the 1960s. And if their fathers were concerned about dividing the firms' assets, why had they not settled their daughters' claims at marriage as bourgeois families had in the past? The reason they did not appears to be that daughters' marriages coincided with sons' entering the firm, which made such settlements extremely difficult. Fathers and sons needed all the firms' earnings to finance the expansion, renovation, and technological modernization undertaken in the sixties and seventies for the survival of the firm. The agreements with sisters about postponing payment until the future thus were a strategy of capital accumulation.

By the early 1980s the future had arrived. In the meantime the circumstances of daughters and mothers had changed. By this time, the eldest of the sisters' children were, like their brothers' children, in their early twenties. Having married men who were salaried managers or professionals with nothing like the assets tied up in their fathers' firms, these sisters could envision putting their share of the patrimony to good use by enhancing their children's futures. Their responsibility for helping their children—through financing their educations and their accumulation of experiences that would identify them as true members of their class—came in direct conflict with their brothers' interests in reinvesting profits in a firm they hoped to pass on to their sons.

The situation of their widowed mothers (and the mothers who were about to become widows), on the other hand, had been significantly altered by changes instituted in Italian family law. When divorce was legalized in 1975, women's property rights were considerably strengthened. With the establishment of spousal community property, widows acquired actual property rights rather than merely rights of usufruct. A woman with two or more children is now entitled to at least one-third of the patrimony if her husband dies intestate and at least one-fourth if he leaves a will disposing of that proportion of his property that he can freely assign to whomever he wishes. This one-fourth is considered her *legittima* or *diritti riservati*. Falling within the community property of spouses are acquisitions made (even separately) during the marriage, the property assigned for the practice of an enterprise of one of the spouses founded after the marriage, and any increase in the enterprise.

With the reform of family law in 1975, widows' acquisition of community property and inheritance rights strengthened their position not only in relation to their husbands but also in relation to their children, in particular their sons. As a consequence, Mother in a propertied family is no longer only a moral force to be reckoned with, but also a political actor who can bring considerable economic pressure to bear on her children. The new family law, moreover, has reformulated the social agency of wives and mothers in such a way as to transform bourgeois women's interests and strategies in the family. These new interests are not motivated by new ideologies of individualism or autonomy, but rather by old gender ideologies about collectivities. The widow Cavalli and her daughters, after all, are not proponents of *la liberazione delle donne* motivated by a feminist vision of autonomy; they are conservative Christian Democrats steeped in a traditional feminine commitment to *la famiglia unita*. What has changed is not their commitment to keeping the family together but the kind of family they are committed to keeping together. The modifications in family and occupational structure have led bourgeois mothers to champion a new kind of collectivity—namely, the inclusive family of parents (or of a widow), their adult children, and their children's spouses, and their grandchildren. Even before they are widowed, wives look beyond their husbands' deaths to their futures in these new inclusive families. Whereas for their husbands, keeping the family together entails consolidating control over the patrimony (that is, capital accumulation), for wives keeping the family together means distributing the patrimony equally among all children. In short, what was emerged is a clash between the cherished projects of the male self and the female self.

Whether the collectivity now being pursued by these women is construed as new depends on the unit we define as the carrier of tradition. If we take actual families and their progeny's families as the carriers of tradition it might be construed as an old idea of collectivity. After all, this was an idea of collectivity that the firm founders' wives learned growing up in petty bourgeois and peasant families and to which their mothers were committed. From the perspective of social class as the carrier of tradition, however, it is a new idea of collectivity, because in the past the old bourgeoisie was more committed to keeping the patrimony intact and to a less-inclusive idea of collectivity. Women raised in these bourgeois families still tend to retain this kind of commitment, but women from the nonbourgeois families have, as it were, imported these ideas into bourgeois family ideology.

Even among new bourgeois families, however, a significant change has occurred. Whereas in the past, among these families, fathers did not have the kind of property or capital to perpetuate their projects through sons, today, like other bourgeois men, they do. The desire of having a son carry on the firm has emerged out of the possibility created by capital joined with a system of means about the gendered self. Together culture and capital have generated desire, as well as conflict between people's projects.

I am not suggesting that mothers are about to take their sons to court over their and their daughters' inheritance rights. Quite the contrary as this is the last thing a mother wants; to enter the domain of the courts is to dissolve the family, and that is what she is trying to avoid. Una famiglia unita can hardly be preserved through a court battle. Nor do husbands and the sons who have taken over the firms have anything to gain by entering into a legal dispute. As the financial consultants mentioned previously are quick to point out, firm owners have everything to lose in a court battle—for litigation paralyzes firms and ultimately destroys them. Particularly in light of the new family law, fathers and their successor sons have every reason to avoid the domain of law. This, I suspect, is why fathers do not leave wills. Given the portion reserved for wives and children, the *quota disponibile* that a husband and father can will away is very restricted. The disposable property of a man with a wife and more than one child, for example, is only one-fourth of his total property. Thus even if he willed his entire disposable property to the sons taking over the firm, the most that a father with one or more daughters could hope to give his sons is one-half of his property—hardly enough to keep afloat a firm under constant pressure to reinvest its profits.

If he writes a will leaving his entire disposable wealth to only some of his children, moreover, a father would be using the legal resources available to him to advance his project and, thereby, risk prodding other family members to do the same. Although mothers are not likely to take sons to court, daughters and nonsuccessor sons are apt to be less restrained. After all, they have their own families to build and their own children to endow. So long as he can remain outside the domain of law and in the domain of the family with its mythological ideology of collectivity, a father can hope that a way will be found to postpone the division of the patrimony until some mythological future when the firm can endow the futures of all his children and grandchildren. If he endows some but not others in his last legacy, he destroys both the possibility of that mythological future and the myth of the collectivity, which is both the material and symbolic basis of his own independence.

THE TRANSFORMATION OF GENDERED INTEREST

The stalemate in which these families find themselves today illustrates how a cultural system of gender and the family can be hoisted by its own petard in the historical transformation of gendered interests. As economic, political, and legal circumstances have changed, so have the interests of wives, daughters, and sons. This transformation is leading them to pursue projects that challenge the collectivities to which fathers have been committed and the strategies of capital accumulation that have enabled fathers to achieve those projects.

But these emergent interests and projects are misconstrued if cast as the goals of individual agents pursuing practical or economic interests fashioned outside of cultural systems of representation. One of the problems with the concept of individual interest that has risen out of the ruins of Durkheimian collectivities is that a concern with strategic agents making their way in a contentious world can easily lead to the assumption that the interests of individuals are focused on themselves in some culturally unmediated fashion. Having discarded a naive notion of altruism, we too often grasp for a naive notion of selfish interest, or at least self-oriented ones.

Such a move, however, blinds us to the collective nature of a good deal of what we call individual interests. I do not mean by this that people are necessarily committed to the same collective goals, but rather that the divergent interests individuals often pursue are motivated as much by cultural representations of collectivities as they are by those of self-interest. In any particular social system, men and women may be structurally predisposed to pursue different kinds of collectivities. Whether these are labeled collective or individual interests is a matter of cultural hegemony. Yet the interests women pursue, which may undermine the collectivities that men pursue and valorize (whether these are agnatic lineages or patrifilial capitalist firms), are no less motivated by cultural representations of collectivities.

In addition, the "selfish" desires and interests that motivate individuals, whether men or women, are no less mythological and ideological constructs than the collective ones. Surely no one knows better than observers of contemporary American society that the interests of Americans in "leading my own life" or "finding myself" are as much the ideological constructions of a system of representations as are the collective goals of "family unity." So, too, are Italian young men's desires for a new kind of independence from fathers as well as padroni. Yet because they are attributed to individuals whom we construe as discrete physiological and motivational entities, individual interests have not been subjected to interpretation as closely as collective ones, which are by definition social.

All interests, whether characterized as selfish or collective, whether elements in a hegemonic system of representations or in one that challenges such a system, are ideologically constructed. Hence it will not suffice to portray Italian male firm owners' strivings for capital accumulation as deriving from the ungendered, purely economic interests of the owners of the means of production. Equally, it will not suffice to portray their wives', daughters', and sisters' strategies as the mere mobilization of bourgeois women's objective interests in the face of changing inheritance laws. For what women and men want is constantly being reformulated as circumstances change in only partially intended ways, and people find themselves pursuing projects they had not previously imagined.

Chapter 18

CAROLINE B. BRETTELL

Property, Kinship, and Gender: A Mediterranean Perspective

Anthropologists and historians share an interest in the relation between the transmission of property from one generation to the next and the nature of family relationships and domestic group structures. Intergenerational flows of wealth involve a series of choices about who is to be the recipient or recipients, when the transfer is to be made, and how it is to be made. Underlying these who, when, and how choices is the fundamental decision of whether to treat all legal heirs equally or to favor one over the others. In this chapter I address the relation between women, property, and family with two goals in mind: first, to demonstrate that the neat labels that have been developed to describe systems of property transmission encompass an enormous range of behaviors; second, to argue that in light of this variation our scholarly focus should be shifted from inheritance systems to the social relationships and cultural values that are expressed and reinforced in association with the transmission of property. Ideas about kinship and gender are embedded in the way in which people transfer wealth.

To place the Italian family into a broader cross-cultural context, I use the countries of the northern Mediterranean as the geographical locus and the literature of anthropology as the material for my discussion. The Mediterranean region has come to be thought of as one characterized by dotal marriage (Goody 1973). Dowry, as defined by Jack Goody, is a form of premortem inheritance whereby a daughter receives her portion at marriage rather than at the death of her parents. It sets up a conjugal fund that ensures a woman's support in widowhood and, in Goody's view, eliminates all further claims on her part to the family patrimony. Goody (1976) has correlated dowry with a range of other aspects of social organization—bilateral kinship, the existence of distinct economic strata within society, in-marriage, delayed marriage for women, and patrivirilocal residence after marriage.

Both the concept of dowry and the unity of the Mediterranean with regard to family and marriage patterns have recently come under serious scrutiny (Bossen 1988; Comaroff 1980; Hirschon 1984; Kertzer and Brettell 1987).[1] Stevan Harrell and Sara Dickey (1985, 106), for example, observe that Goody fails to distinguish families that practice inheritance through dowry from those in which both sons and daughters inherit only at the death or retirement of the parents. Although their criticism does not refer to the Mediterranean in particular, it is nevertheless quite apt for this region. Let us examine why this is so.

DOWRY AND INHERITANCE IN THE MEDITERRANEAN

Within the Mediterranean region, dowry as a mechanism of property transmission is perhaps most characteristic of Greece. The Greek civil code of 1946 defines the dowry as a transfer of property from the girl's family of origin to her and to her husband by means other than inheritance. Although reinforced by legal norms, the centrality of the dowry in Greek culture and society and its continuity is, as many ethnographers have noted, equally sustained by social norms (Lambiri-Dimaki 1985).[2] Within the letter of the law, a number of different strategies have emerged.

The major preoccupation for families in the mainland village of Vasilika (Friedl 1962) is to dower a daughter with both a trousseau, consisting of household items, and land (or its equivalent cash value). Brothers accept that they cannot (or should not) seek wives themselves until their sisters are well settled, and married brothers tend to share houses until they are able to build their own. John Campbell (1964) argues that the implicit purpose of the dowry among Greek Sarakatsani shepherds is to complement the wealth with which the young couple will be endowed by the husband's family. In the first of what becomes a series of socially regulated forms of cooperation between two previously unrelated and therefore hostile families, each kin group bestows a certain amount on a newly formed nuclear family.

On the island of Eressos (Pavlides and Hesser 1986) a girl's family provides

1. Anthropologists once defined the Mediterranean as a unified region, distinguished and dominated by the moral values of honor and shame (Peristiany 1965). This paradigm has also been criticized recently (Gilmore 1987; Herzfeld 1980a, 1987; Pina-Cabral 1989).

2. Jane Lambiri-Dimaki (1985) argues that dowry has survived very well in a modernizing Greece. It is linked to patterns of emigration, saving, and women's work and provides the basis for both interfamilial and intrafamilial relations. See also Couroucli 1987.

her with a house and its furnishings as part of the dowry, either by building a new one or renovating an old one. On Nisi, an island in the Aegean, the bride's father endows his daughter with land and a house, both generally part of his holdings (Casselberry and Valavanes 1976). Thus the newly married couple forms a new household, but in the vicinity of the bride's family.[3] In Piraeus, "a girl with a dowry dwelling but very little personal charm has a better chance of marriage than a girl without her own house" (Hirschon 1983, 306), and the result is a number of coresident families who are linked through female kin. Men, however, retain their authority within separate and autonomous conjugal units. On the Cycladic island of Nisos (Kenna 1976), houses are also part of the dowry, passing from woman to woman as land passes from man to man. No three-generation or joint households of married siblings exist, "but married children work on their parents' land, and married siblings and ritual kinsmen cooperate with each other" (Kenna 1976, 22). On the island of Cyprus, Peter Loizos (1975) has traced a change in residence patterns—from virilocal to uxorilocal—as houses were increasingly included in dowries as an extra lure to bridegrooms.

Houses are quite commonly, but not invariably, a part of dowry throughout Greece, and in some places they are a rather recent phenomenon (Pavlides and Hesser 1986, 95n). The family house in Vasilika goes to the sons, and only when a girl is marrying a townsman is a house part of her dowry. In Glendi, on the island of Crete (Herzfeld 1980b), sons are given houses at the time of their marriage. In the market town of Arnaia, women are given a little land but never a house (Handman 1987).

The other important element of dowry in Greece, besides houses, is the linen trousseau. The value of the trousseau (*rouha*)—primarily comprising linens and other handicrafts—often approximates if not exceeds the family's annual wage-earning power on the island of Amouliani in northern Greece (Salamone and Stanton 1986, 107). In Macedonia, the trousseau of clothing and linen is formally displayed and fingered by everyone as they mentally calculate its worth (Rheubottom 1980). Upon marriage and the bestowing of a dowry (which generally includes a sum of money and some furniture in addition to the trousseau), a Macedonian woman abrogates all further claims on the property of her natal family and takes up residence in her groom's natal household. From a Macedonian perspective, dowry compensates for the girl's labor contributions to her natal household prior to her marriage.

Finally, at least one anthropologist, working in a hill village on the island of Cyprus (Sant Cassia 1982), has documented a significant shift between 1920

---

3. Casselberry and Valavanes in fact describe much more variation in residence patterns.

and 1980 from an inheritance-based system of property transmission to an *inter vivos* dowry system. In the 1920s women brought a house and some land to marriage, whereas a husband "brought his strength and only occasionally some property if there was any left after his sisters' marriages and if his parents could spare it" (Sant Cassia 1982, 644). Today most property is given at marriage, including that to sons, and women still receive a dowry house. Paul Sant Cassia attributes the change to a number of factors: the sale of Church land that put many more plots on the market; the introduction of state-sponsored old age security that encouraged the early release of land; a rise in the rate of emigration that freed up land for those who remained; new employment opportunities for parents; estate duties on land transferred after death; and more cash-crop agriculture, which allows parents to sustain themselves on less land. In conjunction with this shift, Sant Cassia describes major changes in marriage strategies.

Change also has been characteristic of the system of property transmission in Yugoslavia. According to Joel Halpern, the dowry in Serbia is a recent development "springing from Western ideas and reflected in the Serbian Civil Code of the early twentieth century" (1967, 192). Its introduction ultimately led to the dissolution of the *zadruga*—the traditional peasant joint-family farm. Until the late nineteenth century, a groom paid bridewealth, compensating his bride's zadruga for the loss of a girl. Women had no right to share in zadruga property, and a bride took with her only her personal property and household goods when she married into her husband's zadruga. In the 1870s new legislation not only legalized zadruga division but also introduced landownership by women in the form of a dowry that remained the property of a wife and her nuclear family.

A similar shift is described by Jean-François Gossiaux (1987) based on data gathered in the Serbian village of Smedovac close to the Rumanian border. Here, however, dowries consist primarily of household items (sewing machines and knitting machines are currently quite popular), cash, and only rarely of land. Gossiaux refers to it as a "symbolic dowry." In Albanian villages, the Serbian pattern whereby men remain with their father and property is divided only at death has been sustained. Some men, however, bring to their wife's family a marriage gift of a small portion of their own family's land. Once this gift has been bestowed, no further claim on the patrimony can be made.

Like Greece, Italy is a country where the dowry system has deep historical roots (Hughes 1978; Kirshner this volume). Although land is sometimes part of the dowry, in many regions women are excluded from the inheritance of fixed assets and are compensated instead with cash or, more commonly, a trousseau of movable goods. In the *mezzadria* (sharecropping) region of

Tuscany where multiple households prevailed, the wealth of the family was composed of livestock, instruments, tools, and cash, but even here women were excluded from the wealth of production and dowered instead with money or jewelry (Mariottini 1987).

Linens (the *corredo*) were and remain the focal point of a woman's marital portion in many regions of Italy (Pitkin 1960; Silverman 1975). In the southern Lucanian village of Montegrano the minimum corredo for a farm laborer's daughter in the mid-1950s was 12 (12 sheets, 12 nightgowns, 12 towels, and so on), costing about $375 (Banfield 1958). In addition, a bride had to bring land valued at a minimum of $150 and a one-room house. Without such a dowry a girl could not make a successful marriage. Jane Schneider (1980) argues that from the late nineteenth century until the 1930s, trousseaux in the form of embroidered whitewear predominated in the dowries of nonaristocratic Sicilian girls. Though some parents transferred tiny parcels of land or small houses of one or two rooms, the trousseau of linens "nearly equalled and in some cases surpassed the value of these token immovables" (Schneider 1980, 327).[4] Marriage without land, a house, or cash was possible, but it was impossible without a trousseau. That nineteenth-century Sicilian women rarely had access to or control of land is apparent in an 1870 cadastre for the town of Villamaura. Only 161 of 3,288 parcels listed (5 percent) were owned by women, and only 12 of these by untitled women.

John Davis's work on the southern agrotown of Pisticci (1973, 1976) suggests that in the late nineteenth or early twentieth century the relation between women and land may have changed.[5] According to a land cadastre of 1814, whether as spinsters and wives or as widows, women constituted only 13 percent of landowners and controlled only 1 percent of the land. Of all house owners, 20 percent were women. Not only were taxable rights to property transmitted through the male line, but all sons received such rights at the death of their father; daughters received parapherns and, if they were rich, a cash dowry (Davis 1976, 289).

4. Schneider (1980), exploring the late-nineteenth-century elaboration of the embroidered whitewear trousseau among nonaristocratic Sicilians, hypothesizes that such an elaboration may have resulted from (1) a process of status emulation emerging from an increasingly capitalized and class-based rural economy and society; (2) the symbolic association between embroidery and female purity—trousseau production being "make work" that keeps young girls at home; or (3) the liquidity and exchange value of the items produced—trousseau as treasure.

5. Donna Gabaccia (1987, 1988) substantiates this assessment, claiming that prior to the formation of the Italian state married men controlled access to land and few women inherited it or enjoyed rights to its usage. Although the proportion varied by region, by 1881 in general more than a third of property owners in southern Italy were women. They owned land as well as houses.

By the early 1960s the system of land tenure and inheritance in Pisticci was completely different, reflected in a 1961 cadastre in which 53 percent of the people with taxable rights on land were women. Davis further estimates that 60 to 75 percent of houses were owned by women in 1961 and that a further 10 percent were owned by spouses jointly. The bilateral system of inheritance that Davis describes is one wherein houses are considered as one form of property and land as another—the latter divisible and located in the country, the former indivisible and located in the town. Although both forms of property are generally transferred at marriage, houses go to women (along with cash and parapherns) and land to both men and women. The *corredo* that a wife brings as part of her dowry is, according to Davis, sometimes worth as much as the house that she receives, and it is displayed with pride before the wedding. Associated with these practices of the intergenerational transfer of wealth is the tendency for a man to live in his wife's house in her natal neighborhood after marriage. A man also looks for a spouse among those women who have property near his own "in order to counteract the consequences of division" (Davis 1973, 159). Parents disburse this property to their children as they marry, retaining a small portion until their death "to make sure that their children treat them well in their old age" (Davis 1977, 187). Some parents move out of their own house and rent another one, or they pay their son-in-law's rent (Davis 1973, 67).

In his attempt to account for this dramatic change in the transmission of property, Davis raises a number of issues, including the impact of the Piedmontese civil code of 1861, which called for bilateral partible inheritance. Rejecting the legal changes as a single exogenous explanation, Davis instead emphasizes changes in the distribution of property. These changes resulted from new laws and administrative regulations affecting demesne land (land in 1961 was more fragmented and the proportion of property owners in town was higher), population growth (directly related to land redistribution), and a diversification of the local economy, which not only provided opportunities for social mobility but also made land more valuable symbolically than economically for a larger segment of the population. Davis also concludes that because the population did not live on the land it could be deaccessed at marriage rather than retained until death.

It should be emphasized that Davis describes the modern Pisticci pattern, particularly the bestowing of houses on women, as uncharacteristic of other parts of southern Italy. Anthony Galt, however (in this volume), describes a change in the village of Locorotondo in southern Italy from a situation where women brought houses to marriage to one where men did. He attributes this change to a shift in the locus of residence—from town to countryside—itself the result of new emphyteutic contracts. Alternatively, in the Sardinian region of Trexenta (Da Re 1987) men are favored in the inheritance of houses because they are expected to bring a house to a marriage. In spite of an ideology of equality among heirs, differential treatment results because some children provide more services to their parents than others. Such differences are recognized by parents in wills. According to Da Re, daughters inherit both less and lesser quality property, not only because they do not provide agricultural labor but also because sons are expected to contribute to their sisters' trousseaux.

The system of inheritance complemented by dowry that characterizes much of twentieth-century Italy has been associated in some regions with patrilineal joint families and the practice of "expelling" daughters at marriage and in other regions with neolocal and nuclear-family forms and extreme land fragmentation (Banfield 1958; Cronin 1977; Moss and Thompson 1959; Pitkin 1959; Silverman 1968). The peasants of the southern Italian town of Matera (Tentori 1976), for example, divide what little they have and each child sets up an independent household at marriage with the help of their small inheritance. This system has created widespread poverty among children, and old parents are often abandoned. The absence of family cohesion, in Tullio Tentori's view, has encouraged the formation of neighborly ties and of old age homes.[6]

In the countries of the western Mediterranean the *dot*, or *dote*, is quite different from what has been described for Greece, Yugoslavia, and Italy. In regions of southern France (Languedoc, Gascony, Rouergue) where three-generation stem families have been common, a dot was bequeathed to men as well as women (Fine 1987). Those children who left the household (who married out) took money, animals, and small trousseau, or sometimes the usufruct rights to a field. This was, according to Agnes Fine, "the price for renunciating the fixed assets of the patrimony" (1987, 41). Fine describes how who was endowed and with what was determined according to cultural preferences—privileging masculinity, for example, or the eldest.

On the Iberian peninsula dote practices, if they exist at all, vary a good deal by region. Among the cattle-herding Pasiegos of the province of Santander (Freeman 1979, 118), the dote consists of livestock and the opportunity for meadow rental. It "is discussed before banns are announced, but its full extent is not determined, nor is it handed over to the new couple until they have completed the traditional term of co-residence in one or both of the parental

6. Tentori (1976, 283) makes the extremely interesting observation that adopted children show greater humanity than legitimate ones toward the old in expression of gratitude for having been taken in. His discussion of the emergence of neighborly ties is certainly intriguing in light of the debates about "amoral familism" (Banfield 1958; Berkowitz 1984; Silverman 1968) in southern Italy. See Du Boulay and Williams (1987) for a recent reevaluation of amoral familism.

households." The Pasiegos bestow dotes on both sons and daughters and any inequalities are recorded, to be adjusted later when the parental estate is divided. The dote becomes the joint property of the new couple once they have set themselves up as an independent unit. The dote, or marriage portion, is distinguished from the *ajuar,* or trousseau—the domestic equipment that the bride brings with her—bedclothes, blankets, and a mattress. In the Spanish village of Santa Maria del Monte, province of Leon (Behar 1986), the word *dote* refers to a marriage portion from each set of parents. In the past it was an advance on future inheritance, consisting of linens and clothing.

Control of the dote among the Pasiegos tends to pass soon after marriage into the hands of the newly married couple, but in much of the rest of Iberia postmortem inheritance for children of both sexes is emphasized, even when a marriage portion is bestowed. This is frequently associated with powerful ideas about equality, but as João de Pina-Cabral (1986, 67) observes for villages in northwestern Portugal, "this does not mean that [heirs] will inherit the same amount and the same thing."

Although Castilian law permits the free disposition of one-third of inherited property as well as one-half of the remaining two-thirds, in the hamlet of Valdemora in the Sierra Ministra (Freeman 1970) the custom of totally egalitarian division is strictly adhered to. A trousseau (ajuar) of linens and clothing, a bed, and other household equipment and furniture is assembled prior to marriage. It is a gift to daughters, particularly to those who have continued to live with their parents before marrying, working for the household at no salary. Records are supposed to be kept, but Susan Tax Freeman claims that they are avoided because not all gifts are equal and children do not all behave in the same way toward their parents. Coresidence with elders until the first harvest (when the young couple had their own seed to sow) was common in the past, but today independent households are formed. Land is divided at the death of the parents.

Strict and rigid egalitarianism is also characteristic of southern Spain (Pitt-Rivers 1961), adopted in some cases to "combat the competitiveness of rapacious siblings and affines" (Gilmore 1980, 158).[7] Dowry, rarely given, represents an advance on the share of inheritance. Newlyweds usually have their own home, often one rented by the husband. According to J. A. Pitt-Rivers (1961, 100), an older tradition in some parts of Andalusia was for elderly

---

7. The potential conflicts that are associated with property division have been discussed by several anthropologists of Mediterranean Europe (Davis 1977; Herzfeld 1980b; Riegelhaupt 1967). In the wills made by northwestern Portuguese peasants, parents express a hope that their children will "behave themselves," "conserve peace and friendship," "act without discord," and "conduct the apportionment amicably according to God's law."

parents to keep a daughter or daughter-in-law with them for the first year of marriage. The object was "to assist the newly married couple to set up a home" by allowing the husband to save his earnings.

In other regions of Spain an egalitarian ideology does not prevail. Single heirs are chosen by the Basques of northeastern Spain (Douglass 1971, 1974) and in Catalonia (Iszaevich 1975). They live with the parents and acquire rights to the property at the death of the senior generation. In the mountainous regions of eastern Galicia a system of preferential partibility is the rule (Bauer 1987; Lison-Tolosana 1976, 1983). The eldest male or some other male marries at home and receives two-thirds of the total estate and an equal share of the remaining third. He becomes the legal owner while his parents retain usufruct rights during their lifetimes; his obligation is to look after them, working without salary and taking care of their funeral expenses. Unmarried children can remain in the household, exchanging labor for shelter. In coastal Galicia a different system prevails. Daughters are preferential heirs to the house and surrounding fields or to the house and fields and an equal share of the remainder of the property.

Customs of property transmission in southern Portugal reflect those of southern Spain (Cutileiro 1977). Dowries are absent, and the trousseaux that newlyweds bring to a marriage do not represent a major portion of the assets that will come to them at death. Those in northwestern Portugal closely approximate some regions of northwestern Spain. Made to a daughter just prior to marriage, the dote is generally a promise on the part of the senior generation and an expectation on the part of the junior generation that an actual transfer of property that includes fixed assets will occur at the death of one or both members of the senior generation (Pina-Cabral 1986; Dias 1981). In the past, the dote generally included the parental household, and the bequest invariably specified that the daughter and her husband live with the bride's parents. Such promises of future inheritance were revokable in the event that children did not treat parents well. If daughters were given dotes, sons were given *doações,* either at marriage or at another time during their life course. These sometimes involved the actual transfer of property, but the bestowers frequently retained usufruct rights. Property was actually transferred after death, often according to terms outlined in wills. If there was a surviving spouse, he or she retained usufruct rights and thus a degree of authority over the children. Wills emphasized equality, but one child—the one who had contributed the most labor and services to the parents in their advancing age— was the recipient of one-third of the estate in addition to an equal portion of the remaining two-thirds (Brettell 1986).

To summarize, in the southern European countries of the western Mediterranean the dote is quite different from the dowry as defined by Goody. Dowries in the countries of the central Mediterranean conform more closely to his definition, but whereas in some areas it is an institution with deep historical roots (Greece and Italy), in others (Yugoslavia) its practice is more recent. Although a transfer at marriage to a daughter does seem to be common to the dowry practices of Greece and Italy, there are major differences in what and how much is transferred. As a result, patterns of residence and family forms vary enormously, just as they do in the western Mediterranean, where the emphasis is on postmortem inheritance. The neat correlations between systems of inheritance, domestic group structures, and residence and marriage patterns proposed by Goody are hard to uphold. In some cases it is apparent that important changes in the composition of dowry have occurred, and yet use of the term obscures their significance. Furthermore, the degree and timing (is it at marriage or later) of a woman's access to and control of her dowry—if she controls it at all—are not always specified and no doubt also vary. Unless this is made clear, we cannot begin to answer questions about the relation between property and the status and power of women, or about the continuing obligations between parents and children in terms of property devolution.

If a broad regional pattern is no longer sustainable, how are comparison and generalization possible? The myriad local variations that I have just described provide an answer. These variations are different solutions to the common problems faced by families. As Richard Smith (1984, 4) has recently proposed, we need to consider more critically "the direction of causality in the relationship between a society's property distribution, devolution and kinship system." Rather than emphasizing property first as the determinative factor organizing kinship relations and domestic group structures, we should begin with social relations and cultural values and determine how they shape decisions about when property is transferred, what is transferred, and to whom it is transferred. In the context of property transactions, of which the bestowing of dowry is merely one, the rights and obligations among kin and between men and women are both expressed and negotiated.

SOCIAL RELATIONS, CULTURAL VALUES, AND PROPERTY TRANSMISSION

Why do parents in some societies transmit significant shares of their property at the marriages of their children whereas those in others hold onto the major portion until death? If, as Goody (1976) has observed, late timing is directly related to the desire of parents to retain control, why do some parents give this up early? Although a full answer to this question requires more

historical and ethnographic specificity than is possible in this chapter, it is
nevertheless apparent that the difference is partly related to the way in which
the rights and obligations between parents and children are defined.

One such obligation for children is to care for their parents in their advancing years. Though this obligation should be voluntary, arising from emotional
attachments, more often than not incentive and interest play a role. The right to
property is frequently conceived of as a payment for services that have been or
will be rendered. The relationship between server and servee (child and parent)
can be quite businesslike, reinforced through contracts formulated at some
point in the life course—at the marriage of a particular child who is then
designated as the favored heir, at the retirement of parents from active work in
agriculture, or at the death of one parent (in the form of a will).[8] By holding
onto their property rights, actual or usufruct, until death, parents are assured
that their best interests are served.

Even where the law calls for equal division (partibility), parents usually
have the right to bequeath freely a specified portion of their assets. This
discretionary portion not only bolsters parental authority but also is an attractive incentive to the child, single or married, who accepts the role of primary
caretaker. Its importance to some of the peasant populations of Europe is
evident in the results of an 1866 agricultural survey of France. This survey
demonstrated that peasants, unlike the bourgeoisie, did not wholly accept the
concept of equal division specified in the civil code. They "were keen to leave
the father with a larger share of his property to dispose of as he saw fit. Groups
of small owners even got together to petition the senate for this reform" (Zeldin
1973, 144).

Postmortem inheritance in many social contexts perpetuates dependence, of
children on parents as well as of parents on children. As other forms of old age
security (generally from the state) are established, they lay the basis, as Sant
Cassia (1982) argues for Cyprus, for an increasing emphasis on inter vivos
transfers. In addition, when alternative ways to earn a living become possible,
land loses its meaning as the only focus of livelihood. Parents no longer need to
retain the labor and support of their children to survive, and children no longer
see their futures held in the hands of their parents.

8. For further discussion of retirement contracts in particular, see Gaunt (1987) and Plakans
(1989). Though Aage Sørensen (1989) questions the emphasis on property as old age security
(he prefers to stress the goal of maintaining property within the family), there is enough evidence
in wills and other legal documents, as well as in statements made by the informants of anthropological inquiries, to support this view. Richard Saller's observations (chapter 2 this volume) are equally relevant. Ancient Romans had more immediate concerns than making certain
that the patrimony remained in the male line forever.

Substantial premortem payments such as dowry largely concern independence, though whether they disinherit offspring from all further claims to the patrimony varies from one social context to another. In some areas dowry, like postmortem inheritance, is also conceived of as something that parents owe a daughter for the labor she has contributed to their household prior to her marriage. But another obligation is frequently more significant—the obligation of parents, if not brothers as well, to ensure the marriages of their daughters (or sisters). Although further data are necessary to substantiate the claim, dowry may be more fundamental in societies where there is less toleration of spinsterhood. It appears to have greater significance in societies where a woman's role as wife and mother is emphasized more than her role as economic producer or where there are few alternatives to marriage and child rearing. Dowry may be the focus of greater parental effort, as Davis (1977) has suggested, in societies where providing for women is a man's obligation and duty, part of what it means to be an honored male. In this respect the timing of property transmission concerns gender relations as much as intergenerational relations.

I have distinguished the dependence embedded in postmortem transfers of wealth from the independence inherent in marriage portions. This distinction is not pure, which tells us something about culturally specific notions of kinship. What is bequeathed by means of a marriage portion like dowry can in some cases perpetuate social relations. To live in independent households acquired at marriage while continuing to work the family land—land that will be transferred only at death—in cooperation with other kin obviously has different implications for familial relations than if both land and house are transferred at marriage. Furthermore, house and land have different meanings in different cultural contexts.

The house is at the center of kinship and gender relations, both of which vary throughout the Mediterranean. In some regions of northwestern Portugal and Spain, men often marry and move in with their in-laws, accepting, for at least some portion of their life course, the authority of a father-in-law. In other regions of Iberia, as well as in certain localities of Italy, Greece, and Yugoslavia, it is the woman who moves in with her husband's kin, accepting a position of subordination with respect to a mother-in-law and sisters-in-law. Finally, some Greek and Italian men accept the house given to them by their in-laws as part of their wife's dowry. It is generally an independent physical structure, and within it they can establish a household over which they have authority.

These differences reflect varying gender ideologies in the Mediterranean region, ideologies that define not only relationships between the sexes, but also within the sexes. The houses that are provided to daughters at their marriage, for example, create clusters of households linked through female kin. Although such clusters have been explored in some regions of Iberia (Brettell 1988; Pina-Cabral 1986), they have been overlooked in Italy and Greece, where the literature tends to emphasize patrilineality in its analysis of family, property, and gender relations. Only Davis (1977) raises the question of the appropriateness of the term *neolocality* itself when such houses are generally located in proximity to the natal household. Through property transmission, people in different cultures either reinforce existing kinship ties or, as in the case of the Sarakatsani shepherds described by Campbell (1964), forge new alliances.

Houses, like trousseau linens, are symbolic referents of womanhood in particular cultural contexts. When bestowed on women, houses tend to define the domestic and reproductive sphere as opposed to the nondomestic and productive sphere. Land, conversely, represents the latter and is both associated with and inherited by men. The significance of this distinction is most apparent in Davis's (1973) description of change in Pisticci. Once the population moved off the land and found other ways to earn income, land acquired symbolic meaning and was transmitted to women as part of their dowries. Land, like trousseau, became a treasure. Alternatively, in regions like northwestern Portugal where women have worked the land as much as if not more than men, their rights to both inherit and transmit it are of long standing. Both land and women are productive. In addition, the house is more than the center of domestic life; it is part of the unit of production and an extremely valued asset in the distribution of property at the death of the senior generation.

In Sardinia (Da Re 1987) women are given less land because they do not work it. They are also given less because their brothers have contributed to their trousseaux and parents are trying to achieve a measure of equality among all their offspring. The rights and obligations among brothers and sisters are frequently mediated by this principle of equality, which despite the Sardinian solution is best achieved at the death of the senior generation, because the patrimony fluctuates throughout their lifetimes (Davis 1977). If parents transfer very little wealth before their death, their children must ultimately formulate an equitable distribution. In the Spanish province of Leon (Behar 1986) the principle that each offspring should receive a share in every category of property that the parents possess creates a tedious process of evaluation, argument, and maneuvering. Every asset is assigned a monetary value, and the resulting apportionment can be problematic. "In the fluid world of partible inheritance one could own a door without having to own the house it opened onto; just as, in the opposite case, one could own the house and not own the doors through which to enter it" (Behar 1986, 72). When a plot of land is divided into several pieces, one heir may be obligated to give his siblings right of way or access to a water source that is located on the piece he or she has inherited. Though partibility should in principle establish independence, it often requires interdependence and cooperation among siblings.

Within households, the social position of unmarried siblings and widows is clearly substantiated by their rights to both inherit and transmit fixed property. The spinster of the Sierra Caurel (Bauer 1987) who remains in the household of the brother chosen as preferential heir must earn her keep and no doubt has little power in family matters. She is a subordinate, even to a sister-in-law. Alternatively, where no favored heir is designated and both fixed and movable assets are divided among several siblings, a spinster is on equal footing with a brother and sister-in-law who have married in. Indeed, she may use her property rights to foster the attention of a particular nephew or niece, who in turn hopes that the aunt will remember the favors with a bequest at her death.

Inheritance practices are not determinative. One does not have a three-generation stem family because property is transmitted impartibly; one has such a family because parents want at least one child to remain at home, work on the farm, and assist them as they get older. In other words, within the broad context of the law, mechanisms for transferring property are strategies pursued to solve some of the problems faced by families of the past and the present, of Italy, Greece, and Portugal—how to secure support in old age, how to contract a marriage for a child, how to provide for all one's children, how to maintain the social status of all members of the family. Transferring wealth is a form of economic behavior, but as with most economic behavior studied by anthropologists, it has a social dimension as well. Through the transmission of property people make powerful statements about the meanings of parenthood and childhood, of maleness and femaleness, and of kinship and alliance.

REFERENCES

Abouçaya, Claude. 1966. "Les différents conceptions de la *donatio mortis causa* chez les romanistes médiévaux." *Revue historique de droit français et étranger* 44:378–431.

Abt, A. F., and F. H. Garrison. 1965. *History of Pediatrics*. Philadelphia: W. B. Saunders.

Accursius. 1596. *Glossa ordinaria*. Venice.

Alberico da Rosciate. 1586. *In primam Codicis partem commentarii*. Venice.

Alberti, Leon Battista. 1946. *I primi tre libri della famiglia*. Ed. Francesco Carlo Pellegrini. Florence: Sansoni.

Anatra, Bruno, and Giuseppe Puggioni. 1973. "Considerazioni su alcune caratteristiche socio-demographiche della popolazione di Sanluri nel XVII secolo in base alle fonti ecclesiastiche." Pp. 256–279 in *Problemi di utilizzazione delle fonti di demografia storica*. Rome: Comitato Italiano per lo Studio dei Problemi della Popolazione.

Anderson, Alastair. 1984. *Roman Military Tombstones*. Aylesbury, Bucks: Shire Publications.

Angeli, Aurora. 1987. "Strutture familiari e nuzialità nel Bolognese a metà '800." Paper presented at the First Spanish-Portuguese-Italian Conference on Historical Demography, Barcelona, 22–25 April.

Ankum, Hans. 1985. "La 'captive adultera': Problèmes concernant l'*accusatio adulterii* en droit roman classique." *Revue d'histoire des droits de l'antiquité* 32:153–205.

———. 1987. "La 'sponsa adultera': Problèmes concernant l'*accusatio adulterii* en droit roman classique." Pp. 161–196 in *Estudios de derecho romano en honor de A. D'Ors*. Pamplona: EUNSA.

Antoninus of Florence, Saint. 1487. *Summa theologica*. Nuremberg: Anton Koberger.

———. 1581–1582. *Summa sacrae theologiae*. Venice.

Antonius de Bitonto. 1495. *Sermones dominicales per totum annum*. Strasbourg: Johann Gruninger.

Aretinus de Gambilionibus, Angelus. 1551. *De maleficiis*. Lyons: Dionysius Harsaens.

Ariès, Philippe. 1962. *Centuries of Childhood*. Trans. Robert Baldick. New York: Knopf.

———. 1974. *Western Attitudes toward Death: From the Middle Ages to the Present*. Trans. Patricia M. Ranum. Baltimore: Johns Hopkins University Press.

———. 1981. *The Hour of Our Death.* Trans. Helen Weaver. New York: Knopf.

Arlacchi, Pino. 1980. *Mafia, contadini, e latifondo nella Calabria tradizionale.* Bologna: Il Mulino.

Arru, Angiolina. 1987. "La conosco bene perchè è sempre stata a casa mia a servire." Paper presented at the First Spanish-Portuguese-Italian Conference on Historical Demography, Barcelona, 22–25 April.

Astuti, Guido. 1978. "Recezione teorica e applicazione pratica del diritto romano dell'età del Rinascimento giuridico." Pp. 2–25 in *Le droit romain et sa réception en Europe,* edited by Henryk Kupiszewki and Witold Wolodkiewicz. Warsaw: University of Warsaw.

Azimonti, Eugenio. 1909. *Inchiesta parlamentare sulle condizioni dei contadini nelle provincie meridionali e nella Sicilia, Basilicata,* vol. 5, pt. 1. Rome: Tipografia Nazionale di Giovanni Bertero.

Baille, Lodovico. 1967. "Discorso inaugurale della R. Società Agraria ed Economica di Cagliari." In *La Sardegna di Carlo Felice e il problema della terra,* edited by Carlino Sole. Cagliari: Sarda Fossataro.

Balletto, Laura, ed. 1971. *Statuta antiquissima Saone (1345).* 2 vols. Collana Storica di Fonti e Studi nos. 8 and 9. Genoa: Università di Genova, Istituto di Medievistica.

Banfield, Edward C. 1958. *The Moral Basis of a Backward Society.* Glencoe, Ill.: Free Press.

Barbagli, Marzio. 1988. *Sotto lo stesso tetto: Mutamenti della famiglia in Italia dal XV al XX secolo.* 2d ed. Bologna: Il Mulino.

Barnes, J. A. 1964. "Physical and Social Kinship." *Philosophy of Science* 28:296–299.

Bartolo da Sassoferrato. 1570–1571a. *In primam et secundam Infortiati partem.* Venice.

———. 1570–1571b. *In primam et secundam Codicis partem commentaria.* Venice.

———. 1590. *Commentaria in Corpus juris civilis: Tomus IV in secondam Digesti novi partem.* Venice.

Bartolomeo da Saliceto. 1515. *In primam et secundam Codicis libros commentaria.* Lyons.

Bauer, Rainer Lutz. 1987. "Inheritance and Inequality in a Spanish Galician Community." *Ethnohistory* 34:171–193.

Beccaria, Cesare. 1965. *Dei delitti e delle pene.* Ed. F. Venturi. Turin: Einaudi.

Beck, H. G. J. 1950. *The Pastoral Care of Sculs in South-East France during the Sixth Century.* Analecta Gregoriana 51. Rome: Aedes Universitatis Gregorianae.

Becker, Marvin. 1965. "A Study in Political Failure: The Florentine Magnates, 1280–1343." *Medieval Studies* 27:246–308.

Behar, Ruth. 1986. *Santa Maria del Monte: The Presence of the Past in a Spanish Village.* Princeton: Princeton University Press.

Bellomo, Manlio. 1961. *Ricerche sui rapporti patrimoniali tra coniugi: Contributo alla storia della famiglia medievale.* Milan: Giuffrè.

———. 1967. "Familia (diritto intermedio)." Pp. 744–778 in *Enciclopedia del diritto,* vol. 16. Milan: Giuffrè.

Belton, N. R. 1986. "Rickets—Not Only the 'English Disease.'" *Acta Paediatrica Scandinavica* supplement 323:68–75.

Benedict, Saint. 1971–1972. *La règle de Saint Benoît.* Ed. Adalbert de Vogüé and Jean Neufville. 6 vols. Série de Textes Monastiques de l'Occident 24–29. Paris: Cerf.

Benigno, Francesco. 1985. *Una casa, una terra: Ricerche su Paceco, paese nuovo nella Sicilia del sei e settecento.* Catania: Cooperativa Universitaria Editrice Catanese Magistero.

———. 1988. "Per un'analisi del gruppo coresidente nella Sicilia moderna: Il caso di Noto nel 1647." Paper presented at the conference "La famiglia ieri e oggi," Bari, 1–3 December.

———. 1989. "The Southern Italian Family in the Early Modern Period: A Discussion of Co-residential Patterns." *Continuity and Change* 4:165–194.

Bennett, John. 1976. *The Ecological Transition: Cultural Anthropology and Human Adaptation.* New York: Pergamon.

Berkner, Lutz. 1972. "The Stem-Family and the Developmental Cycle of the Peasant Household: An Eighteenth Century Austrian Example." *American Historical Review* 77:398–418.

Berkowitz, Susan G. 1984. "Familism, Kinship and Sex Roles in Southern Italy: Contradictory Ideals and Real Contradictions." *Anthropological Quarterly* 57:83–91.

Berry, B. Midi, and Roger S. Schofield. 1971. "Age at Baptism in Pre-industrial England." *Population Studies* 25:453–463.

Besta, Enrico. 1933. *La famiglia nella storia del diritto italiano.* Milan: Giuffrè.

Bettini, Maurizio. 1988a. *Antropologia e cultura romana: Parentela, tempo, immagini dell'anima.* 2d ed. Rome: La Nuova Italia Scientifica.

———. 1988b. "Il dievieto fino al 'sesto grado' incluso nel matrimonio romano." *Athenaeum* 66:69–98.

Betto, Bianca, ed. 1986. *Gli statuti del comune di Treviso (sec. XIII–XIV).* Fonti per la Storia d'Italia no. 111. Rome: Istituto Storico Italiano per Il Medio Evo.

Biagioli, Giuliana. 1986. "La diffusione della mezzadria nell'Italia centrale: Un modello di sviluppo demografico ed economico." *Bollettino di demografia storica* 3:219–235.

Bianco, Carla. 1988. "The Mezzadria Family: Study of Kinship Roles in the Life Cycle." *Ethnologia europaea* 18:135–148.

Blayney, Jan. 1986. "Theories of Conception in the Ancient Roman World." Pp. 230–236 in *The Family in Ancient Rome: New Perspectives,* edited by Beryl Rawson. Ithaca: Cornell University Press.

Bloch, Marc. 1953. *The Historian's Craft.* Trans. Peter Putnam. New York: Vintage.

Blok, Anton. 1981. "Rams and Billy-Goats: A Key to the Mediterranean Honor Code." *Man* 16:427–440.

Bluhme, Friedrich, ed. 1868. *Leges Langobardorum. Monumenta Germaniae historica,* Legum 4. Hannover.

———. 1875–1889. *Edictum Theodorici regis. Monumenta Germaniae historica,* Legum 5. Hannover.

Bobik, Joseph. 1965. *Aquinas on Being and Essence.* Notre Dame: University of Notre Dame Press.

Bonfield, Lloyd. 1979. "Marriage Settlements and the 'Rise of Great Estates': The Demographic Aspect." *Economic History Review* n.s. 32:483–493.

Bongino, Antonio. 1966. "Relazione dei vari progetti sovra diverse materie che riflettono la Sardegna." Pp. 129–379 in *Il riformismo settecentesco in Sardegna: Relazioni inedite di Piemontesi,* edited by Luigi Bulferetti. Cagliari: Sarda Fossataro.

Boniface, Saint. 1916. *S. Bonifatii et Lulli epistolae.* Ed. M. Tangl. *Monumenta Germaniae historica, Epistolae selectae* 1. Hannover.

Bordiga, Oreste. 1909. *Inchiesta parlamentare sulle condizioni dei contadini nelle provincie meridionali e nella Sicilia, Campania,* vol. 4, pt. 1. Rome: Tipografia Nazionale di Giovanni Bertero.

Borias, André. 1977. "Les relations du moins avec sa famille d'après le Maître et S. Benoît." *Regulae Benedicti studia: Annuarium internationale* 5:13–25.

Bossen, Laurel. 1988. "Toward a Theory of Marriage: The Economic Anthropology of Marriage Transactions." *Ethnology* 27:127–144.

Boswell, John. 1988. *The Kindness of Strangers: The Abandonment of Children in Western Europe from Late Antiquity to the Renaissance.* New York: Pantheon.

Bourdieu, Pierre. 1977. *Outline of a Theory of Practice.* Trans. Richard Nice. London: Cambridge University Press.

Bowring, Sir John. 1838. *Report on the Statistics of Tuscany, Lucca, the Pontifical, and the Lombardo-Venetian States; with a Special Reference to Their Commercial Relations.* London: Her Majesty's Stationery Office.

Boyaval, Bernard. 1976. "Remarques sur les indications d'âges de l'épigraphie funéraire grecque d'Egypte." *Zeitschrift für Papyrologie und Epigraphik* 21:217–243.

———. 1977. "Démographie différentielle et épigraphie funéraire grecque d'Egypte." *Zeitschrift für Papyrologie und Epigraphik* 26:262–266.

Bradley, Keith R. 1980. "Sexual Regulations in Wet-Nursing Contracts from Roman Egypt." *Klio* 62:321–325.

———. 1986. "Wet Nursing at Rome: A Study in Social Relations." Pp. 201–229 in *The Family in Ancient Rome: New Perspectives,* edited by Beryl Rawson. Ithaca: Cornell University Press.

———. 1987a. "Dislocation in the Roman Family." *Historical Reflections/Réflexions historiques* 14:33–62.

———. 1987b. *Slaves and Masters in the Roman Empire: A Study in Social Control.* Oxford: Oxford University Press.

Brain, Peter. 1986. *Galen on Bloodletting.* Cambridge: Cambridge University Press.

Brandes, Stanley, 1975. *Migration, Kinship and Community.* New York: Academic Press.

———. 1980. *Metaphors of Masculinity.* Philadelphia: University of Pennsylvania Press.

———. 1987. "Reflections on Honor and Shame in the Mediterranean." Pp. 121–134 in *Honor and Shame and the Unity of the Mediterranean,* edited by David D. Gilmore. Washington, D.C.: American Anthropological Association.

Bresc, Henri. 1986. *Un monde méditerranéen: Economie et société en Sicile, 1300–1450.* Rome: Ecole Française de Rome.

Bresson, Alain. 1986. "Graphes et réseaux de parenté en Grèce ancienne." Pp. 261–277 in *Informatique et prosopographie: Actes de la Table ronde du CNRS, Paris, 25–26 octobre, 1984.* Paris: Centre National de la Recherche Scientifique.

Brettell, Caroline B. 1986. *Men Who Migrate, Women Who Wait: Population and History in a Portuguese Parish.* Princeton: Princeton University Press.

———. 1988. "Emigration and Household Structure in a Portuguese Parish, 1850–1920." *Journal of Family History* 13:33–58.

Brind'Amour, Lise, and Pierre Brind'Amour. 1971. "La deuxième satire de Perse et le *dies lustricus.*" *Latomus* 30:999–1024.

———. 1975. "Le *dies lustricus,* les oiseaux de l'aurore et l'amphidromie." *Latomus* 34:17–58.

Brown, Peter. 1987. "Late Antiquity." Pp. 253–311 in *A History of Private Life, Vol. 1, From Pagan Rome to Byzantium,* edited by Paul Veyne and translated by Arthur Goldhammer. Cambridge: Harvard University Press.

———. 1988. *The Body and Society: Men, Women, and Sexual Renunciation in Early Christianity.* New York: Columbia University Press.

Brucker, Gene. 1962. *Florentine Politics and Society, 1343–1378.* Princeton: Princeton University Press.

———, ed. 1971. *The Society of Renaissance Florence: A Documentary Study.* New York: Harper Torchbooks.

———, ed. 1977. *The Civic World of Early Renaissance Florence.* Princeton: Princeton University Press.

Bruni, Leonardo. 1978. "Panygyric to the City of Florence." Pp. 135–175 in *The Earthly Republic,* edited by Benjamin G. Kohl and Ronald G. Witt. Philadelphia: University of Pennsylvania Press.

Brunt, P. A. 1971. *Italian Manpower, 225 B.C.–A.D. 14.* Oxford: Clarendon.

———. 1980. "Free Labour and Public Works at Rome." *Journal of Roman Studies* 70:81–100.

———. 1988. *The Fall of the Roman Republic and Related Essays.* Oxford: Clarendon.

Brydone, Patrick. 1774. *A Tour through Sicily and Malta.* 2 vols. London: W. Strahan.

Bullough, Vern L. 1973. "Medieval Medical and Scientific Views of Women." *Viator* 4:485–501.

Buonaccorsi, Biagio. 1976. *Libro di ricordi.* Pp. 169–223 in *Biagio Buonaccorsi: Sa vie—son temps—son oeuvre.* Ed. Denis Fachard. Bologna: Massimiliano Boni.

Bynum, Caroline Walker. 1982. *Jesus as Mother: Studies in the Spirituality of the High Middle Ages.* Berkeley: University of California Press.

Caesarius of Arles. 1937–1941. *Sancti Caesarii episcopi arlelatensis opera omnia.* Ed. Germain Morin. 2 vols. in 3. Maretioli.

———. 1988. *Césaire d'Arles, oeuvres monastiques,* vol. 1, *Oeuvres pour les moniales.* Ed. Adalbert de Vogüé and Joël Courreau. Sources Chrétiennes 345. Paris: Cerf.

Caggese, Romolo, ed. 1910. *Statuti della Repubblica fiorentina,* vol. 1, *Statuto del Capitano del Popolo degli anni 1322–1325.* Florence: Ariani.

———, ed. 1921. *Statuti della Repubblica fiorentina,* vol. 2, *Statuto del Podestà dell'anno 1325.* Florence: Ariani.

Calvinus, Julius Caesar. 1675. *De aequitate.* Milan.

Cammarosano, Paolo. 1977. "Les structures familiales dans les villes de l'Italie communale (XII–XIV s.)." Pp. 181–194 in *Famille et parenté dans l'Occidente médiévale,* edited by Georges Duby and Jacques Le Goff. Rome: Ecole Française de Rome.

Campbell, John. 1964. *Honor, Family and Patronage: A Study of Institutions and Moral Values in a Greek Mountain Community.* Oxford: Clarendon.

Cantarella, Eva. 1976. *Studi sull'omicidio in diritto greco e romano.* Milan: Giuffrè.

Caraccioli, Ivo. 1960. "Causa d'onore." Pp. 580–586 in *Enciclopedia del diritto,* vol. 6. Milan: Giuffrè.

Casalinuovo, Aldo. 1939. *La causa d'onore nella struttura del reato.* Naples: Jovene.

Caso, Anna. 1981. "Per la storia della società milanese: I corredi nuziali nell'ultima età viscontea e nel periodo della repubblica ambrosiana (1433–1450), dagli atti del notaio Protaso Sansoni." *Nuova rivista storica* 65:521–551.

Casselberry, Samuel E., and Nancy Valavanes. 1976. "Matrilocal Greek Peasants and a Reconsideration of Residence Terminology." *American Ethnologist* 3:215–226.

Cavalca, Desiderio. 1967–1968. "Il ceto magnatizio a Firenze dopo gli Ordinamenti di Giustizia." *Rivista di storia del diritto italiano* 40–41:85–132.

Certaldo, Paolo da. 1945. *Libro di buoni costumi.* Ed. Alfredo Schiaffini. Florence: Le Monnier.

Chabot, Isabelle. 1988. "Widowhood and Poverty in Late Medieval Florence." *Continuity and Change* 3:291–311.

Champlin, Edward. 1986. "Miscellanea testamentaria." *Zeitschrift für Papyrologie und Epigraphik* 62:247–255.

Chelotti, Marcella, Rosanna Gaeta, Vincenza Morizio, and Marina Silvestrini. 1985. *Le épigrafi romane di Canosa.* Bari: Regione Puglia.

Chojnacki, Stanley. 1974. "Patrician Women in Early Renaissance Venice." *Studies in the Renaissance* 21:176–203.

———. 1985. "Kinship Ties and Young Patricians in Fifteenth-Century Venice." *Renaissance Quarterly* 38: 240–270.

CISP, ed. 1972–1974. *Le fonti della demografia storica in Italia.* 3 vols. Rome: Comitato Italiano per lo Studio dei Problemi della Popolazione.

Clarus, Julius Alexandrinus. 1583. *Volumen, alias Liber Quintus: In quo omnium criminum materia sub receptis sententiis copiosissime tractatur. . . .* Venice.

Coale, Ansley J., and Paul Demeny. 1983. *Regional Model Life Tables and Stable Populations.* New York: Academic Press.

Cohen, David. 1991. *Law, Sexuality, and Society: The Enforcement of Morals at Classical Athens.* Cambridge: Cambridge University Press.

Cohn, Samuel, Jr. 1989. "Donne e Controriforma a Siena: Autorità e proprietà nella famiglia." *Studi storici* 30:203–224.

Coletti, Francesco. 1908. *La mortalità nei primi anni di età e la vita sociale della Sardegna.* Turin: Fratelli Bocca.

Collier, Jane. 1974. "Women in Politics." Pp. 89–96 in *Women, Culture, and Society,* edited by Michelle Rosaldo and Louise Lamphere. Stanford: Stanford University Press.

Comaroff, John. 1980. *The Meaning of Marriage Payments.* New York: Academic Press.

Constable, Giles. 1987. "The Ceremonies and Symbolism of Entering Religious Life and Taking the Monastic Habit, from the Fourth to the Twelfth Century." *Segni* 2:771–834.

Conti, Elio. 1984. *L'imposta diretta a Firenze nel quattrocento (1427–1494).* Studi Storici fasc. 136–139. Rome: Istituto Storico Italiano per Il Medio Evo.

Corbett, Percy E. 1930. *The Roman Law of Marriage.* Oxford: Clarendon.

Corbier, Mireille. 1982. "Les familles clarissimes d'Afrique proconsulaire (Ier-IIIe siècles)." Pp. 685–754 in *Atti del colloquio internazionale AIEGLSU Epigrafia e ordine senatorio, Roma 14–20 maggio 1981. Series 5,* vol. 2. Rome.

———. 1985. "Idéologie et pratique de l'héritage (Ier s. av J.-C.—IIe s. ap. J.-C.)." *Index* 13:501–528.

———. 1987. "Les comportements familiaux de l'aristocratie romaine (IIe siècle avant J.-C.–IIe siècle après J.-C.)." *Annales E.S.C.* 6:1267–1285.

———. 1988. "Pour une pluralité des approches prosopographiques." *Mélanges de l'Ecole Française de Rome, Moyen-Age, temps modernes* 100:187–197.

———. 1991. "Divorce and Adoption as Roman Familial Strategies." (Le divorce et l'adoption "en plus"). Pp. 47–78 in *Marriage, Divorce, and Children in Ancient Rome,* edited by Beryl Rawson. Oxford: Oxford University Press.

Cornelisen, Ann. 1976. *Women of the Shadows.* New York: Random House.

Cortese, Ennio. 1964. *Appunti sulla storia giuridica sarda.* Milan: Giuffrè.

Couroucli, Maria M. 1987. "Dot et société de Grèce moderne." Pp. 327–348 in *Femmes et patrimoine dans les sociétés rurales de l'Europe méditerranéenne,* edited by G. Ravis-Giordani. Paris: Centre National de la Recherche Scientifique.

Crivellari, Giulio. 1896. *Il codice penale per il Regno d'Italia . . . per l'avvocato Giulio Crivellari.* Turin: Unione Tipografico-Editrice.

Cronin, Constance. 1977. "Illusion and Reality in Sicily." Pp. 67–93 in *Sexual Stratification: A Cross-Cultural View,* edited by Alice Schlegel. New York: Columbia University Press.

Crook, J. A. 1967. *Law and Life of Rome.* Ithaca: Cornell University Press.

———. 1973. "Intestacy in Roman Society." *Proceedings of the Cambridge Philological Society* n.s. 19:38–44.

———. 1986. "Women in Roman Succession." Pp. 58–82 in *The Family in Ancient Rome: New Perspectives,* edited by Beryl Rawson. Ithaca: Cornell University Press.

Csillag, Pal. 1976. *The Augustan Laws on Family Relations.* Budapest: Akademiai Kiado.

Currie, Sarah. Forthcoming. "Paradise Lost: Original Sin and Early Christian Conceptions of Childhood."

Cutileiro, Jose. 1977. *Ricos e pobres no alentejo.* Lisbon: Livraria Sa da Costa.

Daly, Martin, and Margo I. Wilson. 1984. "A Sociobiological Analysis of Human Infanticide." Pp. 487–502 in *Infanticide: Comparative and Evolutionary Perspectives,* edited by G. Hausfater and S. B. Hrdy. New York: Aldine.

D'Amelio, Giuliana. 1965. *Illuminismo e scienza del diritto in Italia.* Milan: Giuffrè.

Da Molin, Giovanna. 1987. "Strutture familiari nell'Italia meridionale." Paper presented at the First Spanish-Portuguese-Italian Conference on Historical Demography, Barcelona, 22–25 April.

Daniélou, Jean. 1960. "La ministère des femmes dans l'Eglise ancienne." *La Maison Dieu* 61:70–96.

Da Re, Maria Gabriella. 1987. "Tous egaux, tous differents: Notes sur le système de transmission des biens materials en Trexenta." Pp. 137–162 in *Femmes et patrimoine dans les sociétés rurales de l'Europe méditerranéenne,* edited by G. Ravis-Giordani. Paris: Centre National de la Recherche Scientifique.

Daube, David. 1956. "The Accuser under the *lex Iulia de adulteriis.*" *Hellenika* 9:15–21.

———. 1972. "The *lex Iulia* concerning Adultery." *Irish Jurist* 7:373–380.

———. 1978. "Biblical Landmarks in the Struggle for Women's Rights." *Juridical Review* 90:177–197.

Davis, James. 1975. *A Venetian Family and Its Fortune, 1500–1900.* Philadelphia: American Philosophical Society.

Davis, John. 1973. *Land and Family in Pisticci.* New York: Humanities Press.

Davis, John. 1976. "An Account of Changes in Rules for Transmission of Property in Pisticci 1814 to 1961." Pp. 287–304 in *Mediterranean Family Structures,* edited by J. G. Peristiany. Cambridge: Cambridge University Press.

———. 1977. *The People of the Mediterranean: An Essay in Comparative Social Anthropology.* London: Routledge and Kegan Paul.

Day, John. 1983. "Problemi di demografia sarda nel periodo spagnolo e piemontese." *Quaderni bolotanesi* 9:31–43.

———. 1986. "La condizione femminile nella Sardegna medievale." Pp. 241–250 in *La famiglia e la vita quotidiana in Europa dal '400 al '600: Fonti e problemi.* Rome: Ministero per i Beni Culturali e Ambientali.

Decianus, Tiberius. 1593. *Tractatus criminalis D. Tiberii Deciani Utinensis.* Augusta Taurinorum: Haeredem Nicolai Beuilaquae.

Delaney, Carol. 1986. "The Meaning of Paternity and the Virgin Birth Debate." *Man* 21:494–513.

Delille, Gérard. 1985. *Famille et Propriété dans le Royaume de Naples (XVe–XIXe siècle).* Rome: Ecole Française de Rome.

Della Pina, Marco. 1986. "Gli insediamenti e la popolazione." Pp. 63–131 in *Prato: Storia di una città,* edited by Elena Fasano Guarini. Prato: Le Monnier.

———. 1987. "Famiglia mezzadrile e celibato: Le campagne di Prato nei secoli XVII e XVIII." Paper presented at the First Spanish-Portuguese-Italian Conference on Historical Demography, Barcelona, 22–25 April.

Del Lungo, Isidoro. 1886. "Una vendetta in Firenze il giorno di San Giovanni del 1295." *Archivio storico italiano,* 4th ser. 18:155–409.

Del Panta, Lorenzo. 1980. *Le epidemie nella storia demografica italiana (secoli XIV–XIX).* Turin: Loescher.

———. 1984. *Evoluzione demografica e popolamento nell'Italia dell'ottocento.* Bologna: Cooperativa Libraria Universitaria Editrice.

Del Panta, Lorenzo, and Massimo Livi Bacci. 1980. "Le componenti naturali dell'evoluzione demografica nell'Italia del settecento." Pp. 71–139 in *La popolazione italiana nel settecento: Relazioni e comunicazioni presentate al convegno su la ripresa demografica del settecento, Bologna, 26–28 aprile 1979,* edited by Società italiana di demografia storica. Bologna: Cooperativa Libraria Universitaria Editrice.

DeMause, Lloyd, ed. 1974. *The History of Childhood.* London: Condor.

Descombes, Françoise. 1985. *Recueil des inscriptions chrétiennes de la Gaule, vol. 15, Viennoise du nord.* Paris: Centre National de la Recherche Scientifique.

De Stefano, Francesco Paolo. 1979. *Romani, Longobardi, e Normanno-Franchi delle Puglie nei secoli XV–XVII: Ricerche sui rapporti patrimoniali fra coniugi fino alla Prammatica "De Antefato" di 1617.* Naples: Jovene.

Deubner, Ludwig. 1959. *Attische Feste.* Hildesheim: Olms.

de Varagine, Jacobus. 1497. *Sermones de sanctis per anni circulum, sermones quadragesimales, sermones de tempore.* Venice: Simon de Luere.

Dias, Jorge. 1981. *Vilharinho da furna,* vol. 2. Lisbon: Imprensa Nacional.

Dibenedetto, Giuseppe. 1976. *Gli archivi di stato di Terra di Bari.* Rome: Centro di Ricerca.

Dickemann, Mildred. 1975. "Demographic Consequences of Infanticide in Man." *Annual Review of Sociology and Systematics* 6:107–137.

Direzione Generale della Statistica. 1878. *Popolazione: Movimento dello stato civile, anno 1875.* Rome: Tipografia Cenniniana.

Dixon, Suzanne. 1984. "Family Finances: Tullia and Terentia." *Antichthon* 18:78–101.

———. 1985a. "The Marriage Alliance in the Roman Elite." *Journal of Family History* 10:353–378.

———. 1985b. "Polybius on Roman Women and Property." *American Journal of Philology* 106:147–170.

———. 1985c. "Breaking the Law to Do the Right Thing: The Gradual Erosion of the Voconian Law in Ancient Rome." *Adelaide Law Review* 9:519–534.

———. 1988. *The Roman Mother.* Norman: University of Oklahoma Press.

Donahue, Charles. 1980. "What Causes Fundamental Legal Ideas? Marital Property in England and France in the Thirteenth Century." *Michigan Law Review* 78:59–88.

Dorini, Umberto. 1923. *Il diritto penale e la delinquenza in Firenze nel sec. XIV.* Lucca: Corsi.

———. 1933. "La vendetta privata ai tempi di Dante." *Giornale Dantesco* 29:105–124.

Douglass, William A. 1971. "Rural Exodus in Two Spanish Basque Villages: A Cultural Explanation." *American Anthropologist* 73:1100–1114.

———. 1974. *Echalar and Murelaga: Opportunity and Rural Exodus in Two Spanish Basque Villages.* New York: St. Martin's.

———. 1980. "The South Italian Family: A Critique." *Journal of Family History* 5:338–359.

———. 1984. *Emigration in South Italian Town: An Anthropological History.* New Brunswick: Rutgers University Press.

Doveri, Andrea. 1987a. "Sposi e famiglie nelle compagne pisane di fine '800: Un caso di matrimonio mediterraneo?" Paper presented at the First Spanish-Portuguese-Italian Conference on Historical Demography, Barcelona, 22–25 April.

———. 1987b. "'Il padre che ha figliuoli grandi fuor li mandi': Una prima valutazione sulla diffusione e sul ruolo dei 'garzoni' nelle campagne pisane dei secoli XVII e XVIII." Paper presented at the meeting of the Society for Italian Historical Demography, Turin, 3–5 September.

Doxiadis, S., C. Angelis, P. Kasatzas, C. Vrettos, and P. Lapatsanis. 1976. "Genetic Aspects of Nutritional Rickets." *Archives of Disease in Childhood* 51:83–90.

Du Boulay, Juliet. 1974. *Portrait of a Greek Mountain Village.* Oxford: Clarendon.

Du Boulay, Juliet, and Rory Williams. 1987. "Amoral Familism and the Image of Limited Good." *Anthropological Quarterly* 60:12–24.

Du Cange, Carolus du Fresne, dominus. 1938. *Glossarium mediae et infimae Latinitatis,* vol. 6 (O–Q). New ed. Paris: Library of Sciences and Arts.

Dumézil, Georges. 1970. *Archaic Roman Religion.* Trans. Philip Krapp. 2 vols. Chicago: University of Chicago Press.

Dumont, François. 1928. *Les donations entre époux en droit romain.* Paris: Sirey.

Duval, Noël. 1975. *Recherches archéologiques à Haïdra.* vol. 1 of *Les inscriptions chrétiennes.* Rome: Ecole Française de Rome.

Elder, Glen H., Jr. 1987. "Families and Lives: Some Developments in Life-Course Studies." Pp. 179–199 in *Family History at the Crossroads: A Journal of Family History Reader,* edited by Tamara Hareven and Andrejs Plakans. Princeton: Princeton University Press.

Elias, Norbert. 1978–1982. *The Civilizing Process.* 2 vols. New York: Urizen.

Ennabli, Liliane. 1975. *Les inscriptions funéraires chrétiennes de la Basilique dite de Sainte-Monique à Carthage.* Rome: Ecole Française de Rome.

————. 1982. *Les inscriptions funéraires chrétiennes de Carthage, vol. 2, La Basilique de Mcidfa.* Rome: Ecole Française de Rome.

Enriques Agnoletti, Anna Maria. 1933. "La vendetta nella vita e nella legislazione fiorentina." *Archivio storico italiano,* 7th ser. 91:90–223.

Epstein, Steven. 1984. *Wills and Wealth in Medieval Genoa, 1150–1250.* Cambridge: Harvard University Press.

Ercole, Francesco. 1908. "La dote romana negli statuti di Parma." *Archivio storico per le provincie parmensi* 8:-106–110.

Esmein, Adhémar. 1929–1935. *Le mariage en droit canonique.* Ed. Robert Génestal and J. Dauvillier. 2d ed. 2 vols. Paris: Sirey.

Etienne, Robert. 1976. "Ancient Medical Conscience and Chidren." *Journal of Psychohistory* 4:131–162.

Eugippius. 1976. *Eugippii regula.* Ed. Fernandus Villegás and Adalbertus de Vogüé. Corpus Scriptorum Ecclesiasticorum Latinorum 87. Vienna: Hoelder-Pichler-Tempsky.

Eyben, Emiel. 1980–1981. "Family Planning in Graeco-Roman Antiquity." *Ancient Society* 11–12:5–82.

Fallers, Lloyd A., and Margaret C. Fallers. 1976. "Sex Roles in Edremit." Pp. 243–260 in *Mediterranean Family Structure,* edited by J. G. Peristiany. Cambridge: Cambridge University Press.

Falsini, Aliberto Benigno. 1971. "Firenze dopo il 1348: Le conseguenze della peste nera." *Archivio storico italiano* 129:425–503.

Fenton, William. 1949. "Collecting Materials for a Political History of the Six Nations." *Proceedings of the American Philosophical Society* 93:233–238.

Ferrua, Antonius. 1964–1983. *Inscriptiones Christianae Urbis Romae*. vols. 4–8. Vatican City: Pontificum Institutum Archaeologiae Christianae.

Festus, S. P. 1975. *De Verborum Significatione Quae Supersunt (Pauli Diac. Excerpta)*. Ed. C. M. Mueller. Reprint. New York: Georg Olms Verlag.

Fildes, Valerie A. 1986. *Breasts, Bottles, and Babies: A History of Infant Feeding*. Edinburgh: Edinburgh University Press.

———. 1988. *Wet Nursing: A History from Antiquity to Present*. Oxford: Basil Blackwell.

Fine, Agnes. 1987. "Hommes dotés, femmes dotées dans la France du sud." Pp. 39–59 in *Femmes et patrimoine dans les sociétés rurales de l'Europe méditerranéenne*, edited by G. Ravis-Giordani. Paris: Centre National de la Recherche Scientifique.

Finley, Moses. 1980. *Ancient Slavery and Modern Ideology*. London: Chatto and Windus.

Forlini, Maria Vittoria. 1983–1984. "Strutture familiari e ceti sociali a Chieti: Una ricerca sul catasto onciario del 1754." Tesi di laurea, University of Bologna.

Fortes, Meyer. 1959. "Descent, Filiation and Affinity: A Rejoinder to Dr. Leach, Part 1." *Man* 59:206–212.

Foucault, Michel. 1984. *Histoire de la sexualité*, vol. 2, *L'usage des plaisirs*. Paris: Gallimard.

———. 1986. *The History of Sexuality, vol. 3, The Care of the Self*. Trans. R. Hurley. New York: Random House.

Fox, Robin. 1967. *Kinship and Marriage: An Anthropological Perspective*. Harmondsworth: Penguin.

Fox-Genovese, Elizabeth. 1988. *Within the Plantation Household: Black and White Women of the Old South*. Chapel Hill: University of North Carolina Press.

Franzoni, Claudio. 1987. *Habius atque habitudo militis: Monumenti funerari di militari nella Cisalpina Romana*. Rome: L'Erma di Bretschneider.

Freeman, Susan Tax. 1970. *Neighbors: The Social Contract in a Castilian Hamlet*. Chicago: University of Chicago Press.

———. 1979. *The Pasiegos: Spaniards in No Man's Land*. Chicago: University of Chicago Press.

Friedl, Ernestine. 1962. *Vasilika: A Village in Modern Greece*. New York: Holt, Rinehart and Winston.

Frier, Bruce. 1982. "Roman Life Expectancy: Ulpian's Evidence." *Harvard Studies in Classical Philology* 86:213–251.

———. 1983. "Roman Life Expectancy: The Pannonian Evidence." *Phoenix* 37:328–344.

Gabaccia, Donna. 1987. "In the Shadows of the Periphery: Italian Women in the Nineteenth Century." Pp. 166–176 in *Connecting Spheres: Women in the Western World, 1500 to the Present*, edited by Marilyn J. Boxer and Jean H. Quataert. New York: Oxford University Press.

———. 1988. "Migrant Sex Ratios and the Women 'Left Behind': The Italian Case." Paper presented at the annual meeting of the Social Science History Association, Chicago, 3–6 November.

Galinski, Karl. 1981–1982. "Augustus' Legislation on Morals and Marriage." *Philologus* 125–126:126–144.

Galmacci, Gianfranco, and Luigi Tittarelli. 1982. "Considerazioni su taluni errori nelle registrazioni dell'età sugli stati d'anime nominativi." *Quaderni dell'Istituto di Statistica dell'Università degli studi di Perugia* 7:29–109.

Galt, Anthony. 1986. "Social Class in a Mid-Eighteenth Century Apulian Town: Indications from the Catasto Onciario." *Ethnohistory* 33:419–447.

———. 1991. *Far from the Bell Towers: Settlement and Society in an Apulian Town.* Cambridge: Cambridge University Press.

García Garrido, Manuel Jesús. 1982. *El patrimonio de la Mujer casada en el derecho civil, vol. 1, La tradition romanistica.* Barcelona: Cento de Estudios Universitarios Ramón Areces.

Gardner, Jane F. 1986. *Woman in Roman Law and Society.* London: Croom Helm.

Garnsey, Peter, ed. 1989. *Food, Health, and Culture in Classical Antiquity.* University of Cambridge Classics Department Working Papers, no 1.

———. In press. "Mass Consumption in the City of Rome." In *Nourrir La Plèbe: Mélanges Van Berchem,* edited by Adalberto Giovannini. Geneva.

Gaudemet, J. 1977. "Le legs du droit roman en matière matrimoniale." *Il matrimonio* 1:139–179.

Gaunt, David. 1987. "Rural Household Organization and Inheritance in Northern Europe." *Journal of Family History* 12:121–141.

Gauthier, Nancy. 1975. *Recueil des inscriptions chrétiennes de la Gaule, vol. 1, Première Belgique.* Paris: Centre National de la Recherche Scientifique.

Gerner, Erich. 1954. *Beiträge zum Recht der Parapherna.* Munich: Beck.

Giacomini, Mariuccia. 1981. *Sposi a Belmonte nel settecento: Famiglia e matrimonio in un borgo rurale Calabrese.* Milan: Giuffrè.

Giddens, Anthony. 1986. *The Constitution of Society.* Berkeley: University of California Press.

Giles of Rome. 1626. *De humani corporis formatione.* Rimini: Joseph Symbenium.

Gilmore, David D. 1980. *The People of the Plain: Class and Community in Lower Andalusia.* Columbia: Columbia University Press.

———. ed. 1987. *Honor and Shame and the Unity of the Mediterranean.* Washington, D.C.: American Anthropological Association.

Giovannini, Maureen. 1986. "Female Anthropologist and Male Informant: Gender Conflict in a Sicilian Town." Pp. 103–116 in *Self, Sex, and Gender in Cross-Cultural Fieldwork,* edited by Tony Whitehead and Mary Ellen Connaway. Urbana: University of Illinois Press.

Gittings, Clare. 1984. *Death, Burial and the Individual in Early Modern England.* London: Croom Helm.

Goar, Robert J. 1987. *The Legend of Cato Uticensis from the First Century B.C. to the Fifth Century A.D.* Brussels: Collection Latomus.

Golden, Mark. 1988. "Did the Ancients Care When Their Children Died?" *Greece and Rome* 35:152–163.

Goody, Esther N., ed. 1982. *From Craft to Industry: The Ethnography of Proto-Industrial Cloth Production.* Cambridge: Cambridge University Press.

Goody, Jack. 1973. "Bridewealth and Dowry in Africa and Eurasia." Pp. 1–58 in *Bridewealth and Dowry,* edited by Jack Goody and S. J. Tambiah. Cambridge: Cambridge University Press.

———. 1976. *Production and Reproduction.* Cambridge: Cambridge University Press.

———. 1983. *The Development of the Family and Marriage in Europe.* Cambridge: Cambridge University Press.

———. 1990. *The Oriental, the Ancient and the Primitive.* Cambridge: Cambridge University Press.

Goody, Jack, Joan Thirsk, and E. P. Thompson, eds. 1976. *Family and Inheritance: Rural Society in Western Europe, 1200–1800.* Cambridge: Cambridge University Press.

Gossiaux, Jean-François. 1987. "Prix de la fiancée et dot dans les villages yugo-slaves." Pp. 291–305 in *Femmes et patrimoine dans les sociétés rurales de l'Europe méditer-ranénne,* edited by G. Ravis-Giordani. Paris: Centre National de la Recherche Scientifique.

Grant, Robert. 1969. "Chains of Being in Early Christianity." Pp. 279–298 in *Myths and Symbols: Studies in Honor of Mircea Eliade,* edited by Joseph M. Kitagawa and Charles H. Long. Chicago: University of Chicago Press.

Gregory I, Pope. 1982. *Registrum epistolarum.* Ed. D. Norberg. 2 vols. Corpus Christianorum 140–140A. Tournhout: Brepols.

Grmek, Mirko D. 1983. *Les maladies à l'aube de la civilisation occidentale.* Paris: Payet.

Guarino, Antonio. 1967. "Manus e potestas." *Labeo* 18:389–391.

Guerra Medici, Maria Teresa. 1986. *I diritti delle donne nella società altomedievale.* Rome: Giuffrè.

Guicciardini, Francesco. 1981. *Ricordi, diari, memorie.* Ed. Mario Spinella. Rome: Ruiniti.

Gülzow, Henneke. 1967. "Kallist von Rom: Ein Beitrag zur Soziologie der römischen Gemeinde." *Zeitschrift für die Neutestamentliche Wissenschaft* 58:102–121.

Hager, Joseph. 1799. *Gemälde von Palermo.* Berlin: Froelich.

Hahn, István. 1981. "Freie Arbeit und Sklavenarbeit in der spätantiken Stadt." Pp. 128–154 in *Sozial- und Wirtschaftsgeschichte der römischen Kaiserzeit,* edited by H. Schneider. Darmstadt.

Hajnal, John. 1965. "European Marriage Patterns in Perspective." Pp. 101–143 in *Population and History: Essays in Historical Demography,* edited by D. V. Glass and D. E. C. Eversley. London: Edward Arnold.

———. 1983. "Two Kinds of Pre-industrial Household Formation System." Pp. 65–104 in *Family Forms in Historic Europe,* edited by Richard Wall, Jean Robin, and Peter Laslett. Cambridge: Cambridge University Press.

Hallam, H. E. 1985. "Age at First Marriage and Age at Death in the Lincolnshire Fenland, 1252–1478." *Population Studies* 39:55–69.

Hallett, Judith P. 1984. *Fathers and Daughters in Roman Society: Women and the Elite Family.* Princeton: Princeton University Press.

Halpern, Joel. 1967. *A Serbian Village.* New York: Harper and Row.

Hamilton, Richard. 1984. "Sources for the Athenian Amphidromia." *Greek, Roman and Byzantine Studies* 25:243–251.

Hammel, Eugene A. 1972. "The Zadruga as Process." Pp. 335–373 in *Household and Family in Past Time,* edited by Peter Laslett and Richard Wall. Cambridge: Cambridge University Press.

Handman, Marie-Elisabeth. 1987. "Ni terre ni maison mais un métier à tisser, ou les femmes et la monnaie en Chalcidique." Pp. 349–363 in *Femmes et patrimoine dans les sociétés rurales de l'Europe méditerranéenne,* edited by G. Ravis-Giordani. Paris: Centre National de la Recherche Scientifique.

Hareven, Tamara, and Kanji Masaoka. 1988. "Turning Points and Transitions: Perceptions of the Life Course." *Journal of Family History* 13:271–289.

Harrell, Stevan, and Sara A. Dickey. 1985. "Dowry Systems in Complex Societies." *Ethnology* 24:105–120.

Harris, Marvin, and Eric B. Ross. 1987. *Death, Sex and Fertility: Population Regulation in Preindustrial and Developing Societies.* New York: Columbia University Press.

Hart, H. L. A. 1961. *The Concept of Law.* Oxford: Oxford University Press.

Herlihy, David. 1985. *Medieval Households.* Cambridge: Harvard University Press.

———. 1987. "The Florentine Merchant Family of the Middle Ages." Pp. 179–201 in *Studi di storia economica Toscana nel Medievo e nel Rinascimento memoria di Federigo Melis.* Pisa: Pacini.

Herlihy, David, and Christiane Klapisch-Zuber. 1978. *Les Toscans et leurs familles: Une étude du catasto florentin de 1427.* Paris: Foundation Nationale des Sciences Politiques, Ecole des Hautes Etudes en Sciences Sociales.

Herzfeld, Michael. 1980a. "Honor and Shame: Some Problems in the Comparative Analysis of Moral Systems." *Man* 15:339–351.

———. 1980b. "Social Tension and Inheritance by Lot in Three Greek Villages." *Anthropological Quarterly* 53:91–100.

———. 1984. "The Horns of the Mediterraneanist Dilemma." *American Ethnologist* 11:439–454.

———. 1987. "As in Your Own House: Hospitality, Ethnography and the Stereotype of Mediterranean Society." Pp. 75–89 in *Honor and Shame and the Unity of the Mediterranean,* edited by David D. Gilmore. Washington, D.C.: American Anthropological Association.

Hewson, M. Anthony. 1975. *Giles of Rome and the Medieval Theory of Conception.* London: Athlone.

Hickey, A. E. 1986. *Women of the Roman Aristocracy as Christian Monastics.* Ann Arbor, Mich.: UMI Research Press.

Hilaire, Jean. 1973. "Vie en commun, famille et esprit communautaire." *Revue historique de droit français et étranger* 51:8–53.

Hinde, Robert A. 1987. *Individuals, Relationships and Culture.* Cambridge: Cambridge University Press.

Hirschon, Renée. 1983. "Under One Roof: Marriage, Dowry and Family Relations in Piraeus." Pp. 299–323 in *Urban Life in Mediterranean Europe: Anthropological Perspectives,* edited by Michael Kenny and David I. Kertzer. Urbana: University of Illinois Press.

——, ed. 1984. *Women and Property: Women as Property.* New York: St. Martin's.

Hopkins, Keith. 1964–1965. "The Age of Roman Girls at Marriage." *Population Studies* 18:309–327.

——. 1966. "On the Probable Age Structure of the Roman Population." *Population Studies* 20:245–264.

——. 1980. "Brother-Sister Marriage in Roman Egypt." *Comparative Studies in Society and History* 22:303–354.

——. 1983. *Death and Renewal: Sociological Studies in Roman History.* Cambridge: Cambridge University Press.

——. 1987. "Graveyards for Historians." Pp. 113–126 in *La mort, les morts et l'au-delà dans le monde romain: Actes du colloque de Caen, 20–22 novembre 1985,* edited by François Hinard. Caen: Centre de Publications de l'Université de Caen.

Howell, Martha. 1989. *Women, Production and Patriarchy in Late Mediaeval Cities.* Chicago: University of Chicago Press.

Hughes, Diane Owen. 1976. "Struttura familiare e sistemi di successione ereditaria nei testamenti dell'Europa medievale." *Quaderni storici* 33:929–952.

——. 1978. "From Brideprice to Dowry in Mediterranean Europe." *Journal of Family History* 3:262–296.

——. 1983. "Sumptuary Law and Social Relations in Renaissance Italy." Pp. 69–99 in *Disputes and Settlements: Law and Human Relations in the West,* edited by John Bossy. Cambridge: Cambridge University Press.

Humbert, Michael. 1972. *Le remariage à Rome: Etude d'histoire juridique et sociale.* Milan: Giuffrè.

Hunecke, Volker. 1989. *I trovatelli di Milano.* Bologna: Il Mulino.

Hunt, David. 1972. *Parents and Children in History: The Psychology of Family Life in Early Modern France.* New York: Harper Torchbooks.

Isidore of Seville. 1911. *Etymologiarum sive originum libri XX.* Ed. W. M. Lindsay. 2 vols. Oxford: Clarendon.

Istituto Centrale di Statistica. 1967. *Popolazione residente e presente dei comuni ai censimenti dal 1861 al 1961.* Rome: ISTAT.

Iszaevich, Abraham. 1975. "Emigrants, Spinsters and Priests: The Dynamics of Demography in Spanish Peasant Societies." *Journal of Peasant Studies* 2:292–312.

Ius graeco-romanum. 1962. Ed. J. and P. Zepos. Reprint. Aalen: Scientia.

Jacques, François. 1986. "L'ordine senatorio attraverso la crisi del III secolo." Pp. 81– 285 in *Società romana e impero tardoantico,* vol. 1, *Istituzioni, ceti, economie,* edited by Andrea Giardina. Bari: Istituto Gramsci.

Jamous, Raymond. 1981. *Honneur et Baraka: Les structures traditionelles dans le Rif.* Cambridge: Cambridge University Press.

Jelliffe, D. M., and E. F. P. Jelliffe. 1978. *Human Milk.* Oxford: Oxford University Press.

Jenal, Georg. 1986. "Grégoire le Grand et la vie monastique dans l'Italie de son temps." Pp. 147–157 in *Grégoire le Grand,* edited by Jacques Fontaine, Robert Gillet, and Stan Pollistrandi. Paris: Colleques Internationaux du Centre National de la Recherche Scientifique.

Johnston, David. 1988. *The Roman Law of Trust.* Oxford: Oxford University Press.

Jolowicz, H. F. 1947. "The Wicked Guardian." *Journal of Roman Studies* 37:82–90.

Jones, Philip. 1956. "Florentine Families and Florentine Diaries in the Fourteenth Century." *Papers of the British School at Rome* 24:183–205.

Kajanto, Iiro. 1969. *On the Problem of the Average Duration of Life in the Roman Empire.* Annales Academiae Scientiarum Fennicae, ser. B, vol. 153.2. Helsinki: Suomalainen Tiedeakatemia.

Kampen, Natalie. 1981. *Image and Status: Roman Working Women in Ostia.* Berlin: Gebr. Mann.

Kenna, Margaret E. 1976. "Houses, Fields, and Graves: Property and Ritual Obligation on a Greek Island." *Ethnology* 15:21–34.

Kent, Francis William. 1977. *Household and Lineage in Renaissance Florence: The Family Life of the Capponi, Ginori, and Ruccellai.* Princeton: Princeton University Press.

Kertzer, David I. 1984. *Family Life in Central Italy.* New Brunswick: Rutgers University Press.

———. 1987. "Anthropology and History." *Historical Methods* 19:119–120.

———. 1989. "The Joint Family Household Revisited: Demographic Constraints and Household Complexity in the European Past." *Journal of Family History* 14:1– 15.

———. 1991. "Household History and Sociological Theory." *Annual Review of Sociology* 17: 155–179.

Kertzer, David I., and Caroline B. Brettell. 1987. "Advances in Italian and Iberian Family History." *Journal of Family History* 12:85–120.

Kirshner, Julius. 1974. "Ars imitatur naturam: A Consilium of Baldus on Naturalization in Florence." *Viator* 5:289–331.

———. 1976. "A Consilium of Rosello dei Roselli on the Meaning of 'Florentinus,' 'de Florentia' and 'de populo.'" *Bulletin of Medieval Canon Law* n.s. 6:87–91.

———. 1985. "Wives' Claims against Insolvent Husbands in Late Medieval Italy." Pp. 256–303 in *Women of the Medieval World,* edited by Julius Kirshner and Suzanne F. Wemple. Oxford: Basil Blackwell.

———. Forthcoming. "*Maritus Lucretur Dotem Uxoris Sue Premortue* in Late Medieval Florence." In *Zeitschrift der Savigny-Stiftung für Rechtsgeschichte, Kanonistische Abteilung.*

Kirshner, Julius, and Anthony Molho. 1978. "The Dowry Fund and the Marriage Market in Early Quattrocento Florence." *Journal of Modern History* 58:403–438.

Kirshner, Julius, and Jacques Pluss. 1979. "Two Fourteenth-Century Opinions on Dowries, Paraphernalia and Non-Dotal Goods." *Bulletin of Medieval Canon Law* 9:65–77.

Klapisch-Zuber, Christiane. 1985. "The Griselda Complex: Dowry and Marriage Gifts in the Quattrocento." Pp. 213–246 in *Women, Family, and Ritual in Renaissance Florence,* translated by Lydia G. Cochrane. Chicago: University of Chicago Press.

———. 1988a. "Ruptures de parenté et changements d'identité chez les magnats florentins du XIVe siècle." *Annales E.S.C.* 43:1205–1240.

———. 1988b. "Le zane della sposa: La donna fiorentina e il suo corredo nel rinascimento." Pp. 193–211 in *La famiglia e le donne nel rinascimento a Firenze,* edited by Christiane Klapisch-Zuber. Bari: Laterza.

Kleiner, Diana. 1977. *Roman Group Portraiture: The Funerary Reliefs of the Late Republic and Early Empire.* New York: Garland.

———. 1987a. *Roman Imperial Funerary Altars with Portraits.* Rome: G. Bretschneider.

———. 1987b. "Women and Family Life on Roman Imperial Funerary Altars." *Latomus* 46:545–554.

Koestermann, Erich, ed. 1963. *Cornelius Tacitus, Annalen,* vol. 1. Heidelberg: C. Winter.

Köhler, Josef, and Giustiniano Degli Azzi-Vitelleschi, eds. 1909. *Das Florentiner Strafrecht des XIV Jahrhunderts, mit einem Anhang über den Strafprozess der italienischen Statuten.* Mannheim and Leipzig: Bensheimer.

Kuehn, Thomas. 1981. "Women, Marriage and *Patria Potestas* in Late Medieval Florence." *Revue d'histoire du droit* 49:127–147.

———. 1982a. "'Cum Consensu Munduali': Legal Guardianship of Women in Quattrocento Florence." *Viator* 13:309–333.

———. 1982b. *Emancipation in Late Medieval Florence.* New Brunswick: Rutgers University Press.

Kussmaul, Ann Sturm. 1981. *Servants in Husbandry in Early-Modern England.* Cambridge: Cambridge University Press.

Lambiri-Dimaki, Jane. 1985. "Dowry in Modern Greece: An Institution at the Crossroads between Persistence and Decline." Pp. 165–178 in *The Marriage Bargain: Women and Dowries in European History,* edited by Marion Kaplan. New York: Harrington Park.

Lansing, Carol. 1985. *The Florentine Magnates: Lineage and Faction in a Thirteenth-Century Commune.* Ph.D. diss., University of Michigan.

Lapatsanis, Peter, Vasso Deliyanni, and Spyros Doxiadis. 1968. "Vitamin D Deficiency Rickets in Greece." *Journal of Pediatrics* 73:195–202.

La Roncière, Charles de. 1977. "Une famille florentine au XIVe siècle: Les Velluti." Pp. 227–248 in *Famille et parenté dans l'Occident médiéval,* edited by Georges Duby and Jacques Le Goff. Rome: Ecole Française de Rome.

Laslett, Peter. 1972. "The History of the Family." Pp. 1–89 in *Household and Family in*

Past Time, edited by Peter Laslett and Richard Wall. Cambridge: Cambridge University Press.

———. 1977. *Family Life and Illicit Love in Earlier Generations: Essays in Historical Sociology.* Cambridge: Cambridge University Press.

———. 1983. "Family and Household as Work Group and Kin Group: Areas of Traditional Europe Compared." Pp. 513–587 in *Family Forms in Historic Europe,* edited by Richard Wall, Jean Robin, and Peter Laslett. Cambridge: Cambridge University Press.

Laslett, Peter, and Richard Wall, eds. 1972. *Household and Family in Past Time.* Cambridge: Cambridge University Press.

Leicht, Pier S. 1960. *Storia del diritto italiano: Il diritto privato.* Milan: Giuffrè.

Lemay, Helen. 1981. "William of Saliceto on Human Sexuality." *Viator* 12:165–181.

Le Play, Frédéric. 1871. *L'organisation de la famille.* Paris: Tours.

Leprotti, Carlo Felice. 1966. "Libro primo delle cagioni dello spopolamento della Sardegna." In *Il riformismo settecentesco in Sardegna: Relazioni inedite di Piemontesi,* edited by Luigi Bulferetti. Cagliari: Sarda Fossataro.

Leti, Giuseppe, and Luigi Tittarelli. 1976. *Le fonti per lo studio della popolazione della diocesi di Perugia dalla metà del XVI secolo al 1860.* 3 vols. *Vol. 1, Guida alle fonti.* Gubbio: Oderisi.

Lévi-Strauss, Claude. 1973. "Réflexions sur l'atome de parenté." Chapter 7 in *Anthropologie structurale deux.* Paris: Plon.

———. 1983a. *Le regard éloigné.* Paris: Plon.

———. 1983b. "Histoire et ethnologie." *Annales E.S.C.* 38:1217–1231.

Levy, Jean-Philippe. 1974. "L'évolution du droit familial depuis 1789." Pp. 485–504 in *Recueil de mémoires et travaux publié par la Société d'histoire du droit et des Institutions des anciens pays de droit écrit,* vol. 9, edited by Roger Aubenas. Montpellier: Faculté de Droit et des Sciences Economiques de Montpellier.

Lewis, A. W. 1981. *Royal Succession in Capetian France.* Cambridge: Harvard University Press.

Lewis, Naphtali. 1983. *Life in Egypt under Roman Rule.* Oxford: Clarendon.

Leyser, K. J. 1968. "The German Aristocracy from the Ninth to the Early Twelfth Century: A Historical and Cultural Sketch." *Past and Present* 41:25–53.

———. 1970. "Maternal Kin in Early Medieval Germany: A Reply." *Past and Present* 49:126–134.

Lisón-Tolosana, Carmelo. 1976. "The Ethics of Inheritance." Pp. 305–316 in *Mediterranean Family Structure,* edited by J. G. Peristiany. Cambridge: Cambridge University Press.

———. 1983. *Belmonte de los Caballeros.* Princeton: Princeton University Press.

Livi Bacci, Massimo. 1981. "On the Frequency of Remarriage in Nineteenth-Century Italy: Methods and Results." Pp. 347–361 in *Marriage and Remarriage in Populations of the Past,* edited by Jacques Dupâquier et al. London: Academic Press.

Loizos, Peter. 1975. "Changes in Property Transfer among Greek Cypriot Villagers." *Man* 10:503–523.

Lorenzoni, Giovanni. 1910. *Inchiesta parlamentare sulle condizioni dei contadini nelle provincie meridionali e nella Sicilia*, vol. 5, pt. 2. Rome: Tipografia Nazionale di Giovanni Bertero.

Lowe, N. J. 1988. "Sulpicia's Syntax." *Classical Quarterly* 38:193–205.

Lutz, Cora. 1947. "Musonius Rufus: The Roman Socrates." Yale Classical Studies 10:3–147.

Lynch, J. M. 1986. *Godparents and Kinship in Early Medieval Europe*. Princeton: Princeton University Press.

Macfarlane, Alan. 1980. "Demographic Structures and Cultural Regions in Europe." *Cambridge Anthropology* 6:1–17.

———. 1986. *Marriage and Love in England: Modes of Reproduction, 1300–1840*. Oxford: Basil Blackwell.

Macinghi-Strozzi, Alessandra. 1877. *Lettere di una gentildonna fiorentina ai figliuoli esuli*. Ed. Cesare Guasti. Florence: Sansoni.

Maclean, Ian. 1980. *The Renaissance Notion of Woman*. Cambridge: Cambridge University Press.

McManners, John. 1981. *Death and the Enlightenment: Changing Attitudes to Death among Christians and Unbelievers in Eighteenth Century France*. Oxford: Clarendon.

MacMullen, Ramsay. 1988. *Corruption and the Decline of Rome*. New Haven: Yale University Press.

Maher, Vanessa. 1974. *Women and Property in Morocco*. Cambridge: Cambridge University Press.

Maine, Henry S. 1861. *Ancient Law*. London: Murray.

Malinowski, Bronislaw. 1929. *The Sexual Life of Savages*. London: Routledge.

Mansi, J. D. 1759–1798. *Sacrorum conciliorum nova et amplissima collectio*. 31 vols. Florence.

Maraspini, A. L. 1968. *The Study of an Italian Village*. Paris: Mouton.

Marcillet-Jaubert, Jean. 1968. *Les inscriptions d'Altava*. Gap: Editions Ophrys.

Mariottini, Jean-Marc. 1987. "Il corredo e la legittima." Pp. 163–188 in *Femmes et patrimoine dans les sociétés rurales de l'Europe méditerranéenne*, edited by G. Ravis-Giordani. Paris: Centre National de la Recherche Scientifique.

Morongiu, Antonio. 1975. *Saggi di storia giuridica e politica sarda*. Padova: Milani.

———. 1981. "Il matrimonio 'alla sardesca.'" *Archivio storico sardo di Sassari* 7:85–93.

Marsilius of Padua. 1980. *Defensor Pacis*. Trans. Alan Gewirth. Toronto: University of Toronto Press.

Martimort, A. G. 1982. *Les diaconesses: Essai historique*. Bibliotheca Ephemerides Liturgicae, Subsidia 24. Rome: Edizioni Liturgiche.

Masciadri, Maria Adele Manca, and Orsolina Montevecchi. 1982. "Contratti di baliatico e vendite fiduciarie." *Aegyptus* 62:148–161.

Massetto, G. P. 1979a. "La prassi giuridica lombarda nell'opera di Giulio Claro." Pp. 491–546 in *Confluences des droits savants et des pratiques juridiques: Actes du colloque de Montpellier 1977*. Milan: Giuffré.

———. 1979b. "I reati nell'opera di Giulio Claro." *Studia et documenta historiae et iuris* 45:328–503.

Matthaeus, Antonius. [1644] 1803. *Antonii Matthaei Commentarius ad lib. XLVII et XLVIII Dig. De criminibus.* Ticini.

Mayali, Laurent. 1987. *Droit savant et coutumes: L'exclusion des filles dotées XIIème–XVème siècles.* Frankfurt am Main: Vittorio Kostermann.

Mayer-Maly, Theo. 1964. "Adulterium." Cols. 78–80 in *Der Kleine Pauly,* vol. 1, edited by K. Ziegler and W. Southeimer. Stuttgart: A. Druckenmüller.

Meli, Giovanni. 1884. *Puisii Siciliani.* Palermo: Lauriel.

Mengoni, Luigi. 1961. *Successioni per causa di morte.* Milan: Giuffré.

Mernissi, Fatima. 1975. *Beyond the Veil: Male-Female Dynamics in a Modern Muslim Society.* Cambridge, Mass.: Schenkman.

Merzario, Raul. 1981. *Il paese stretto.* Turin: Einaudi.

Metz, Réné. 1954. *La consécration des vierges dans l'eglise romaine: Etude d'histoire de la liturgie.* Bibliothèque de l'Institut de Droit Canonique de l'Université de Strasbourg 4. Paris: Presses Universitaries de Frances.

Meyvaert, P. 1971. "Bede's Text of the 'Libellus Responsionum' of Gregory the Great to Augustine of Canterbury." Pp. 15–33 in *England before the Conquest: Studies in Primary Sources Presented to Dorothy Whitelock,* edited by Peter Clemoes and Kathleen Hughes. Cambridge: Cambridge University Press.

Millar, Fergus. 1983. "Epigraphy." Pp. 80–136 in *Sources for Ancient History,* edited by Michael Crawford. Cambridge: Cambridge University Press.

———. 1986. "Italy and the Roman Empire: Augustus to Constantine." *Phoenix* 40:295–318.

Molho, Anthony. 1987. "L'amministrazione del debito pubblico a Firenze nel quindicesimo secolo." Pp. 191–208 in *I ceti dirigenti della Toscana del quattrocento,* edited by Riccardo Fubini. Florence: Francesco Papafava.

Momigliano, Arnaldo. 1966. *Studies in Historiography.* London: Weidenfeld and Nicolson.

Mommsen, Theodore. 1955. *Römisches Strafrecht.* Graz: Akademische Druck-und Verlagsanthalt.

Mommsen, Theodor. and P. M. Meyer. 1905. *Theodosiani libri XVI cum constitutionibus sirmondianis et leges novellae ad theodosianum pertinentes.* 2 vols. Berlin: Weidermann.

Monleone, Giovanni. 1941. *Iacopo da Varagine e la sua cronaca di Genova dalle origini al MCCXCVII.* 2 vols. Rome: Tipografia del Senato.

Moreau, Philippe. 1983. "Structures de parenté et d'alliance à Larinum d'après le *Pro Cluentio.*" Pp. 99–123 in *Les "Bourgeoisies": Municipales italiennes aux IIe et Ier siècles av J.-C.* Naples: Centre Jean Bérard.

———. 1986. "Patrimoines et successions à Larinum au Ier sieècle av J.-C." *Revue historique de droit français et étranger* 64:169–189.

Moretti, Piero. 1989. "'Un uomo per famiglia': Servi, contadini e famiglie nella diocesi di Reggio Emilia nel settecento." *Quaderni storici* 71:405–442.

Morton, Ann Crabb. 1980. *A Patrician Family in Renaissance Florence: The Family Relations of Alessandra Strozzi and Her Sons, 1440–1491.* Ph.D. diss., Washington University.

Moss, Leonard, and Walter H. Thompson. 1959. "The South Italian Family: Literature and Observation." *Human Organization* 18:35–47.

Munier, Charles. 1960. *Les Statuta ecclesiae antiquae: Edition, études critiques.* Bibliothèque de l'Institut de Droit Canonique de l'Université de Strasbourg 5. Paris: Presses Universitaires de France.

———. 1963. *Concilia Galliae A. 314–A. 506.* Tournhout: Brepols.

Münzer, Friedrich. 1920. *Römische Adelsparteien und Adelsfamilien.* Stuttgart: Metzler.

Needham, Joseph. 1959. *A History of Embryology.* 2d rev. ed. New York: Abelard-Schuman.

Neilsen, Hanne Sigismund. 1987. *"Alumnus:* A Term of Relation Denoting Quasi-Adoption." *Classica et mediaevalia* 38:141–188.

Néraudau, Jean-Pierre. 1984. *Etre enfant à Rome.* Paris: Les Belles Lettres.

———. 1987. "La loi, la coutume et le chagrin: Réflexions sur la mort des enfants." Pp. 195–208 in *La mort, les morts et l'au-delà dans le monde romain: Actes de colloque de Caen, 20–22 Novembre 1985,* edited by François Hinard. Caen: Centre de Publications de l'Université de Caen.

Netting, Robert, Richard Wilk, and Eric Arnould, eds. 1984. *Households: Comparative and Historical Studies of the Domestic Group.* Berkeley and Los Angeles: University of California Press.

Nevizzanus Astensis, Johannes. 1573. *Silva Nuptialis libri sex.* Venice.

Nitti, Francesco. 1910. *Inchiesta parlamentare sulle condizioni dei contadini nelle provincie meridionali e nella Sicilia, Basilicata e Calabria,* vol. 5, pt. 3. Rome: Tipografia Nazionale di Giovanni Bertero.

Nörr, Dieter. 1977. "Planung in der Antike." Pp. 309–334 in *Freiheit und Sachzwang: Beiträge zu Ehren Helmut Schelskys.* Opladen.

Odofredus. 1552. *Lectura super Codice.* Lyons.

Oppo, Anna. 1983. "La domesticità nella famiglia tradizionale sarda." In *Fonti orali e politica delle donne: Storia, ricerca, racconto.* Bologna: Centro di Documentazione delle Donne.

Orlandi, Stefano. 1960. "Il convento di S. Domenico di Fiesole." *Memorie Domenicane* 4:3–180.

Ortner, Sherry. 1984. "Theory in Anthropology since the Sixties." *Comparative Studies in Society and History* 26:126–166.

Pandimiglio, Leonida. 1981. "Giovanni di Pagolo Morelli e la continuità familiare." *Studi medievali, 3d ser.* 22:129–181.

Papa, Cristina. 1985. *Dove sono molte braccia è molto pane.* Foligno: Umbra.

———. 1987. "La famiglia mezzadrile come ambito normativo specifico e luogo di conflitto 'di diritti.'" In *Annali dell'Istituto Alcide Cervi,* vol. 9. Bologna: Il Mulino.

Papias Grammaticus. 1496. *Papias vocabulista.* Venice: Philip de Pincis.

Parker, Robert. 1983. *Miasma: Pollution and Purification in Early Greek Religion.* Oxford: Clarendon.

Patterson, Cynthia. 1985. "'Not Worth the Rearing': The Causes of Infant Exposure in Ancient Greece." *Transactions of the American Philological Association* 115:103–123.

Patterson, Orlando. 1982. *Slavery and Social Death: A Comparative Study.* Cambridge: Harvard University Press.

Paul, A. A., A. E. Black, J. Evans, T. J. Cole, and R. G. Whitehead. 1988. "Breastmilk Intake and Growth in Infants from Two to Ten Months." *Journal of Human Nutrition and Dietetics* 1:437–450.

Pavlides, Eleftherios, and Jana Hesser. 1986. "Women's Roles and House Form and Decoration in Eressos, Greece." Pp. 68–96 in *Gender and Power in Rural Greece,* edited by Jill Dubisch. Princeton: Princeton University Press.

Peristiany, John. 1965. *Honour and Shame: The Values of Mediterranean Society.* London: Weidenfeld and Nicolson.

Pertile, Antonio. 1893. *Storia del diritto italiano,* vol. 4, *Storia del diritto privato.* 2d ed. Turin: Unione Tipografica.

Pina-Cabral, João de. 1986. *Sons of Adam, Daughters of Eve: The Peasant World View of the Alto Minho.* Oxford: Clarendon.

———. 1989. "The Mediterranean as a Category of Regional Comparison: A Critical View." *Current Anthropology* 30:399–406.

Piore, Michael J., and Charles F. Sabel. 1984. *The Second Industrial Divide: Possibilities for Prosperity.* New York: Basic Books.

Pitkin, Donald S. 1959. "Land Tenure and Family Organization in an Italian Village." *Human Organization* 18:169–173.

———. 1960. "Marital Property Considerations among Peasants: An Italian Example." *Anthropological Quarterly* 33:33–39.

———. 1985. *The House That Giacomo Built.* New York: Cambridge University Press.

Pitt-Rivers, J. A. 1961. *The People of the Sierra.* Chicago: University of Chicago Press.

———. 1977. *The Fate of Shechem, or the Politics of Sex.* Cambridge: Cambridge University Press.

Plakans, Andrejs. 1989. "Stepping Down in Former Times: A Comparative Assessment of 'Retirement' in Traditional Europe." Pp. 175–195 in *Age Structuring in Comparative Perspective,* edited by David I. Kertzer and K. Warner Schaie. Hillsdale, N.J.: Lawrence Erlbaum.

Pollock, Linda A. 1983. *Forgotten Children: Parent-Child Relations from 1500–1900.* Cambridge: Cambridge University Press.

———. 1987. *A Lasting Relationship: Parents and Children over Three Centuries.* London: Fourth Estate.

Powell, Anton. 1988. *Athens and Sparta: Constructing Greek Political and Social History from 478 B.C.* London: Routledge.

Prévot, Françoise. 1984. *Recherches archéologiques franco-tunisiennes à Mactar. Vol. 5 of Les inscriptions chrétiennes.* Rome: Ecole Française de Rome.

Quale, Gladys Robina. 1988. *A History of Marriage Systems.* Westport, Conn.: Greenwood.

Raditsa, L. F. 1980. "Augustus' Legislation Concerning Marriage, Procreation, Love

Affairs and Adultery." Pp. 278–339 in *Aufsteig und Niedergang der römischen Welt*, edited by H. Temporini, vol. 2, pt. 13. Berlin and New York: de Gruyter.

Raepsaet-Charlier, M.-Th. 1981–1982. "Ordre sénatorial et divorce sous le haut-empire: Un chapitre de l'histoire des mentalités." *Acta classica universitatis scientiarum debreceniensis* 17–18:161–173.

Raimondi, Raffaele. 1576. *Consilia.* Venice.

Rawson, Beryl. 1974. "Roman Concubinage and Other 'De Facto' Marriages." *Transactions and Proceedings of the American Philological Association* 104:280–305.

———, ed. 1986. *The Family in Ancient Rome: New Perspectives.* Ithaca: Cornell University Press.

Renier, E. 1942. *Etude sur l'histoire de la querela inofficiosi en droit romain. Liège.*

Rettaroli, Rosella. 1987. *Modelli di nuzialità nell'Italia rurale del XIX secolo.* Ph.D. thesis, University of Bologna.

Reydellet, Marc, ed. and trans. 1984. *Isidore de Séville, Etymologies livre IX.* Paris: Les Belles Lettres.

Rheubottom, David B. 1980. "Dowry and Wedding Celebrations in Macedonia: The Meaning of Marriage Payments." Pp. 221–249 in *The Meaning of Marriage Payments*, edited by J. L. Comaroff. New York: Academic Press.

Ricchioni, Vincenzo. 1958. "Miracoli del lavoro contadino: I vigneti della Murgia dei 'Trulli.'" *Annali della Facoltà di Agraria dell'Università di Bari* 14:347–381.

Richlin, Amy. 1981. "Approaches to the Sources on Adultery at Rome." *Women's Studies* 8:225–250.

Riegelhaupt, Joyce F. 1967. "Saloio Women: An Analysis of Informal and Formal Political Economic Roles of Portuguese Peasant Women." *Anthropological Quarterly* 40:109–126.

Riesenberg, Peter. 1974. "Citizenship at Law in Late Medieval Italy." *Viator* 5:333–346.

Rinaldi, Evelina. 1909. "La donna negli statuti del comune di Forlì, sec. XIV." *Studi storici* 18:185–200.

Ritzer, Korbinian. 1970. *Le mariage dans les églises chrétiennes du Ier au XIe siècle.* Paris: Cerf.

Roberti, Francesco. 1957. "Adulterio (diritto canonico)." Pp. 333–335 in *Novissimo digesto italiano*, vol. 1. Turin: UTET.

Roberti, Michele. 1908. "Per una storia dei rapporti patrimoniali fra i coniugi in Sardegna." *Archivio storico sardo* 99:273–292.

Rocke, Michael J. 1987. "Il controllo dell'omosessualità a Firenze nel XV secolo: Gli 'Ufficiali di Notte.'" *Quaderni storici* 66:701–723.

Roda, Sergio. 1979. "Il matrimonio fra cugini germani nella legislazione tardoimperiale." *Studia et documenta historiae et iuris* 45:289–309.

Rogers, Susan. 1975. "Female Forms of Power and the Myth of Male Dominance." *American Ethnologist* 2:727–756.

Rosenthal, Elaine. 1989. "The Position of Women in Renaissance Florence: Neither

Autonomy nor Subjection." Pp. 369–381 in *Florence and Italy: Renaissance Studies in Honour of Nicolai Rubinstein,* edited by Peter Denley and Caroline Elam. Westfield Publications in Medieval Studies, vol. 2. London: Westfield College, University of London.

Rouche, Michel. 1987a. "Des mariages païens au mariage chrétien: Sacré et sacrament." *Segni* 2:835–880.

———. 1987b. "The Early Middle Ages in the West." Pp. 411–549 in *A History of Private Life, vol. 1, From Pagan Rome to Byzantium,* edited by Paul Veyne and translated by Arthur Goldhammer. Cambridge: Harvard University Press.

Rousselle, Aline. 1983. *Porneia: De la maîtrise du corps à la privation sensorielle, IIe–IVe siècles de l'ère chrétienne.* Paris: Presses Universitaires de France.

———. 1988. *Porneia: On Desire and the Body in Antiquity.* Trans. Felicia Pheasant. Oxford: Basil Blackwell.

Rowland, Robert. 1983. "Sistemas matrimoniales en la peninsula ibérica: Una perspectiva regional." In *La demografia historica de la peninsula ibérica,* edited by Vicente Pérez Moreda and David Sven Reher. Madrid: Tecnos.

———. 1986. "Matrimonio y familia en el Mediterraneo occidental: Algúnas interrogaciónes." Seminar paper, University of Murcia.

———. 1987. "Nupcialidade, familia, Mediterraneo." *Bollettino di demografia storica* 5:128–143.

Rubinstein, Nicolai. 1942. "The Beginnings of Political Thought in Florence: A Study in Mediaeval Historiography." *Journal of the Warburg and Courtauld Institutes* 5:198–227.

Ruggiero, Guido. 1985. *The Boundaries of Eros: Sex Crime and Sexuality in Renaissance Venice.* New York: Oxford University Press.

Ruggles, Steven. 1987. *Prolonged Connections: The Rise of the Extended Family in Nineteenth-Century England and America.* Madison: University of Wisconsin Press.

Saint-Simon, Louis de Rouvroy, duc de. 1953–1958. *Mémoires.* Paris: Gallimard, Bibliothèque de la Pléiade.

Salamone, S. D., and J. B. Stanton. 1986. "Introducing the Nikomyra: Ideality and Reality in Social Process." Pp. 97–120 in *Gender and Power in Rural Greece,* edited by Jill Dubisch. Princeton: Princeton University Press.

Salaris, Francesco. 1895. *Atti della giunta per l'inchiesta agraria e sulle condizioni della classe agricola,* vol. 14, fol. 1. Rome: Forzani.

Saller, Richard P. 1982. *Personal Patronage under the Early Empire.* Cambridge: Cambridge University Press.

———. 1984. "*Familia, Domus,* and the Roman Conception of the Family." *Phoenix* 38:336–355.

———. 1986. "*Patria Potestas* and the Stereotype of the Roman Family." *Continuity and Change* 1:7–22.

———. 1987. "Men's Age at Marriage and Its Consequences in the Roman Family." *Classical Philology* 82:21–34.

———. 1988. "Pietas, Obligation and Authority in the Roman Family." Pp. 393–410 in

Alte Geschichte und Wissenschaftsgeschichte: Festschrift für Karl Christ, edited by Peter Kneissl and Volker Losemann. Darmstadt: Wissenschaftliche Buchgesellschaft.

————. 1991. "Corporal Punishment, Authority, and Obedience in the Roman Household." Pp. 144–165 in *Marriage, Divorce, and Children in Ancient Rome,* edited by Beryl Rawson. Oxford: Oxford University Press.

Saller, Richard P., and Brent D. Shaw. 1984. "Tombstones and Roman Family Relations in the Principate: Civilians, Soldiers and Slaves." *Journal of Roman Studies* 74:124–156.

Salvemini, Gaetano. [1899] 1966. *Magnati e popolani in Firenze dal 1280 al 1295.* Milan: Feltrinelli.

Sanders, Irwin T. 1962. *The Rainbow in the Rock.* Cambridge: Harvard University Press.

Sandeus, Felinus. 1547. *Secunda in quinque decretalium libros pars.* Lyons.

Sant Cassia, Paul. 1982. "Property in Greek Cypriot Marriage Strategies, 1920–1980." *Man* 17:643–663.

Santini, Pietro. 1886. "Appunti sulla vendetta privata e sulle rappresaglie in occasione di un documento inedito." *Archivio storico italiano,* 4th ser. 18:162–176.

————. 1895. *Documenti dell'antica costituzione del comune di Firenze.* Documenti di Storia Italiana 10. Florence: Vieusseux.

Sapori, Armando. 1938. "Il libro di amministrazione dell'eredità di Baldovino Iacopi Riccomanni (1272–1274)." *Archivio storico italiano* 1938:88–113.

Sarton, George. 1927. *Introduction to the History of Science,* vol. 1. Carnegie Institution of Washington Publication no. 376. Baltimore: Williams and Wilkins.

Schama, Simon. 1987. *The Embarrassment of Riches: An Interpretation of Dutch Culture in the Golden Age.* London: Collins.

Scheper-Hughes, Nancy. 1985. "Culture, Scarcity and Maternal Thinking: Maternal Detachment and Infant Survival in a Brazilian Shantytown." *Ethos* 13:291–317.

Schneider, Jane. 1971. "Of Vigilance and Virgins." *Ethnology* 9:1–24.

————. 1980. "Trousseau as Treasure: Some Contradictions of Late Nineteenth Century Change in Sicily." Pp. 323–355 in *Beyond the Myths of Culture: Essays in Cultural Materialism,* edited by Eric B. Ross. New York: Academic Press.

Schneider, Jane, and Peter Schneider. 1976. *Culture and Political Economy in Western Sicily.* New York: Academic Press.

Schofield, Sue. 1979. *Development and the Problem of Village Nutrition.* London: Croom Helm.

Schwartzenberg, Claudio. 1960. "Parentela, a: Storia." Pp. 638–676 in *Enciclopedia del diritto,* vol. 31. Milan: Giuffrè.

Scrimshaw, Susan. 1983. "Infanticide as Deliberate Fertility Control." Pp. 245–266 in *Determinants of Fertility in Developing Countries: Fertility Regulation and Institutional Influences,* vol. 2, edited by Rodolpho A. Bulatao and Ronald D. Lee. New York: Academic Press.

Sercambi, Giovanni. 1972. *Novelle.* Ed. Giovanni Sinicropi. 2 vols. Scrittori d'Italia 250–251. Bari: Laterza.

Seymour, Michael C., ed. 1975. *On the Properties of Things: John of Trevisa's Translation of Bartholomaeus Anglicus "De proprietatibus rerum,"* vol. 1. Oxford: Clarendon.

Shaw, Brent. 1982. "The Elders of Christian Africa." Pp. 207–226 in *Mélanges offerts à R. P. Etienne Gareau: Cahiers des études anciennes,* edited by Pierre Brind'Amour. Ottawa: Editions de l'Université d'Ottawa.

———. 1984. "Latin Funerary Epigraphy and Family Life in the Later Roman Empire." *Historia* 33:457–497.

———. 1987a. "The Age of Roman Girls at Marriage: Some Reconsiderations." *Journal of Roman Studies* 77:30–46.

———. 1987b. "The Family in Late Antiquity: The Experience of Augustine." *Past and Present* 115:3–51.

Shaw, Brent D., and Richard P. Saller. 1984. "Close-Kin Marriage in Roman Society?" *Man* n.s. 19:432–444.

Sheehan, M. M. 1988. "Theory and Practice: Marriage of the Unfree and the Poor in Medieval Society." *Mediaeval Studies* 50:457–487.

Shorter, Edward. 1975. *The Making of the Modern Family.* New York: Basic Books.

Sieder, Reinhard, and Michael Mitterauer. 1983. "The Reconstruction of the Family Life Course: Theoretical Problems and Empirical Results." Pp. 309–345 in *Family Forms in Historic Europe,* edited by Richard Wall, Jean Robin, and Peter Laslett. Cambridge: Cambridge University Press.

Silverman, Sydel F. 1968. "Agricultural Organization, Social Structure, and Values in Italy: Amoral Familism Reconsidered." *American Anthropologist* 70:1–20.

———. 1975. *Three Bells of Civilization: The Life of an Italian Hill Town.* New York: Columbia University Press.

Smalley, Beryl. 1952. *The Study of the Bible in the Middle Ages.* Oxford: Basil Blackwell.

Smith, James E. 1989 "Method and Confusion in the Study of the Household." *Historical Methods* 22:57–60.

Smith, Richard M. 1979 "Some Reflections on the Evidence for the Origins of the 'European Marriage Pattern' in England." Pp. 74–112 in *The Sociology of the Family: New Direction for Britain,* edited by Chris Harris. Sociological Review Monograph no. 28. Chester: Bemrose.

———. 1981a. "Fertility, Economy and Household Formation over Three Centuries." *Population and Development Review* 8:595–622.

———. 1981b. "The People of Tuscany and Their Families: Medieval or Mediterranean?" *Journal of Family History* 6:107–128.

———. 1983. "Hypothèses sur la nuptialité en Angleterre aux XIIIe-XIVe siècles." *Annales E.S.C.* 38:107–136.

———. 1984. "Some Issues concerning Families and Their Property in Rural England, 1250–1800." Pp. 1–86 in *Land, Kinship and Life-Cycle,* edited by Richard Smith. Cambridge: Cambridge University Press.

Socinus Junior, Marianus. 1561. *Consiliorum sive malis responsorum.* Venice.

Somogyi, Stefano. 1965. "Nuzialità." Pp. 321–397 in *Annali di statistica,* vol. 17, *Sviluppo della popolazione italiana dal 1861 al 1961.* Rome: Istituto Centrale di Statistica.

Sørensen, Aage B. 1989. "Old Age, Retirement, and Inheritance." Pp. 197–213 in *Age Structuring in Comparative Perspective*, edited by David I. Kertzer and K. Warner Schaie. Hillsdale, N.J.: Lawrence Erlbaum.

Spadoni, Domenico. 1899. *Alcune costumanʒe e curiosità storiche marchigiane*. Turin and Palermo: Clausen.

Spawforth, A. J. S. 1985. "Family at Roman Sparta and Epidaurus: Some Prosopographical Notes." *Annual of the British School of Athens* 80:228–230.

Statuta. [1504] 1616. *Statuta civitatis Forlolivii*. Forlì.

Statuta. [1415] 1778–1781. *Statuta populi et communis Florentie . . . anno Salutis MCCCCXV*. 4 vols. Freiburg.

Statuti. [1325] 1910–1921. *Statuti della Repubblica fiorentina*. Ed. Romolo Caggese. 2 vols. Florence: Comune de Firenze.

Statutorum magnificae civitatis et communis Feltriae. [1439] 1749. Venice.

Still, G. F. 1931. *The History of Pediatrics*. London: Oxford University Press.

Stini, W. A. 1985. "Growth Rates and Sexual Dimorphism in Evolutionary Perspective." Pp. 191–226 in *The Analysis of Prehistoric Diets*, edited by Robert I. Gilbert, Jr., and James H. Mielke. Orlando, Fla.: Academic Press.

Stone, Lawrence. 1977. *The Family, Sex and Marriage in England, 1500–1800*. London: Wiedenfeld and Nicholson.

Storti Storchi, Claudia. 1980. "La tradizione longobarda nel diritto bergamesco: I rapporti patrimoniali tra coniugi (secoli XII-XIV)." Pp. 481–554 in *Diritto comune e diritto locali nella storia dell'Europa*. Milan: Giuffrè.

———, ed. 1986. *Lo statuto di Bergamo del 1331*. Milan: Giuffrè.

Syme, Ronald. 1958. *Tacitus*. 2 vols. Oxford: Clarendon.

———. 1982. "Clues to Testamentary Adoption." Pp. 397–410 in *Atti del colloquio internaʒionale AIEGL su Epigrafia e ordine senatorio, Roma 14–20 maggio 1981*. Series 4, vol. 1. Rome.

———. 1986. "Les alliances dynastiques dans l'aristocratie romaine." *Diogène* 135:3–13.

Szilàgyi, János. 1961. "Beiträge zur statistik der Sterblichkeit in den westeuropäischen Provinzen des römischen Imperiums." *Acta Archaeologica Academiae Scientiarum Hungaricae* 13:125–155.

———. 1962. "Beiträge zur Statistik der Sterblichkeit in der Illyrischen Provinzgruppe und in Norditalien (Gallia Padana)." *Acta Archaeologica Academiae Scientiarum Hungaricae* 14:297–396.

———. 1963. "Die Sterblichkeit in den Städen Mittel- und Süd-Italiens sowie in Hispanien." *Acta Archaeologica Academiae Scientiarum Hungaricae* 15:129–224.

———. 1965. "Die Sterblichkeit in den nordafrikanischen Provinzen, I." *Acta Archaeologica Academiae Scientiarum Hungaricae* 17:309–334.

———. 1966. "Die Sterblichkeit in den nordafrikanischen Provinzen, II." *Acta Archaeologica Academiae Scientiarum Hungaricae* 18:235–277.

———. 1967. "Die Sterblichkeit in den nordafrikanischen Provinzen, III." *Acta Archaeologica Academiae Scientiarum Hungaricae* 19:25–29.

Tamassia, Giovanni. 1910. *La famiglia italiana nei secoli decimoquinto e decimosesto.* Milan: R. Sestan.

Tartagni, Alessandro. 1548. *Consiliorum.* . . . Lyons.

Tentori, Tullio. 1976. "Social Classes and Family in a Southern Italian Town: Matera." Pp. 273–285 in *Mediterranean Family Structures,* edited by J. G. Peristiany. Cambridge: Cambridge University Press.

Thomas, J. A. C. 1961. "Accusation adulterii." *Iura* 12:70–75.

———. 1976. *Texbook of Roman Law.* Amsterdam: North-Holland.

Thomas, Keith. 1971. *Religion and the Decline of Magic: Studies in Popular Belief in Sixteenth and Seventeenth Century England.* London: Weidenfeld and Nicolson.

Thomas, Yan. 1980. "Mariages endogamiques à Rome: Patrimoine, pouvoir et parenté depuis lépoque archaique." *Revue historique de droit français et étranger* 58:345–382.

———. 1986. "Le 'ventre': Corps maternel, droit paternel." *Le genre humain* 14:211–236.

Thomasset, Claude. 1981. "La représentation de la sexualité et de la génération dans la pensée scientifique médiévale." Pp. 1–17 in *Love and Marriage in the Twelfth Century,* edited by Willy van Hoecke and Andries Welkenhuysen. Mediaevalia Lovaniensia Series 1, studia 8. Louvain: Louvain University Press.

Tittarelli, Luigi. 1977. "Sulle crisi di mortalità in Perugia nei secoli XVII, XVIII et XIX." *Quaderni dell'Istituto di Statistica dell'Università degli studi di Perugia* 1:65–92.

———. 1980. "Alcuni aspetti della struttura della popolazione del contado perugino nel 1782." *Quaderni dell'Istituto di Statistica dell'Università degli studi di Perugia* 5:1–76.

———. 1984. "La struttura della famiglia urbana e rurale a Perugia nei secoli XVIII e XIX." *Quaderni dell'Istituto di Statistica dell'Università degli studi di Perugia* 9:115–155.

———. 1985. "I servi domestici a Perugia a metà dell'ottocento." *Quaderni dell'Istituto di Statistica dell'Università degli studi di Perugia* 10:25–86.

———. 1987. "Gli esposti all'ospedale di S. Maria della Misericordia in Perugia nei secoli XVIII e XIX." *Bollettino della Deputazione di Storia Patria per l'Umbria* 82 (1985):23–130.

Torelli, Marina. 1973. "Une nuova iscrizione di Silla da Larino." *Athenaeum* 61:336–354.

Treggiari, Susan. 1975. "Family Life among the Staff of the Volusii." *Transactions and Proceedings of the American Philological Association* 105:393–401.

———. 1981a. "Concubinae." *Papers of the British School at Rome* 39:59–81.

———. 1981b. "Contubernales in *CIL* 6." *Phoenix* 35:42–69.

———. 1982a. "Consent to Roman Marriage: Who, Why and How?" *Classical Views/Echos du monde classique* 1:34–44.

———. 1982b. "Urban Labour in Rome: Mercenarii and Tabernarii." Pp. 48–64 in *Non-Slave Labour in the Greco-Roman World,* edited by Peter Garnsey. Cambridge: Cambridge Philological Society, supplementary volume, no. 6.

———. 1984. "*Digna condicio:* Betrothals in the Roman Upper Class." *Classical Views/Echos du monde classique* 3:419–451.

———. 1985. "*Iam proterva fronte:* Matrimonial Advances by Roman Women." Pp. 331––

352 in *The Craft of the Ancient Historian: Essays in Honor of Chester G. Starr,* edited by J. W. Eadie and J. Ober. Lanham, Md.: University Press of America.

———. 1991. *Roman Marriage: Iusti coniuges from the Time of Cicero to the Time of Ulpian.* Oxford: Clarendon.

Trexler, Richard C. 1973a. "Infanticide in Florence: New Sources and First Results." *History of Childhood Quarterly* 1:98–116.

———. 1973b. "The Foundlings of Florence, 1395–1455." *History of Childhood Quarterly* 1:259–284.

Turner, C. M. 1916. "Arles and Rome: The First Development of Canon Law in Gaul." *Journal of Theological Studies* 17:236–247.

———. 1931. "Ministries of Women in the Primitive Church: Widow, Deaconess, and Virgin in the First Four Christian Centuries." Pp. 316–351 in *Catholic and Apostolic: Collected Papers by the Late Cuthbert Hamilton Turner,* edited by H. N. Bate. London: A. R. Mowbray.

Tuzet, Hélène. 1955. *La Sicile au XVIIIe siècle vue par les voyageurs étrangers.* Strasbourg: P. H. Heitz.

Ubaldi, Angelo degli. 1548. *Lectura super Codice.* Lyons.

———. 1551. *Consilia.* Lyons.

Ubaldi, Baldo degli. 1498. *Commentaria super I–V libris Codicis.* Lyons.

———. 1575. *Consilia.* 6 vols. Venice.

Ungari, Paolo. 1970. *Il diritto di famiglia in Italia dalle costituzioni "giacobine" al codice civile del 1942.* Bologna: Il Mulino.

———. 1974. *Storia del diritto di famiglia in Italia (1796–1942).* Bologna: Il Mulino.

Van Gennep, Arnold. 1960. *The Rites of Passage.* London: Routledge.

Velluti, Donato. 1914. *La cronica domestica.* Ed. Isidoro Del Lungo and Guglielmo Volpi. Florence: Sansoni.

Vernant, Jean-Pierre. 1983. *Myth and Thought among the Greeks.* London: Routledge.

Veyne, Paul. 1987. "The Roman Empire." Pp. 5–233 in *A History of Private Life, vol. 1, From Pagan Rome to Byzantium,* edited by Paul Veyne and translated by Arthur Goldhammer. Cambridge: Harvard University Press.

Villani, Giovanni. 1537. *Cronica.* Venice: Bartolomeo Zanetti.

Violante, Cinzio. 1977. "Quelques caractéristiques des structures familiales en Lombardie, Emilie et Toscane aux XIe et XIIe siècles." Pp. 87–147 in *Famille et parenté dans l'Occident médiéval,* edited by Georges Duby and Jacques Le Goff. Rome: Ecole Française de Rome.

———. 1981. "Le strutture familiari, parentali e consortili delle aristocrazie in Toscana durante i secoli X–XII." Pp. 1–57 in *I ceti dirigenti in Toscana nell'età precomunale,* edited by Comitato di Studi sulla Storia dei Ceti Dirigenti in Toscana. Pisa: Pacini.

Vismara, Giulio. 1962. "I patti successori nella dottrina di Bartolo." Pp. 755–783 in *Bartolo da Sassoferrato: Studi e documenti per il VI centenario,* vol. 2. Milan: Giuffrè.

———. 1971. "Momenti della storia della famiglia sarda." Pp. 170–191 in *Studi Sassaresi II: Famiglia e società sarda,* edited by Società sassarese per le scienze giuridiche. Milan: Giuffré.

————. 1988. "Scritti di storia giuridica." Pp. 65–137 in *La famiglia,* vol. 5. Milan:Giuffrè.

Vives, José. 1969. *Inscripciones cristianas de la España, Romana y Visigoda.* 2d ed. *Monumenta Hispaniae sacra,* serie patristica, vol. 2. Barcelona: Hospitalet.

Vogel, Cyrille. 1977. "Les rites de la célébration du mariage: Leur signification dans la formation du lien durant le haut moyen âge." *Il matrimonio* 1:397–472.

Vogüé, Adalbert de, ed. 1964–1965. *La règle du maître.* 3 vols. Sources chrétiennes 105–107; Série de textes monastiques de l'Occident 14–16. Paris: Cerf.

Volterra, Edoardo. 1928. "Per la storia dell'*accusatio adulterii iure mariti vel patris.*" *Studi economici-giuridici dell'Università di Cagliari* 17:1–62.

————. 1930. "In tema di 'Accusatio Adulterii.'" Pp. 111–122 in *Studi Bonfante,* vol. 2. Milan: Fratelli Treves.

————. 1966. "Nuove richerche sulla conventio *in manum.*" Pp. 1–105 in *Atti della Accademia dei Lincei: Memorie* 8, vol. 12, fasc. 4.

Vovelle, Michel. 1974. *Mourir autrefois: Attitudes collectives devant la mort aux XVIIᵉ et XVIIIᵉ siècles.* Paris: Gallimard.

————. 1980. "A Century and One-Half of American Epitaphs (1660–1813): Toward the Study of Collective Attitudes about Death." *Comparative Studies in Society and History* 22:534–547.

————. 1982. "Encore la mort: Un peu plus qu'une mode?" *Annales E.S.C.* 37:276–287.

————. 1983. *La mort et l'Occident de 1300 à nos jours.* Paris: Gallimard.

Wall, Richard, Jean Robin, and Peter Laslett, eds. 1983. *Family Forms in Historic Europe.* Cambridge: Cambridge University Press.

Watson, Alan. 1967. *The Law of Persons in the Later Roman Republic.* Oxford: Clarendon.

————. 1971. *The Law of Succession in the Later Roman Republic.* Oxford: Oxford University Press.

————. 1975. *Roman Law of the XII Tables.* Princeton: Princeton University Press.

Watson, Paul F. 1979. *The Garden of Love in Tuscan Art of the Early Renaissance.* Philadelphia: Art Alliance Press.

Weaver, Paul R. C. 1972. *Familia Caesaris: A Social Study of the Emperor's Freedmen and Slaves.* Cambridge: Cambridge University Press.

Weiner, Annette. 1976. *Women of Value, Men of Reknown.* Austin: University of Texas Press.

Weinstein, Donald. 1968. "The Myth of Florence." Pp. 15–44 in *Florentine Studies: Politics and Society in Renaissance Florence,* edited by Nicolai Rubinstein. London: Faber and Faber.

Werminghoff, A. 1906. *Concilia aevi karolini 1. Monumenta Germaniae historica,* Leges 3 Concilia 2. Hannover.

Wharton, Brian, ed. 1986. "Flood for the Weanling." Special issue. *Acta paediatrica scandinavica* supplement 323.

Whitehead, Roger G. 1980. "The Better Use of Food Resources for Infants and Mothers." *Proceedings of the Royal Society of London* B 209:59–69.

Whitehead, Roger G., and Alison A. Paul. 1981. "Infant Growth and Human Milk Requirements: A Fresh Approach." *Lancet* 2:161–163.

————. 1988. "Comparative Infant Nutrition in Man and Other Animals." Pp. 199–213 in *Comparative Nutrition,* edited by Kenneth Blaxter and Ian MacDonald. London: Libbey.

Whitehead, Roger G., Alison A. Paul, and Timothy J. Cole. 1982. "How Much Breast Milk Do Babies Need?" *Acta Paediatrica Scandinavica,* supplement 299:43–50.

————. 1989. "Diet and the Growth of Healthy Infants." *Journal of Human Nutrition and Dietetics* 2:73–84.

Wiedemann, Thomas. 1989. *Adults and Children in the Roman Empire.* New Haven: Yale University Press.

Wiesehöfer, Josef. 1988. *Zur Ernährung von Säuglingen in der Antike.* Typescript.

Wiseman, T. Peter. 1971. *New Men in the Roman Senate, 139 B.C.–A.D. 14.* Oxford: Clarendon.

Wolff, Hans Julius. 1955. "Zer Geschichte der Parapherna." *Zeitschrift der Savigny: Stiftung für Rechtsgeschichte (Romanistische Abteilung)* 72:335–347.

Wrightson, Keith. 1982a. "Infanticide in English History." *Criminal Justice History* 1:1–20.

————, 1982b. *English Society, 1580–1680.* London: Hutchinson.

Wrigley, Anthony. 1978. "Fertility Strategy for the Individual and the Group." Pp. 135–154 in *Historical Studies of Changing Fertility,* edited by Charles Tilly. Princeton: Princeton University Press.

Wrigley, E. A., and Roger S. Schofield. 1981. *The Population History of England: A Reconstruction.* Cambridge: Harvard University Press.

Yanagisako, Sylvia, and Jane Collier. 1987. "Toward a Unified Analysis of Gender and Kinship." Pp. 14–50 in *Gender and Kinship: Essays toward a Unified Analysis,* edited by Jane Collier and Sylvia Yanagisako. Stanford: Stanford University Press.

Zanker, Paul. 1975. "Grabreliefs römischer Freigelassener." *Jahrbuch des Deutschen Archäologischen Instituts* 90:267–315.

Zeldin, Theodore. 1973. *France, 1848–1945, vol. 1, Ambition, Love and Politics.* Oxford: Oxford University Press.

Zordan, Giorgio. 1966. "I vari aspetti della comunione familiare di beni nella Venezia dei secoli XI–XII." *Studi veneziani* 8:127–194.

Zulueta, Francis de, ed. 1946–1953. *The Institutes of Gaius.* Parts 1 and 2. Oxford: Clarendon.

INDEX

Abandonment of infants: parental attitudes
toward, 15–16, 49, 50, 51; and Christianity, 15, 50n; and Egyptians, 15; and
Jews, 15, 50n; grounds for, 54–56; rights
of father, 135

Abraham, 157

Accursius, 238

Adam, 165, 169

Adfines, 136, 137

Adoption, 128, 135, 137, 142–43, 346n

Adultery: and honor, 116, 148; as assertion of
masculinity, 121; attitude toward men's,
121–23, 148; attitude toward women's,
122; in Bible, 124; as grounds for divorce,
137; prevalence of, 148–49; Church and,
148, 176–77, 237–38; defined in *lex Julia,*
229–30; and *jura propria,* 236–37; and
public denunciation, 239. *See also* Homicides of honor; *Lex Julia de adulteriis*

Aetius, 63

Africa: valuation of children and elderly, 75–
79 passim; gender preferences in, 84–85

Agde, Council of, 178

Age: effect of on inheritance, 36–37; specified
by *fideicommissum,* 43; in epitaphs, 68–69,
73–80

Age at marriage, 7, 36, 272; model Tuscan
family, 4; family type, 5; life-cycle service,
9–10; girl's choice of partner, 106; Hajnal
household systems theory, 250–53, 256–
59; regional differences, 253–55; and servants, 255–59 passim, 266–67; of landowning stem families, 259–60; relation to
number of celibates, 259–64 passim; of
sharecropping complex families, 260–63;

in Sicily and Sardinia, 263–70; sharecroppers, Perugia and Cortona, 276–77; regional and socioeconomic factors, 281;
regional and temporal differences, 295;
and joint family, 295; and postnuptial
residence, 295–96

Agnates: inheritance law, 31; guardianship,
32; move toward cognatic succession, 32;
familia, 129; *gentilicium,* 131; association
with blood, 155; solidarity of, 208; and
Roman kinship reckoning, 210–14 passim; revenge, 216

Agnone, 6; family structure in, 286–303

Agrippa, M., 100–01

Agrippina the Younger, 98, 134

Ahala, 100

Alaric II, 234

Albania, 343

Albergotti, Francesco, 188, 190n, 191

Albertus Magnus, 161

Alexander II (pope), 216n

Algeria, 119, 324

Alliances: political, 137; representations of,
137–39; and names, 138–39; preserving,
139; importance for Romans, 143–44

Allifae, 131–32

Amoral familism, 346n

Amouliana, Greece, 342

Ancona, 263

Ancyra, Council of, 177

Andalusia, 115, 119–20, 347

Antonius de Bitonto, 166

Antoninus Pius, 234

Antony, Mark, 104, 137, 141

Apostolic Canons, 179